FAIRY TAIL

42

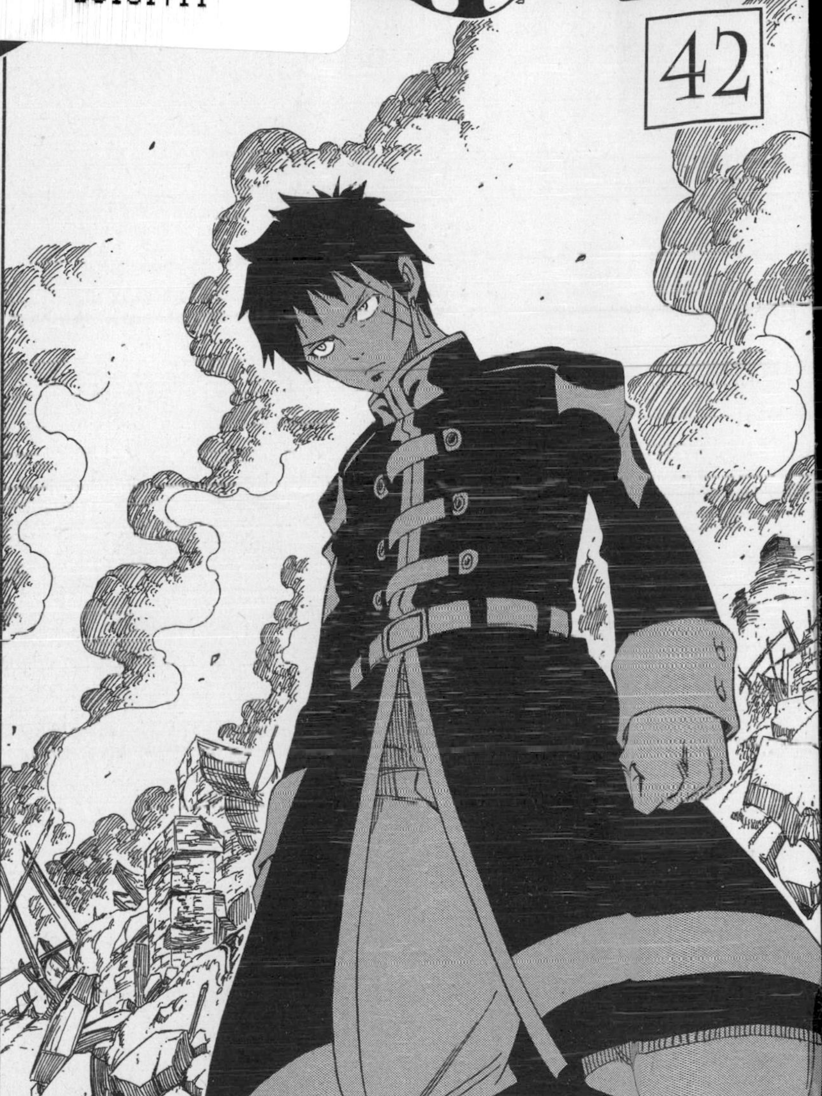

HIRO MASHIMA

FAIRYTAIL 42
CONTENTS

Contents

FAIRY TAIL

Chapter 354: Kyôka

LAMIA SCALE

Name: **Toby Horhorta**   Age: **25**

Magic:
Paralyzing Claws of the Mega-Jellyfish

Likes: Dislikes:
Sashimi   **Socks**

Remarks

Normally, he seems rather cheerful, but he has a history of suddenly getting angry for no good reason. Still, he is one of the more capable wizards in Lamia, helping lead the guild to second place in last year's Grand Magic Games even though Lyon and Jura did not take part.

He spent three months looking for a lost sock only to have it torn apart by Kurohebi of Raven Tail during a match in the Games. After that, they say he soon lost his other sock.

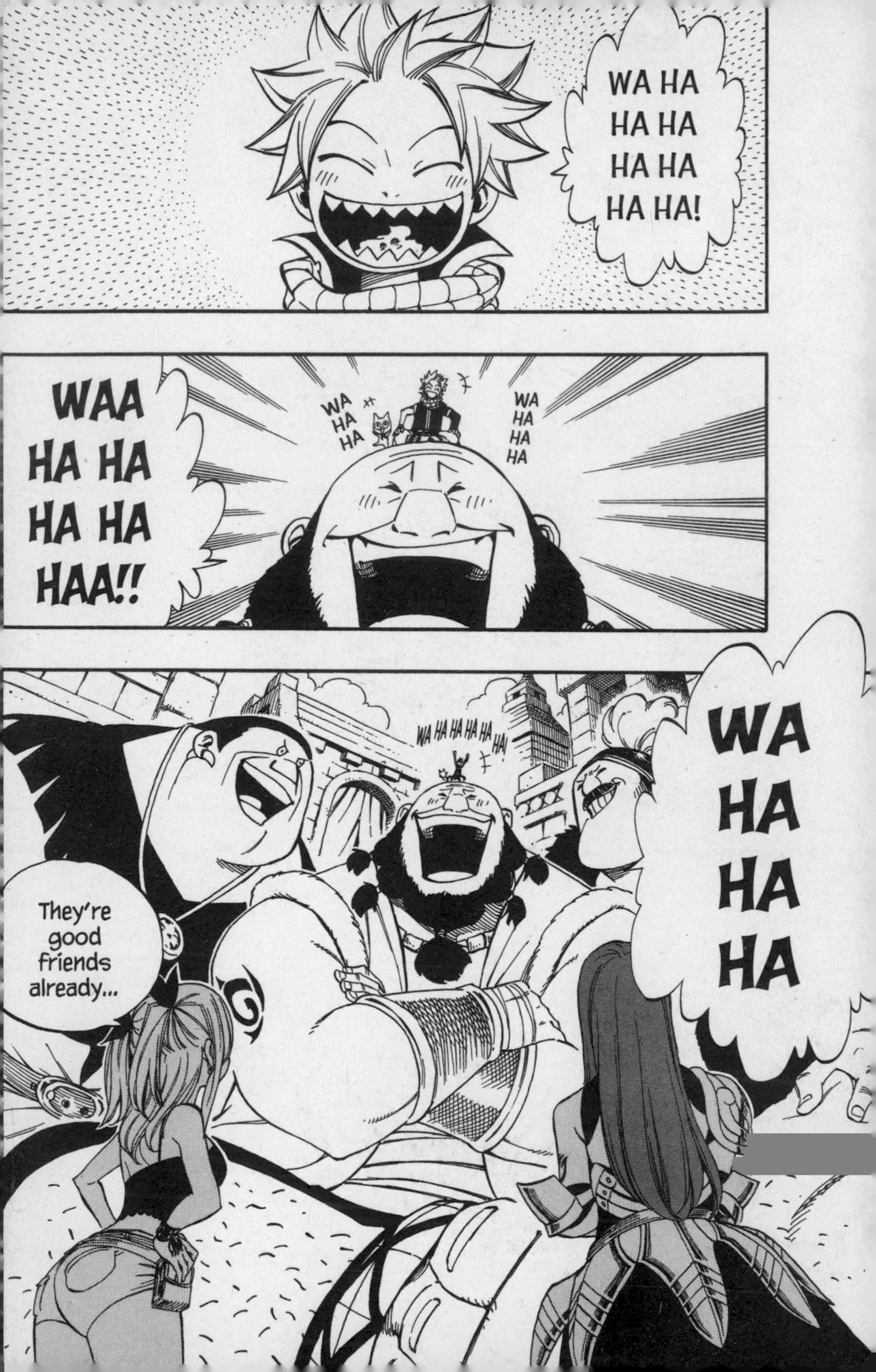
WA HA HA HA HA HA HA HA!
WA HA HA HA
WA HA HA
WAA HA HA HA HA HAA!!
WA HA HA HA HA
WA HA HA HA HA HA HA!
They're good friends already...

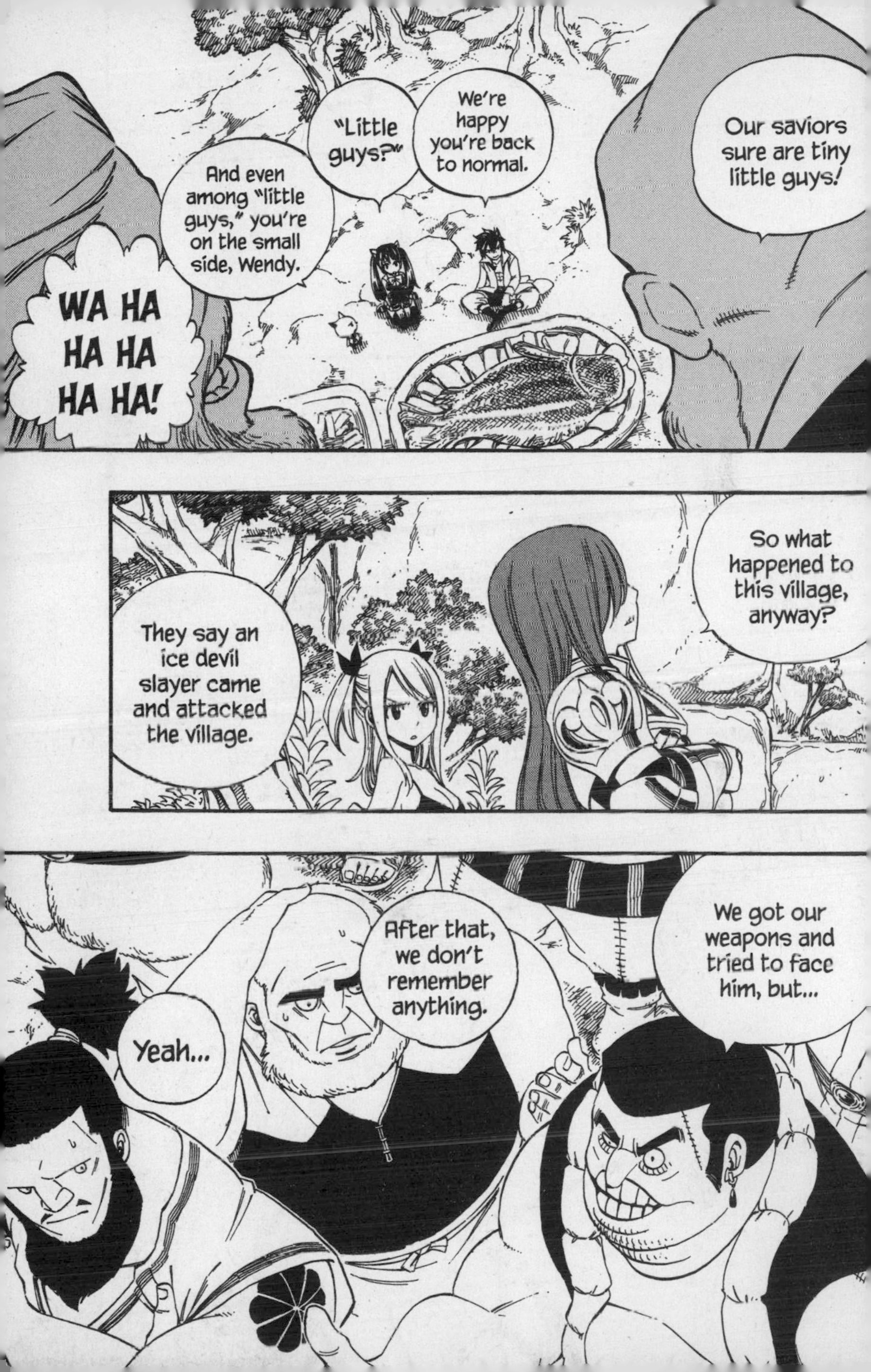
Our saviors sure are tiny little guys!
We're happy you're back to normal.
"Little guys?"
And even among "little guys," you're on the small side, Wendy.
WA HA HA HA HA HA!
So what happened to this village, anyway?
They say an ice devil slayer came and attacked the village.
We got our weapons and tried to face him, but...
After that, we don't remember anything.
Yeah...

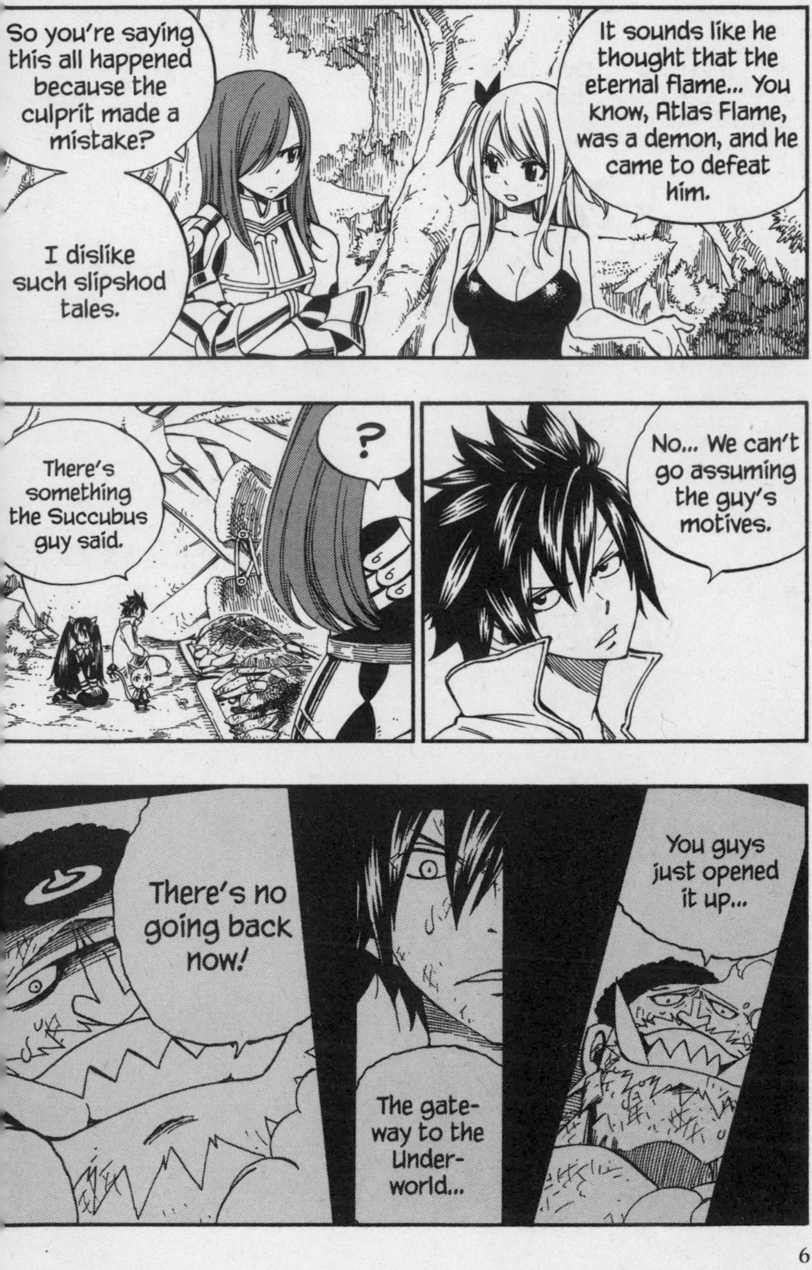
It sounds like he thought that the eternal flame... You know, Atlas Flame, was a demon, and he came to defeat him.
So you're saying this all happened because the culprit made a mistake?
I dislike such slipshod tales.
No... We can't go assuming the guy's motives.
?
There's something the Succubus guy said.
You guys just opened it up...
There's no going back now!
The gate-way to the Under-world...

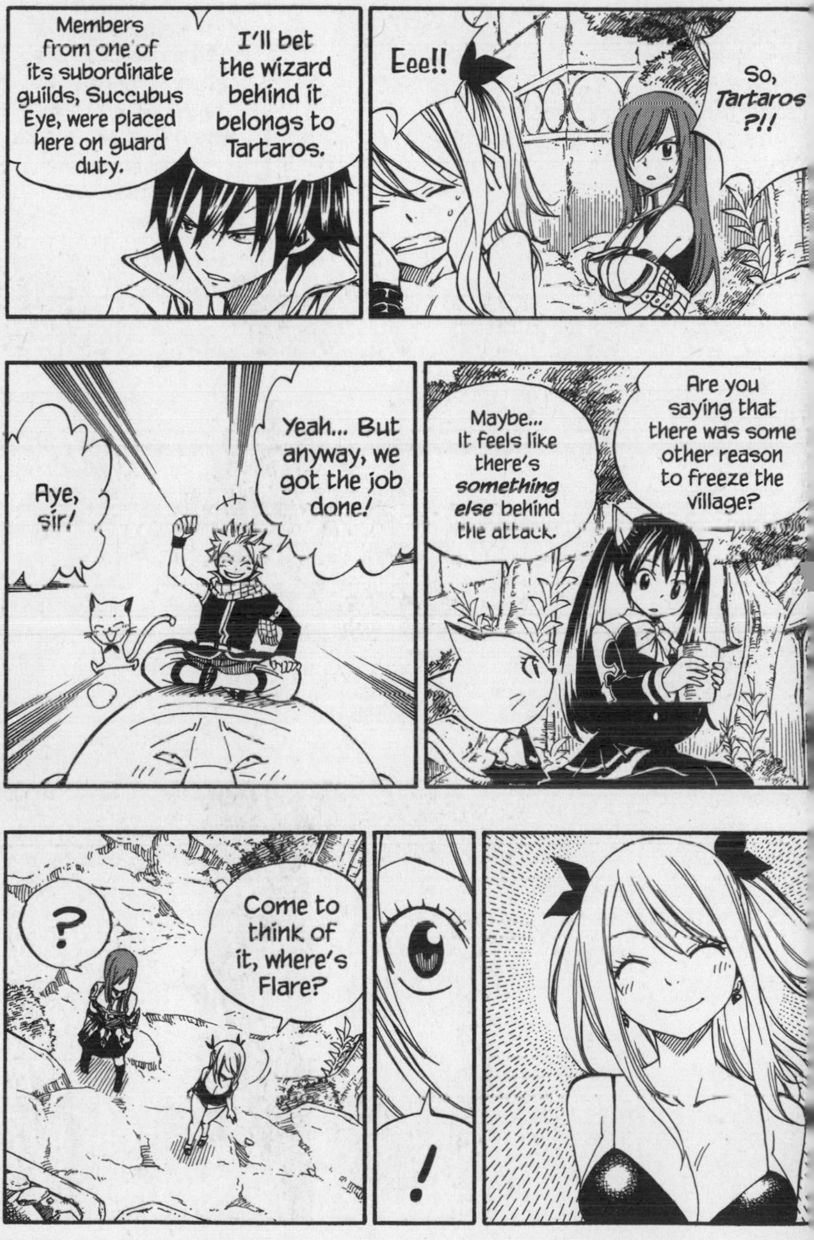
So, Tartaros ?!!
Eee!!
I'll bet the wizard behind it belongs to Tartaros.
Members from one of its subordinate guilds, Succubus Eye, were placed here on guard duty.
Are you saying that there was some other reason to freeze the village?
Maybe... It feels like there's *something else* behind the attack.
Yeah... But anyway, we got the job done!
Aye, sir!
!
Come to think of it, where's Flare?
?

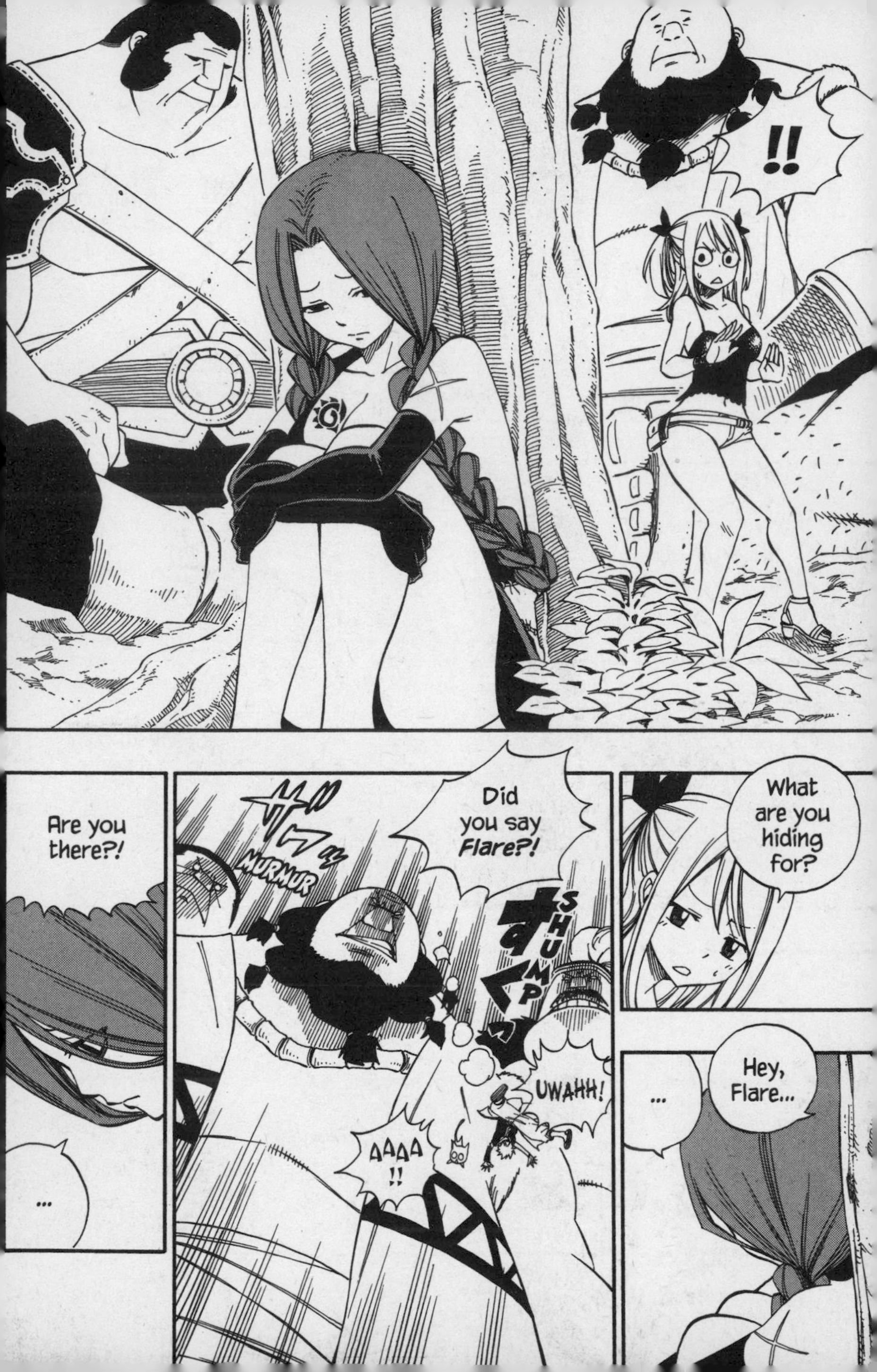
!!
What are you hiding for?
Hey, Flare...
...
Did you say Flare?!
MURMUR
SHUMP
UWAHH!
AAAA !!
Are you there?!
...

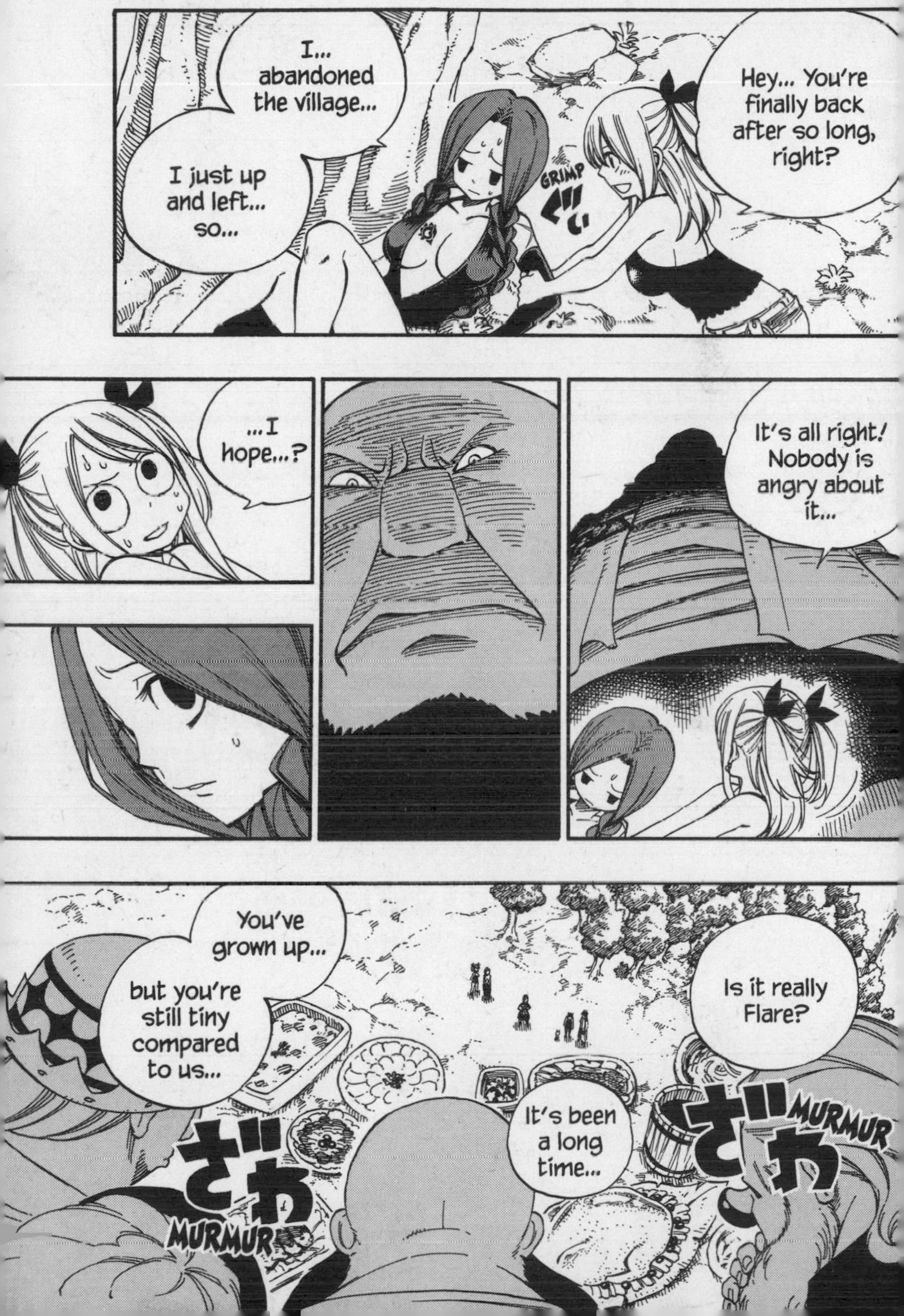
Hey... You're finally back after so long, right?
GRIMP
I... abandoned the village...
I just up and left... so...
It's all right! Nobody is angry about it...
...I hope...?
Is it really Flare?
MURMUR
You've grown up...
but you're still tiny compared to us...
It's been a long time...
MURMUR

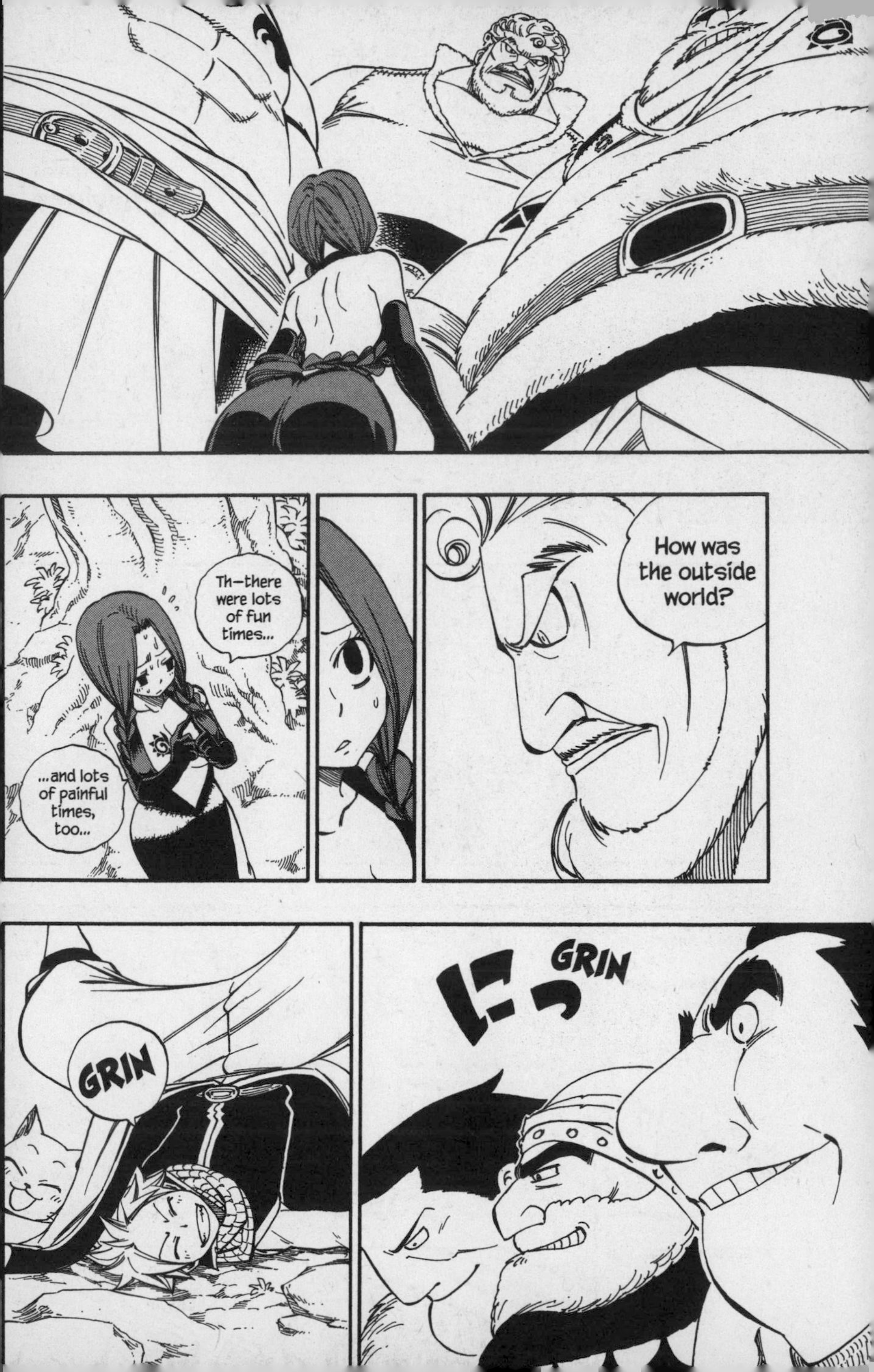
How was the outside world?
Th—there were lots of fun times...
...and lots of painful times, too...
にっ
GRIN
GRIN

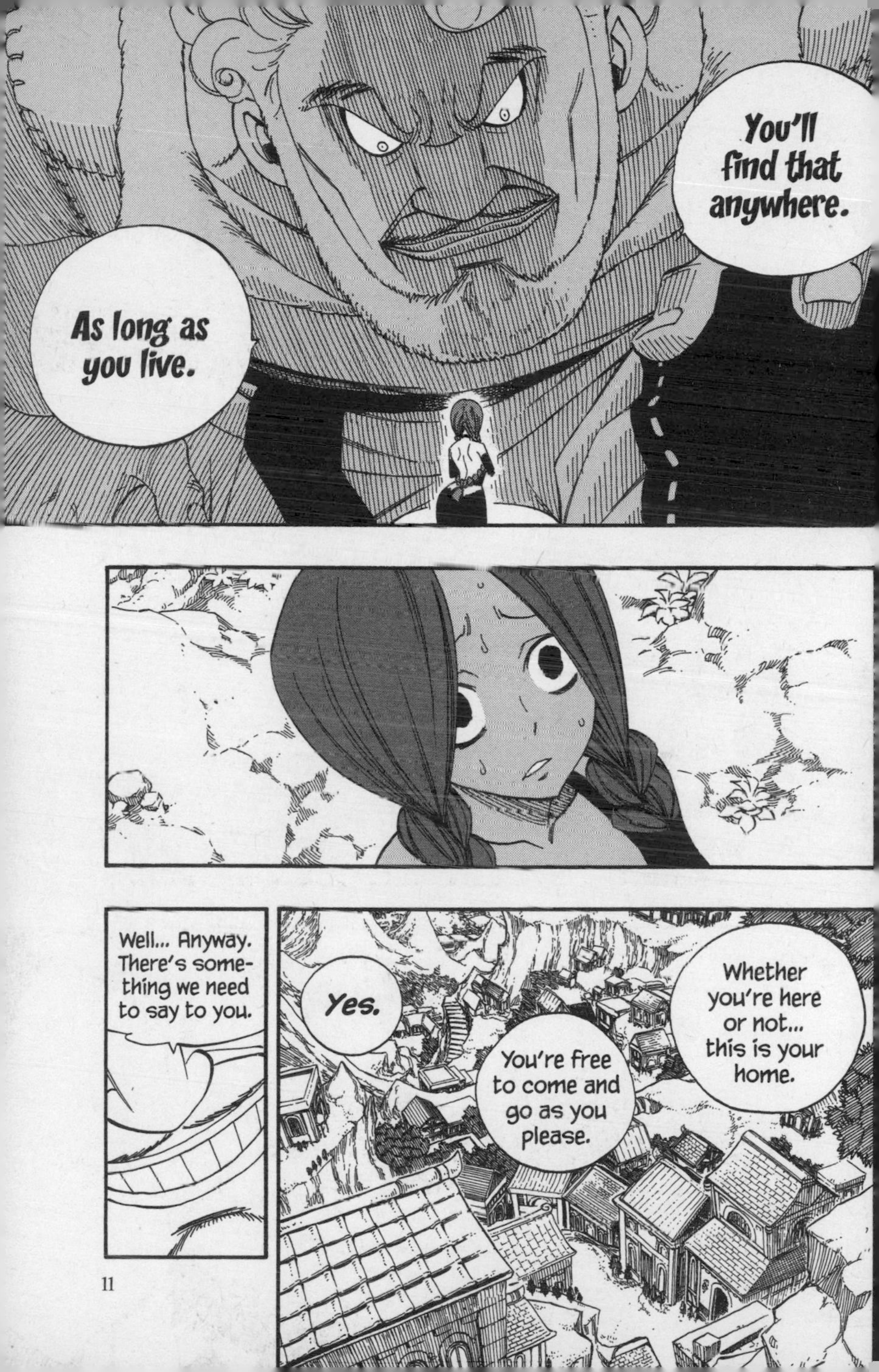
You'll find that anywhere.
As long as you live.
Whether you're here or not... this is your home.
You're free to come and go as you please.
Yes.
Well... Anyway. There's some-thing we need to say to you.

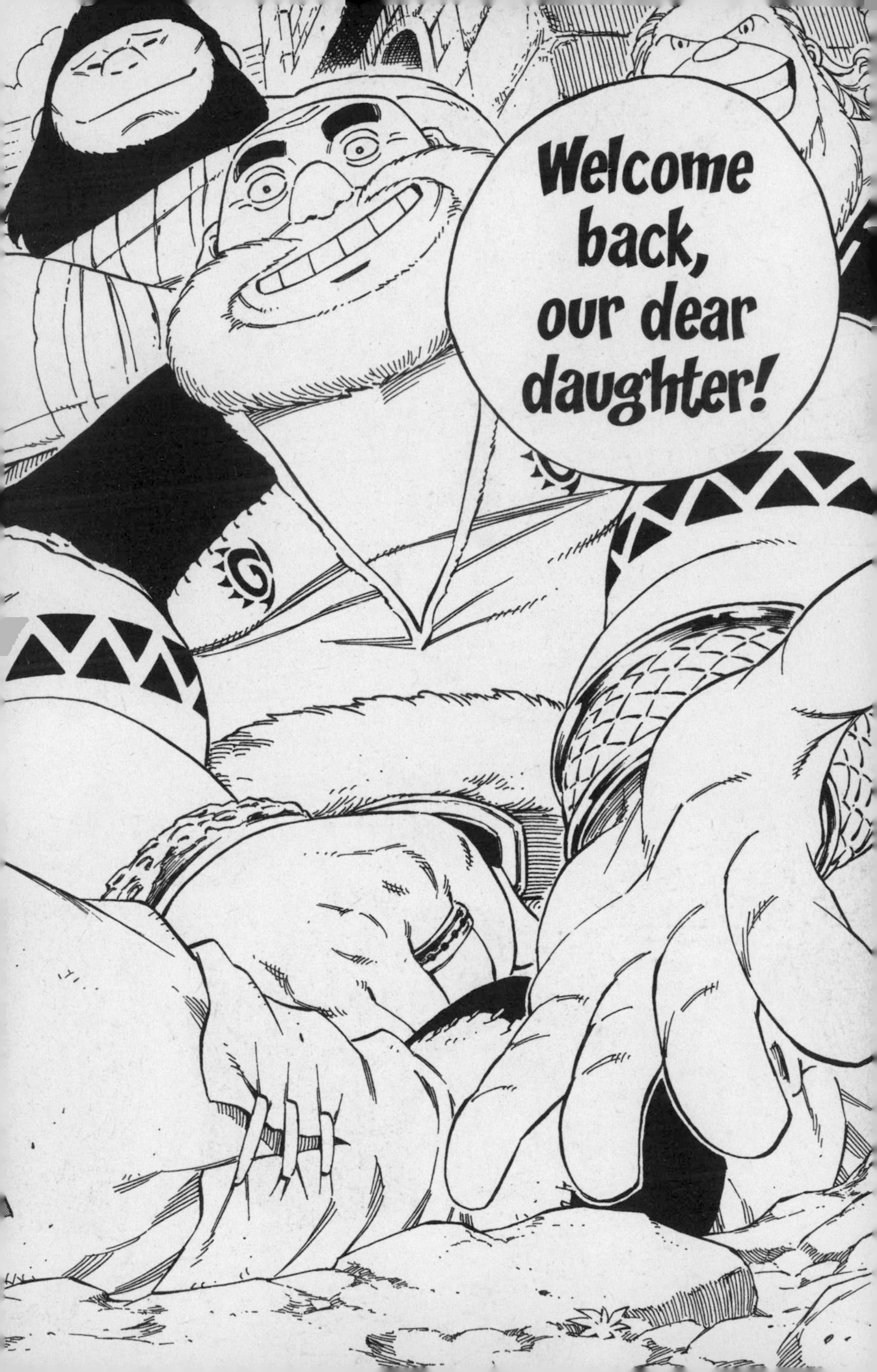
Welcome back, our dear daughter!

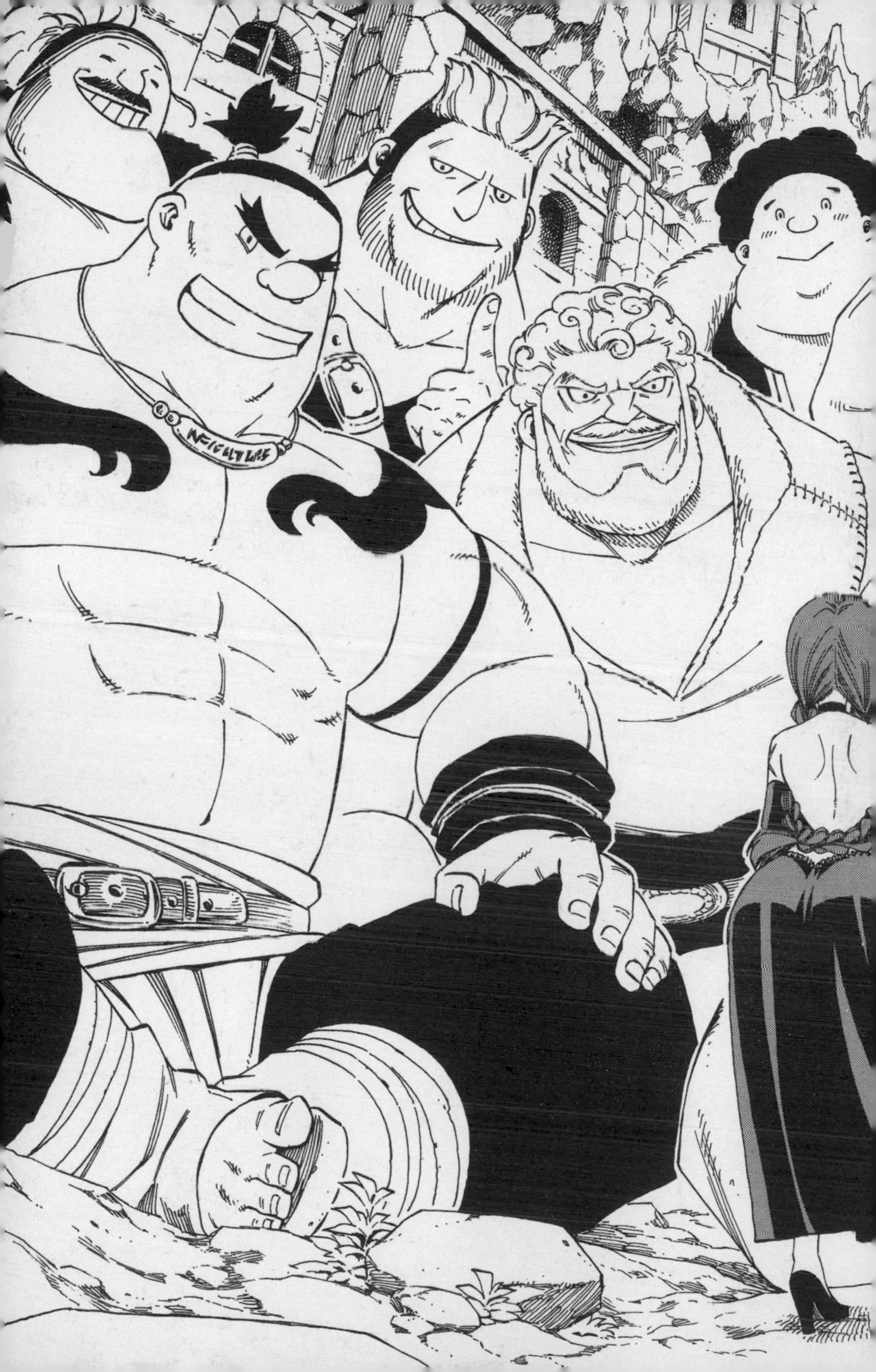

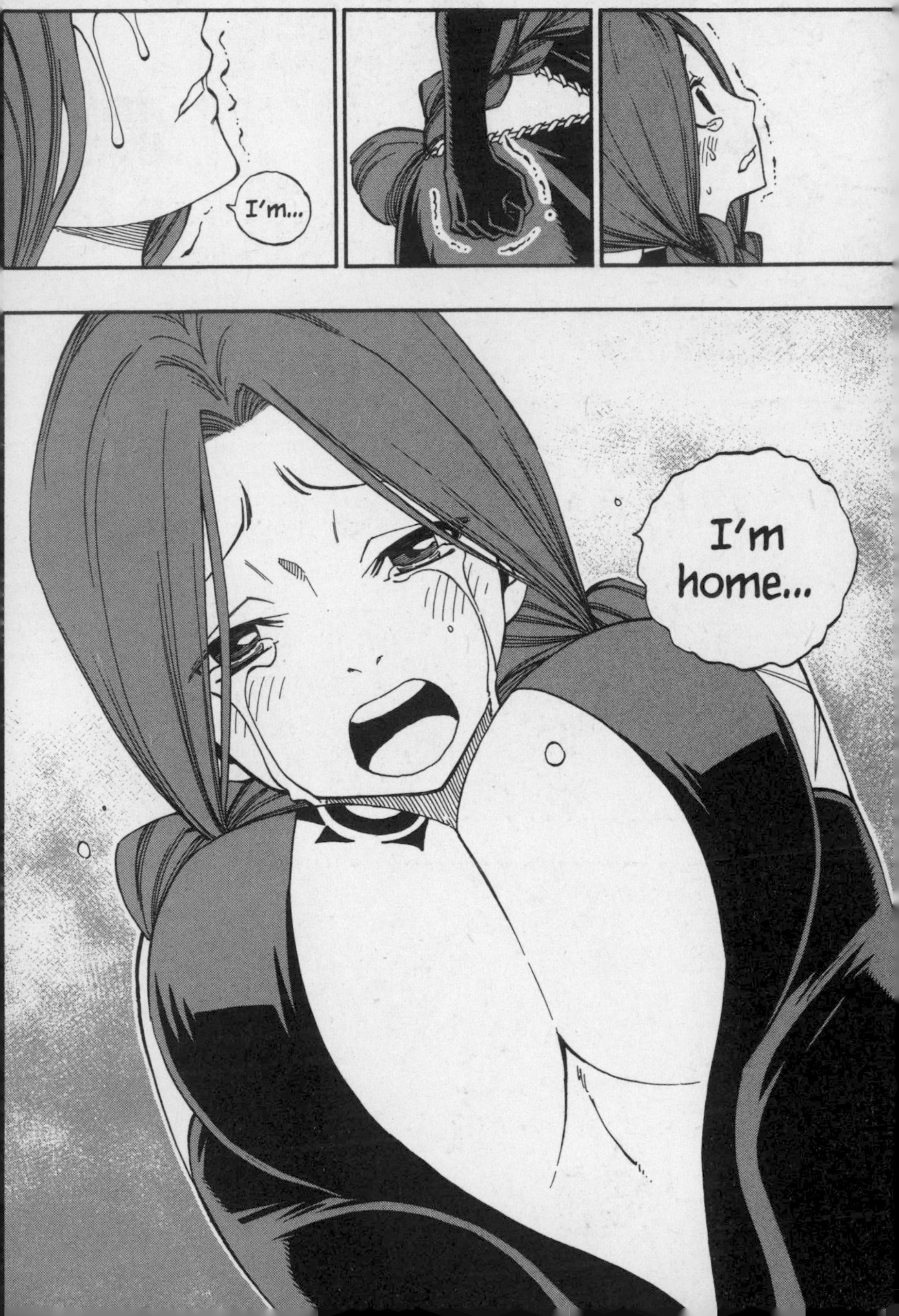
I'm...
I'm home...

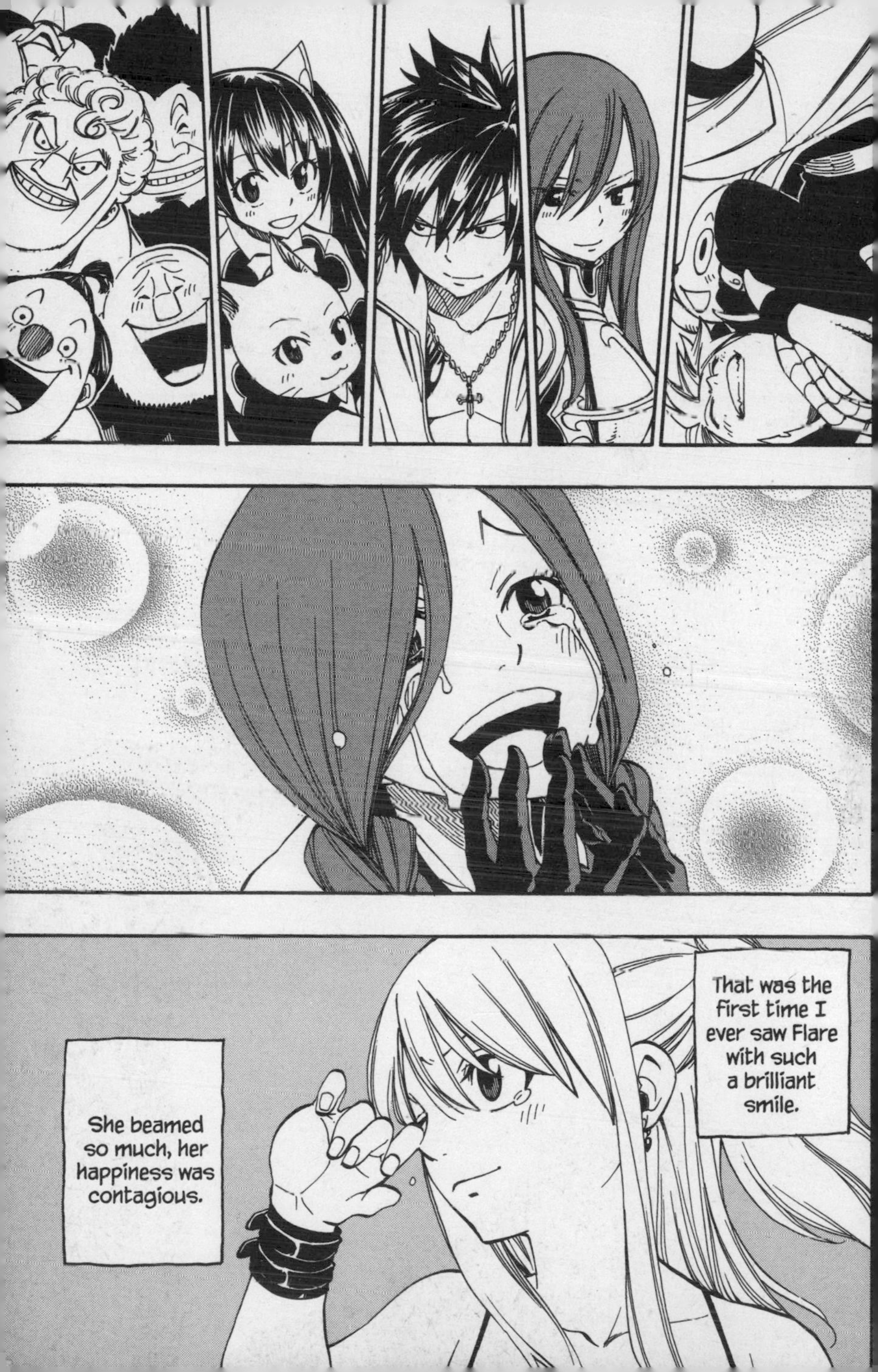
That was the first time I ever saw Flare with such a brilliant smile.
She beamed so much, her happiness was contagious.

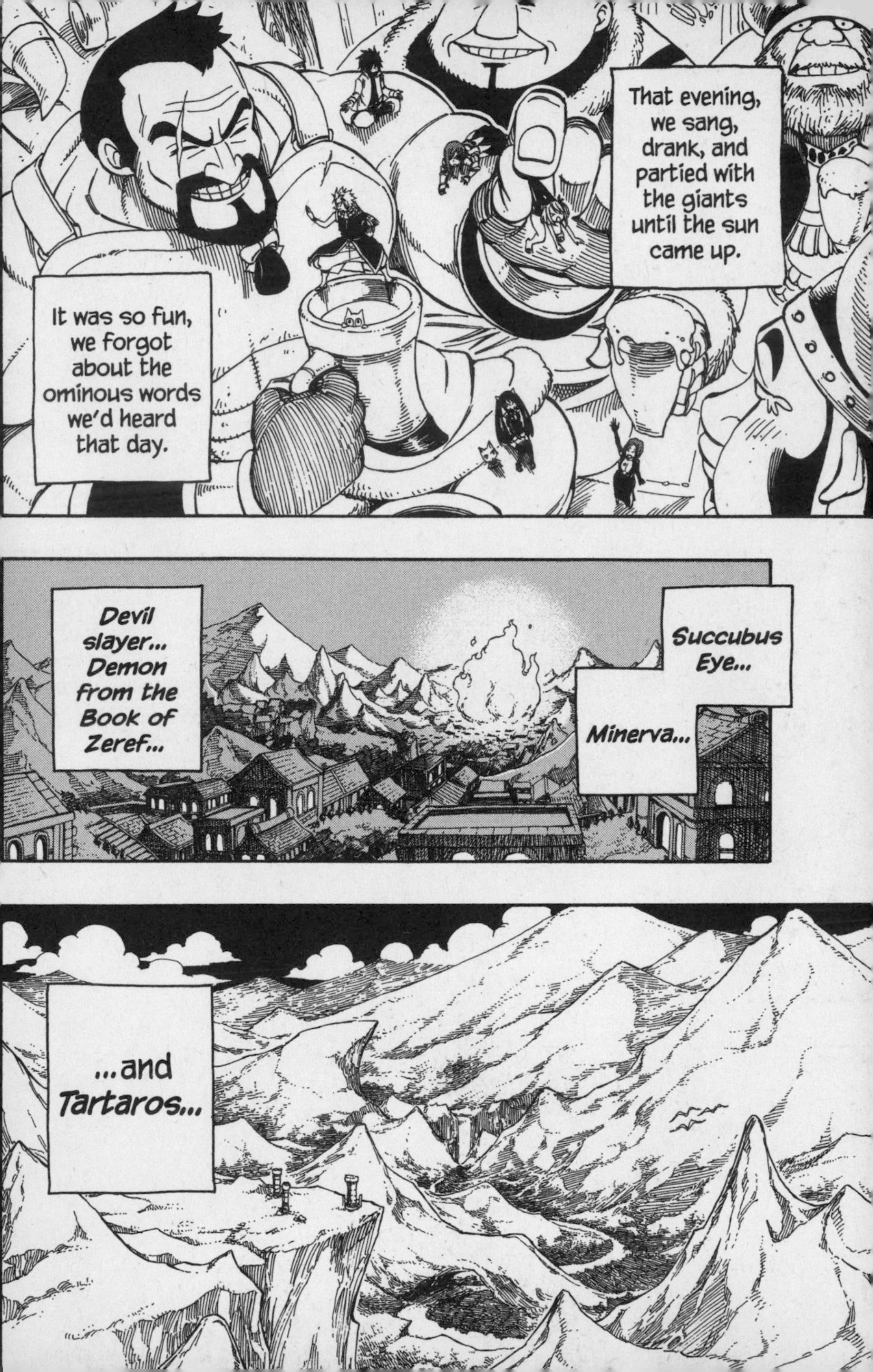
That evening, we sang, drank, and partied with the giants until the sun came up.
It was so fun, we forgot about the ominous words we'd heard that day.
Succubus Eye...
Minerva...
Devil slayer... Demon from the Book of Zeref...
...and Tartaros...

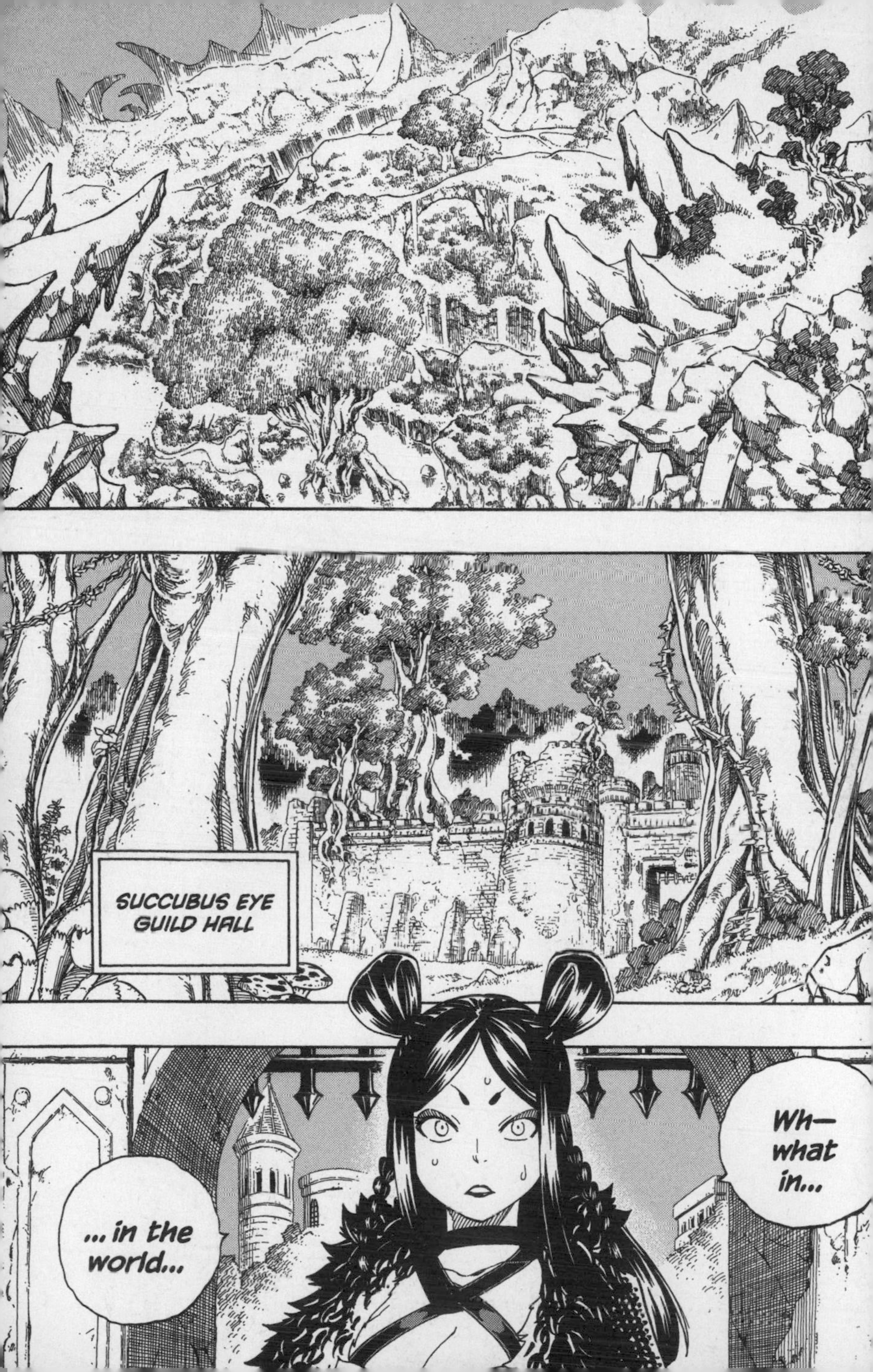
SUCCUBUS EYE GUILD HALL
Wh— what in...
...in the world...

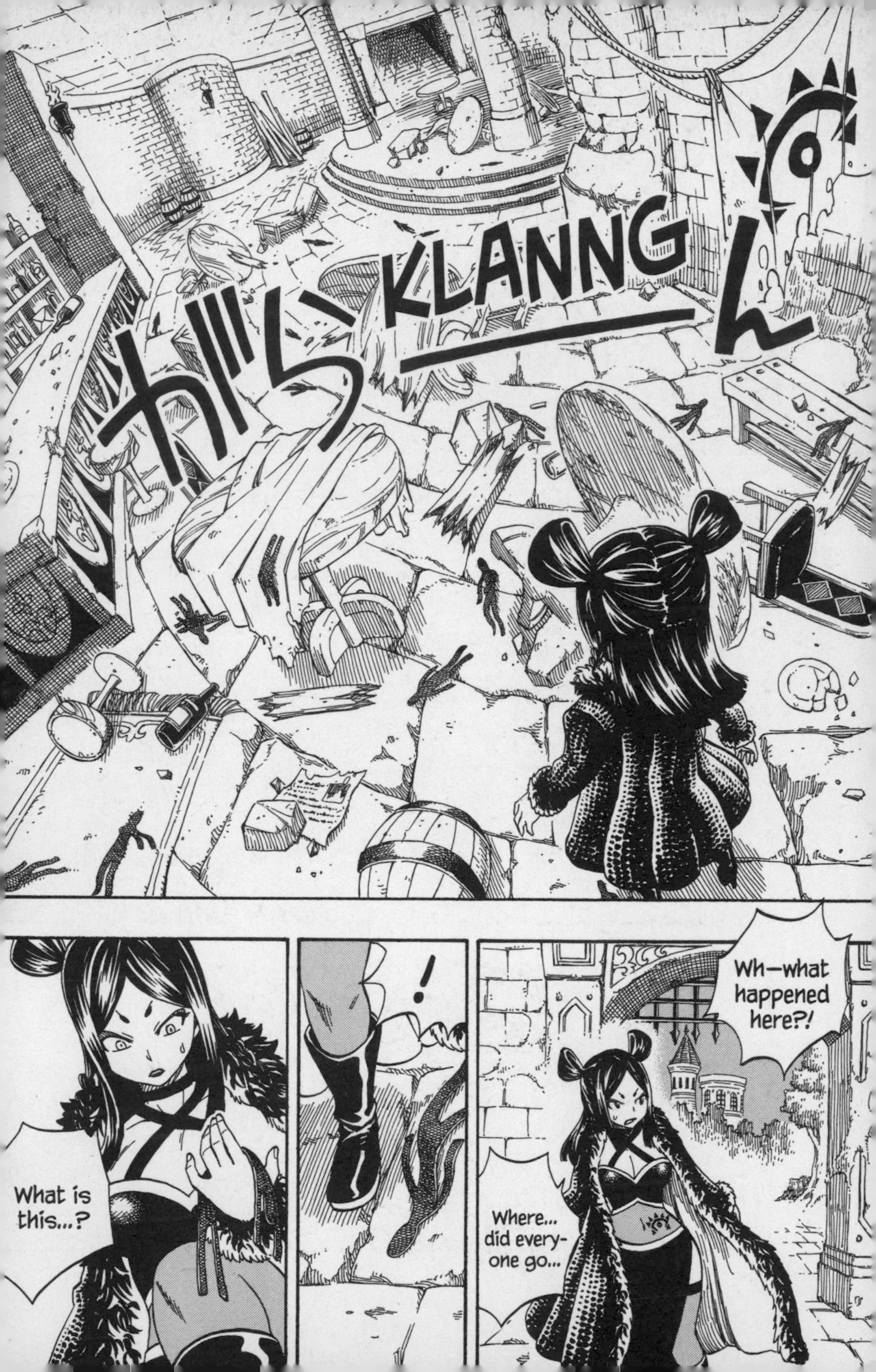
がらん
KLANNG
Wh—what happened here?!
Where... did every-one go...
!
What is this...?

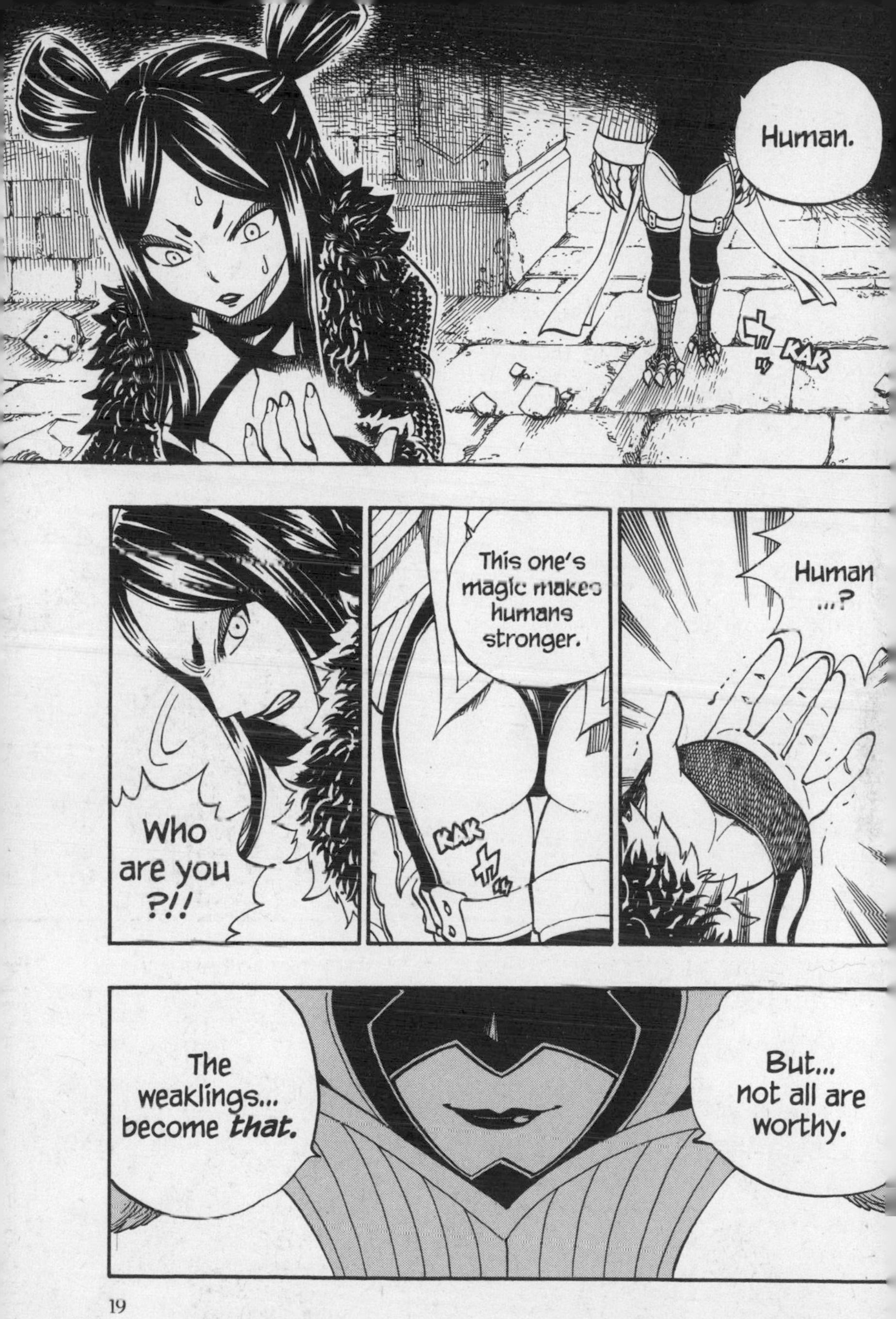
Human.
KAK
Human ...?
This one's magic makes humans stronger.
KAK
Who are you ?!!
But... not all are worthy.
The weaklings... become *that.*

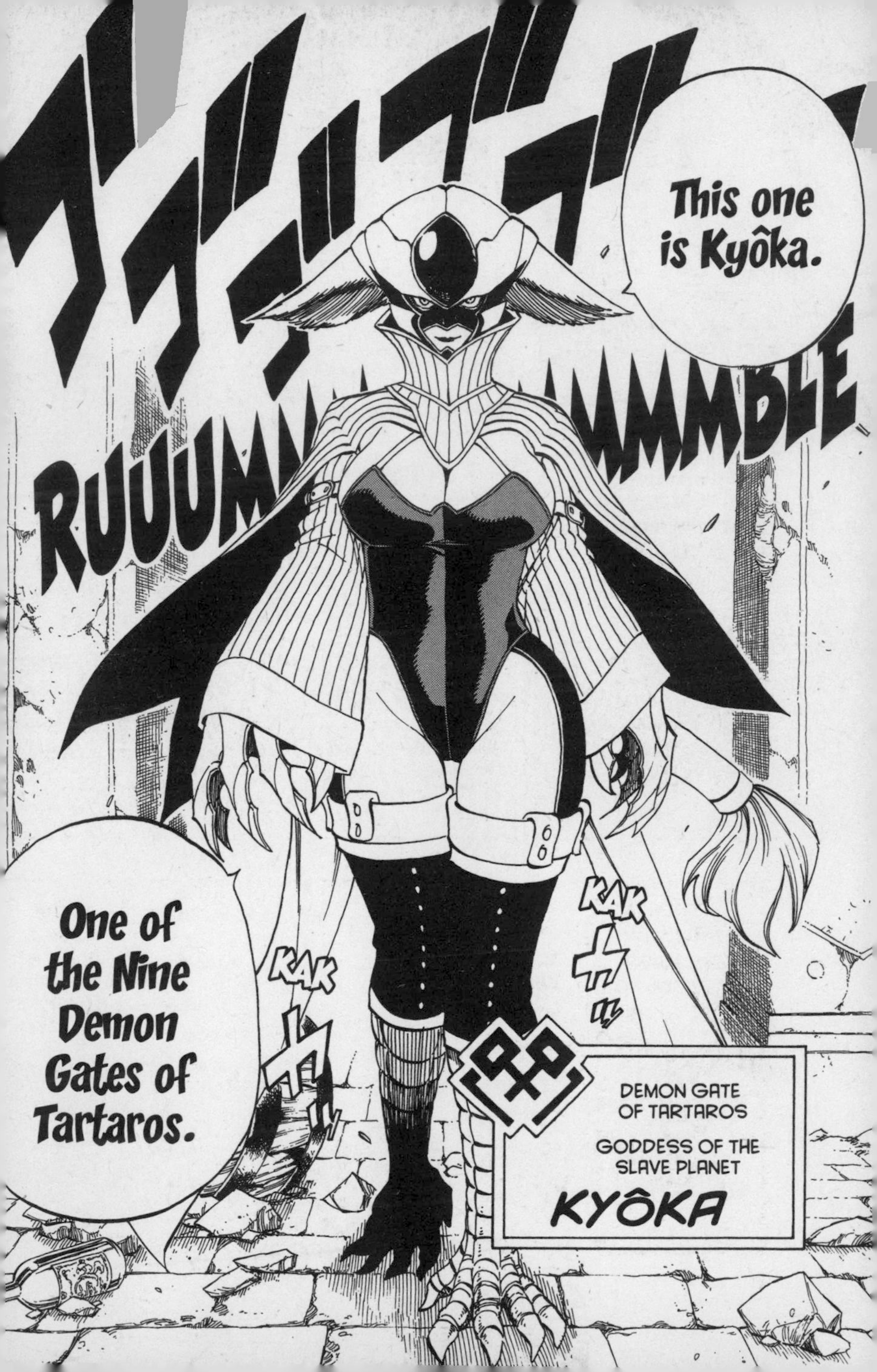
This one is Kyôka.
RUUUM
MMMBLE
KAK
DEMON GATE OF TARTAROS
GODDESS OF THE SLAVE PLANET
KYÔKA
KAK
One of the Nine Demon Gates of Tartaros.

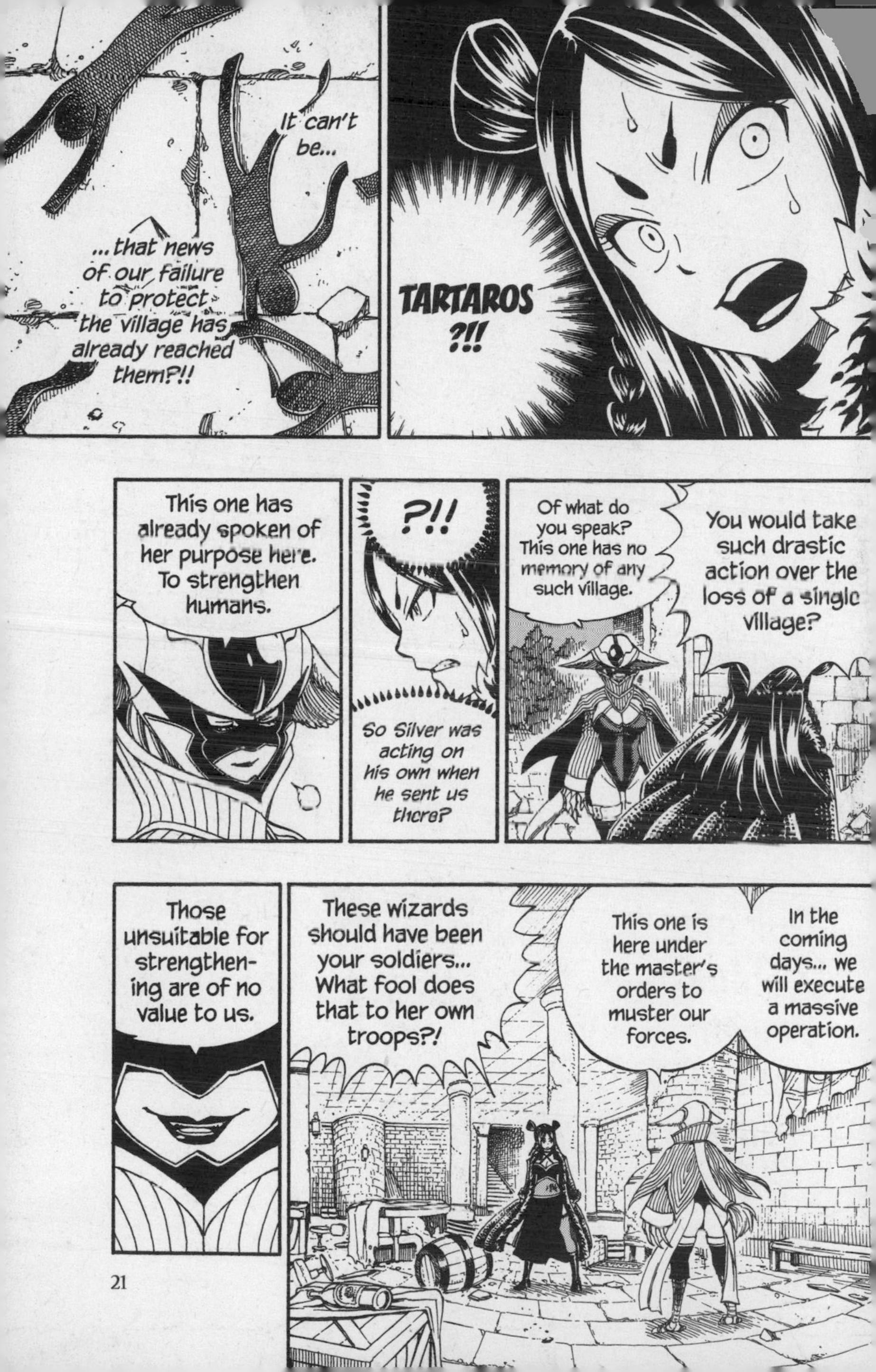
TARTAROS ?!!
It can't be...
...that news of our failure to protect the village has already reached them?!!
You would take such drastic action over the loss of a single village?
Of what do you speak? This one has no memory of any such village.
?!!
So Silver was acting on his own when he sent us there?
This one has already spoken of her purpose here. To strengthen humans.
In the coming days... we will execute a massive operation.
This one is here under the master's orders to muster our forces.
These wizards should have been your soldiers... What fool does that to her own troops?!
Those unsuitable for strengthen-ing are of no value to us.

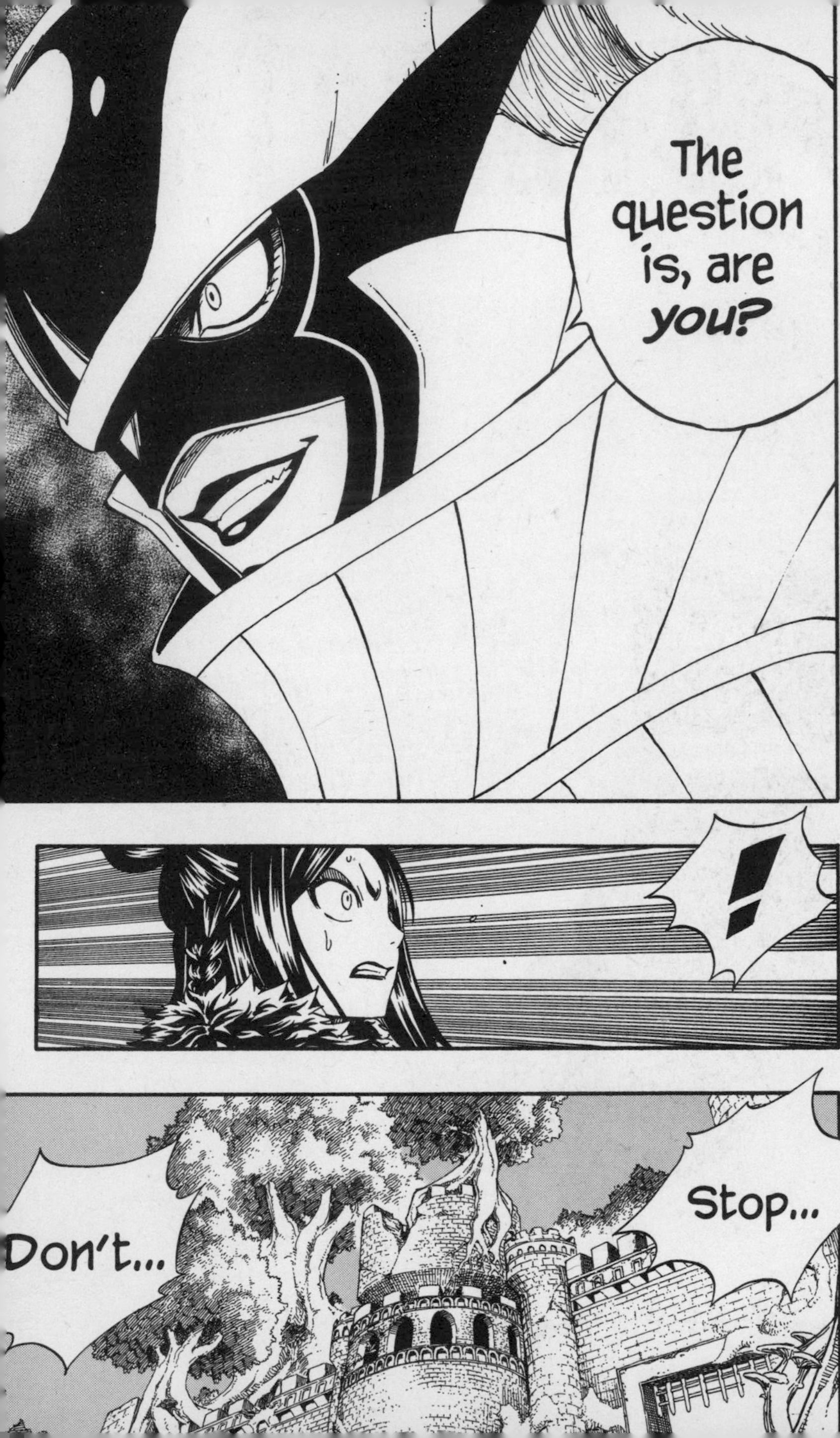
The question is, are *you?*
!
Stop...
Don't...

FAIRY TAIL

Chapter 355:
Song of the Fairies

LAMIA SCALE

Name: **Yûka Suzuki**   Age: **25**

Magic:
Wave Motion

Likes: Dislikes:
Eyebrows   **Salty foods**

Remarks

His magic creates a wave form that eliminates his opponent's magic abilities, and because of that, most of the jobs he goes on set him against other wizards. For a little while, he, Toby, and Sherry did too much evil and were expelled from their guild. Then they met Lyon and committed even more evil acts.

But after they met Natsu and the Fairy Tail members, they were reinstated, and with Jura's lectures, they've matured quite a bit.

He has too-prominent eyebrows. A long time ago, he played a game to see how many matchsticks he could balance on top of them.

*Shirt Patch: Eyebrows

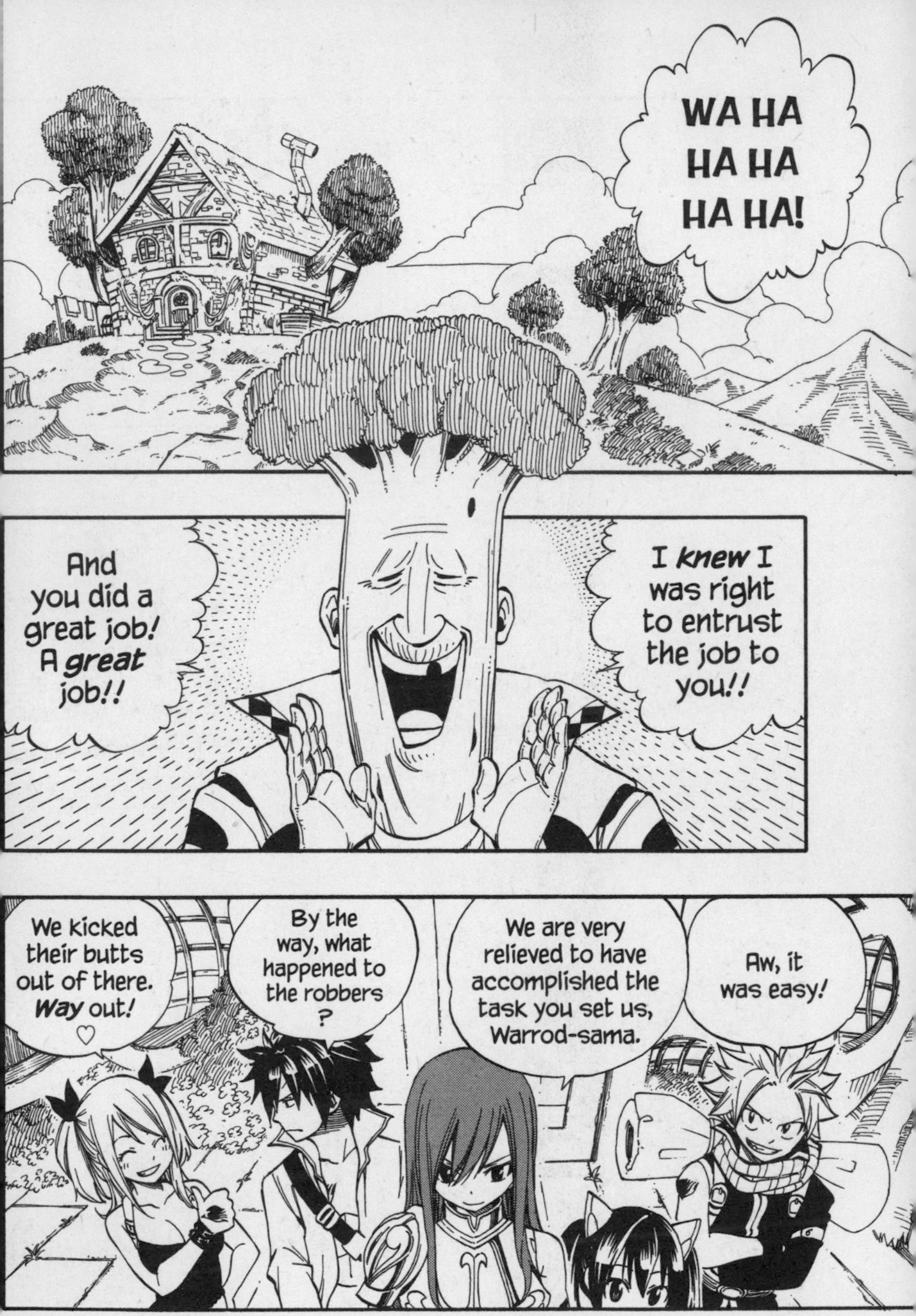
WA HA HA HA HA HA!
I *knew* I was right to entrust the job to you!!
And you did a great job! A *great* job!!
Aw, it was easy!
We are very relieved to have accomplished the task you set us, Warrod-sama.
By the way, what happened to the robbers?
We kicked their butts out of there. *Way* out! ♡

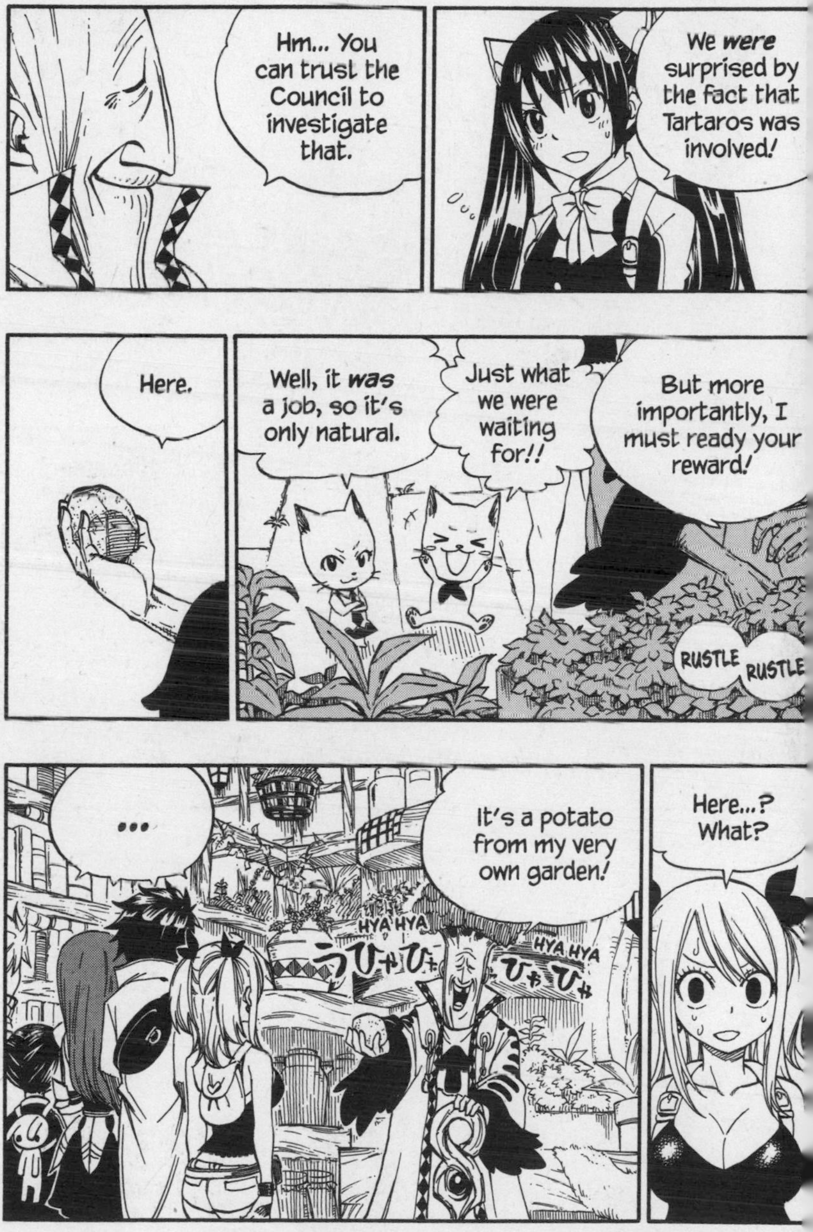
We *were* surprised by the fact that Tartaros was involved!
Hm... You can trust the Council to investigate that.
But more importantly, I must ready your reward!
RUSTLE
RUSTLE
Just what we were waiting for!!
Well, it *was* a job, so it's only natural.
Here.
Here...? What?
It's a potato from my very own garden!
HYA HYA
HYA HYA
...

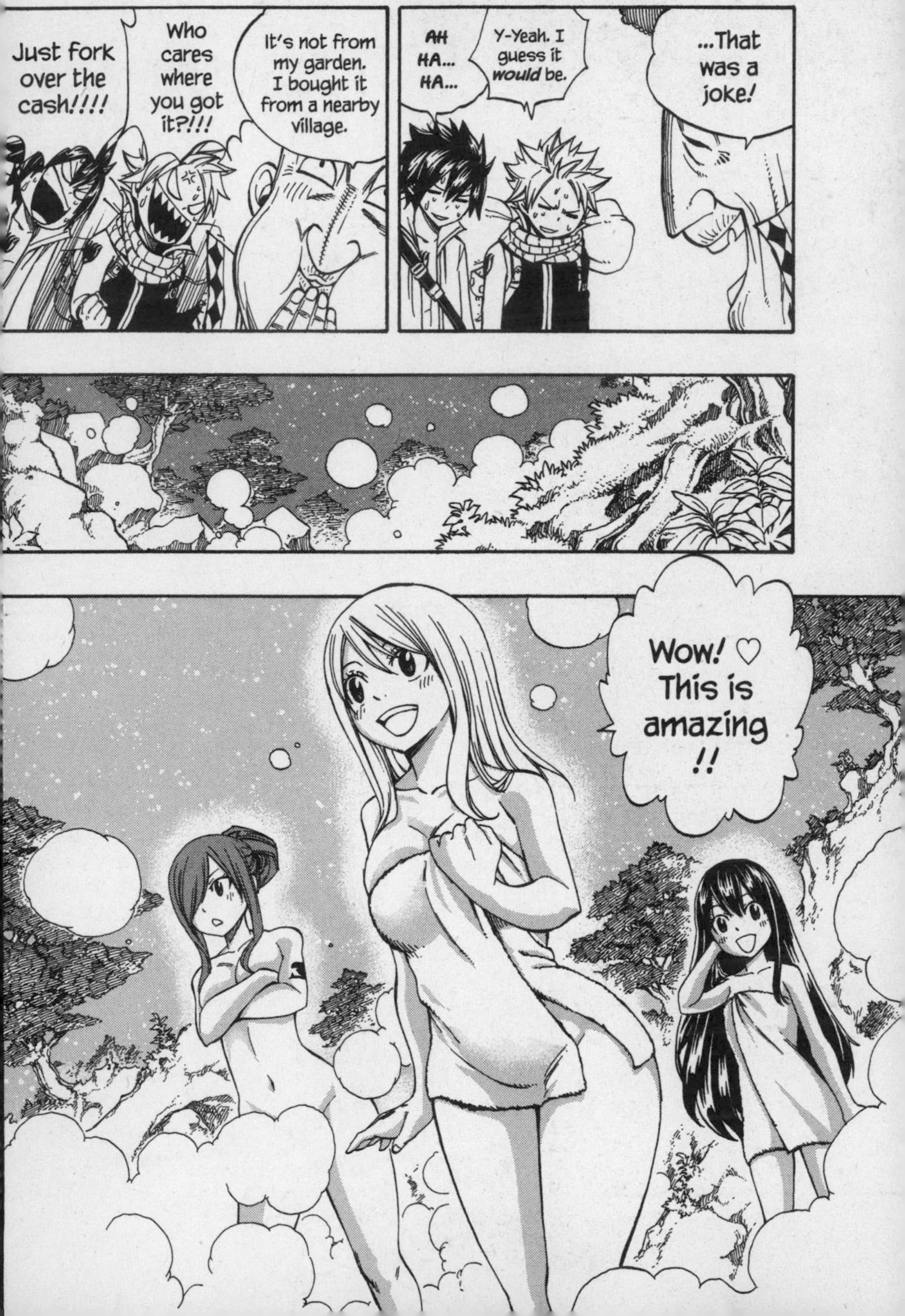
...That was a joke!
Y-Yeah. I guess it *would* be.
AH HA... HA...
It's not from my garden. I bought it from a nearby village.
Who cares where you got it?!!!
Just fork over the cash!!!!
Wow! ♡ This is amazing!!

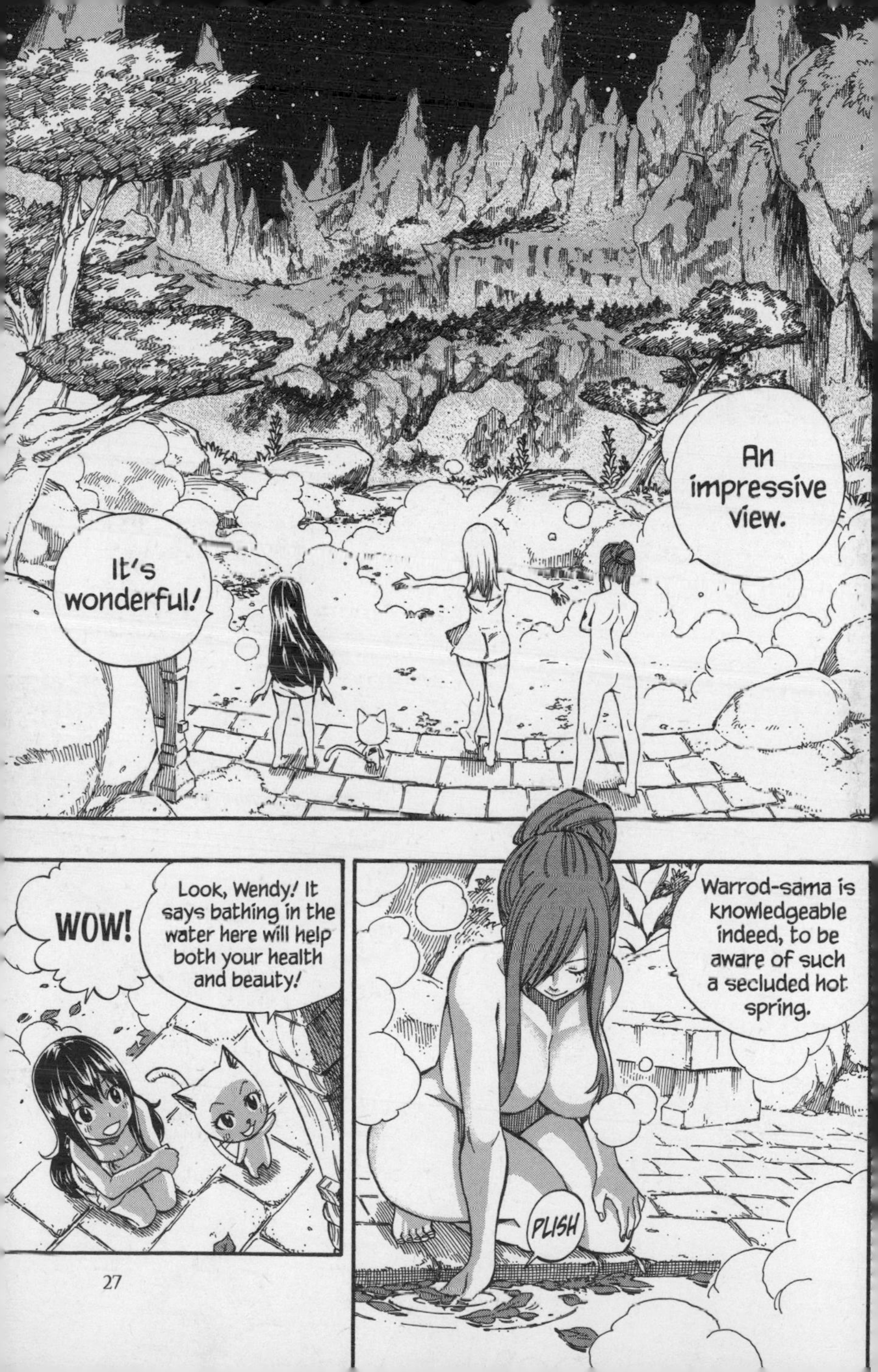
An impressive view.
It's wonderful!
Warrod-sama is knowledgeable indeed, to be aware of such a secluded hot spring.
PLISH
Look, Wendy! It says bathing in the water here will help both your health and beauty!
WOW!

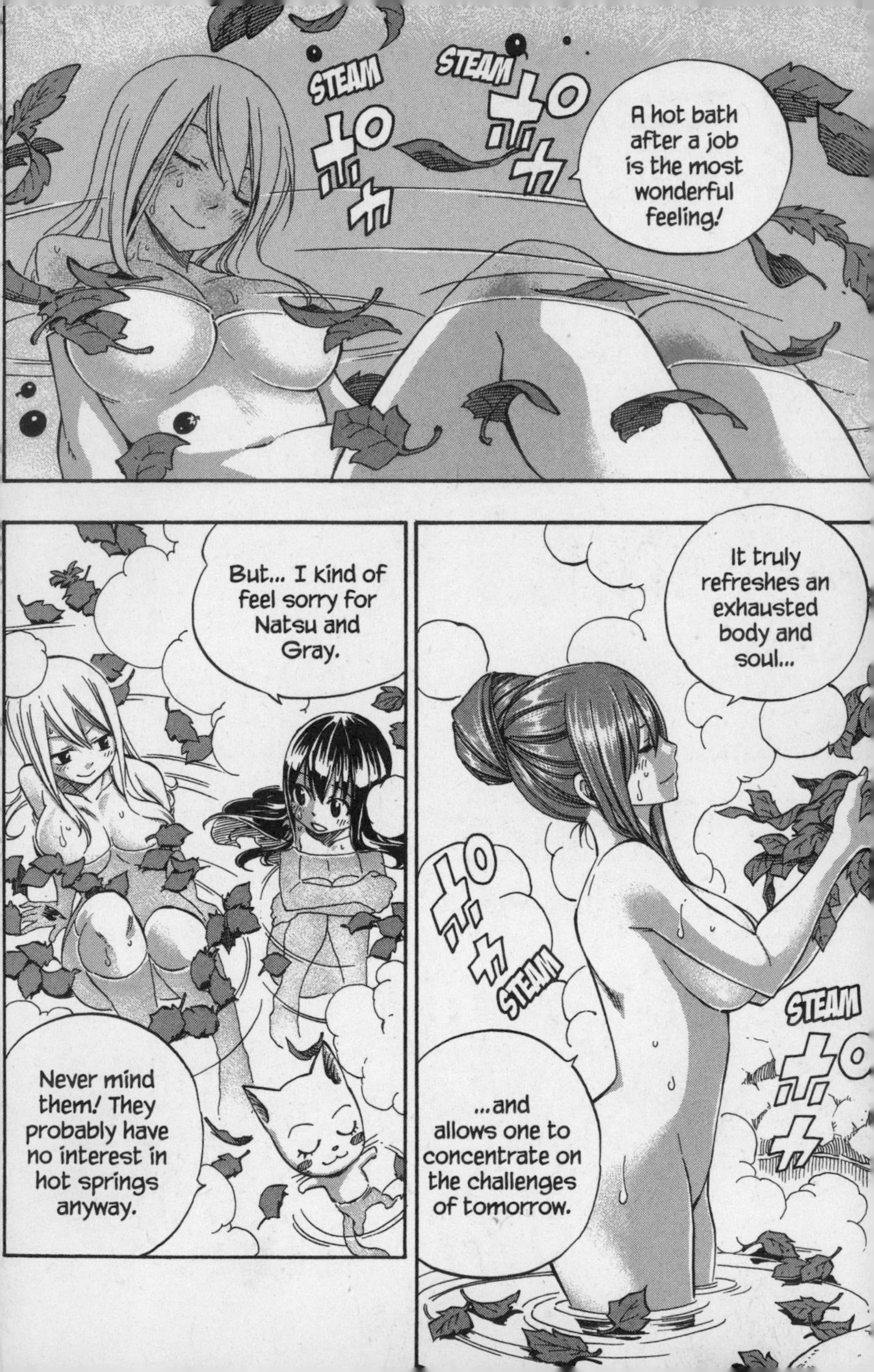
A hot bath after a job is the most wonderful feeling!
STEAM
STEAM
It truly refreshes an exhausted body and soul...
STEAM
STEAM
...and allows one to concentrate on the challenges of tomorrow.
But... I kind of feel sorry for Natsu and Gray.
Never mind them! They probably have no interest in hot springs anyway.

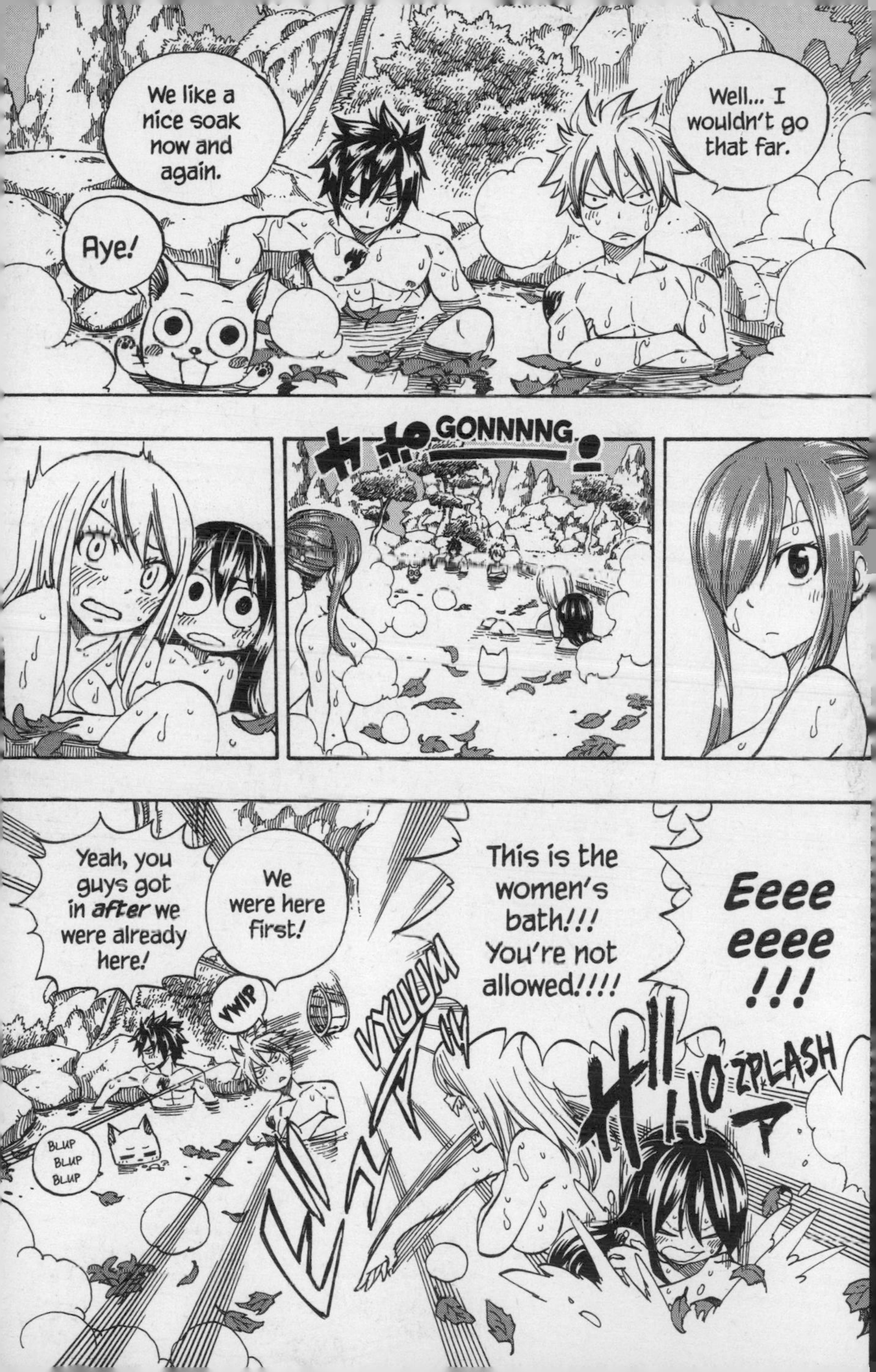

Well... I wouldn't go that far.
We like a nice soak now and again.
Aye!
GONNNNG
Eeee eeee !!!
This is the women's bath!!! You're not allowed!!!!
We were here first!
Yeah, you guys got in *after* we were already here!
ZPLASH
VYUUM
VWIP
BLUP BLUP BLUP

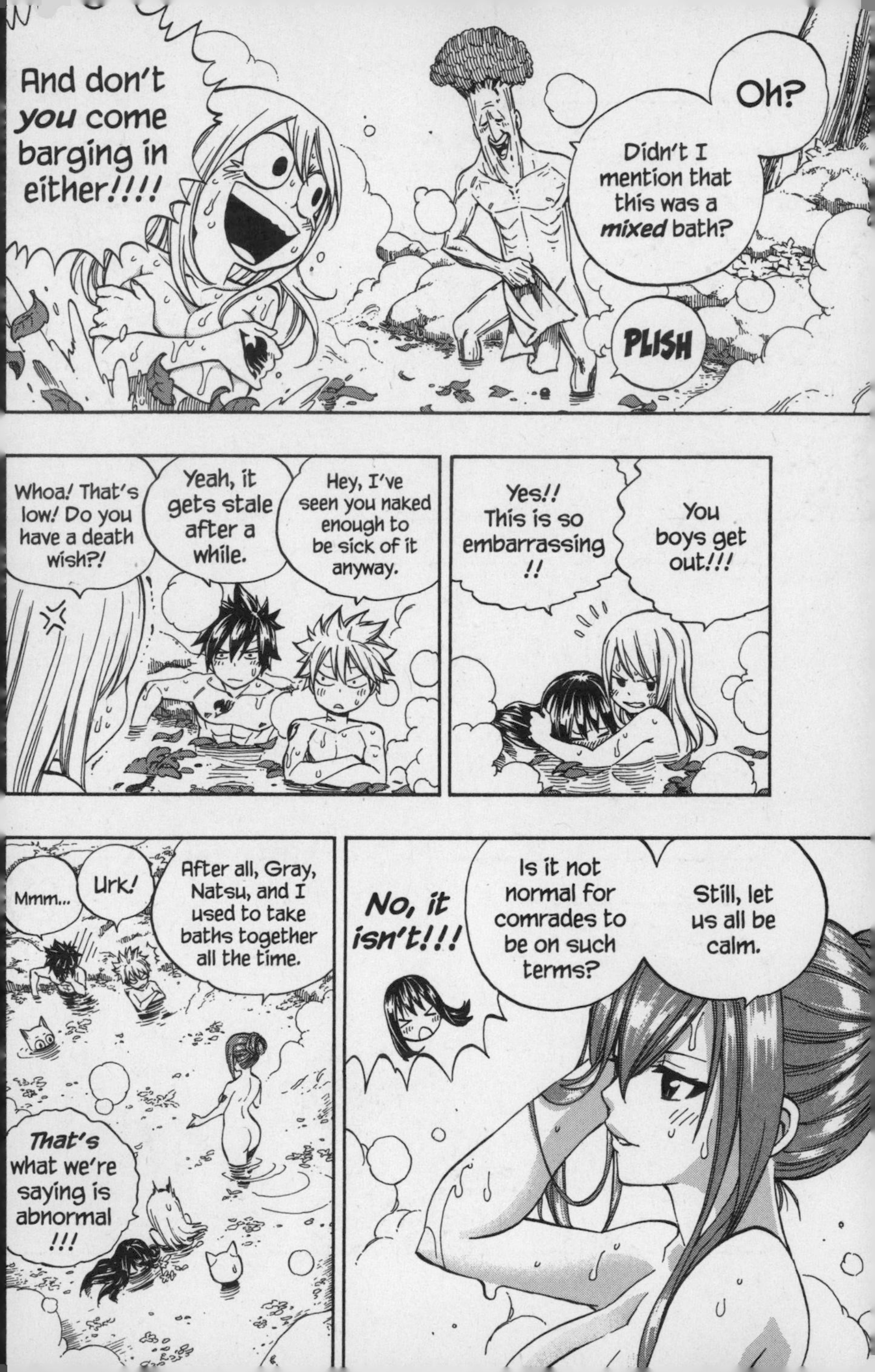

Oh?
Didn't I mention that this was a *mixed* bath?
PLISH
And don't *you* come barging in either!!!!
You boys get out!!!
Yes!! This is so embarrassing !!
Hey, I've seen you naked enough to be sick of it anyway.
Yeah, it gets stale after a while.
Whoa! That's low! Do you have a death wish?!
Still, let us all be calm.
Is it not normal for comrades to be on such terms?
No, it isn't!!!
After all, Gray, Natsu, and I used to take baths together all the time.
Urk!
Mmm...
That's what we're saying is abnormal !!!

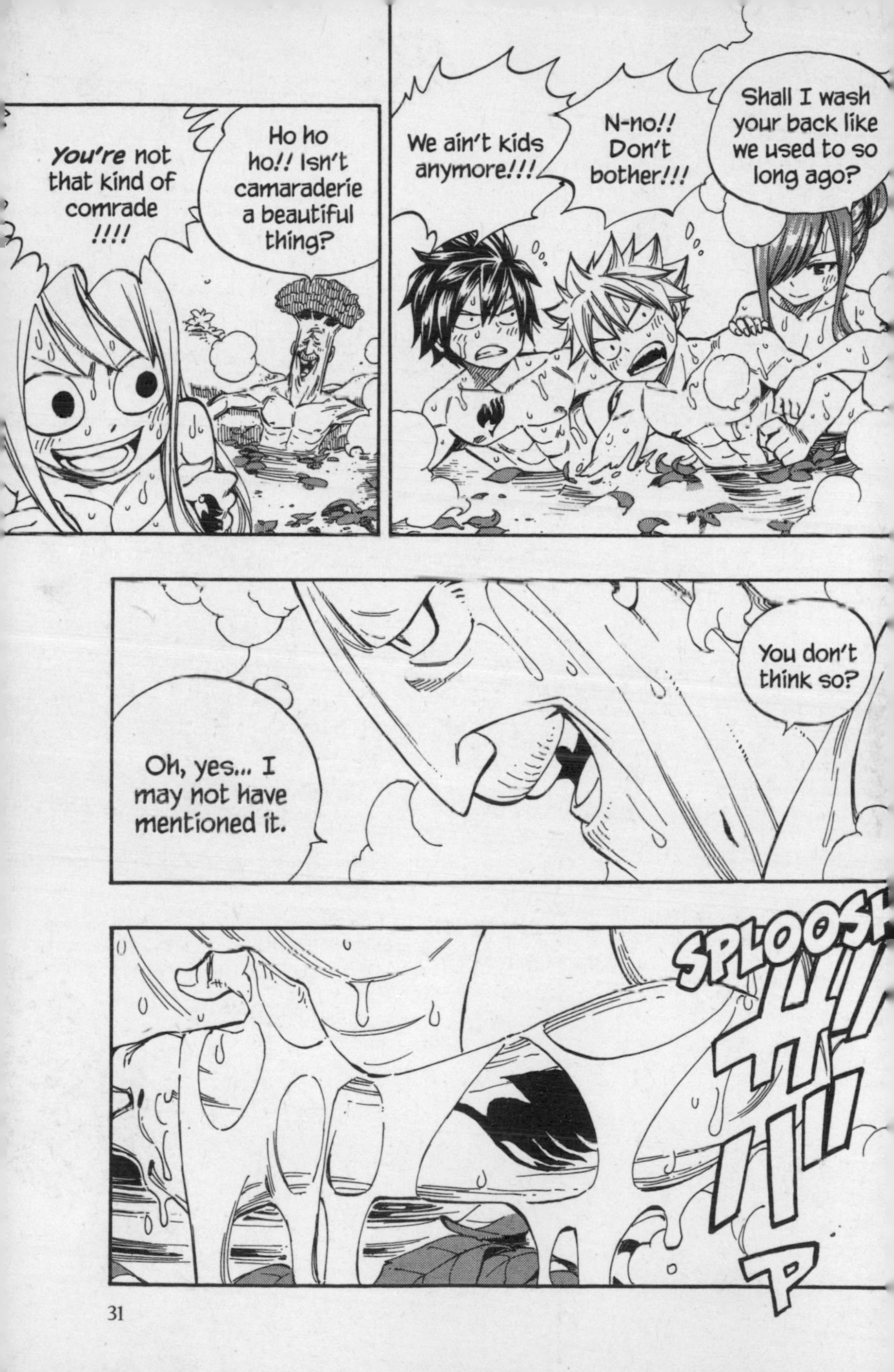
Shall I wash your back like we used to so long ago?
N-no!! Don't bother!!!
We ain't kids anymore!!!
Ho ho ho!! Isn't camaraderie a beautiful thing?
You're not that kind of comrade!!!!
You don't think so?
Oh, yes... I may not have mentioned it.
SPLOOS

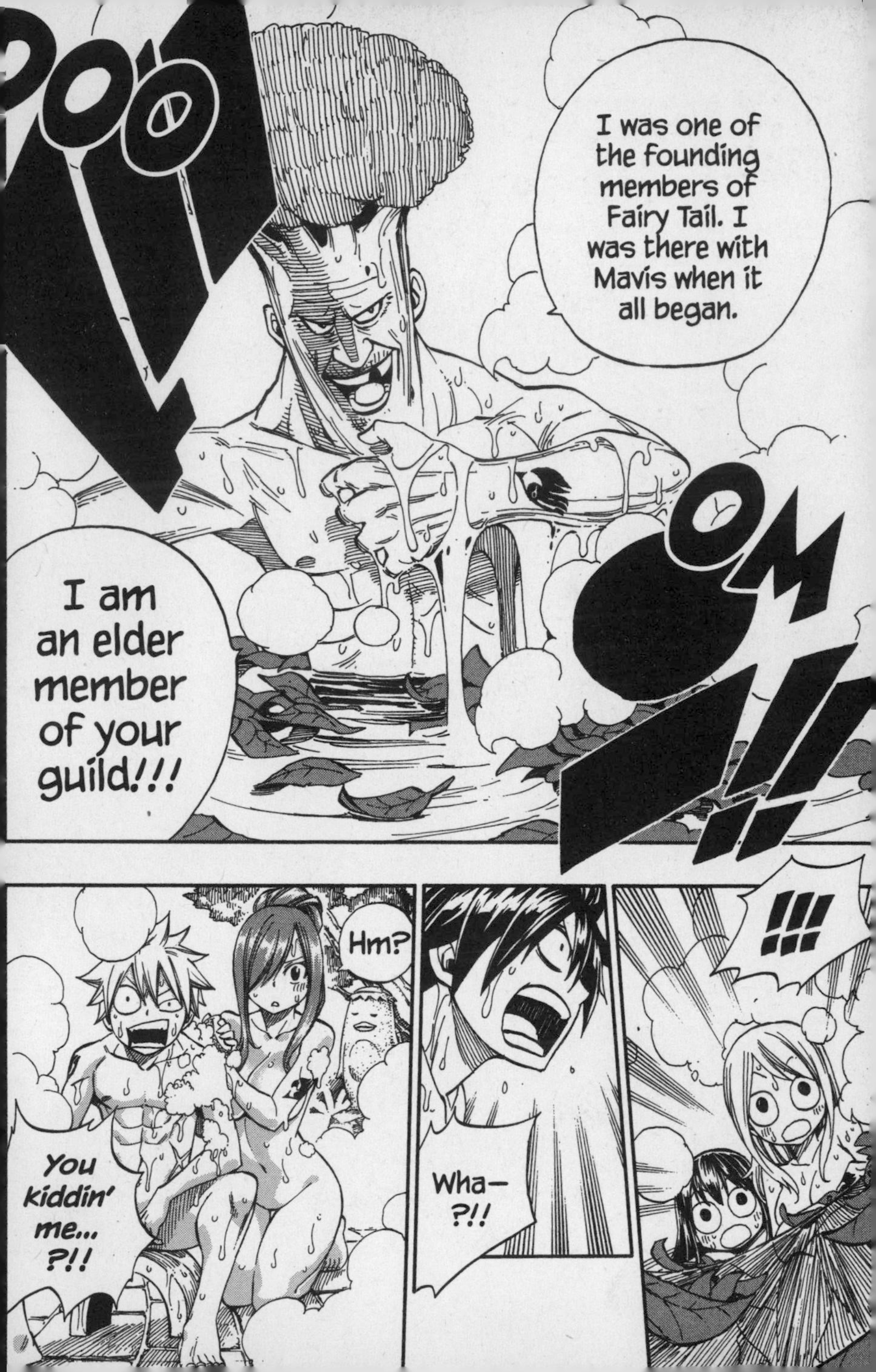
I was one of the founding members of Fairy Tail. I was there with Mavis when it all began.
I am an elder member of your guild!!!
!!!
Wha— ?!!
Hm?
You kiddin' me... ?!!

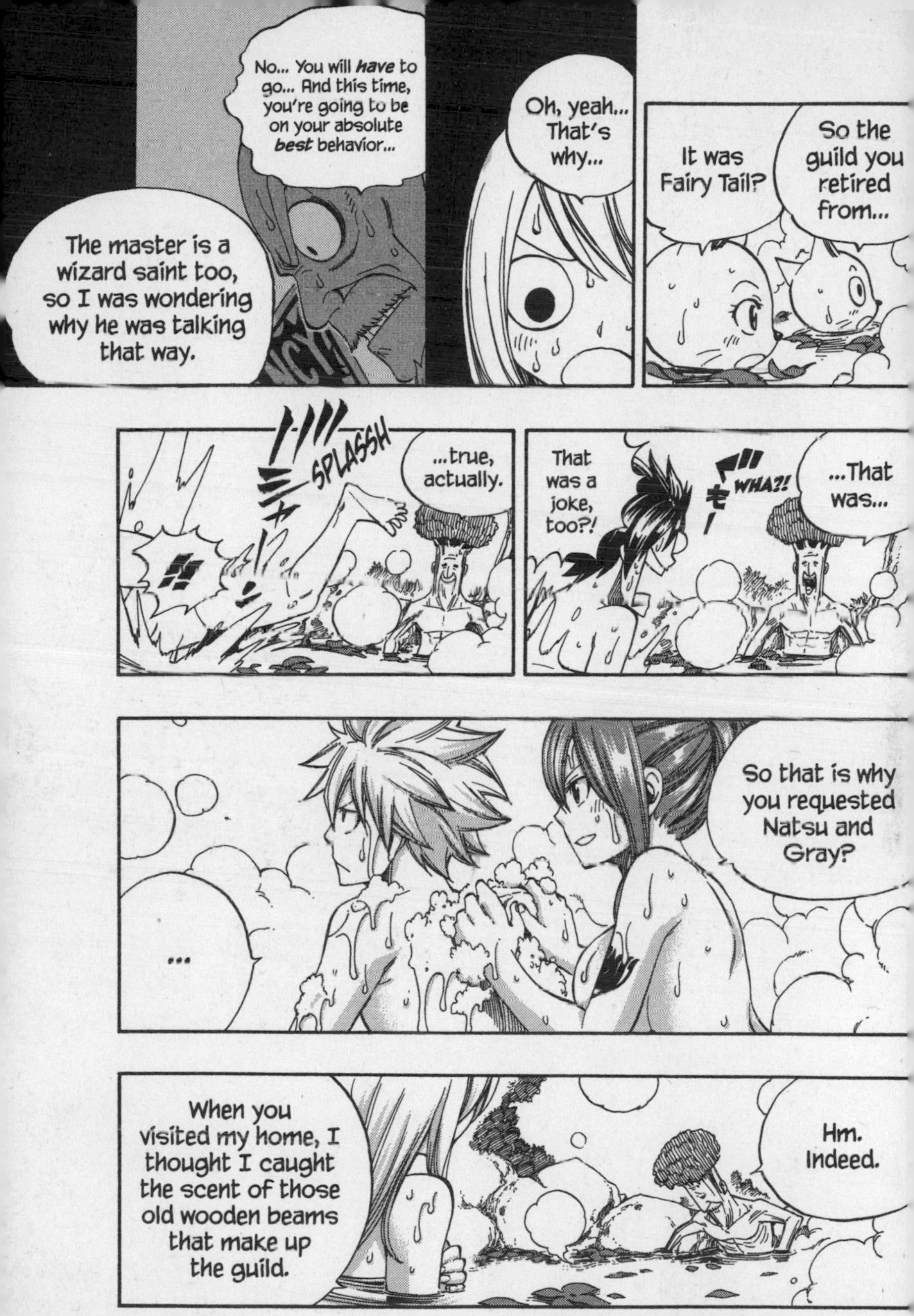
So the guild you retired from...
It was Fairy Tail?
Oh, yeah... That's why...
No... You will *have* to go... And this time, you're going to be on your absolute *best* behavior...
The master is a wizard saint too, so I was wondering why he was talking that way.
...That was...
WHA?!
That was a joke, too?!
...true, actually.
SPLASSH
So that is why you requested Natsu and Gray?
...
Hm. Indeed.
When you visited my home, I thought I caught the scent of those old wooden beams that make up the guild.

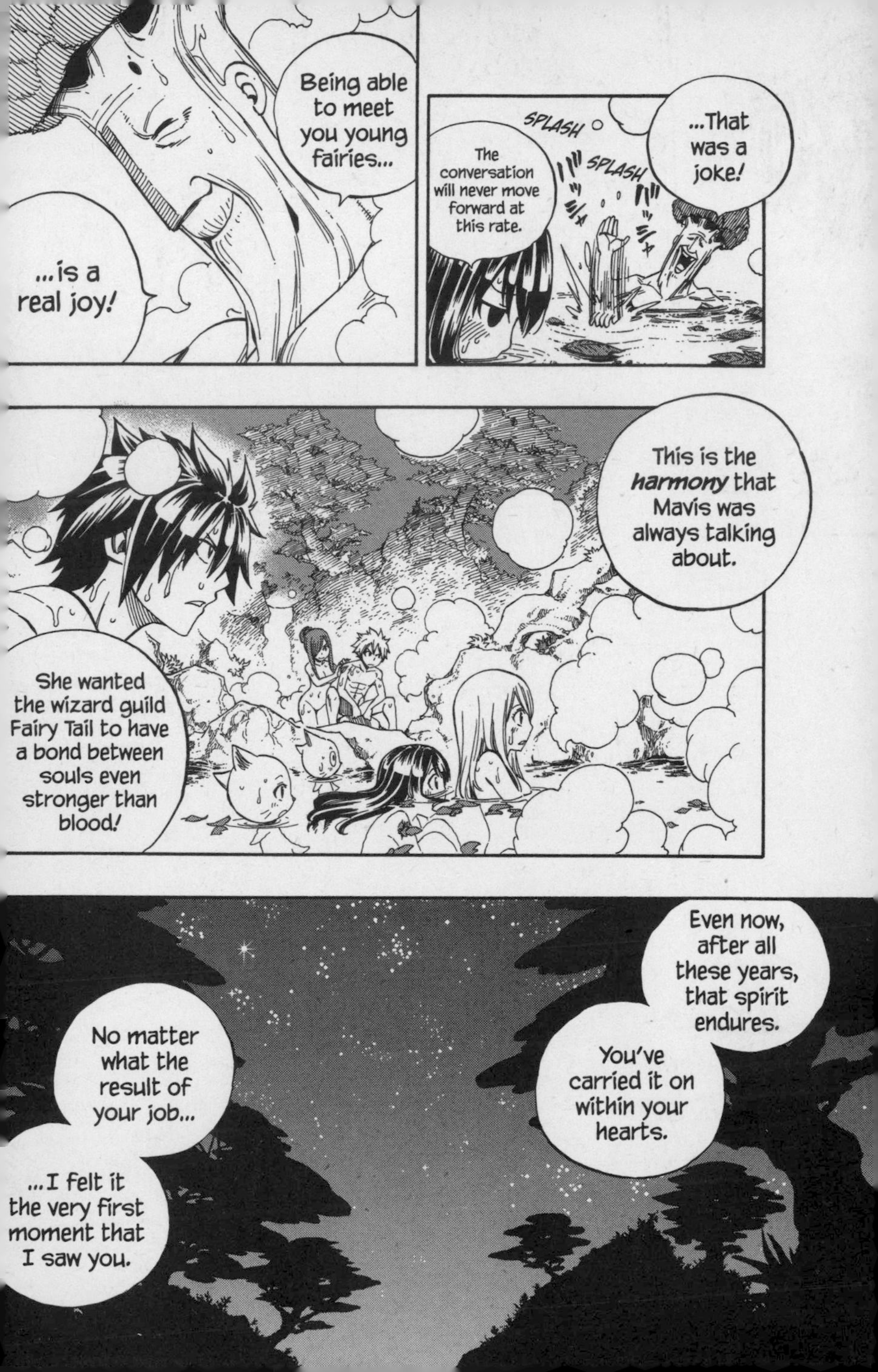
...That was a joke!
SPLASH
SPLASH
The conversation will never move forward at this rate.
Being able to meet you young fairies...
...is a real joy!
This is the *harmony* that Mavis was always talking about.
She wanted the wizard guild Fairy Tail to have a bond between souls even stronger than blood!
Even now, after all these years, that spirit endures.
You've carried it on within your hearts.
No matter what the result of your job...
...I felt it the very first moment that I saw you.

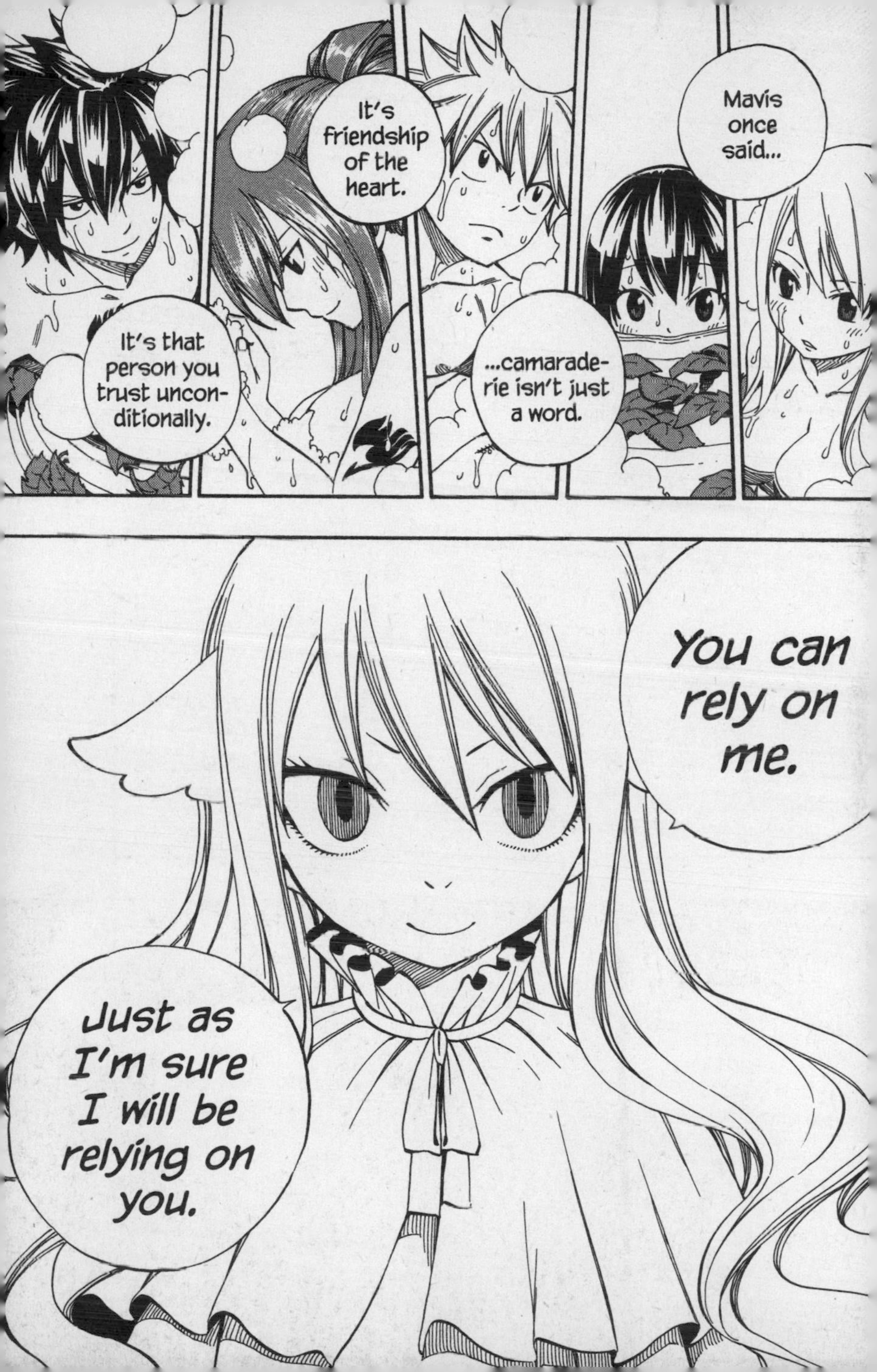
Mavis once said...
...camaraderie isn't just a word.
It's friendship of the heart.
It's that person you trust uncon-ditionally.
You can rely on me.
Just as I'm sure I will be relying on you.

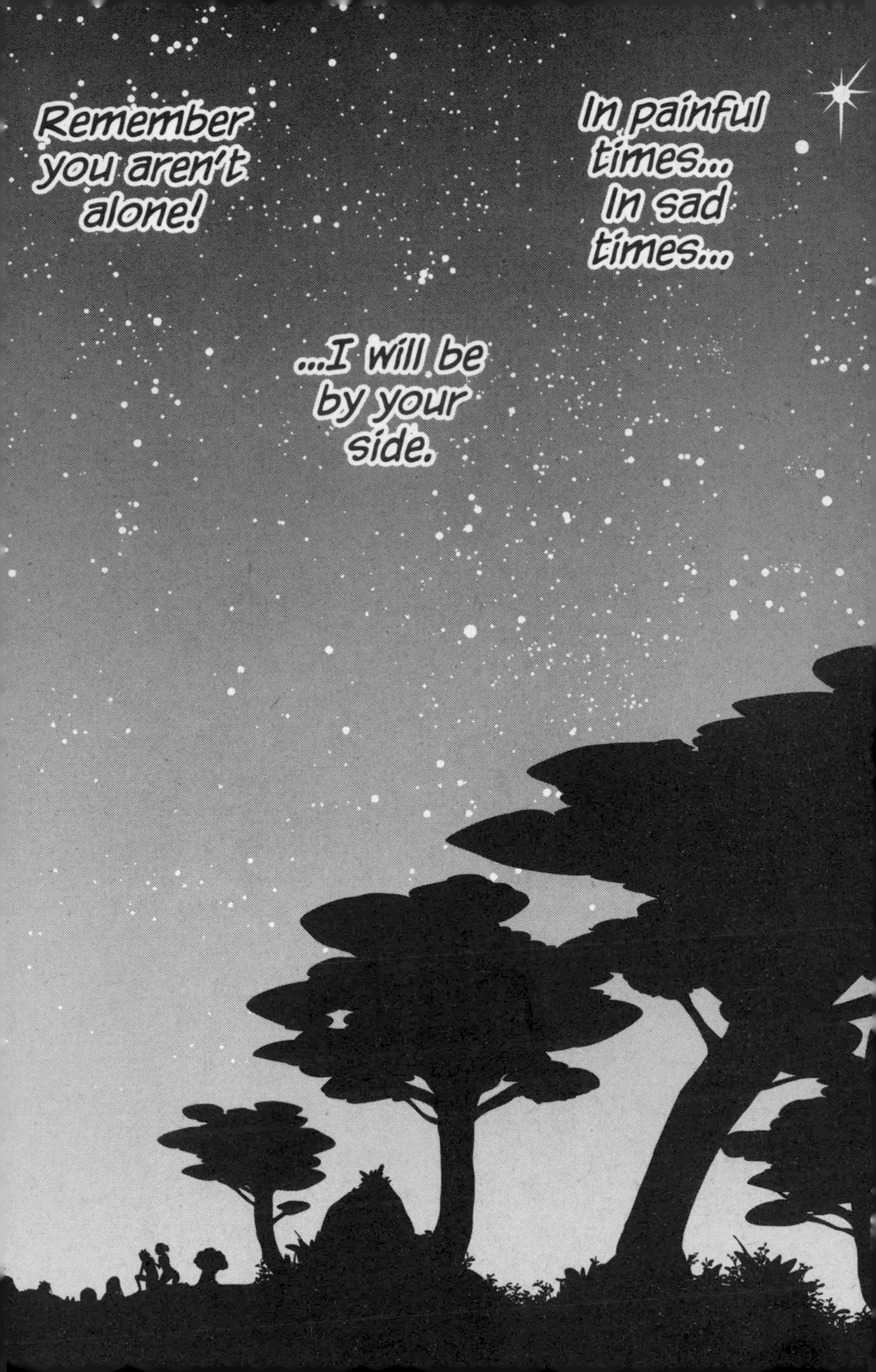
In painful times... In sad times...
...I will be by your side.
Remember you aren't alone!

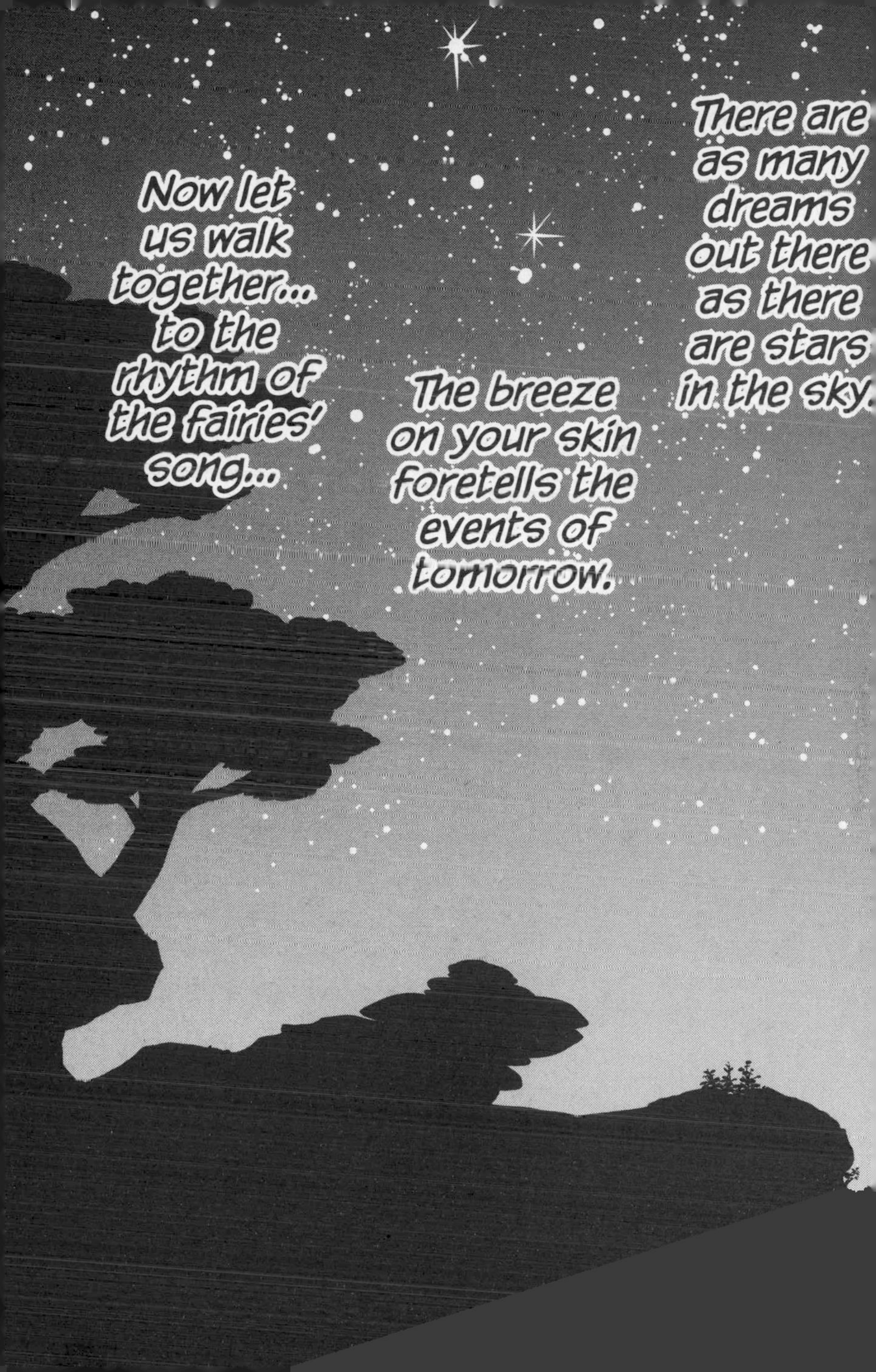
There are as many dreams out there as there are stars in the sky.
The breeze on your skin foretells the events of tomorrow.
Now let us walk together... to the rhythm of the fairies' song...

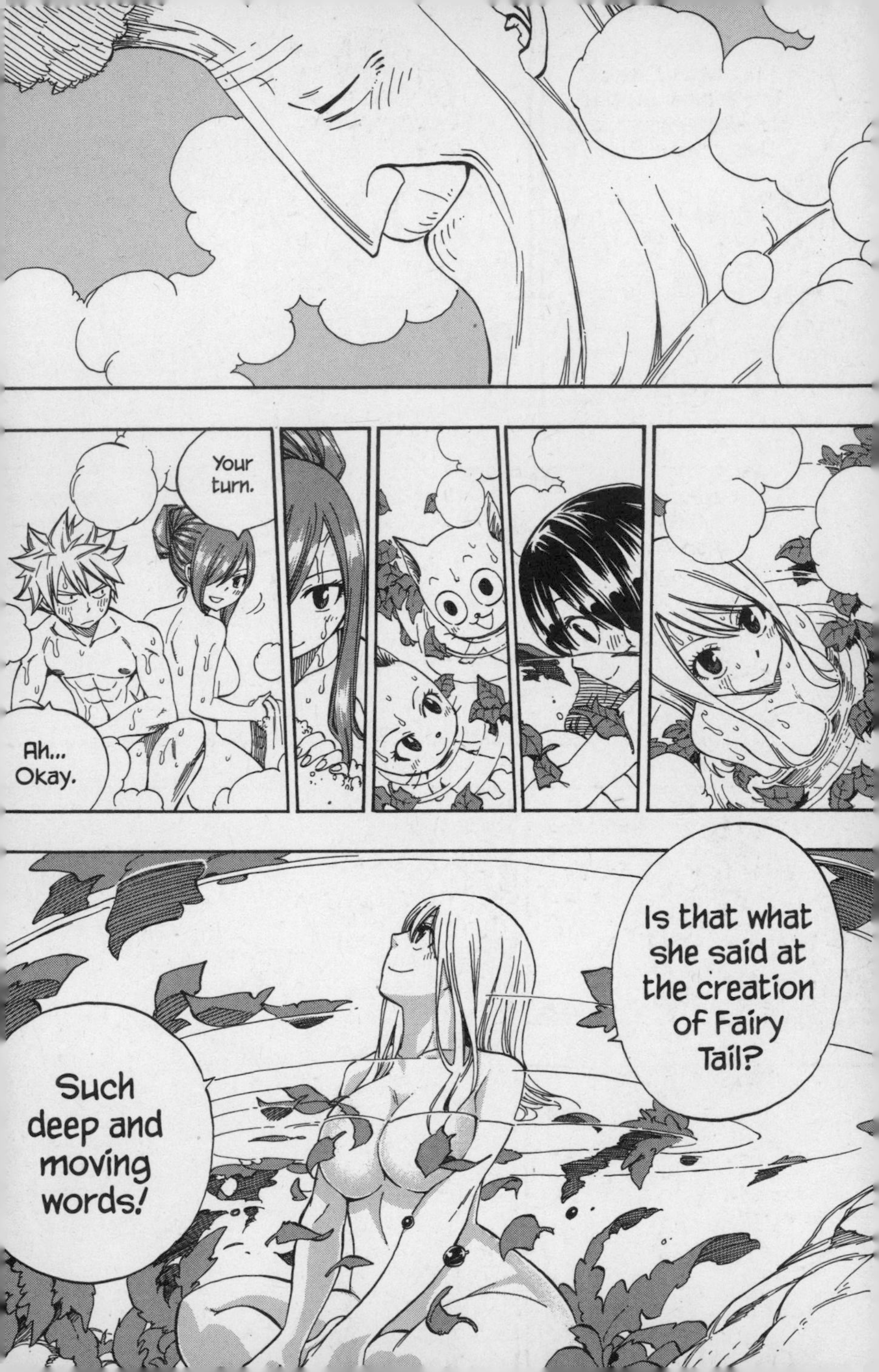
Your turn.
Ah... Okay.
Is that what she said at the creation of Fairy Tail?
Such deep and moving words!

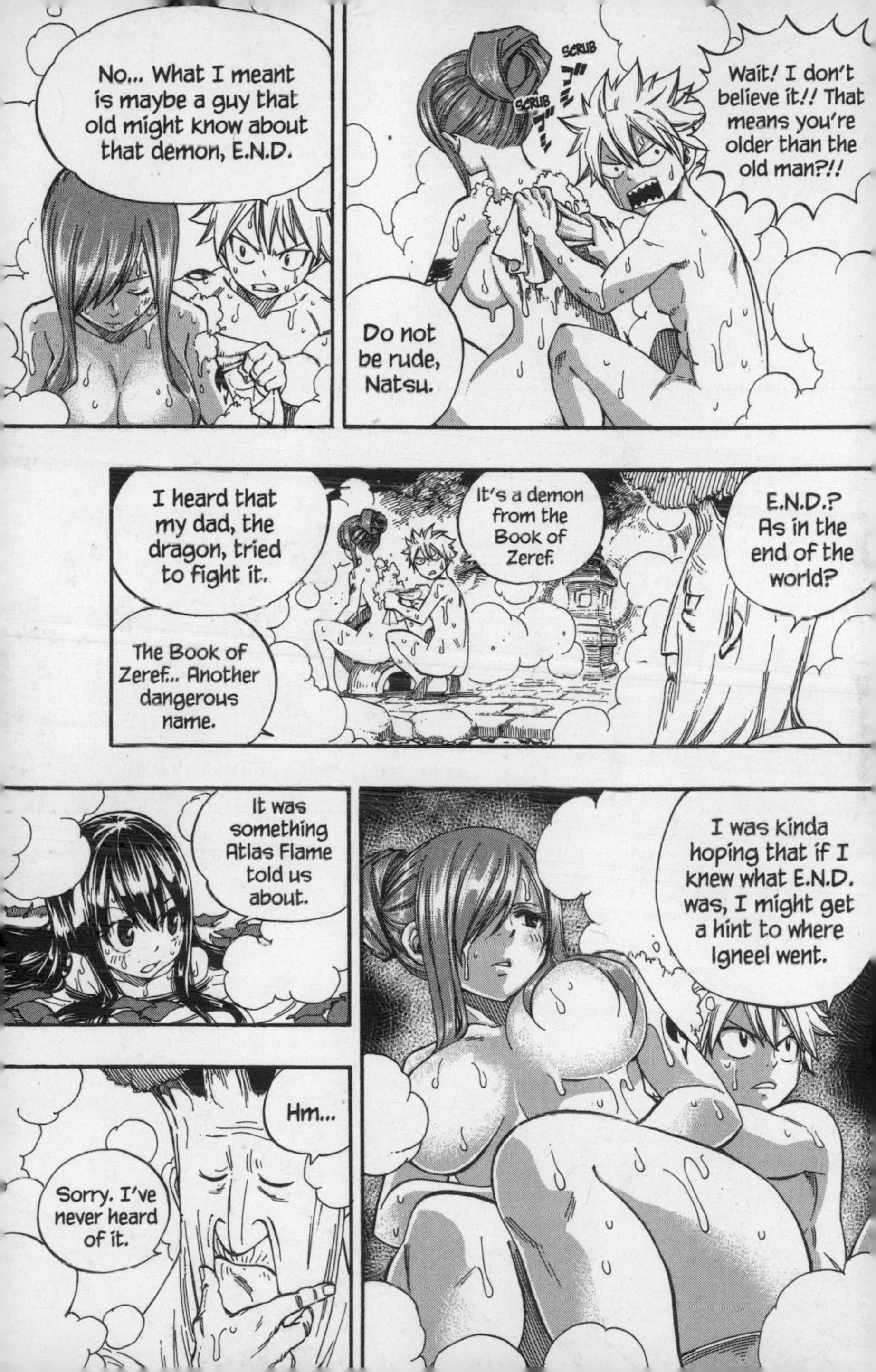
Wait! I don't believe it!! That means you're older than the old man?!!
SCRUB
SCRUB
Do not be rude, Natsu.
No... What I meant is maybe a guy that old might know about that demon, E.N.D.
E.N.D.? As in the end of the world?
It's a demon from the Book of Zeref.
I heard that my dad, the dragon, tried to fight it.
The Book of Zeref... Another dangerous name.
I was kinda hoping that if I knew what E.N.D. was, I might get a hint to where Igneel went.
It was something Atlas Flame told us about.
Hm...
Sorry. I've never heard of it.

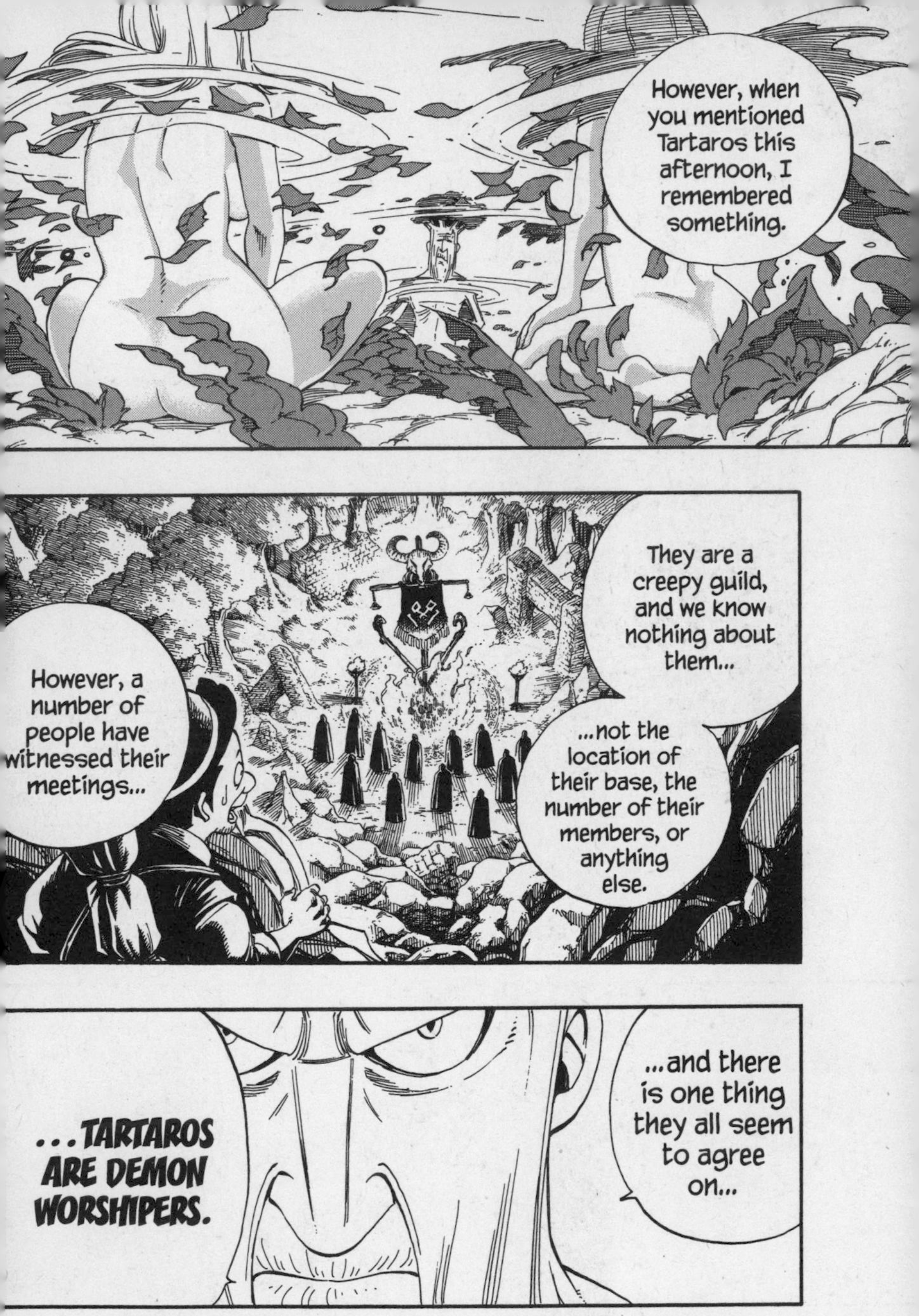
However, when you mentioned Tartaros this afternoon, I remembered something.
They are a creepy guild, and we know nothing about them...
...not the location of their base, the number of their members, or anything else.
However, a number of people have witnessed their meetings...
...and there is one thing they all seem to agree on...
...TARTAROS ARE DEMON WORSHIPERS.

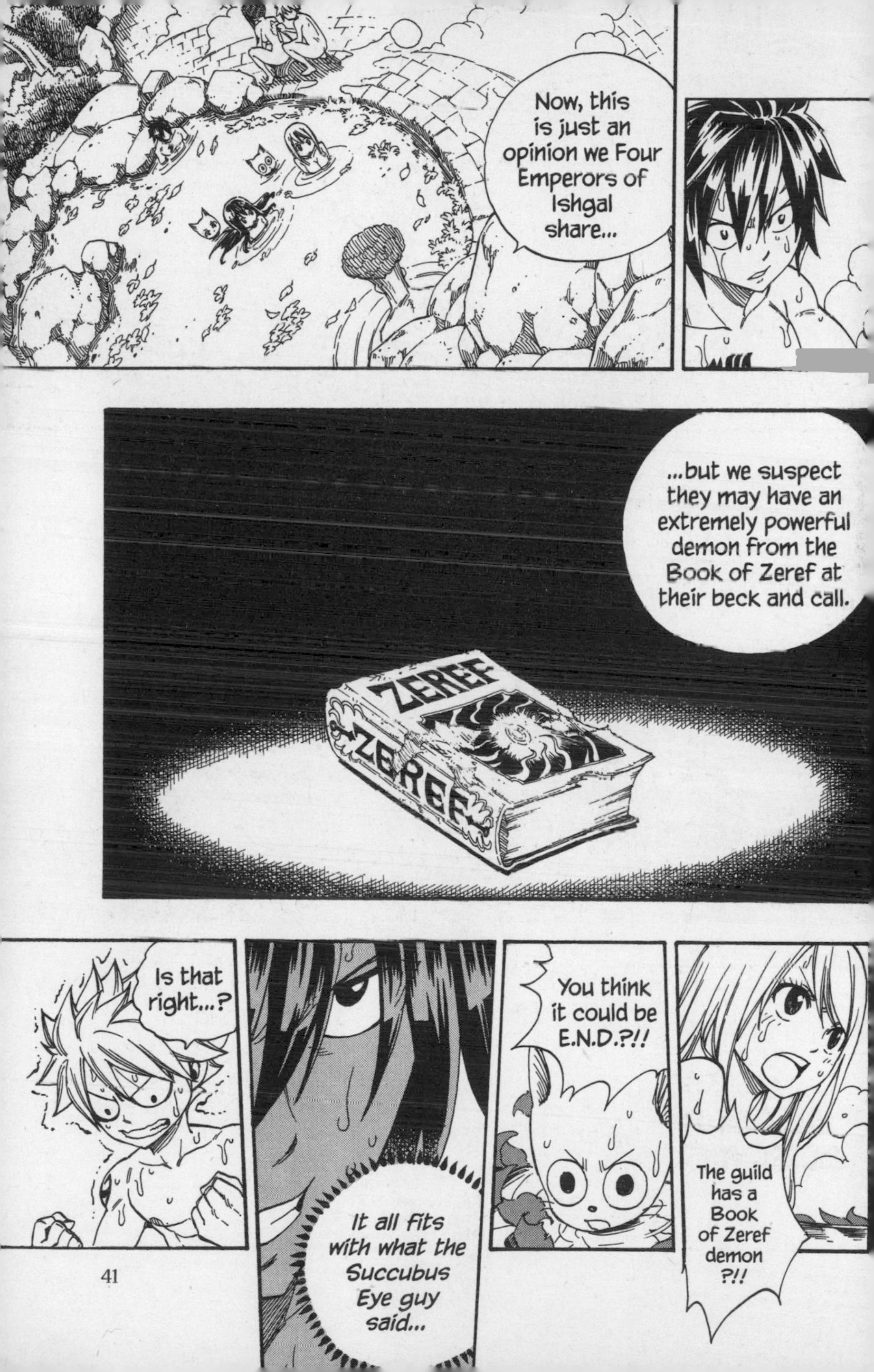
Now, this is just an opinion we Four Emperors of Ishgal share...
...but we suspect they may have an extremely powerful demon from the Book of Zeref at their beck and call.
ZEREF
ZEREF
The guild has a Book of Zeref demon ?!!
You think it could be E.N.D.?!!
It all fits with what the Succubus Eye guy said...
Is that right...?

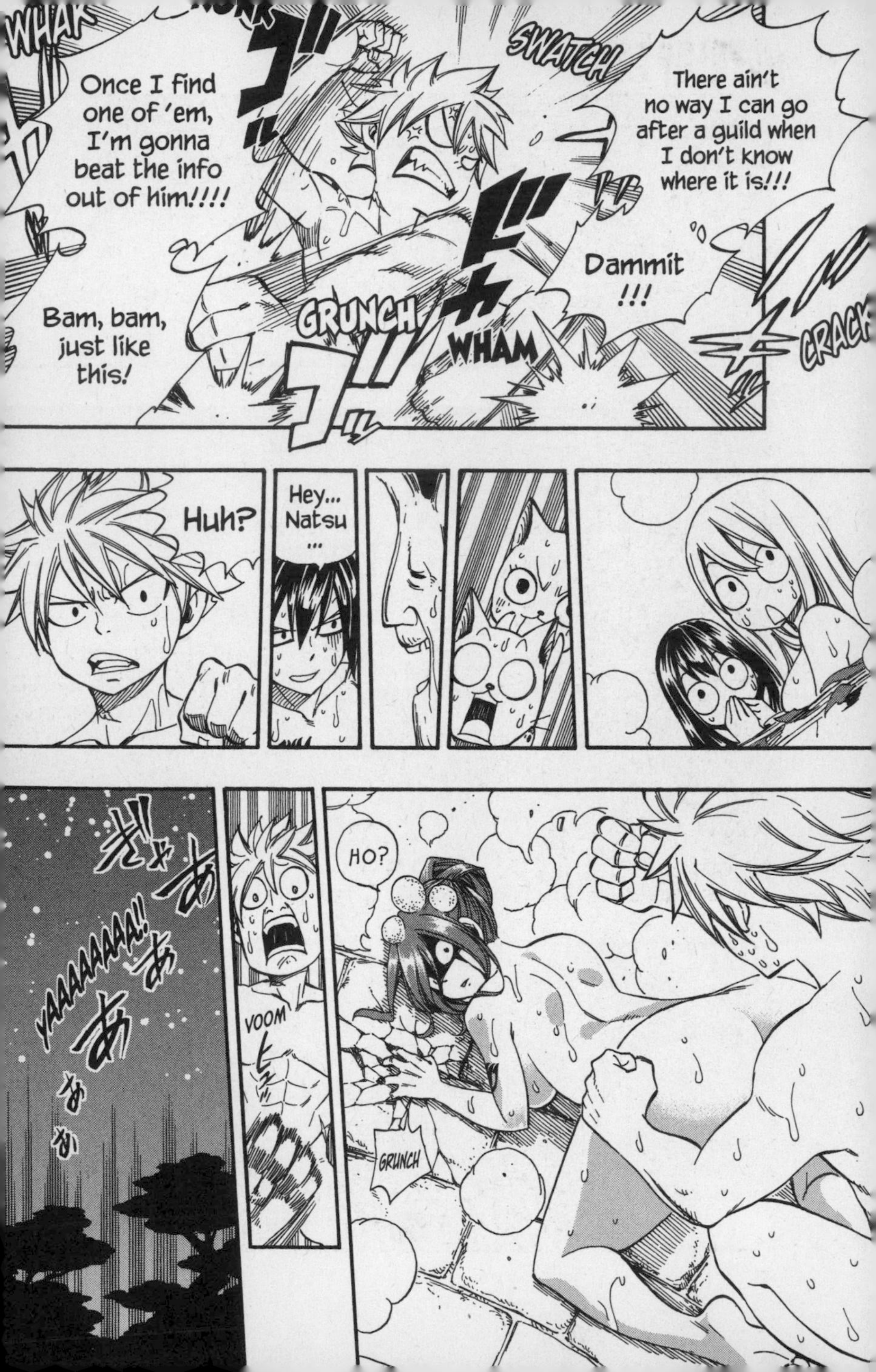
There ain't no way I can go after a guild when I don't know where it is!!!
SWATCH
Once I find one of 'em, I'm gonna beat the info out of him!!!!
Dammit!!!
CRACK
WHAM
GRUNCH
Bam, bam, just like this!
Hey... Natsu ...
Huh?
HO?
GRUNCH
VOOM
YAAAAAAAA!!

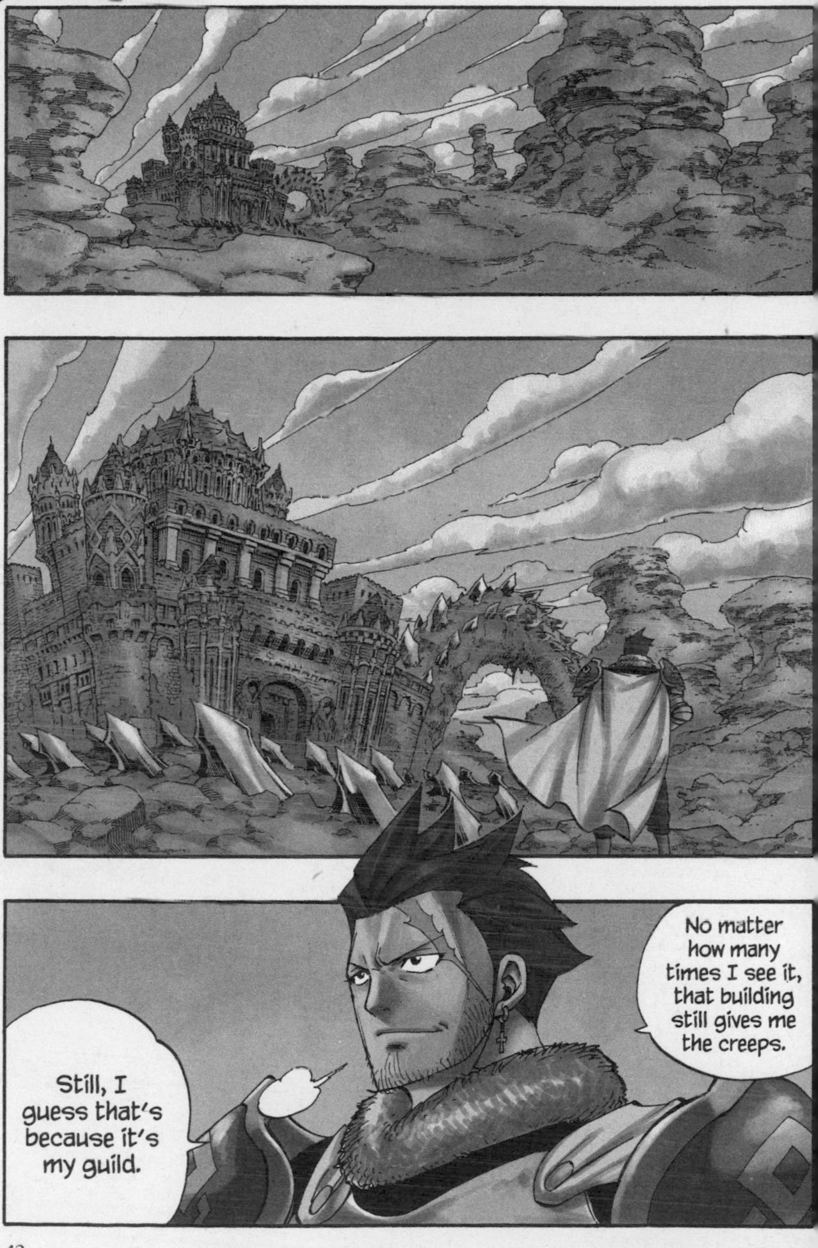
No matter how many times I see it, that building still gives me the creeps.
Still, I guess that's because it's my guild.

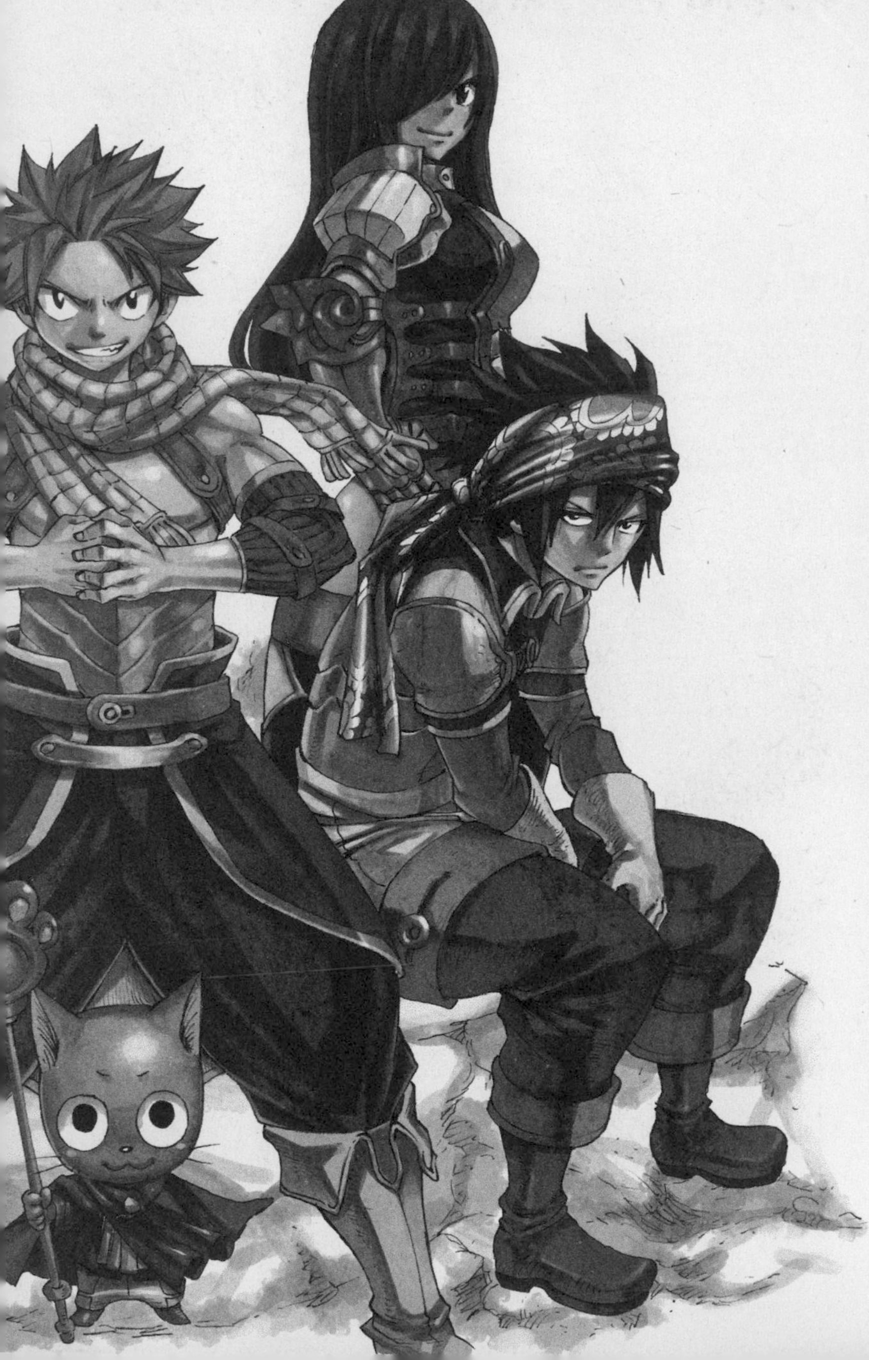

Chapter 356: Tartaros Arc Prologue

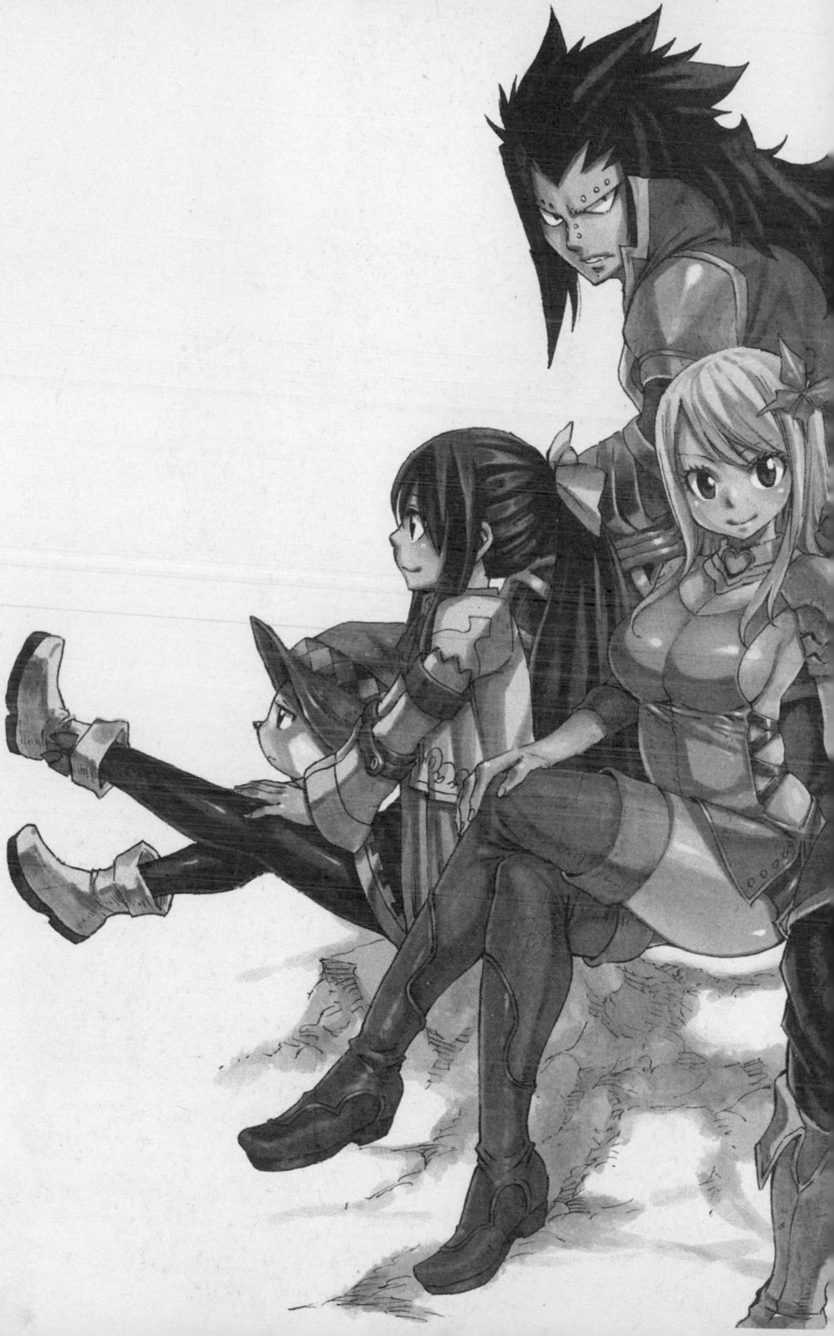

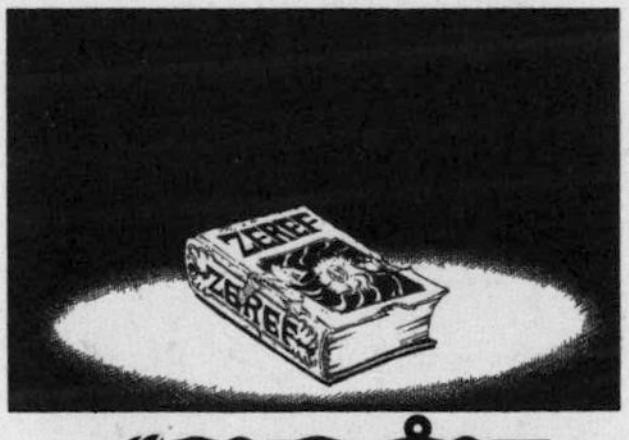
ZEREF
ZEREF

FAIRY TAIL

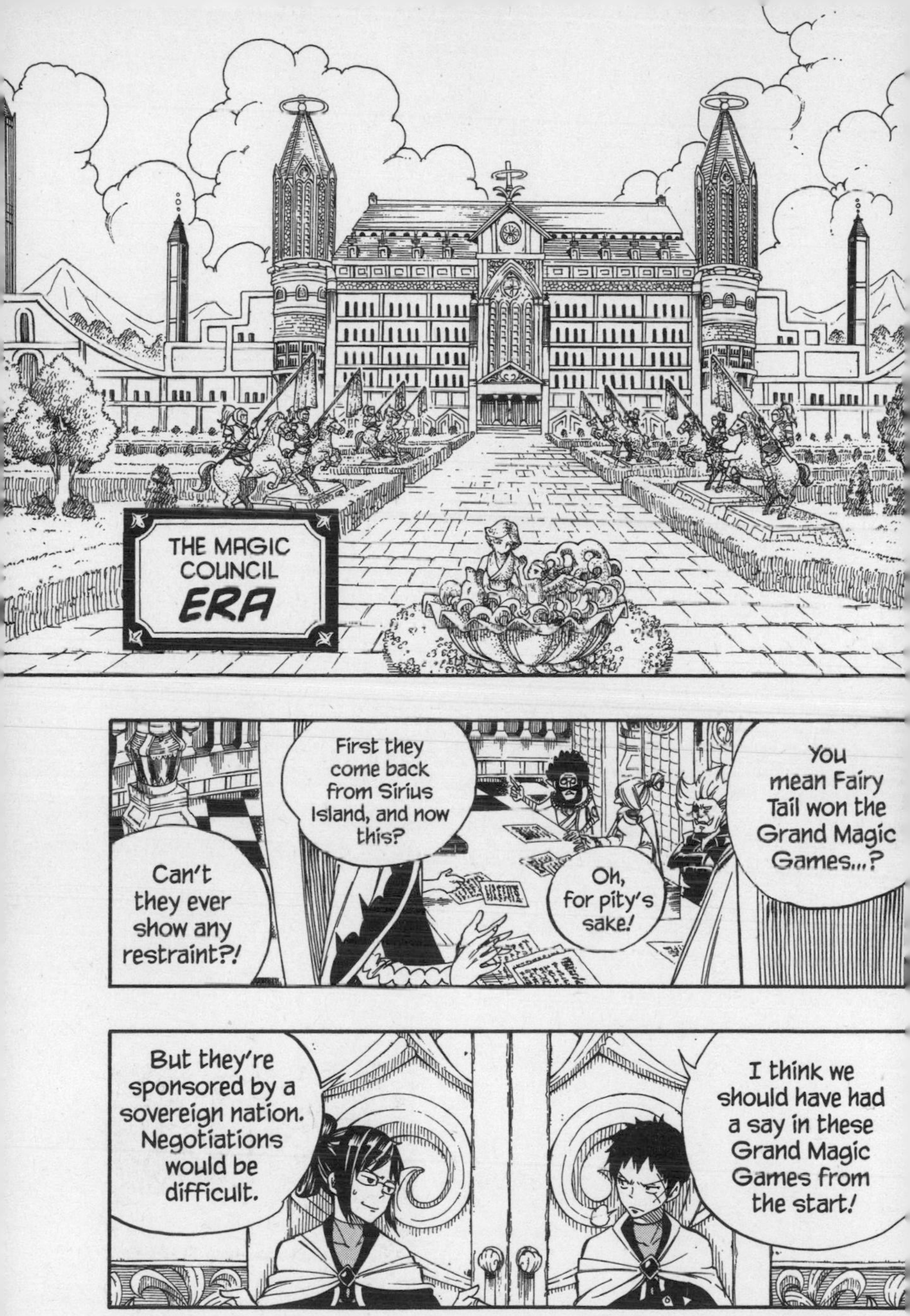
THE MAGIC COUNCIL ERA
You mean Fairy Tail won the Grand Magic Games...?
First they come back from Sirius Island, and now this?
Oh, for pity's sake!
Can't they ever show any restraint?!
I think we should have had a say in these Grand Magic Games from the start!
But they're sponsored by a sovereign nation. Negotiations would be difficult.

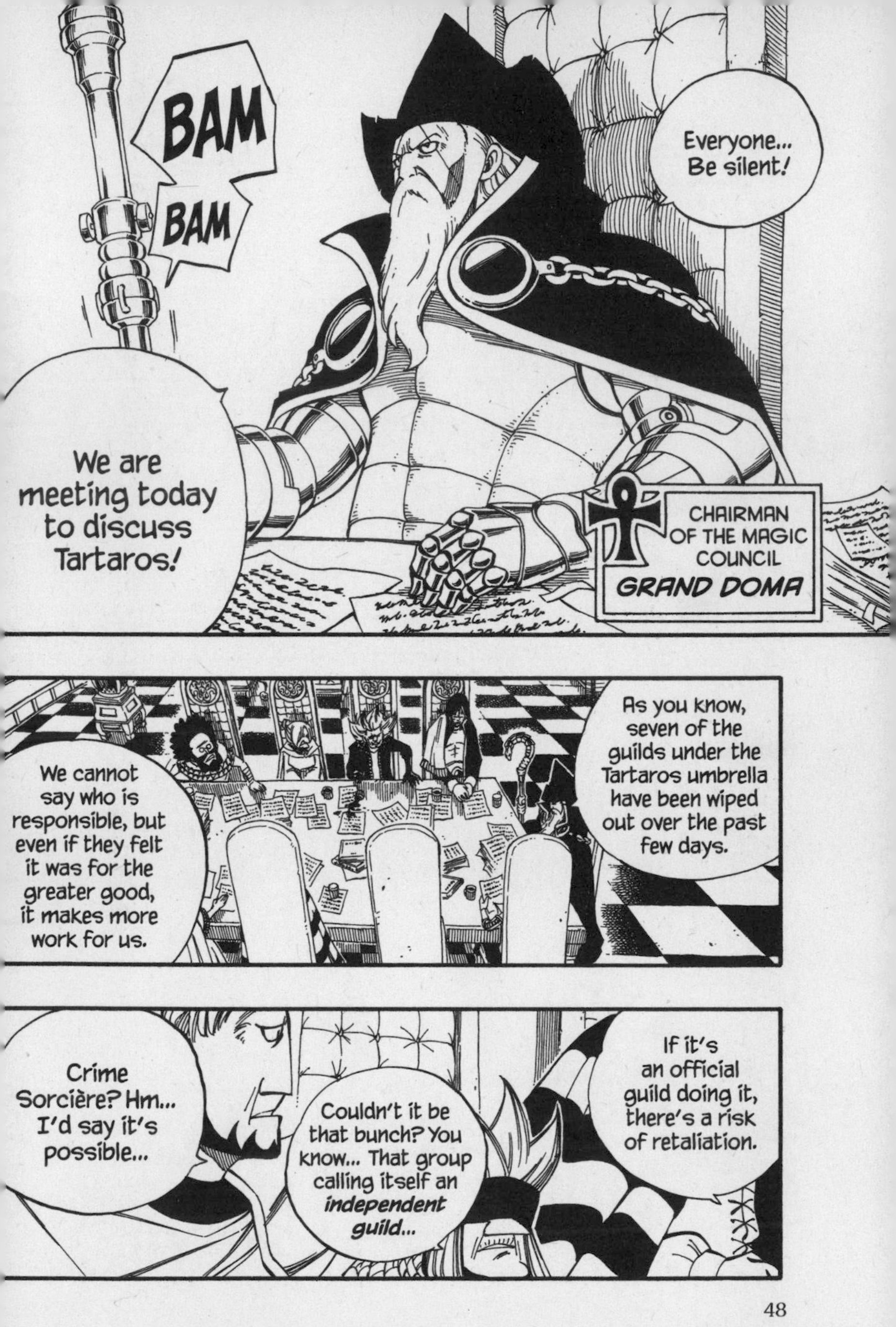
Everyone... Be silent!
BAM
BAM
We are meeting today to discuss Tartaros!
CHAIRMAN OF THE MAGIC COUNCIL
GRAND DOMA
As you know, seven of the guilds under the Tartaros umbrella have been wiped out over the past few days.
We cannot say who is responsible, but even if they felt it was for the greater good, it makes more work for us.
If it's an official guild doing it, there's a risk of retaliation.
Couldn't it be that bunch? You know... That group calling itself an *independent guild*...
Crime Sorcière? Hm... I'd say it's possible...

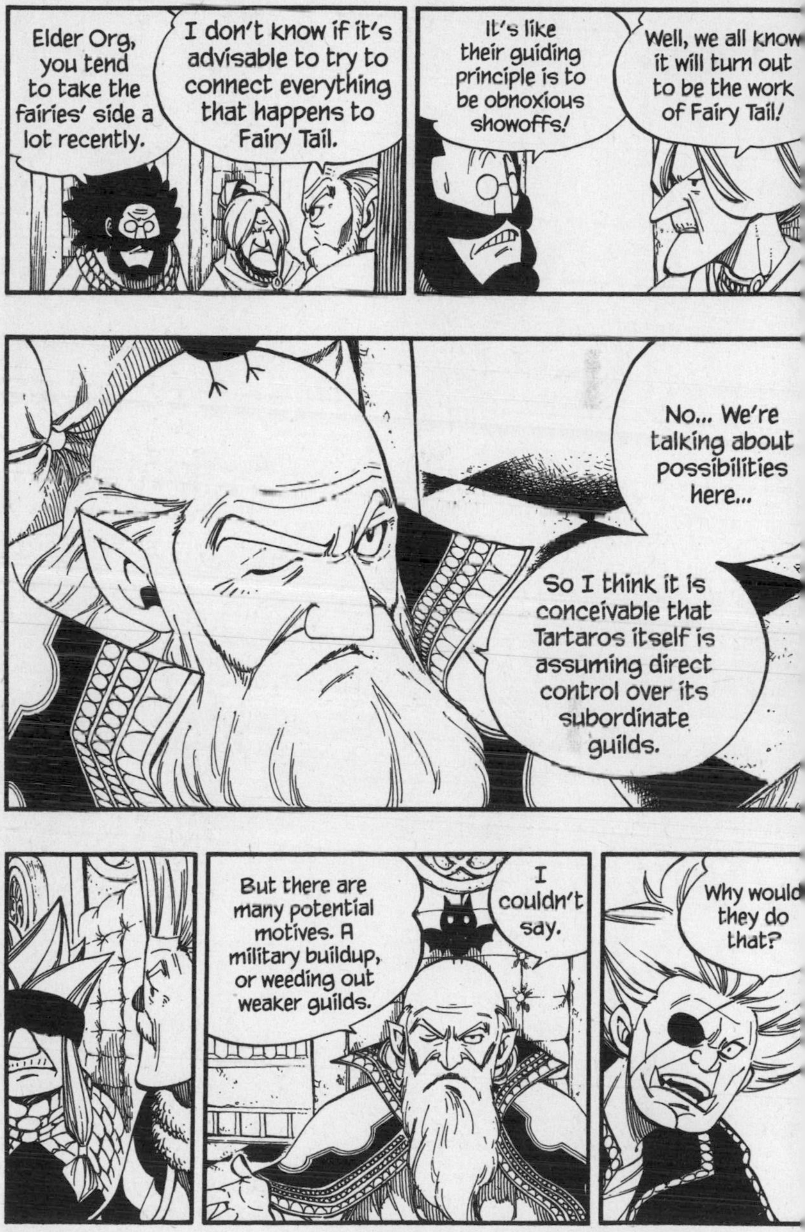

Well, we all know it will turn out to be the work of Fairy Tail!
It's like their guiding principle is to be obnoxious showoffs!
I don't know if it's advisable to try to connect everything that happens to Fairy Tail.
Elder Org, you tend to take the fairies' side a lot recently.
No... We're talking about possibilities here...
So I think it is conceivable that Tartaros itself is assuming direct control over its subordinate guilds.
Why would they do that?
I couldn't say.
But there are many potential motives. A military buildup, or weeding out weaker guilds.

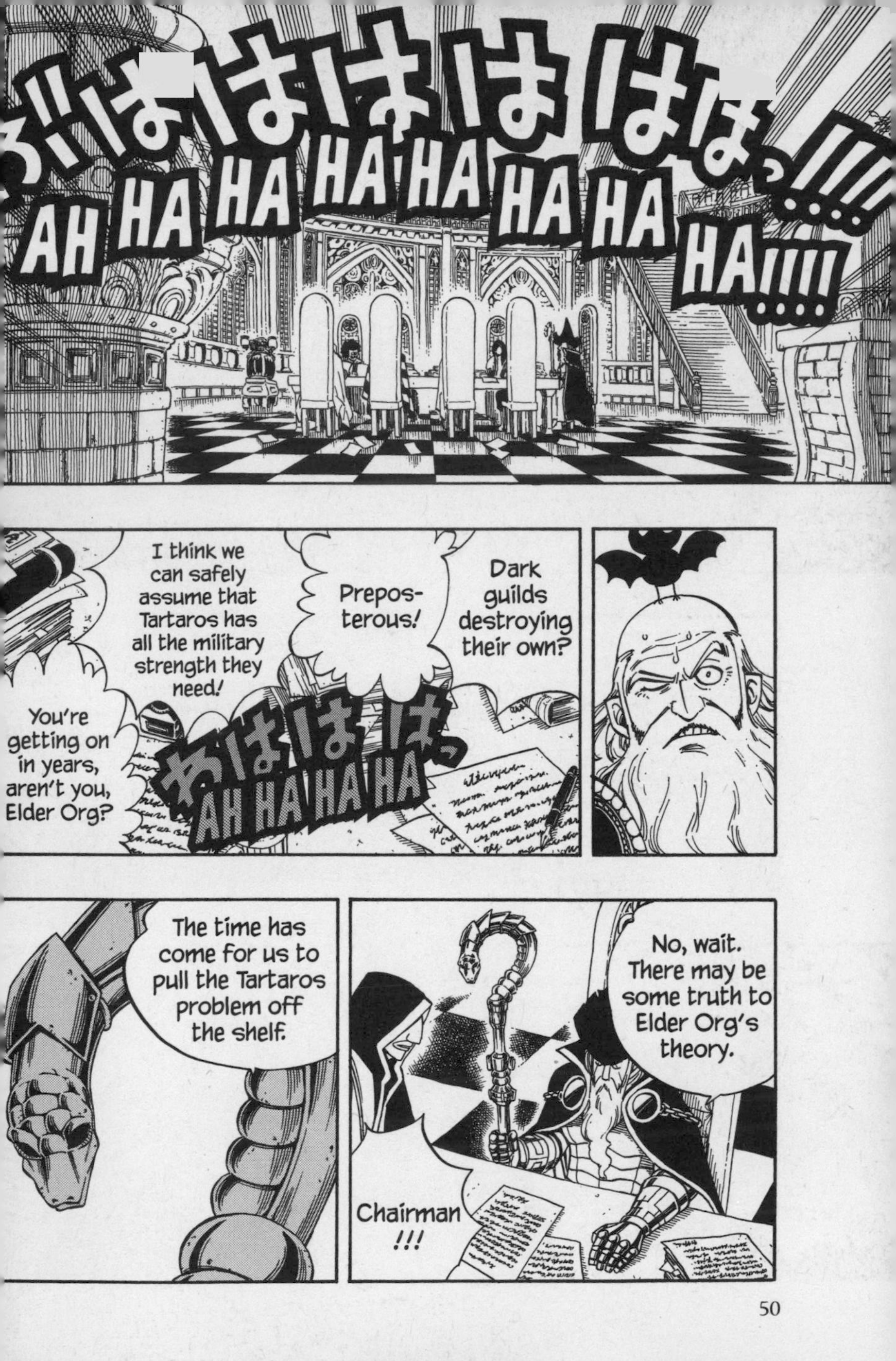
AH HA HA HA HA HA HA HA!!!!
Dark guilds destroying their own?
Prepos-terous!
I think we can safely assume that Tartaros has all the military strength they need!
You're getting on in years, aren't you, Elder Org?
AH HA HA HA
No, wait. There may be some truth to Elder Org's theory.
Chairman!!!
The time has come for us to pull the Tartaros problem off the shelf.

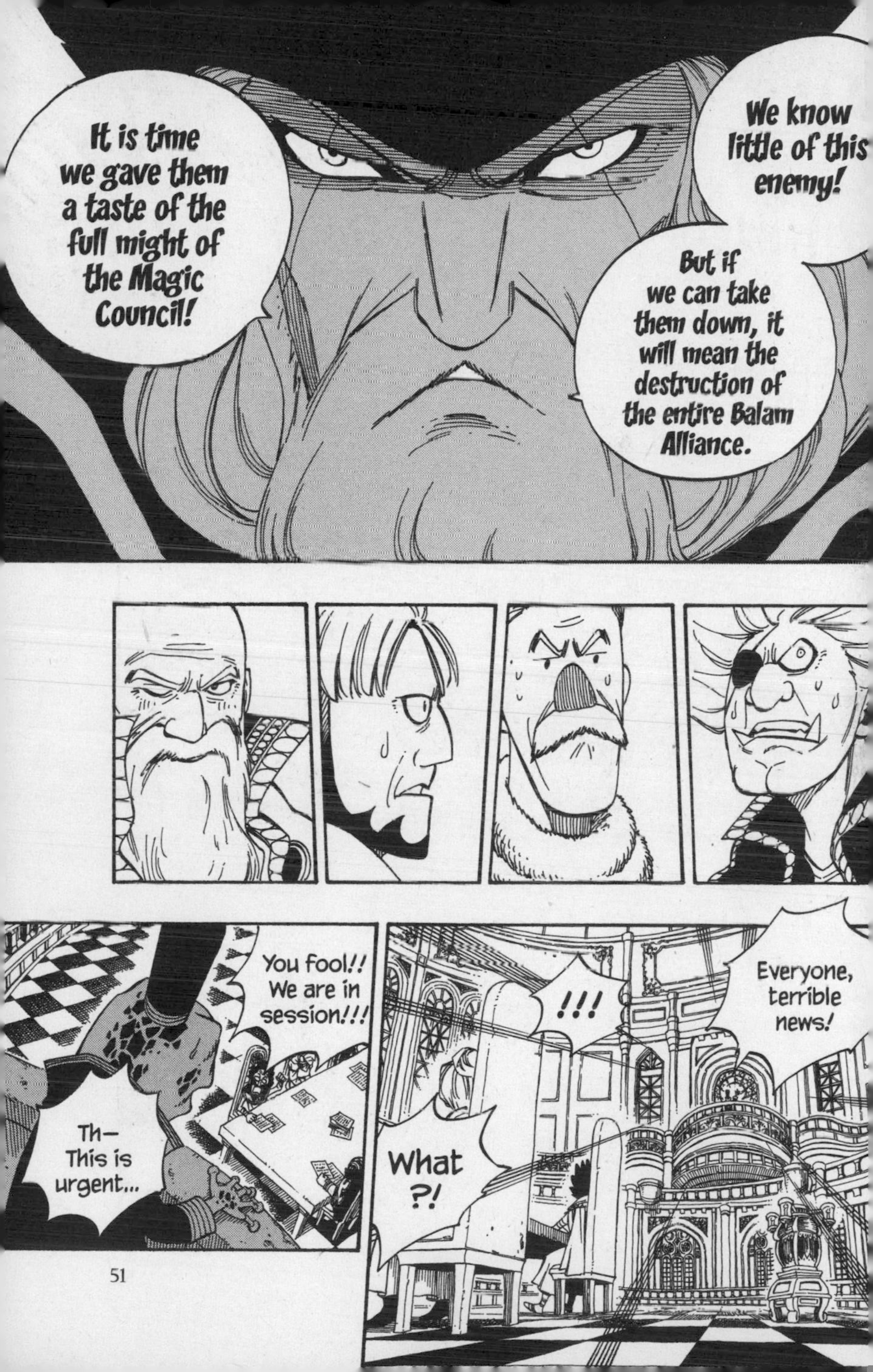
We know little of this enemy!
But if we can take them down, it will mean the destruction of the entire Balam Alliance.
It is time we gave them a taste of the full might of the Magic Council!
Everyone, terrible news!
!!!
What?!
You fool!! We are in session!!!
Th— This is urgent...

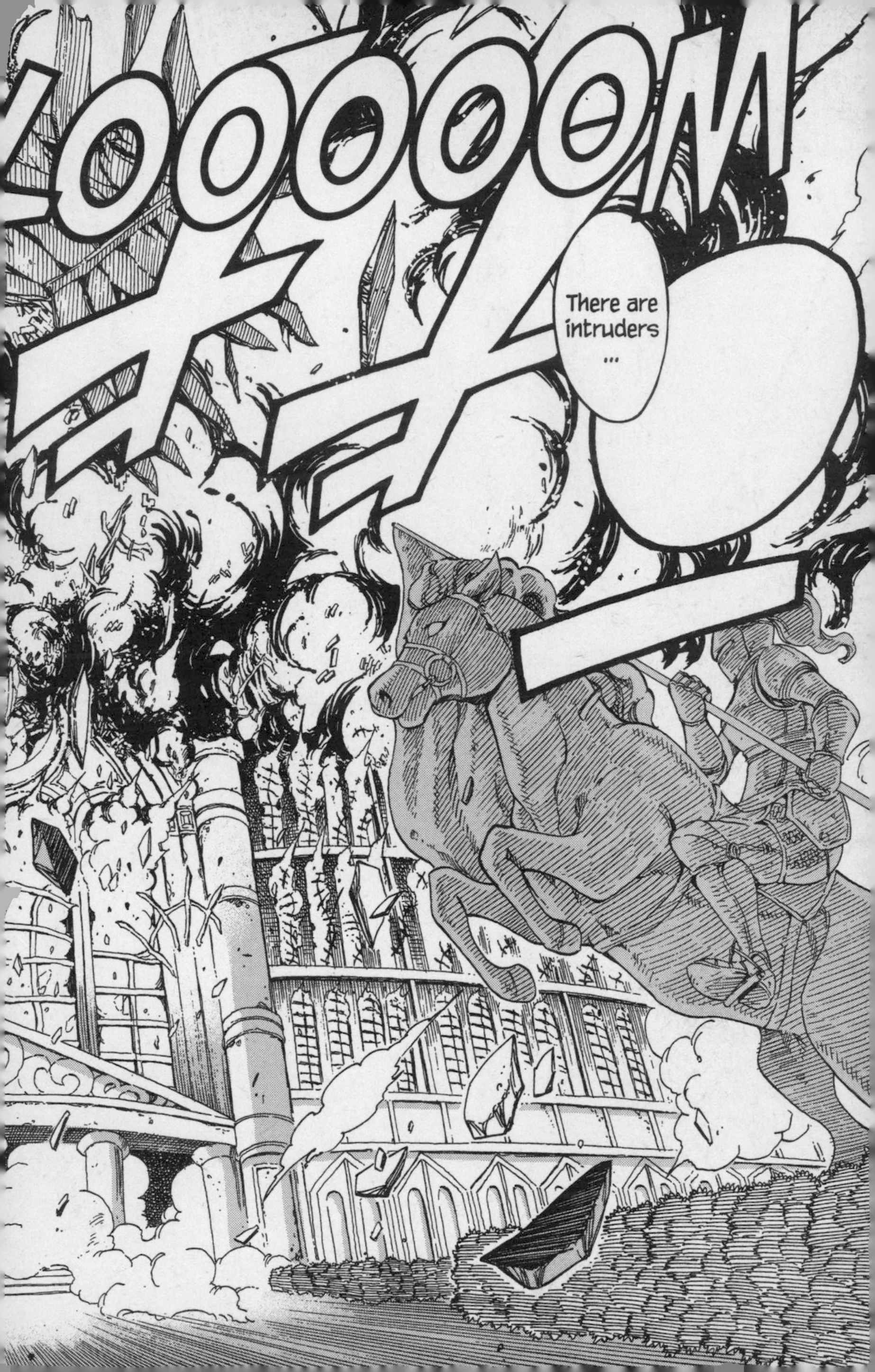
OOOOOM
There are intruders ...

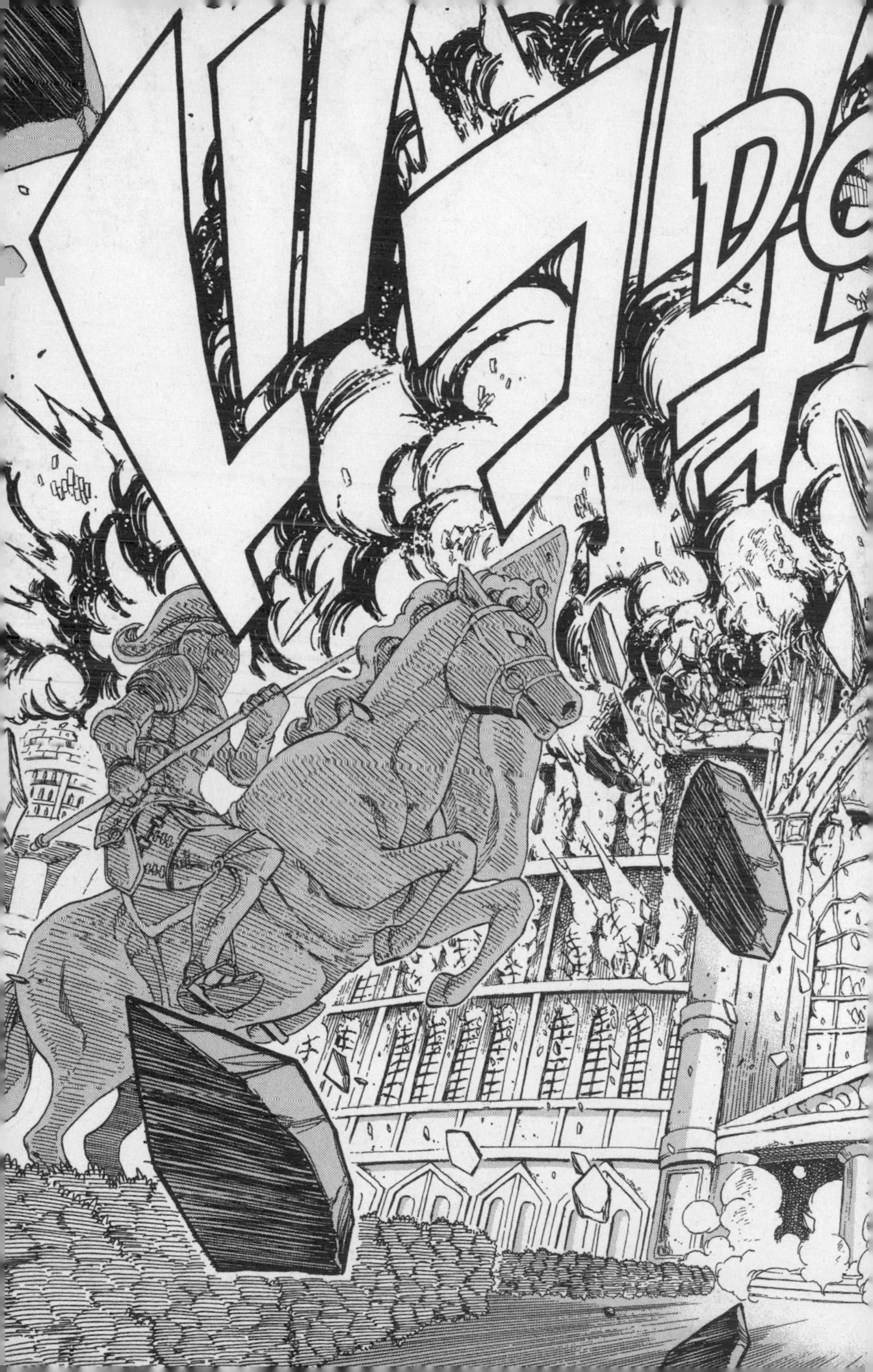
DO

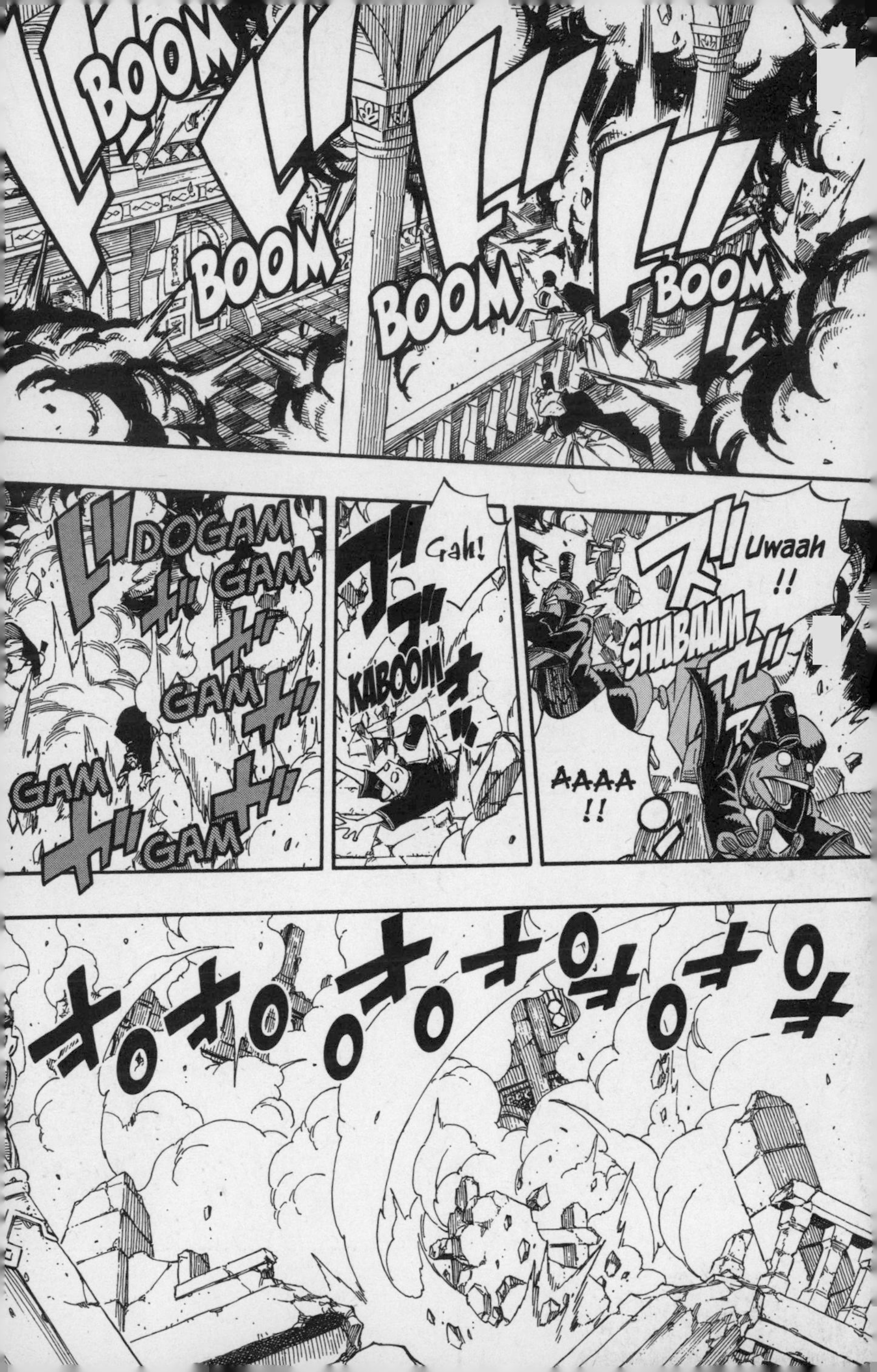
BOOM
BOOM
BOOM
BOOM
Uwaah !!
SHABAAM
AAAA !!
Gah!
KABOOM
DOGAM
GAM
GAM
GAM
GAM

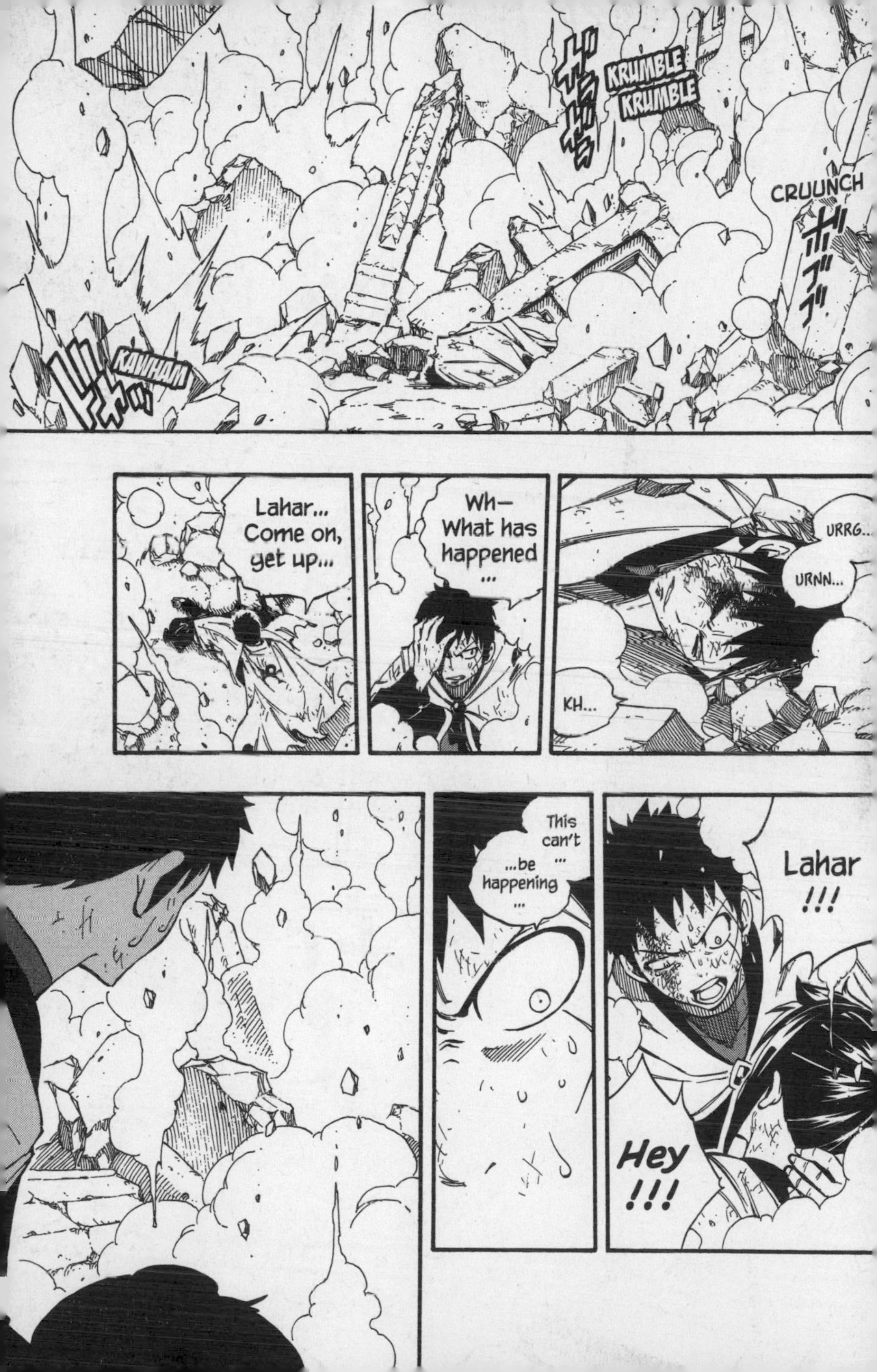
CRUUNCH
KRUMBLE KRUMBLE
KAWHAM
URRG...
URNN...
KH...
Wh— What has happened ...
Lahar... Come on, get up...
Lahar !!!
Hey !!!
This can't ...
...be happening ...

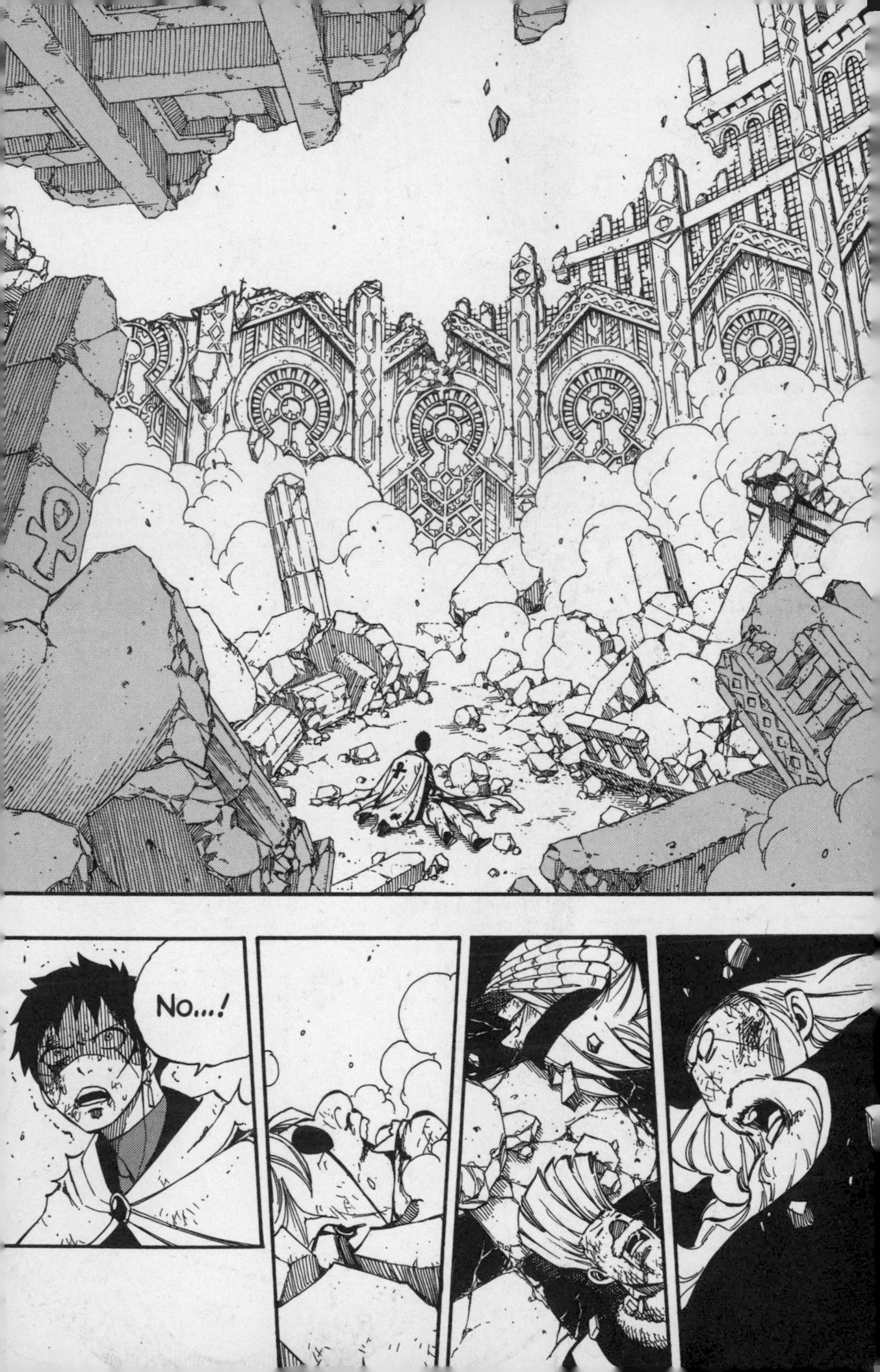
No...!

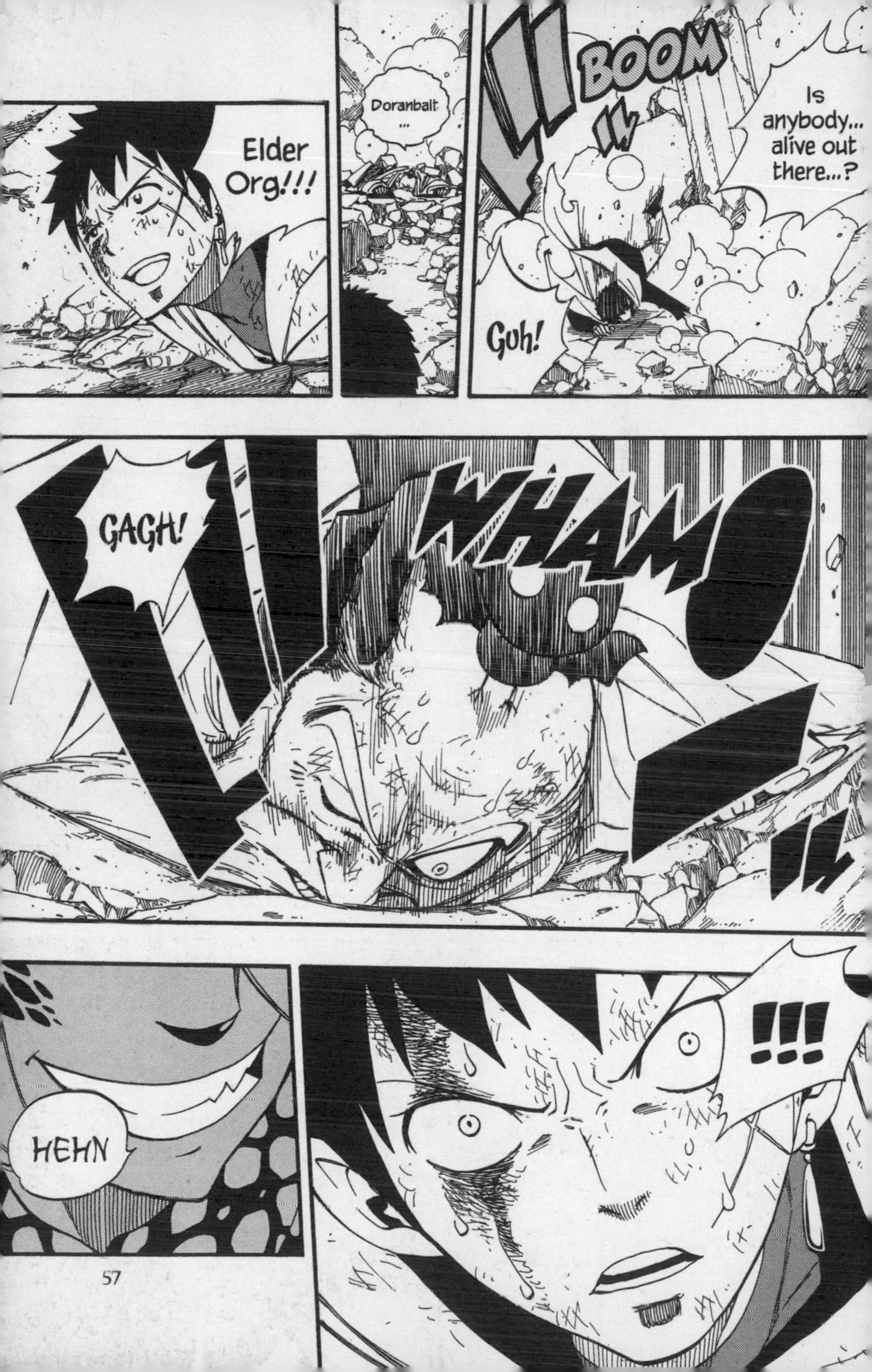

Is anybody... alive out there...?
BOOM
Guh!
Doranbalt ...
Elder Org!!!
WHAM
GAGH!
!!!
HEHN

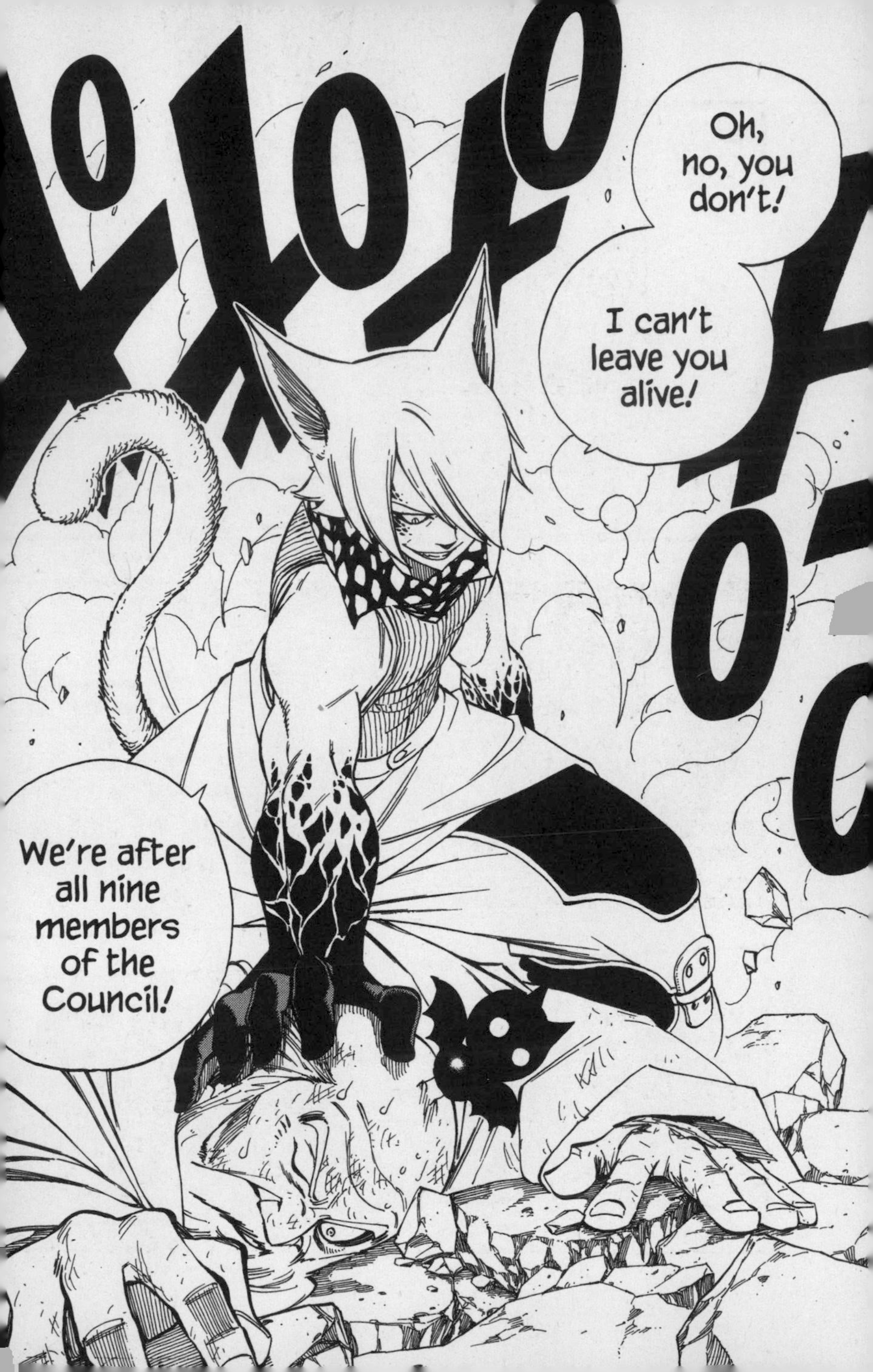
Oh, no, you don't!
I can't leave you alive!
We're after all nine members of the Council!

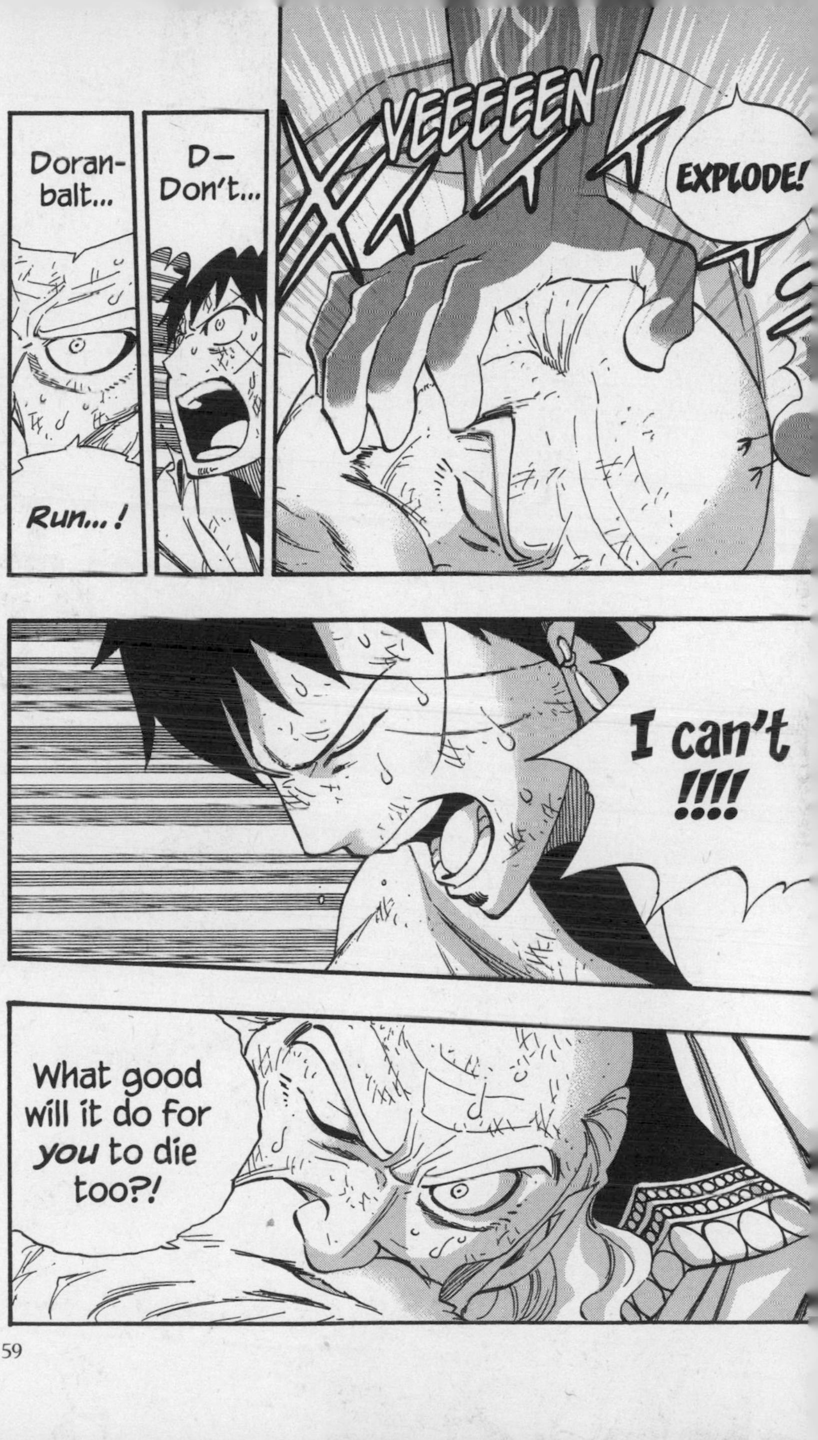
EXPLODE!
VEEEEEEN
D— Don't...
Doran-balt...
Run...!
I can't !!!!
What good will it do for *you* to die too?!

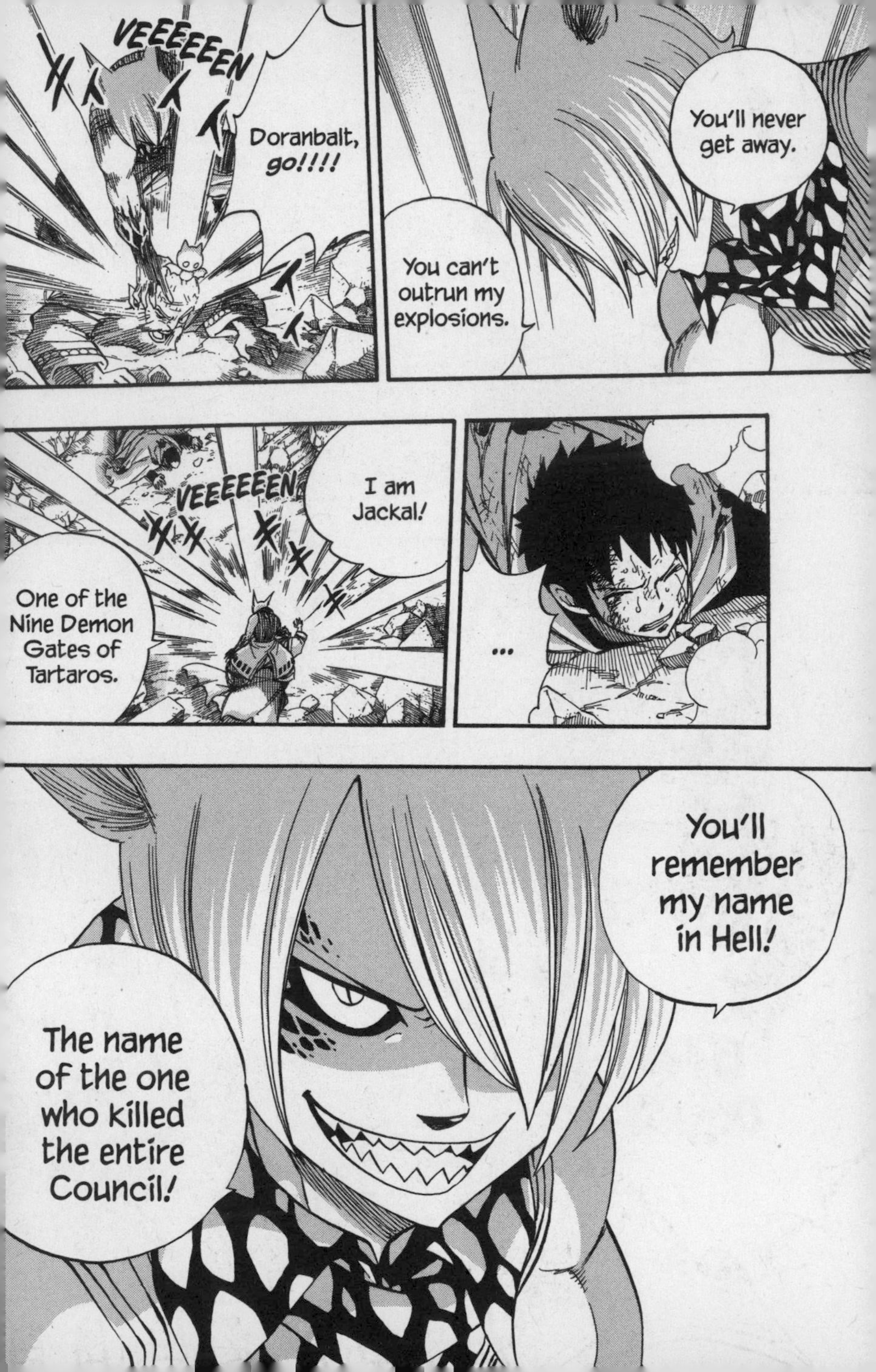
You'll never get away.
You can't outrun my explosions.
VEEEEEEN
Doranbalt, go!!!!
...
I am Jackal!
VEEEEEEN
One of the Nine Demon Gates of Tartaros.
You'll remember my name in Hell!
The name of the one who killed the entire Council!

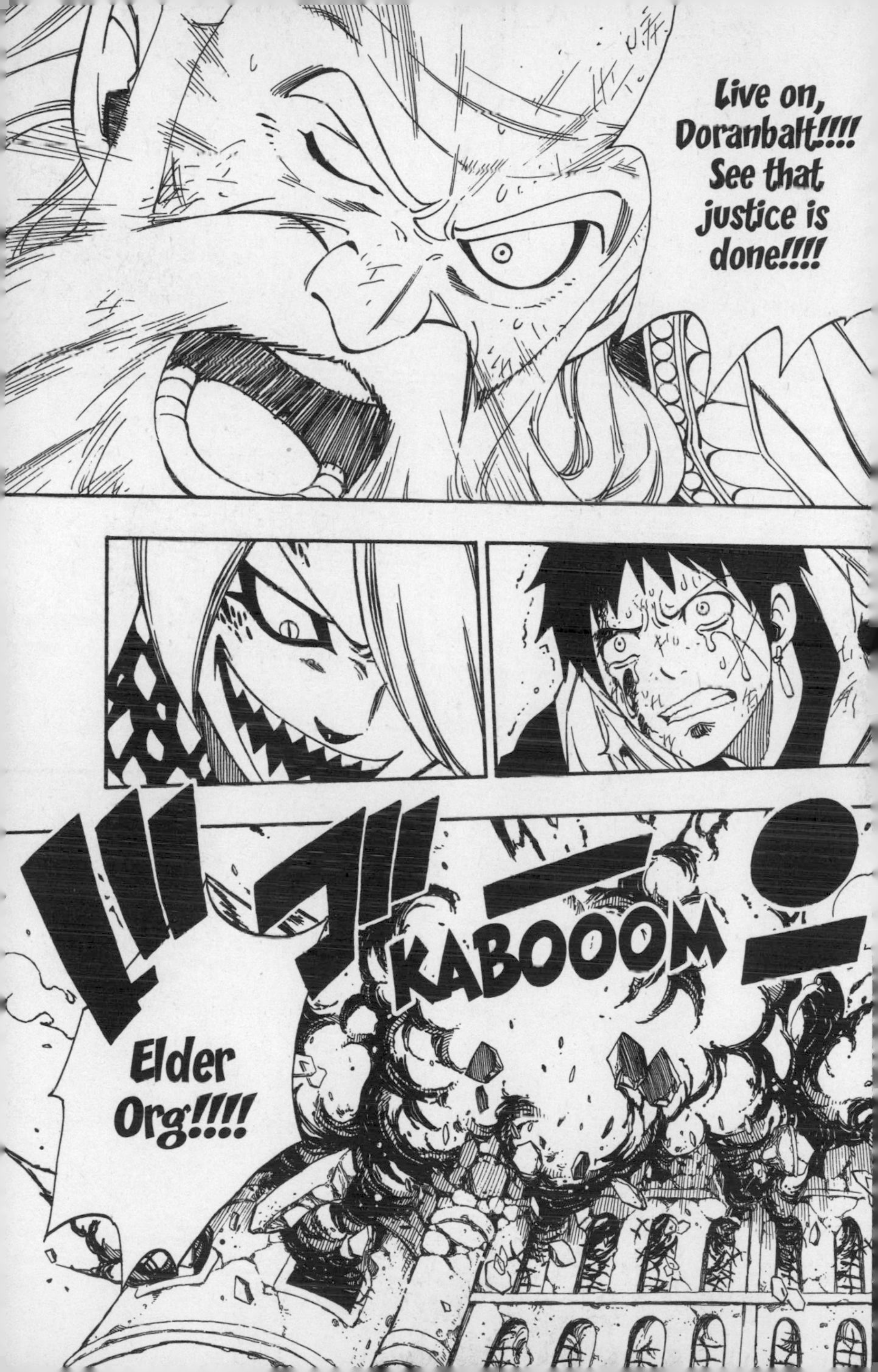
Live on, Doranbalt!!!! See that justice is done!!!!
KABOOOM
Elder Org!!!!

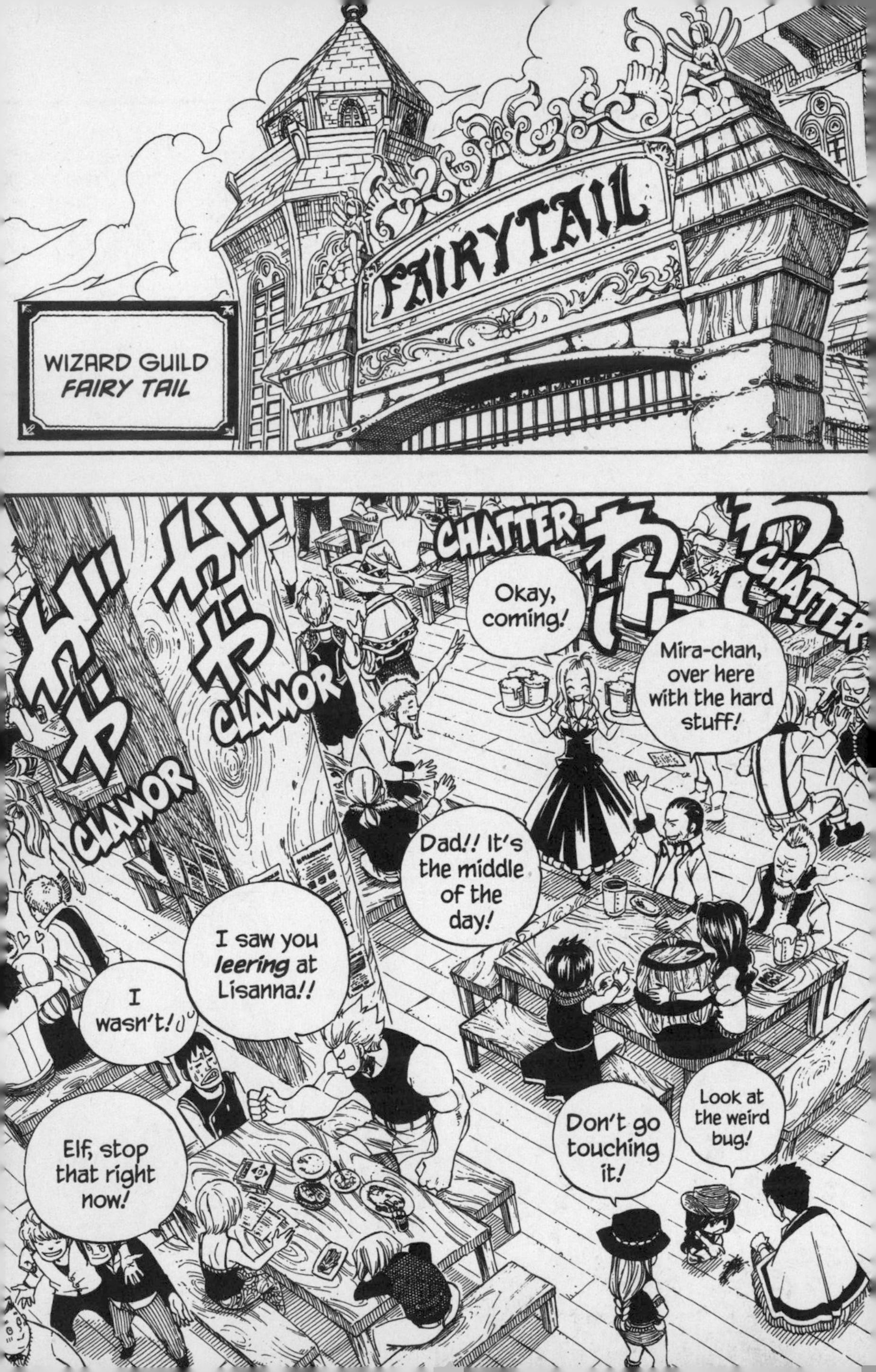
FAIRYTAIL
WIZARD GUILD *FAIRY TAIL*
CHATTER
CHATTER
Mira-chan, over here with the hard stuff!
Okay, coming!
CLAMOR
CLAMOR
Dad!! It's the middle of the day!
I saw you *leering* at Lisanna!!
I wasn't!
Look at the weird bug!
Don't go touching it!
Elf, stop that right now!

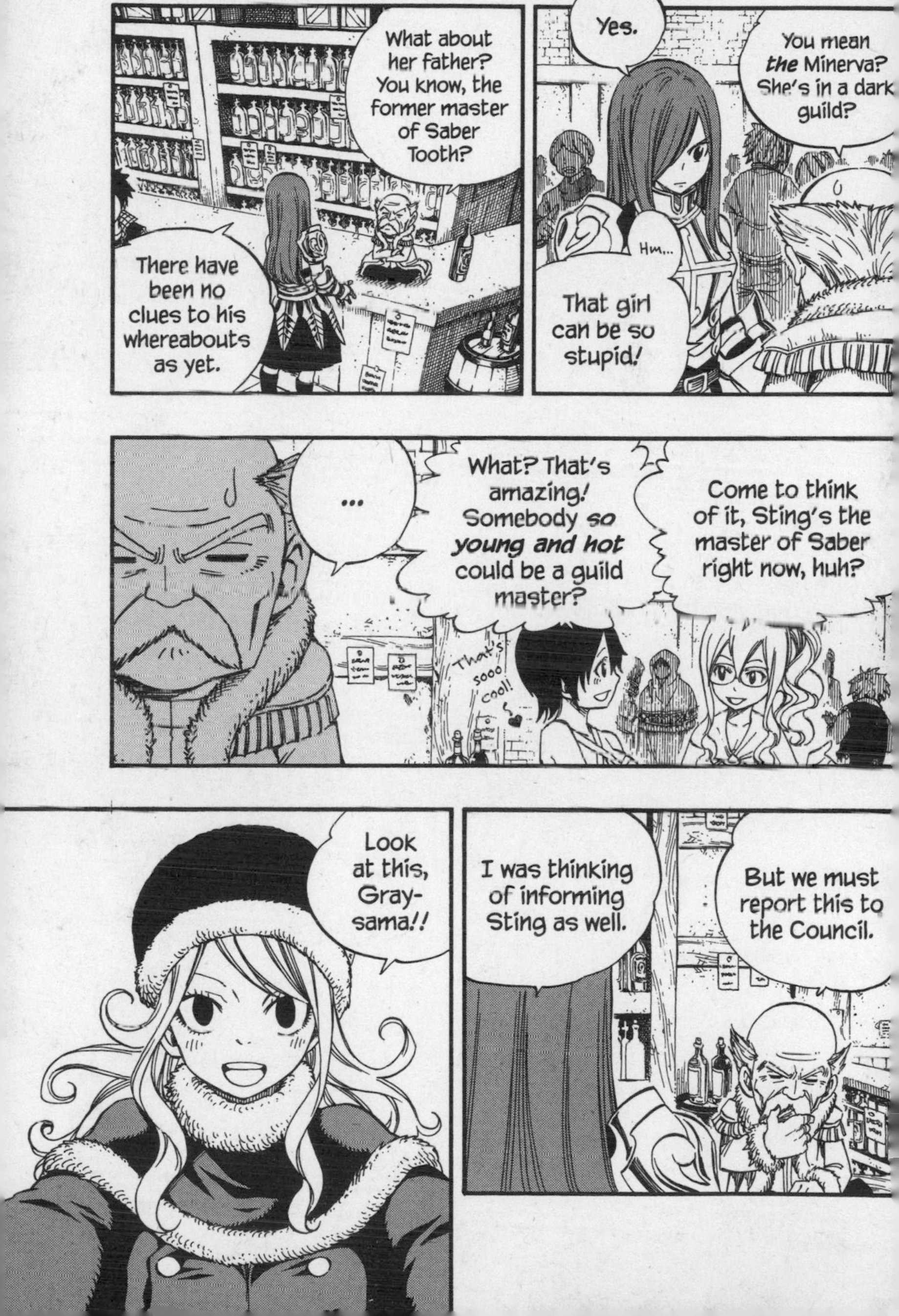
You mean *the* Minerva? She's in a dark guild?
Yes.
Hm...
That girl can be so stupid!
What about her father? You know, the former master of Saber Tooth?
There have been no clues to his whereabouts as yet.
Come to think of it, Sting's the master of Saber right now, huh?
What? That's amazing! Somebody *so young and hot* could be a guild master?
That's sooo cool!
...
But we must report this to the Council.
I was thinking of informing Sting as well.
Look at this, Gray-sama!!

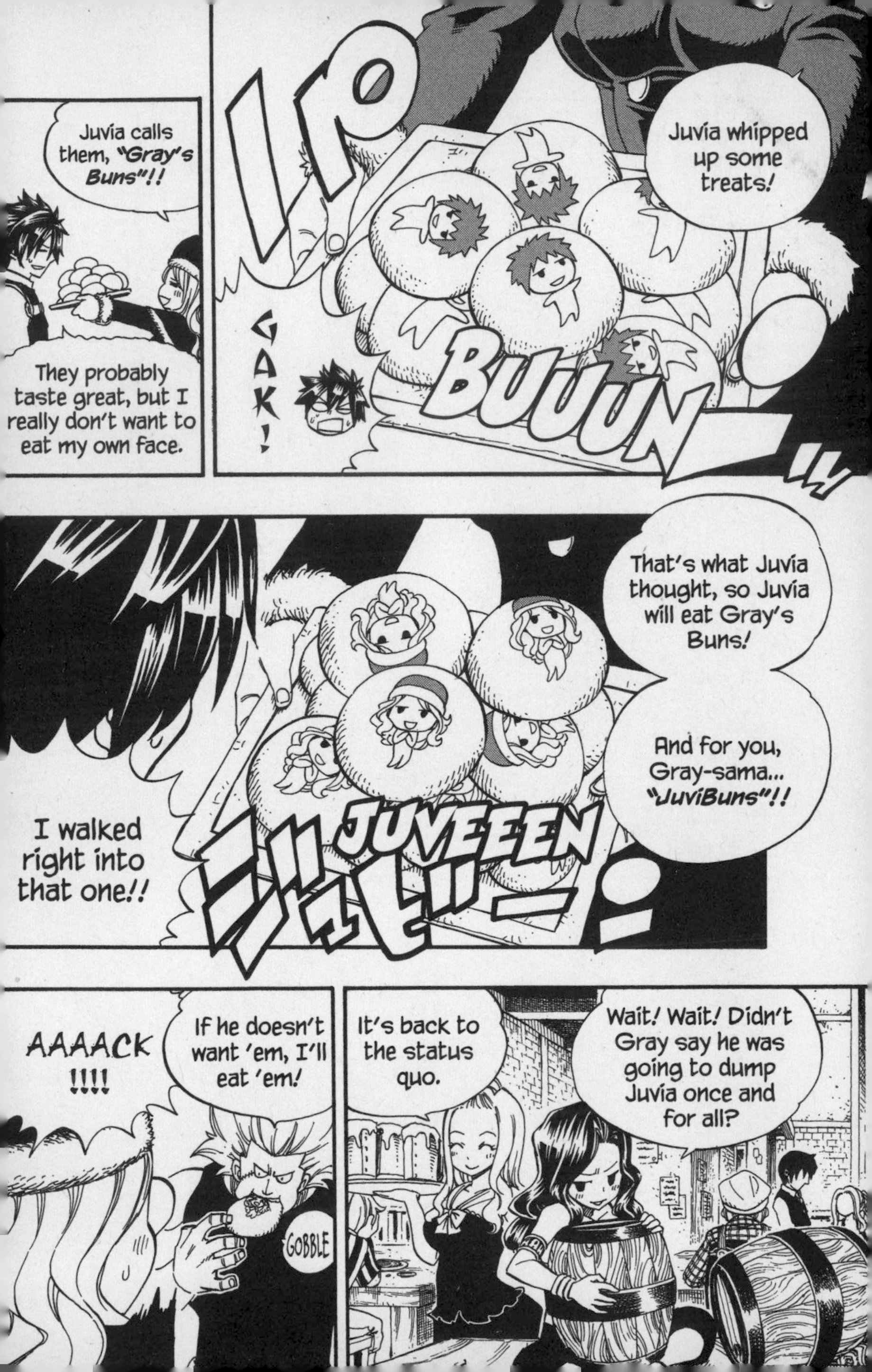
Juvia whipped up some treats!
BUUUN!!
GAK!
Juvia calls them, "Gray's Buns"!!
They probably taste great, but I really don't want to eat my own face.
That's what Juvia thought, so Juvia will eat Gray's Buns!
And for you, Gray-sama... "JuviBuns"!!
JUVEEEN
I walked right into that one!!
Wait! Wait! Didn't Gray say he was going to dump Juvia once and for all?
It's back to the status quo.
If he doesn't want 'em, I'll eat 'em!
GOBBLE
AAAACK !!!!

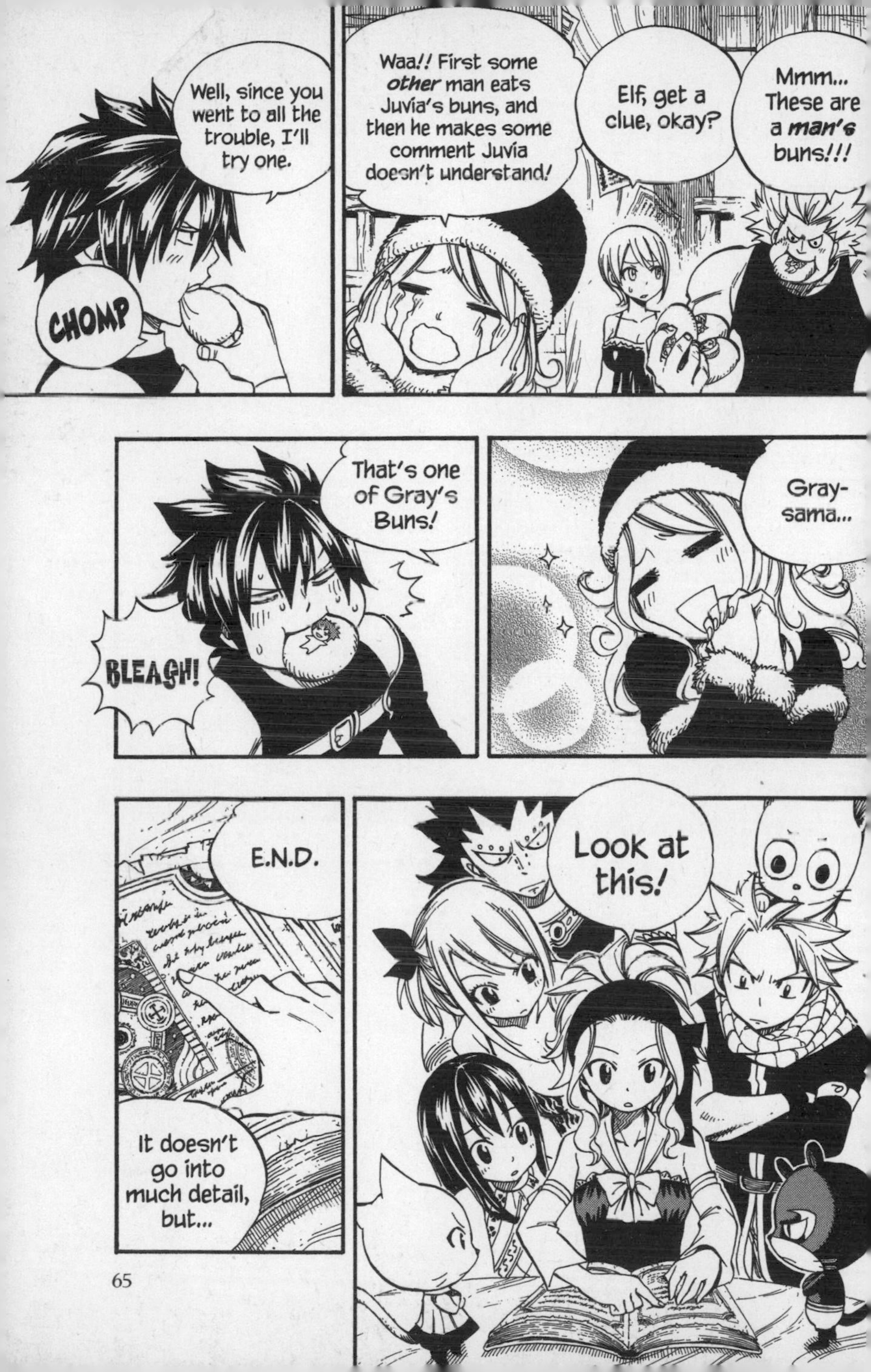
Mmm... These are a man's buns!!!
Elf, get a clue, okay?
Waa!! First some other man eats Juvia's buns, and then he makes some comment Juvia doesn't understand!
Well, since you went to all the trouble, I'll try one.
CHOMP
Gray-sama...
That's one of Gray's Buns!
BLEAGH!
Look at this!
E.N.D.
It doesn't go into much detail, but...

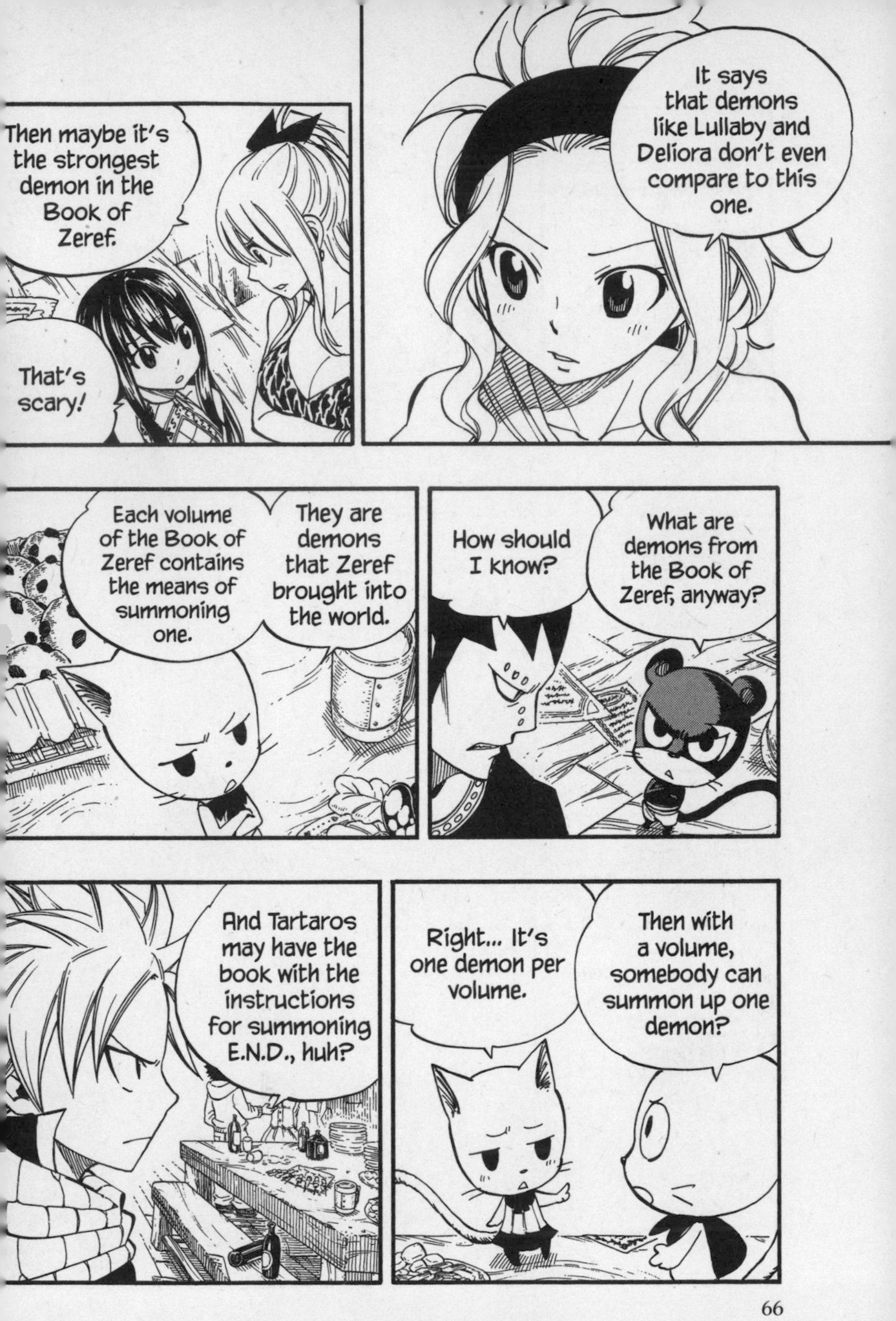
It says that demons like Lullaby and Deliora don't even compare to this one.
Then maybe it's the strongest demon in the Book of Zeref.
That's scary!
What are demons from the Book of Zeref, anyway?
How should I know?
They are demons that Zeref brought into the world.
Each volume of the Book of Zeref contains the means of summoning one.
Then with a volume, somebody can summon up one demon?
Right... It's one demon per volume.
And Tartaros may have the book with the instructions for summoning E.N.D., huh?

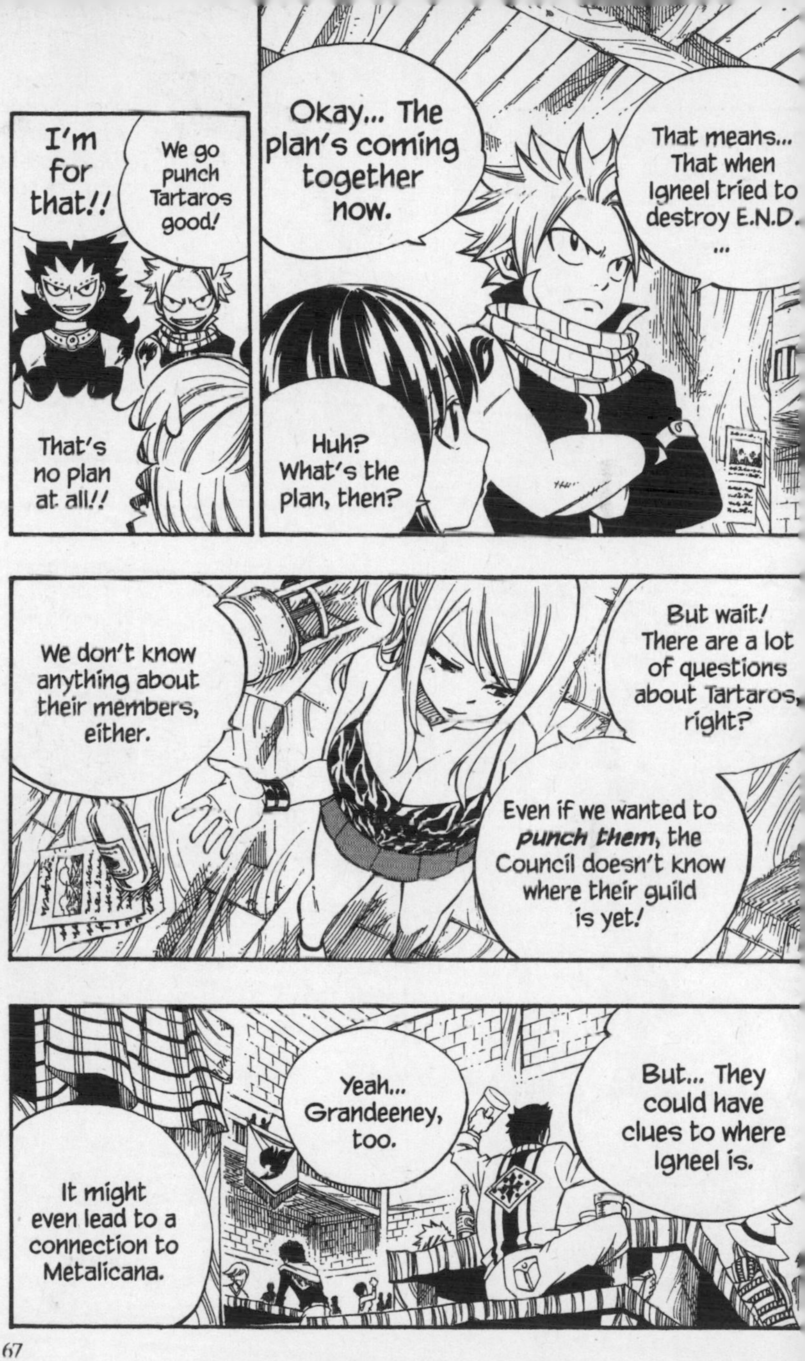
That means... That when Igneel tried to destroy E.N.D. ...
Okay... The plan's coming together now.
Huh? What's the plan, then?
We go punch Tartaros good!
I'm for that!!
That's no plan at all!!
But wait! There are a lot of questions about Tartaros, right?
Even if we wanted to *punch them*, the Council doesn't know where their guild is yet!
We don't know anything about their members, either.
But... They could have clues to where Igneel is.
Yeah... Grandeeney, too.
It might even lead to a connection to Metalicana.

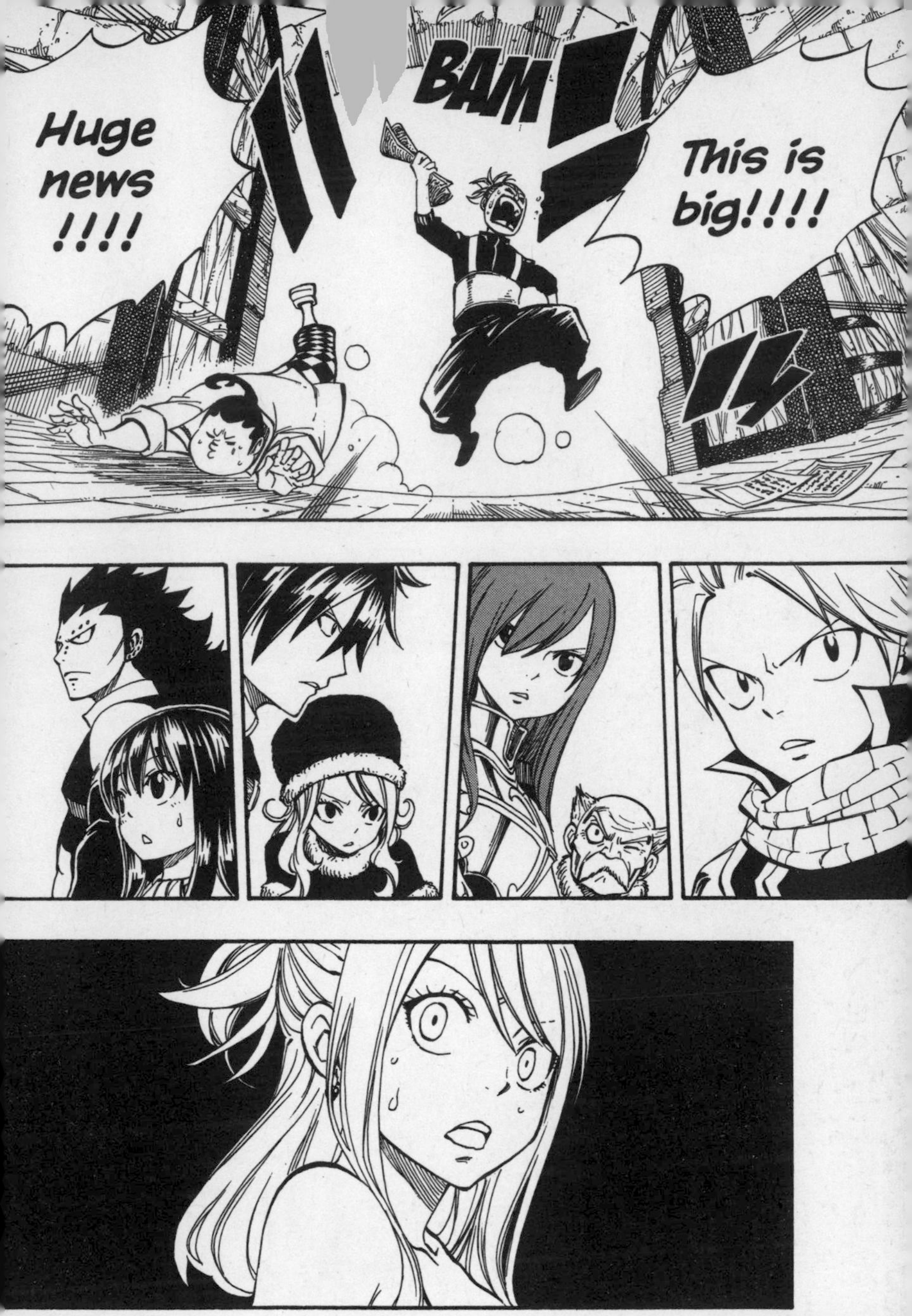
BAM
This is big!!!!
Huge news!!!!

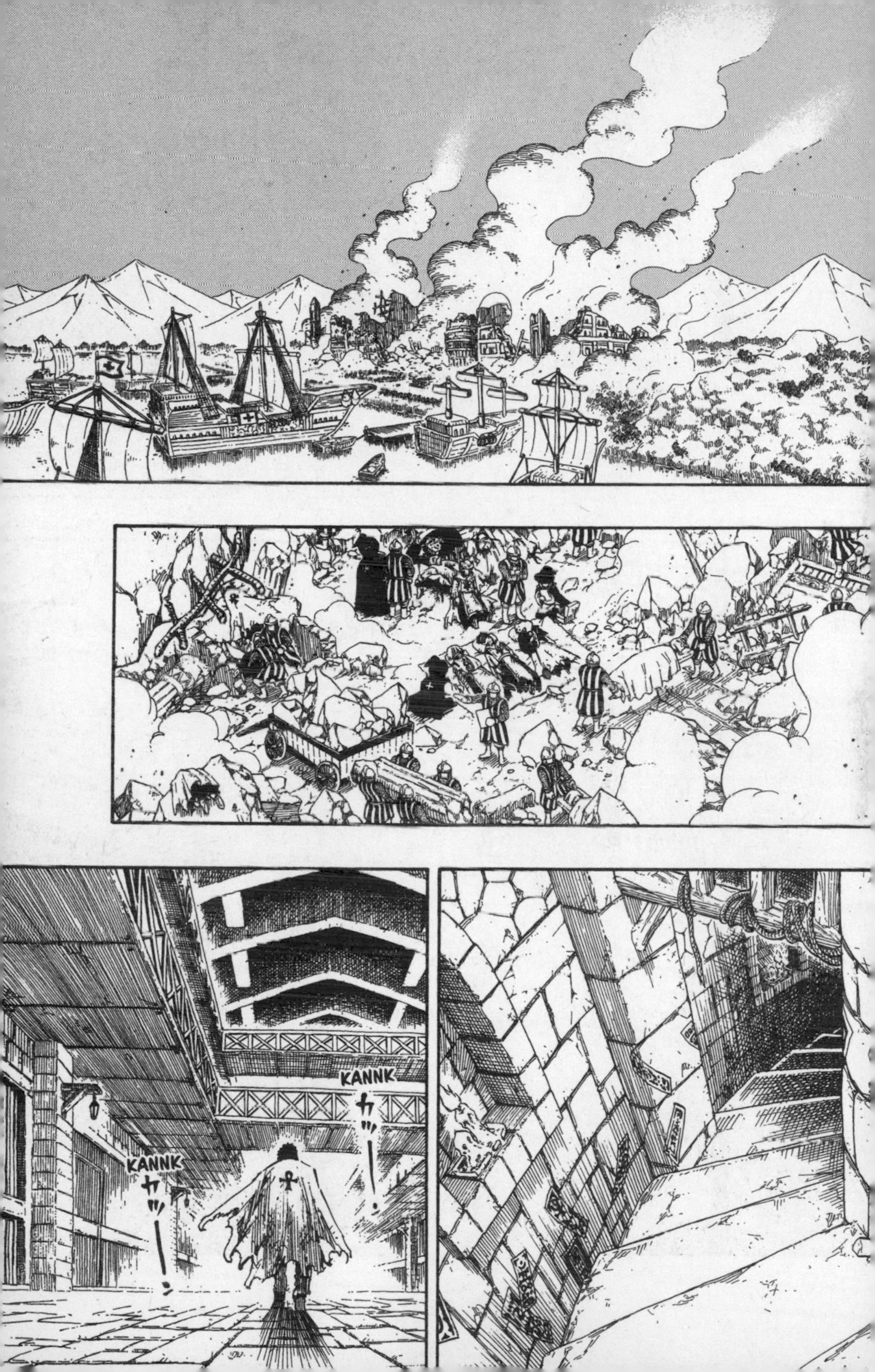
KANNK
KANNK

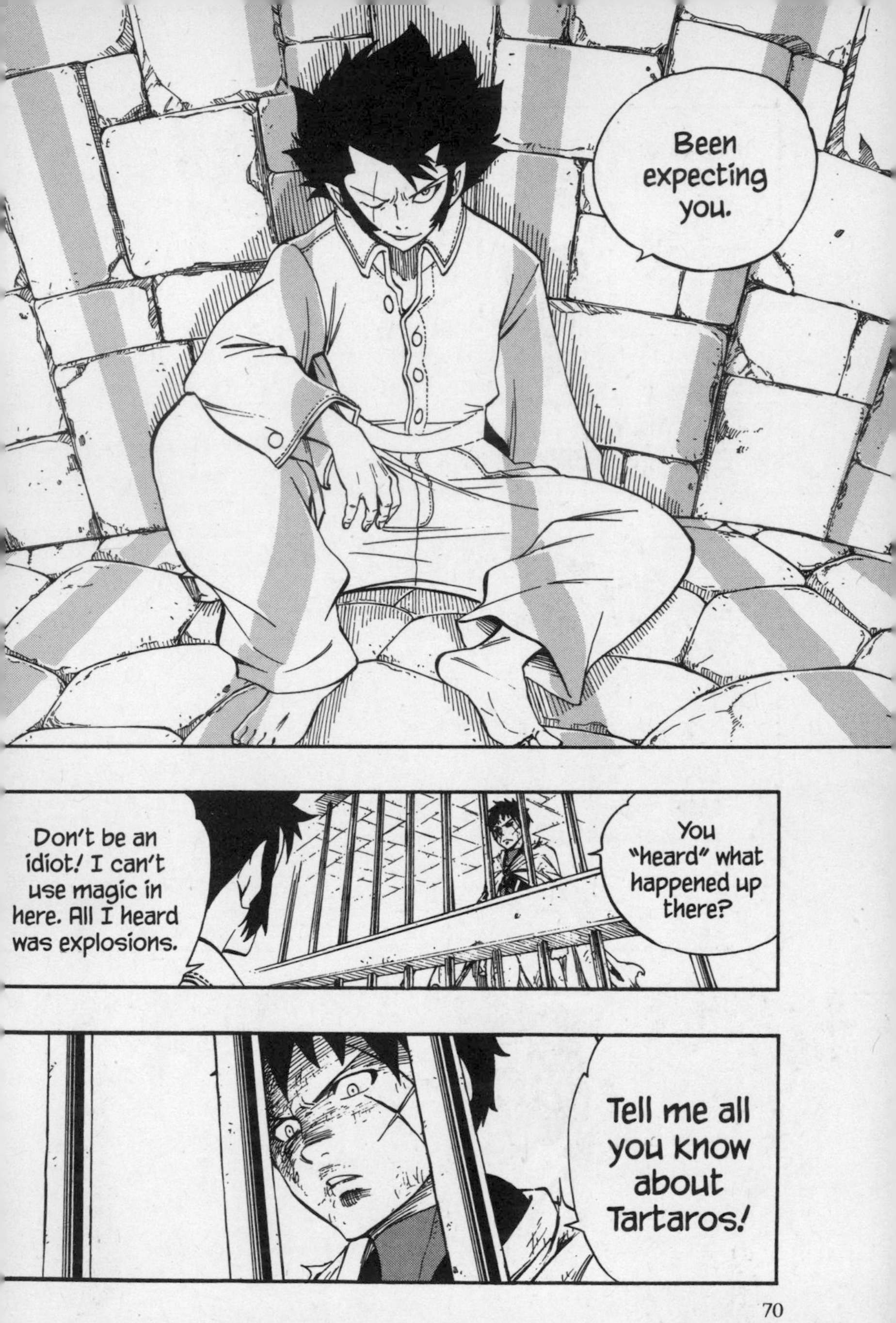
Been expecting you.
You "heard" what happened up there?
Don't be an idiot! I can't use magic in here. All I heard was explosions.
Tell me all you know about Tartaros!

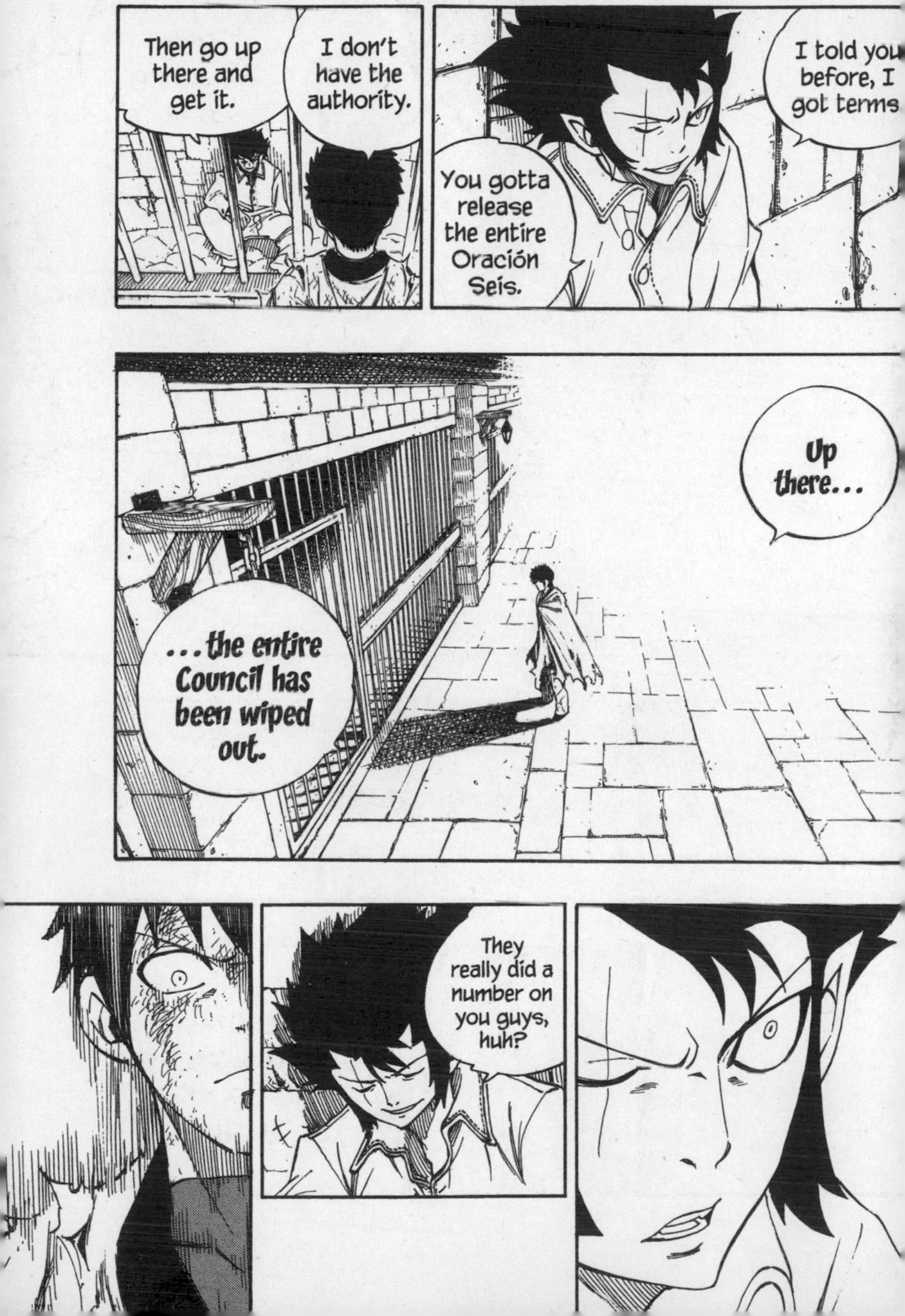
I told you before, I got terms
You gotta release the entire Oración Seis.
I don't have the authority.
Then go up there and get it.
Up there...
...the entire Council has been wiped out.
They really did a number on you guys, huh?

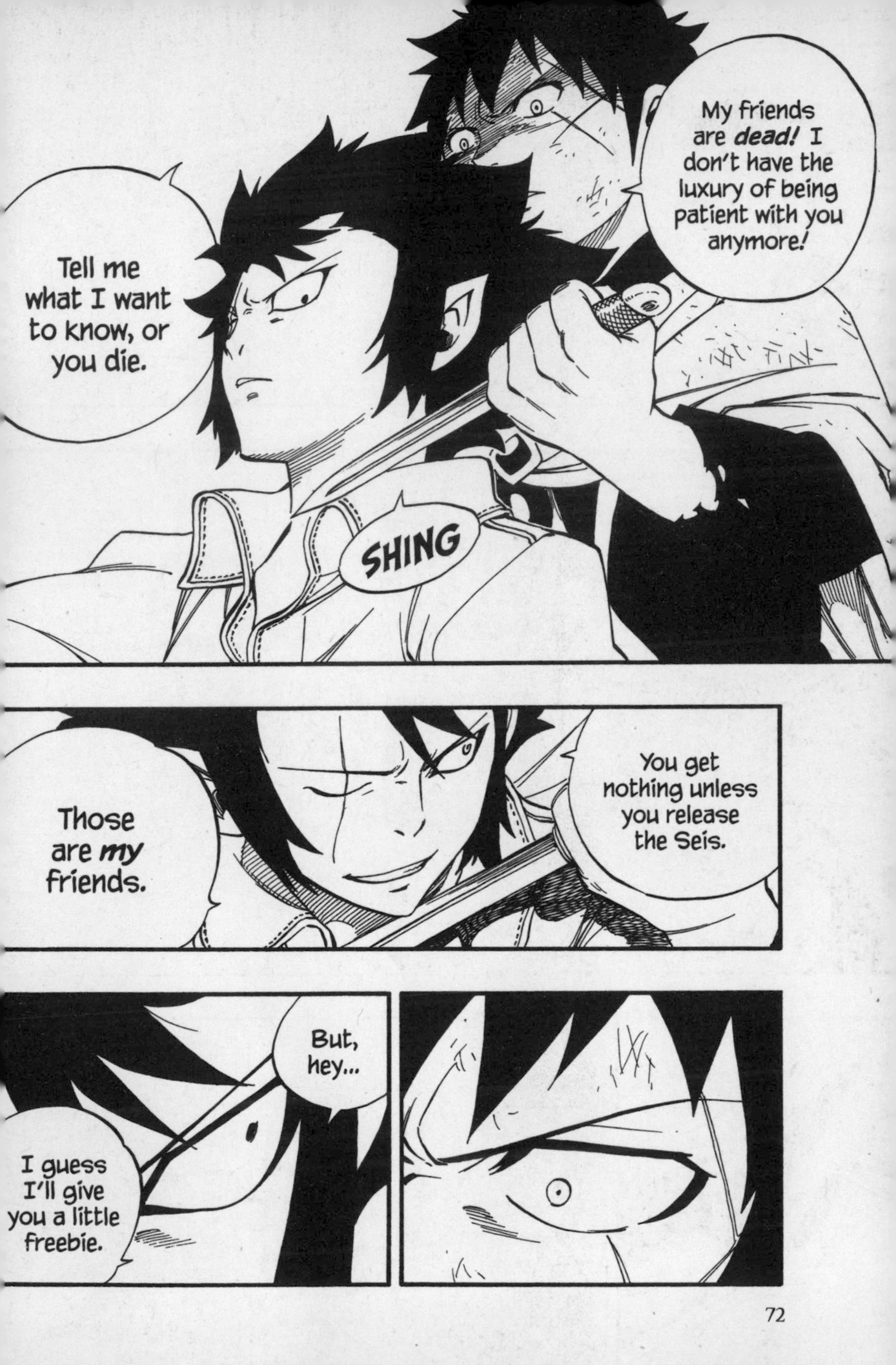
My friends are *dead!* I don't have the luxury of being patient with you anymore!
Tell me what I want to know, or you die.
SHING
You get nothing unless you release the Seis.
Those are *my* friends.
But, hey...
I guess I'll give you a little freebie.

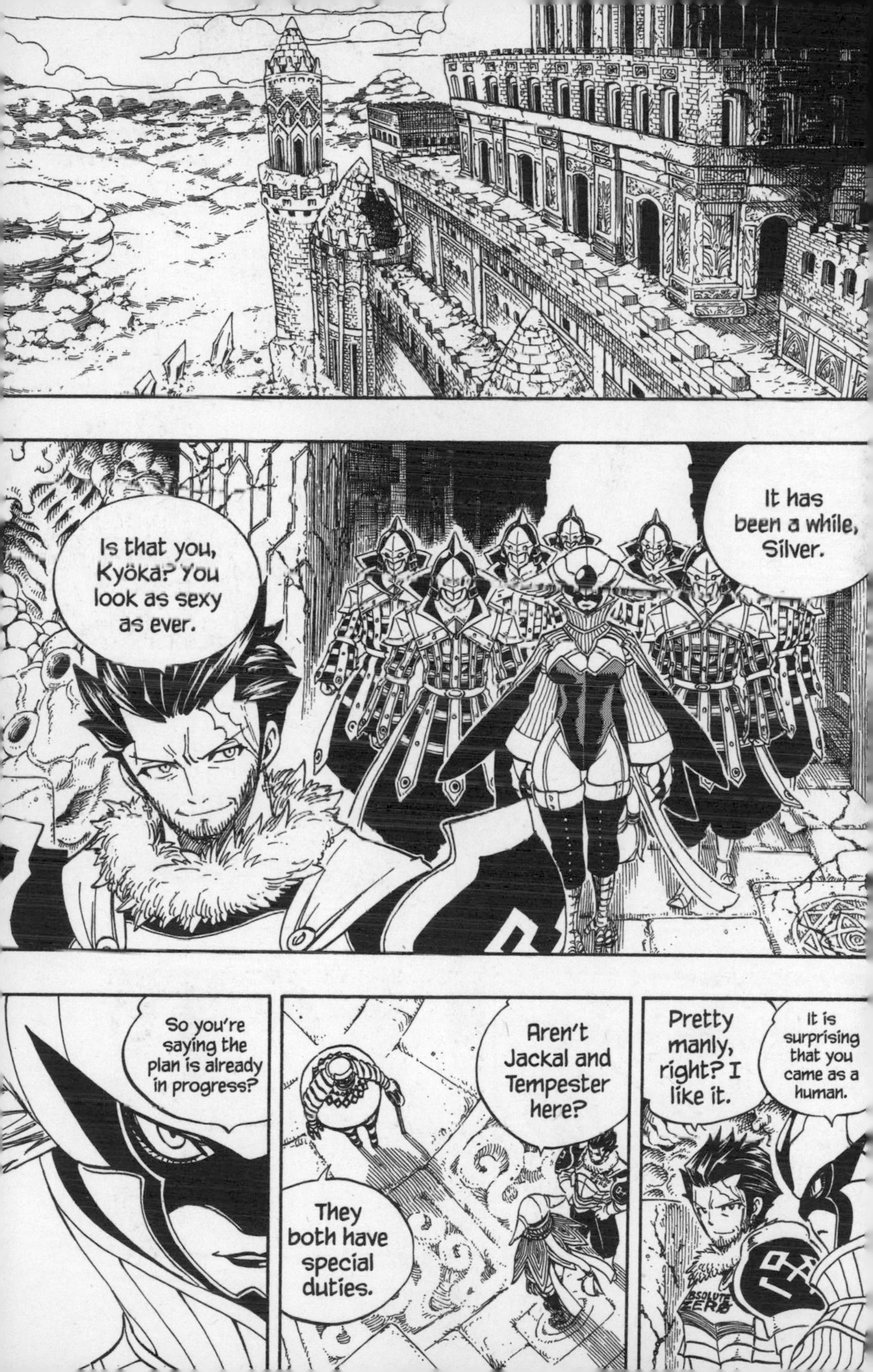
It has been a while, Silver.
Is that you, Kyōka? You look as sexy as ever.
It is surprising that you came as a human.
Pretty manly, right? I like it.
Aren't Jackal and Tempester here?
They both have special duties.
So you're saying the plan is already in progress?

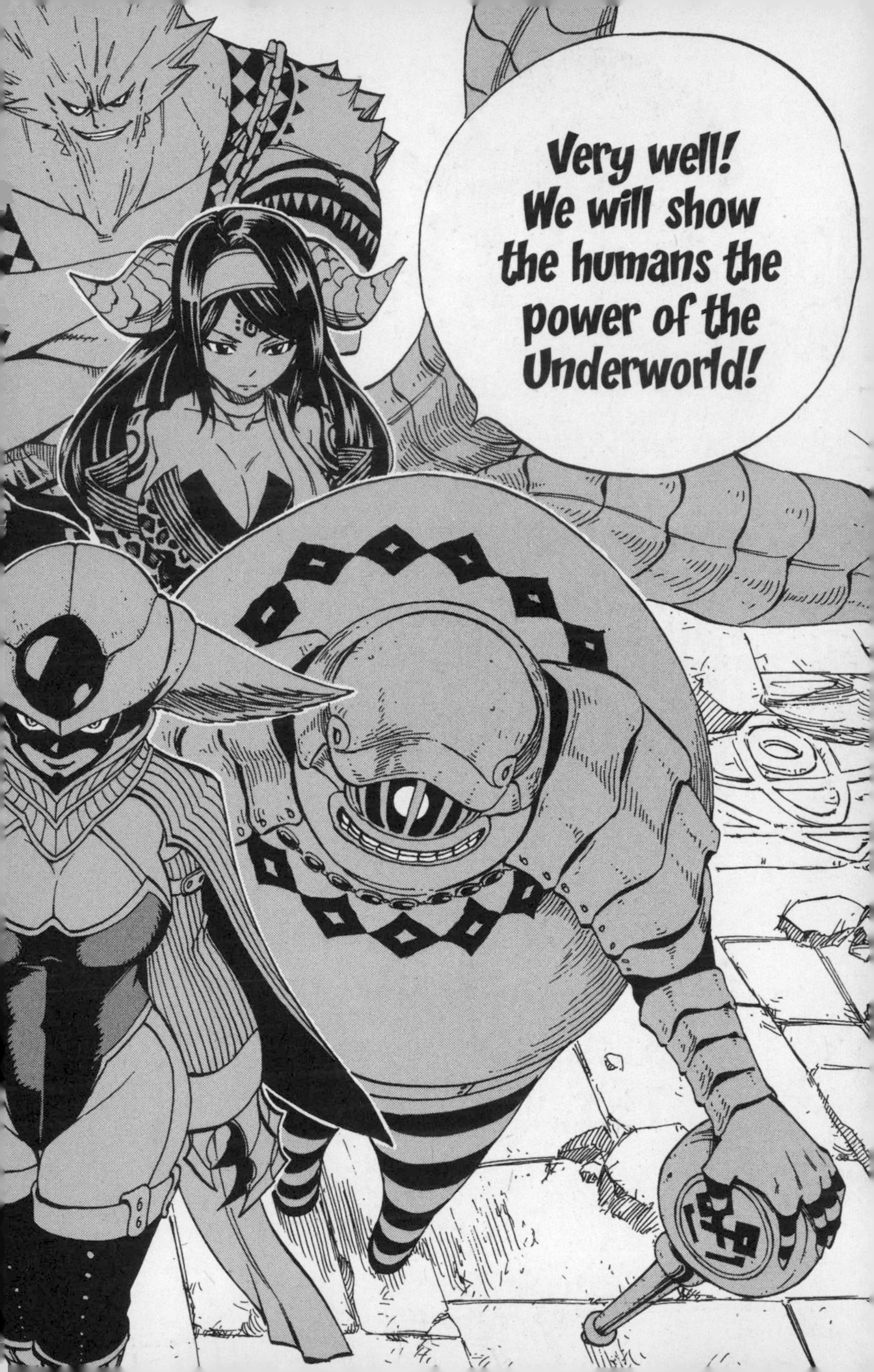
Very well! We will show the humans the power of the Underworld!

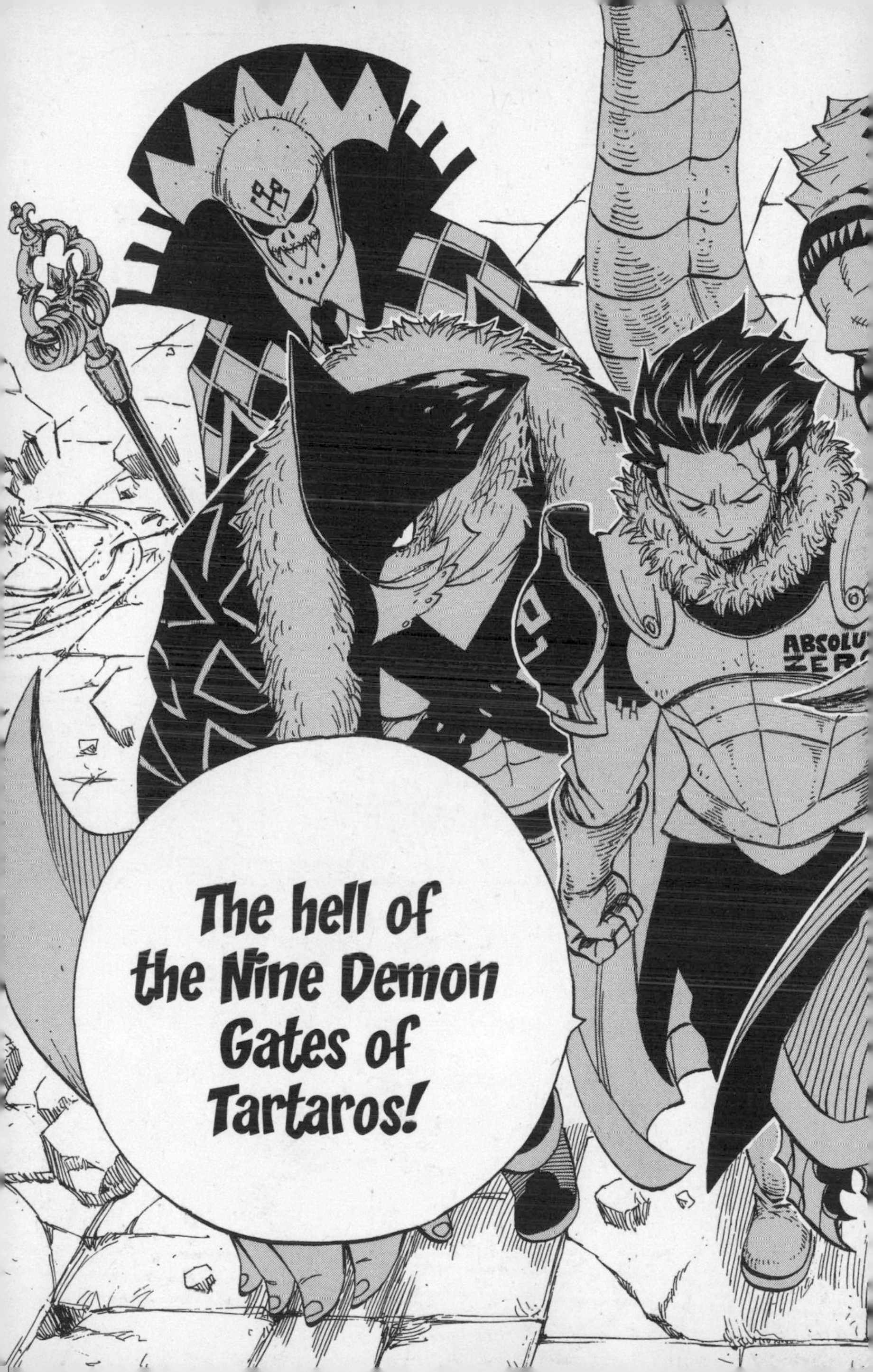
The hell of the Nine Demon Gates of Tartaros!

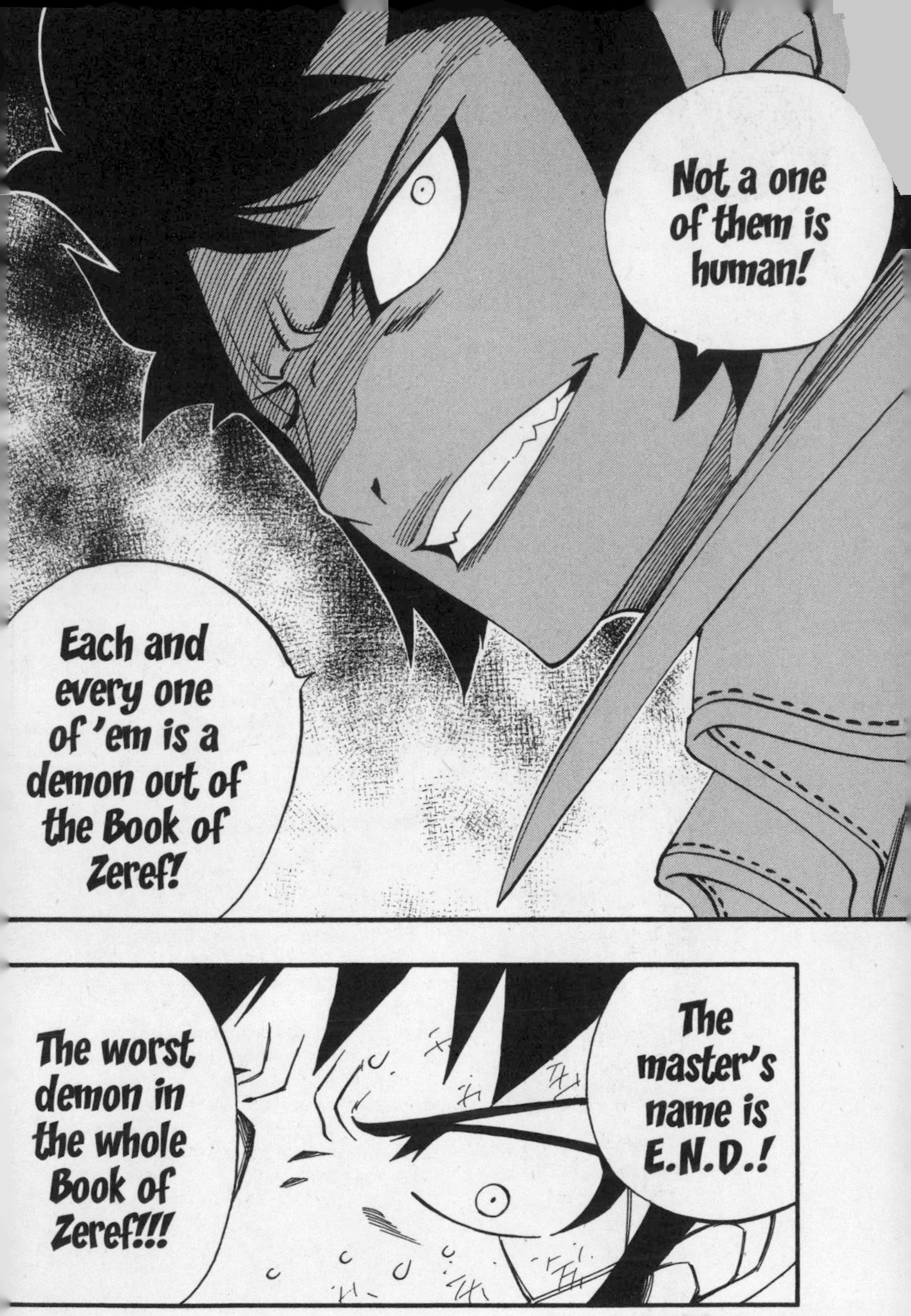
Not a one of them is human!
Each and every one of 'em is a demon out of the Book of Zeref!
The master's name is E.N.D.!
The worst demon in the whole Book of Zeref!!!

FAIRY TAIL

Chapter 357:
The Nine Demon Gates

LAMIA SCALE

Name: Sherry Blendy   **Age:** 24

Magic:
Doll Attack

Likes: **Dislikes:**
Love   Water

Remarks

Seven years ago, she fought Lucy on Galuna Island, and was reinstated into Lamia Scale afterward. She met the Blue Pegasus member Ren when fighting for the allied guilds against the Oración Seis, and the two started dating. Now they are engaged.

During the Grand Magic Games, she was secretly rooting more for Ren than for her own guild, but when her guild master (Ooba Babasaama) found out, she hit Sherry with her twirl-twirl magic.

She wants to teach her cousin Sherria what true "love" is.

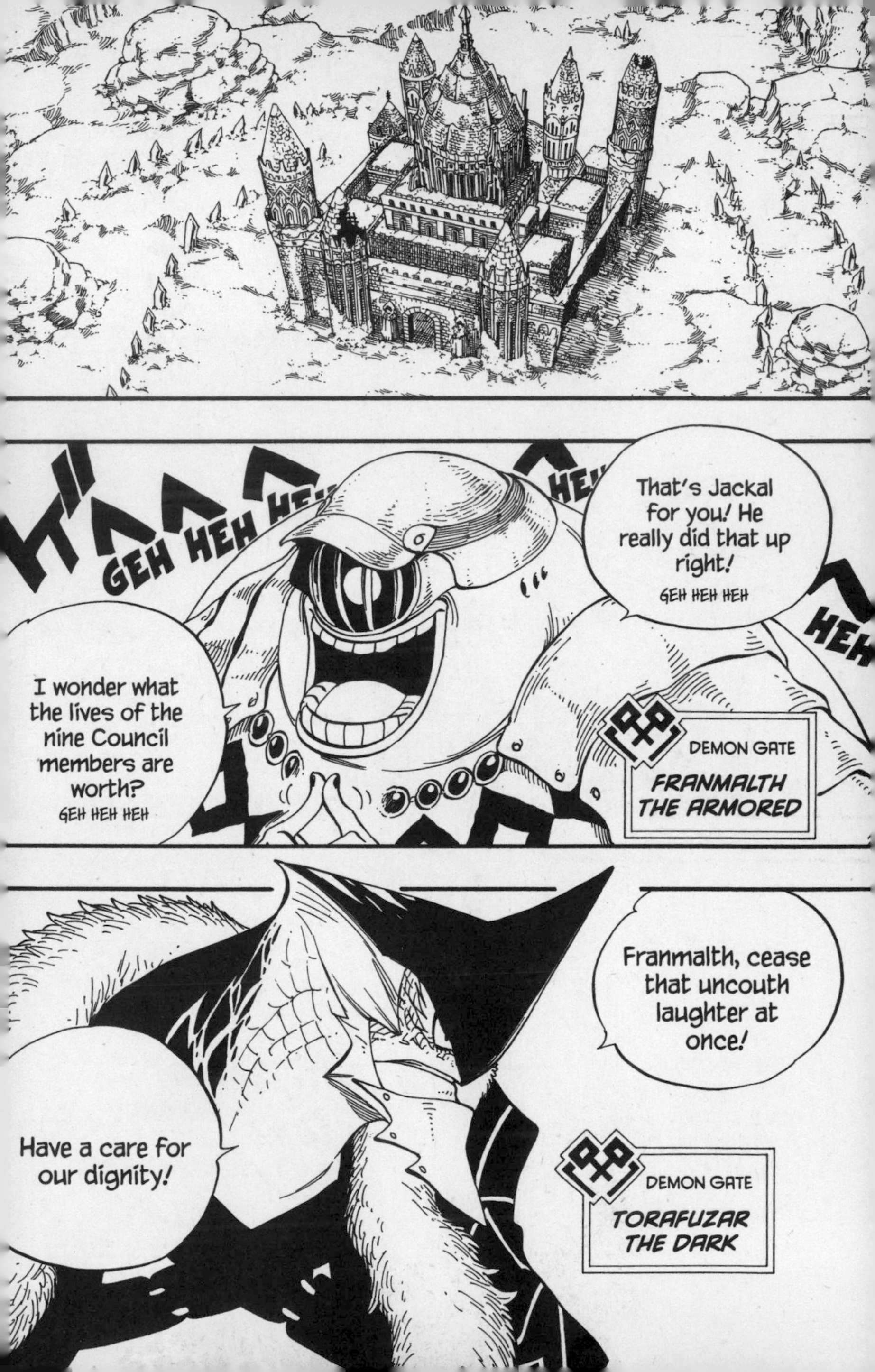
That's Jackal for you! He really did that up right!
GEH HEH HEH
HEH
GEH HEH
DEMON GATE
FRANMALTH THE ARMORED
I wonder what the lives of the nine Council members are worth?
GEH HEH HEH
Franmalth, cease that uncouth laughter at once!
DEMON GATE
TORAFUZAR THE DARK
Have a care for our dignity!

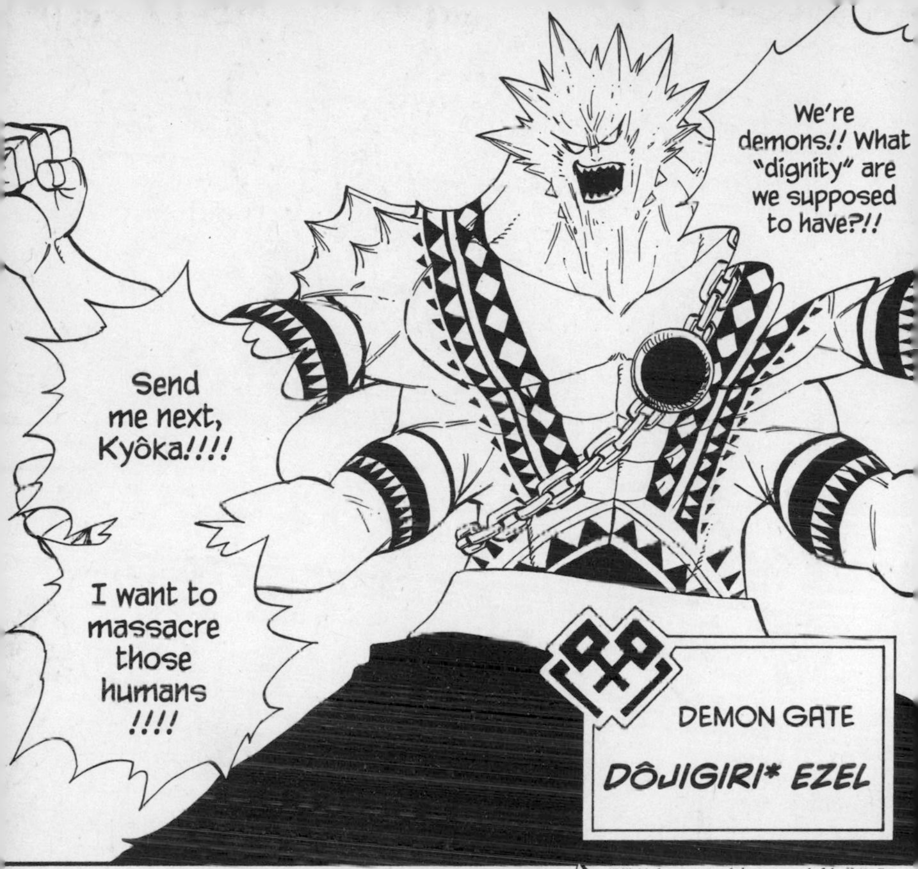
We're demons!! What "dignity" are we supposed to have?!!
Send me next, Kyôka!!!!
I want to massacre those humans !!!!
DEMON GATE
DÔJIGIRI* EZEL

*Dôjigiri, the greatest and sharpest sword of the Heian Era.

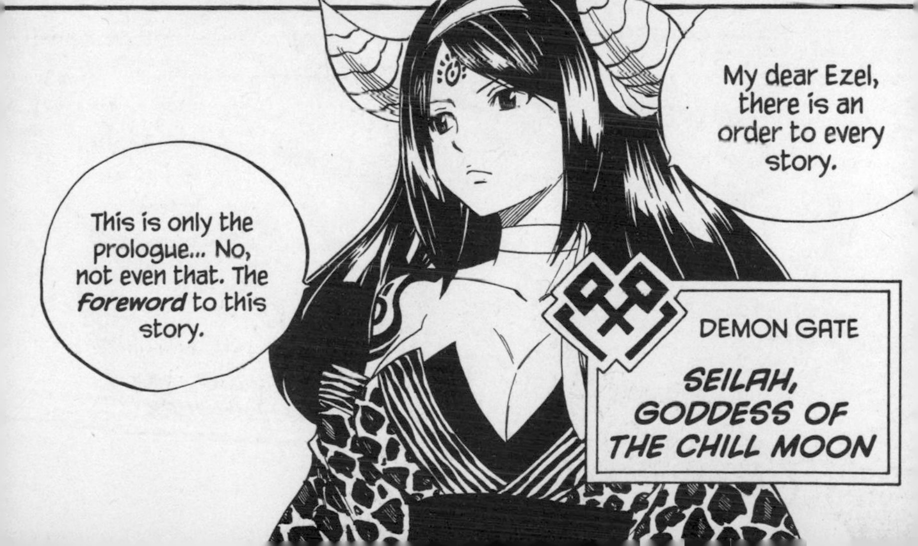
My dear Ezel, there is an order to every story.
This is only the prologue... No, not even that. The *foreword* to this story.
DEMON GATE
SEILAH, GODDESS OF THE CHILL MOON

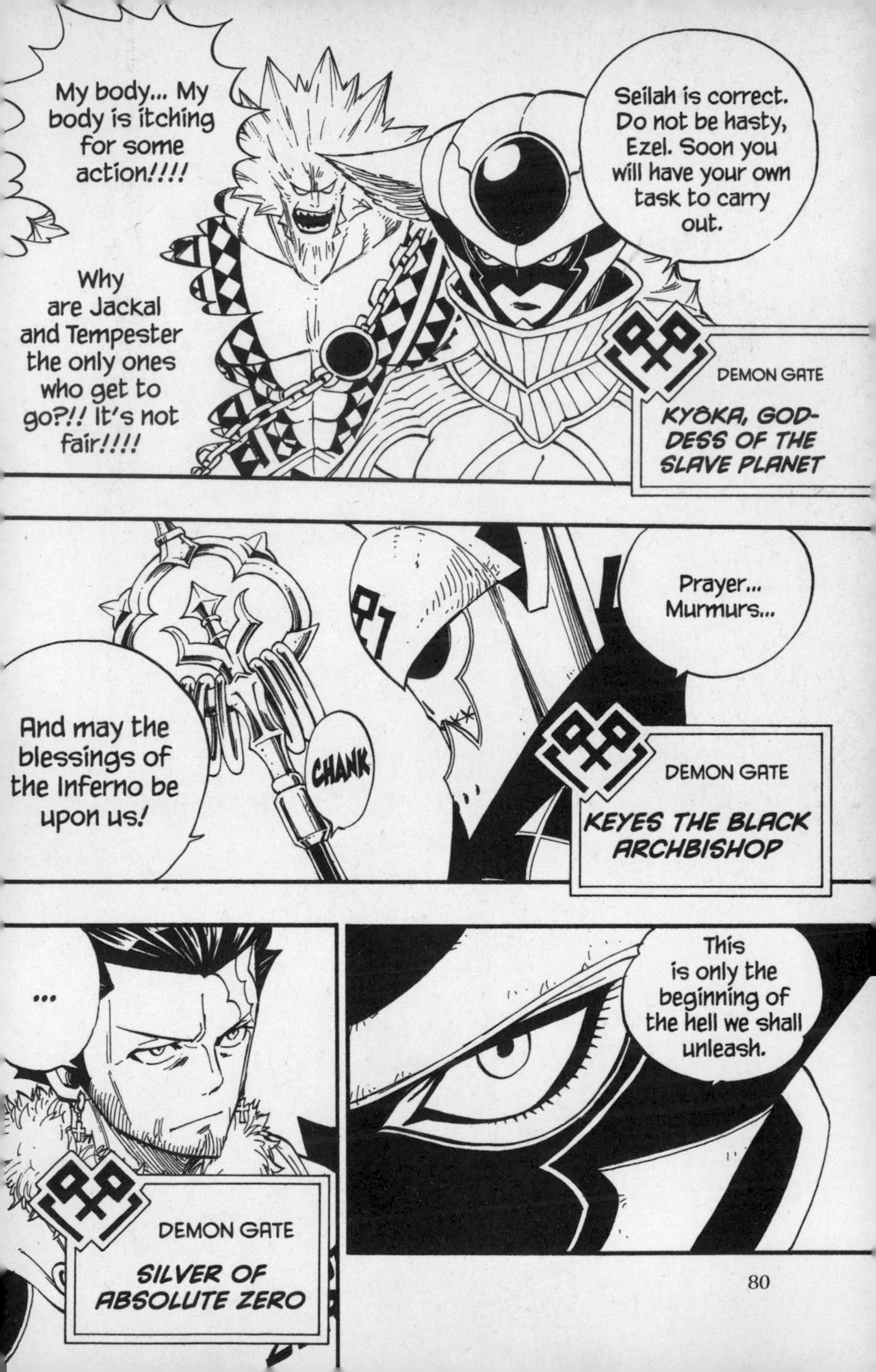

Seilah is correct. Do not be hasty, Ezel. Soon you will have your own task to carry out.
DEMON GATE
KYÔKA, GODDESS OF THE SLAVE PLANET
My body... My body is itching for some action!!!!
Why are Jackal and Tempester the only ones who get to go?!! It's not fair!!!!
Prayer... Murmurs...
DEMON GATE
KEYES THE BLACK ARCHBISHOP
CHANK
And may the blessings of the Inferno be upon us!
This is only the beginning of the hell we shall unleash.
...
DEMON GATE
SILVER OF ABSOLUTE ZERO

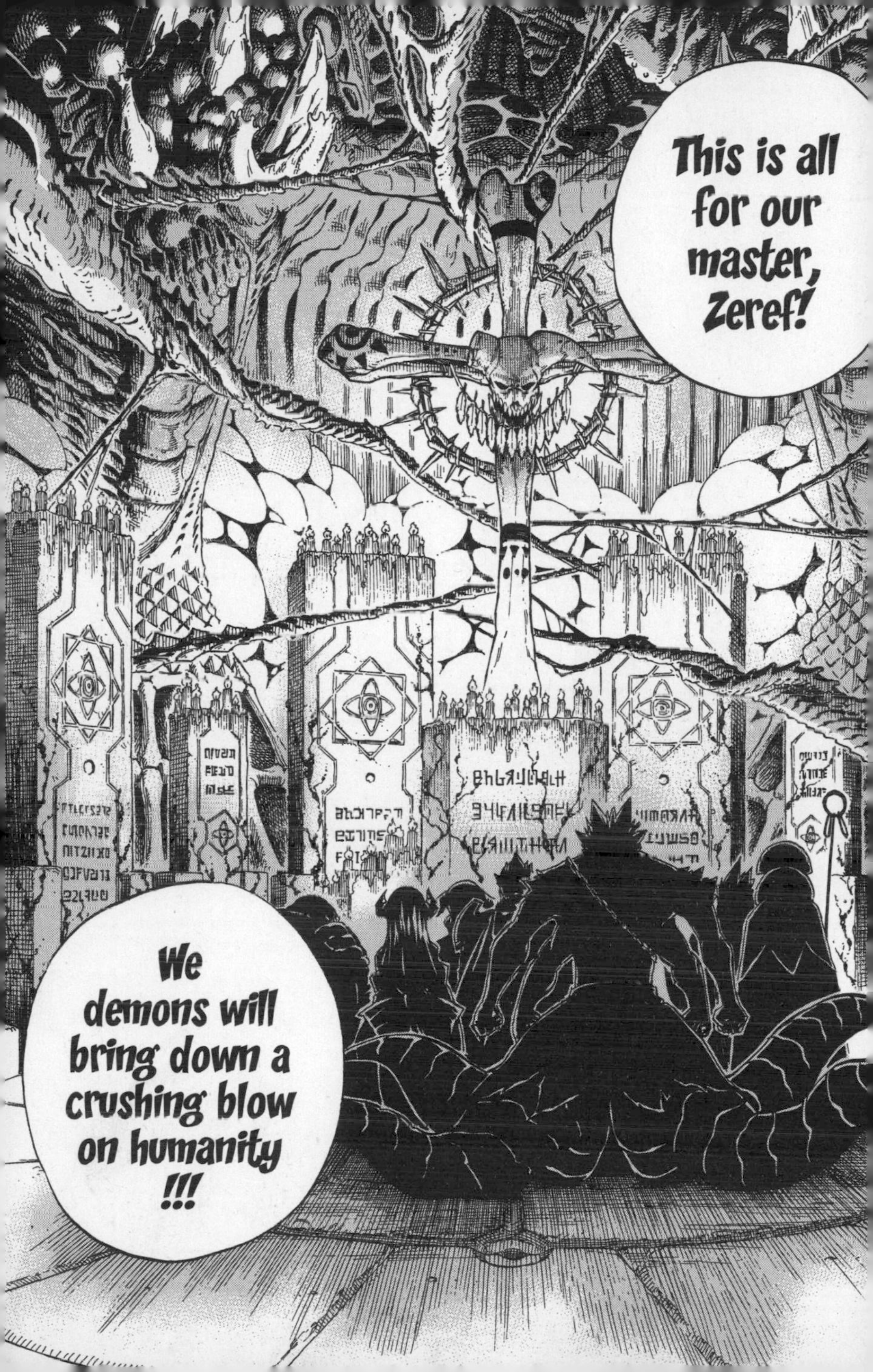
This is all for our master, Zeref!
We demons will bring down a crushing blow on humanity !!!

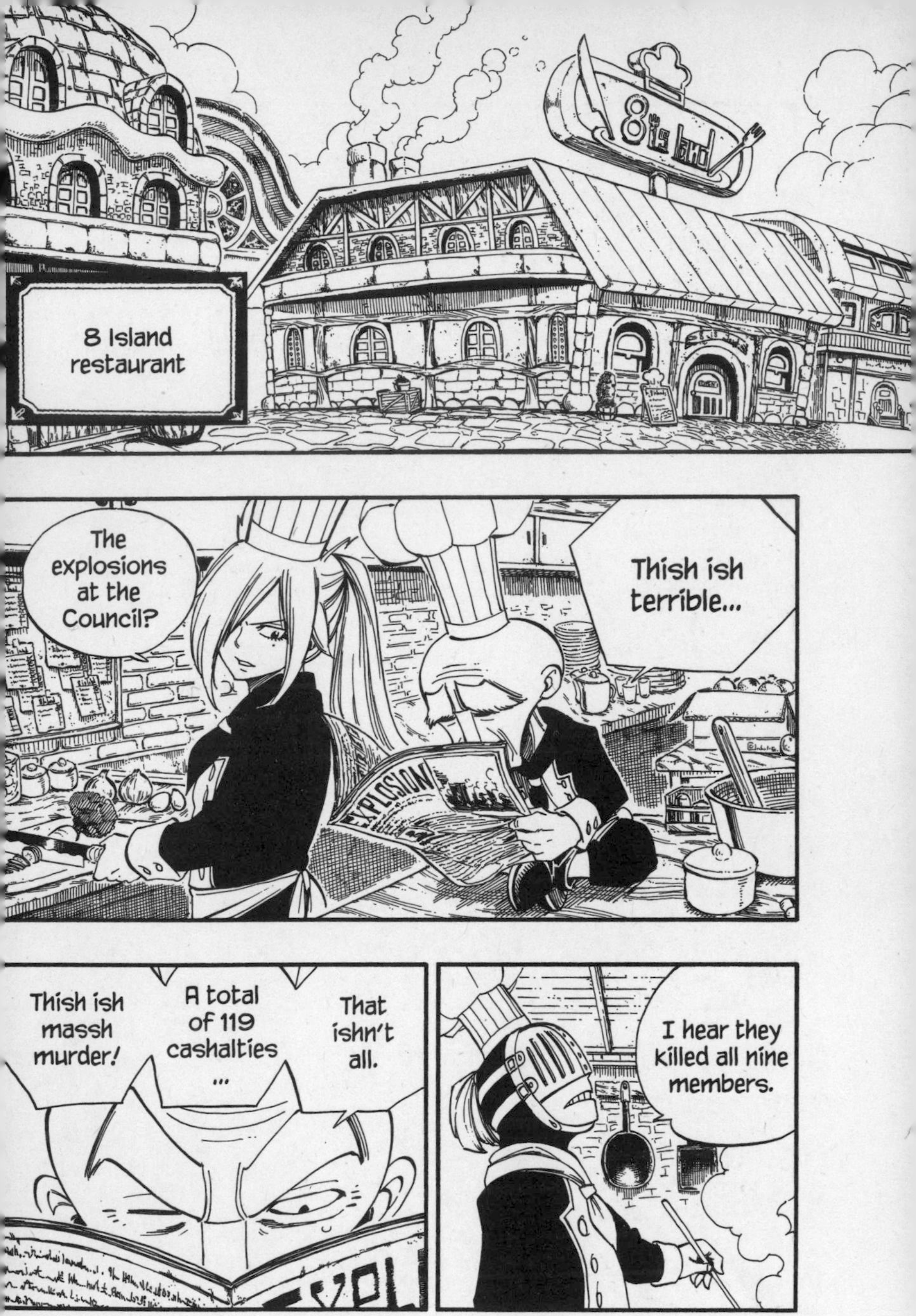
8 is land
8 Island restaurant
Thish ish terrible...
The explosions at the Council?
EXPLOSION
I hear they killed all nine members.
That ishn't all.
A total of 119 cashalties ...
Thish ish massh murder!

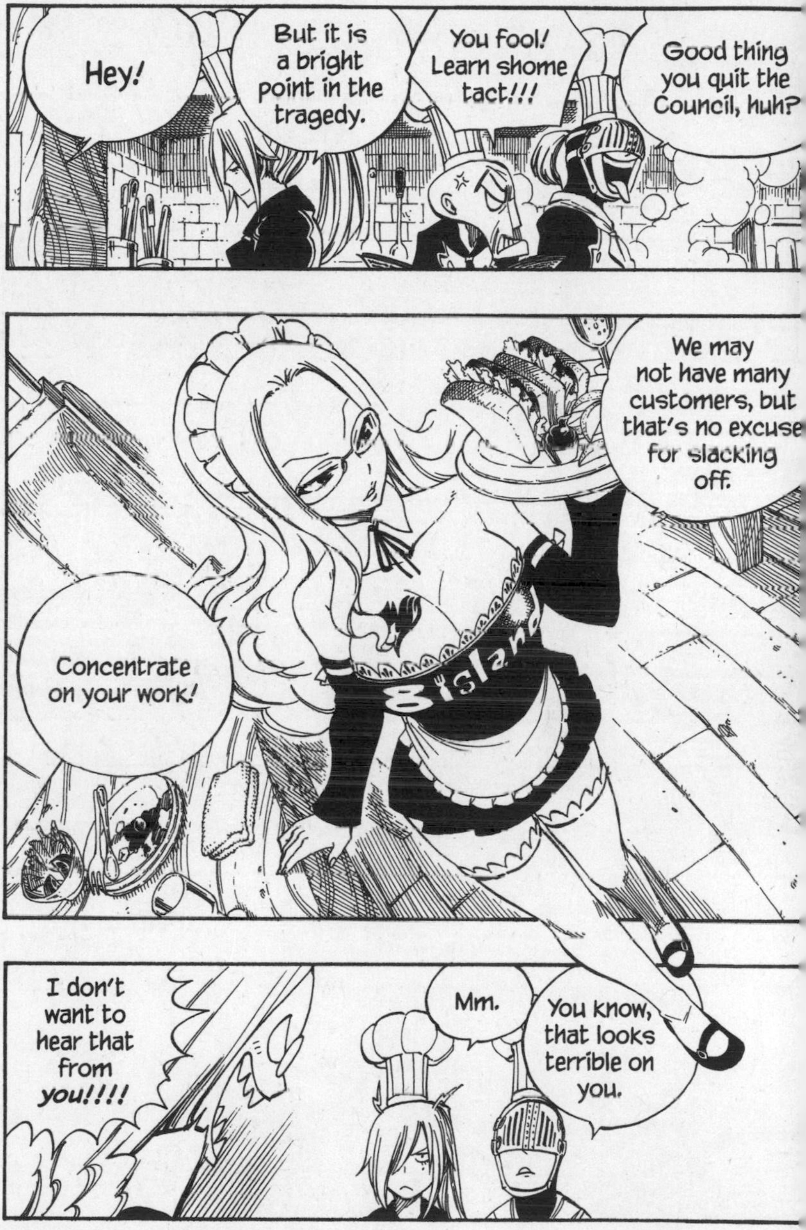
Good thing you quit the Council, huh?
You fool! Learn shome tact!!!
But it is a bright point in the tragedy.
Hey!
We may not have many customers, but that's no excuse for slacking off.
Concentrate on your work!
8 Island
You know, that looks terrible on you.
Mm.
I don't want to hear that from *you!!!!*

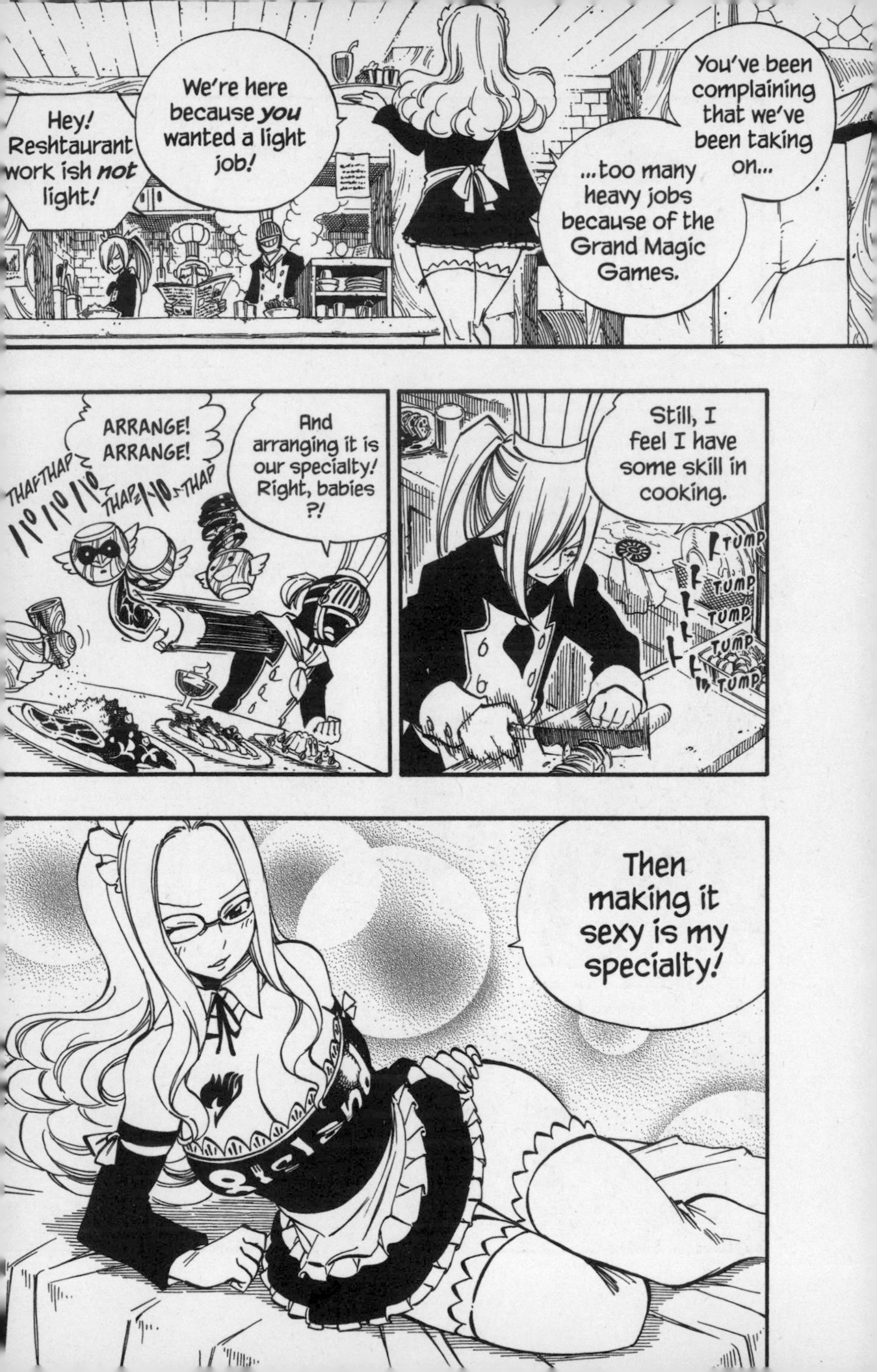
You've been complaining that we've been taking on...
...too many heavy jobs because of the Grand Magic Games.
We're here because *you* wanted a light job!
Hey! Reshtaurant work ish *not* light!
Still, I feel I have some skill in cooking.
TUMP
TUMP
TUMP
TUMP
TUMP
And arranging it is our specialty! Right, babies?!
ARRANGE! ARRANGE!
THAPTHAP
THAP
THAP
Then making it sexy is my specialty!

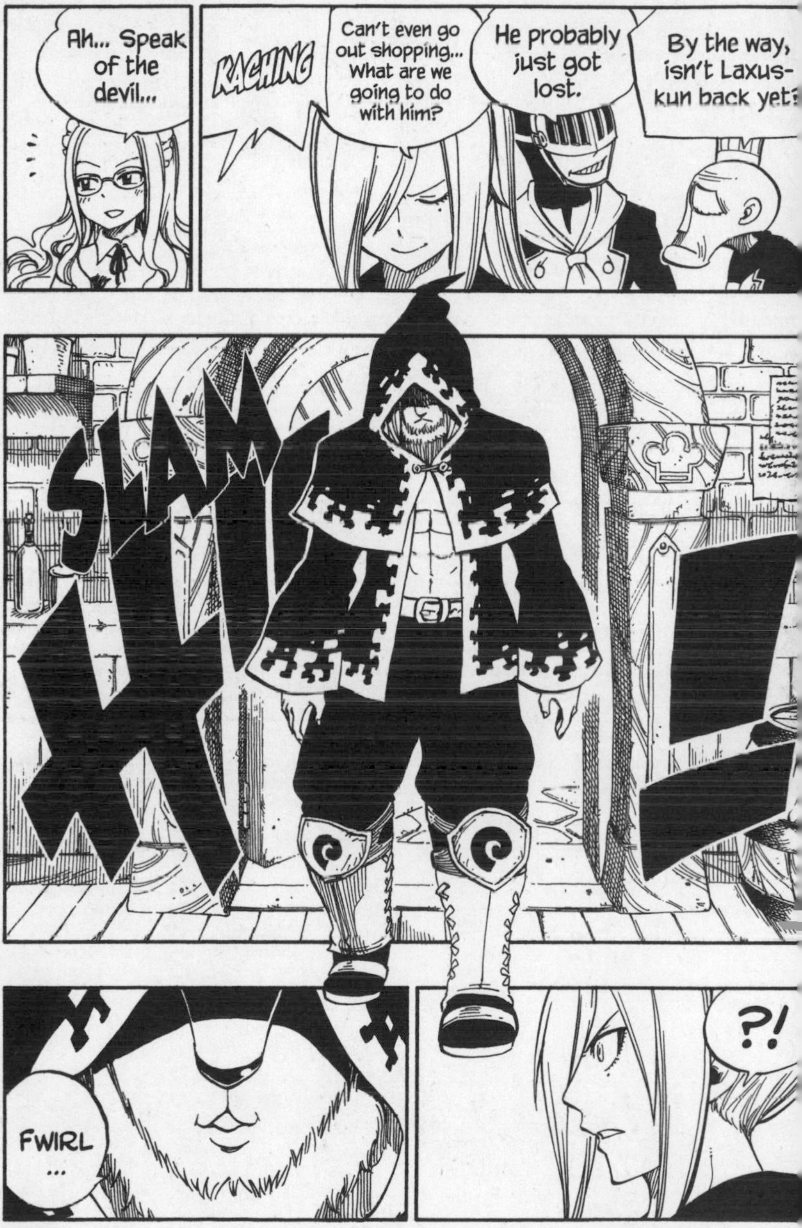
By the way, isn't Laxus-kun back yet?
He probably just got lost.
Can't even go out shopping... What are we going to do with him?
KACHING
Ah... Speak of the devil...
SLAM
?!
FWIRL ...

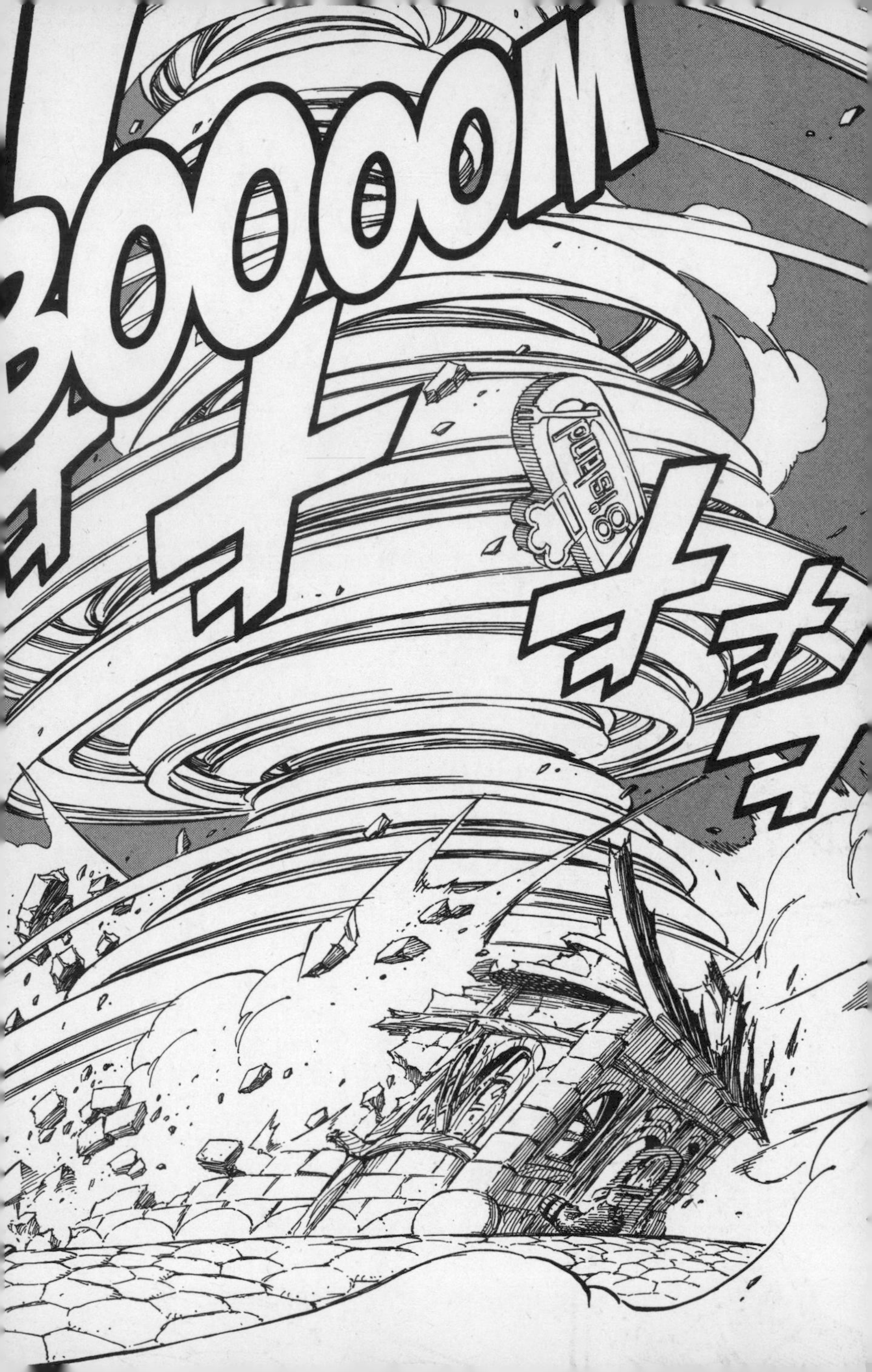
BOOOOM

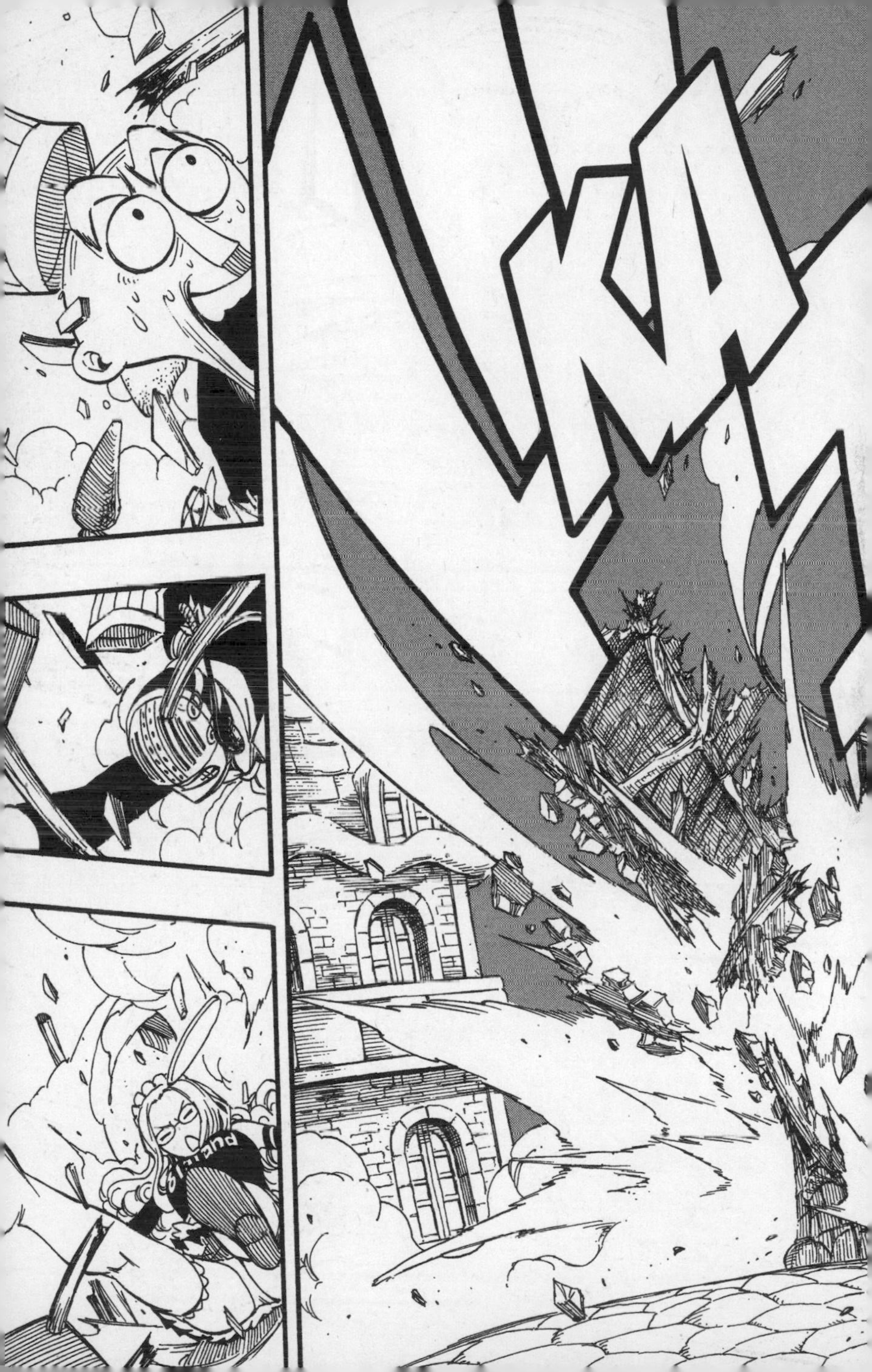

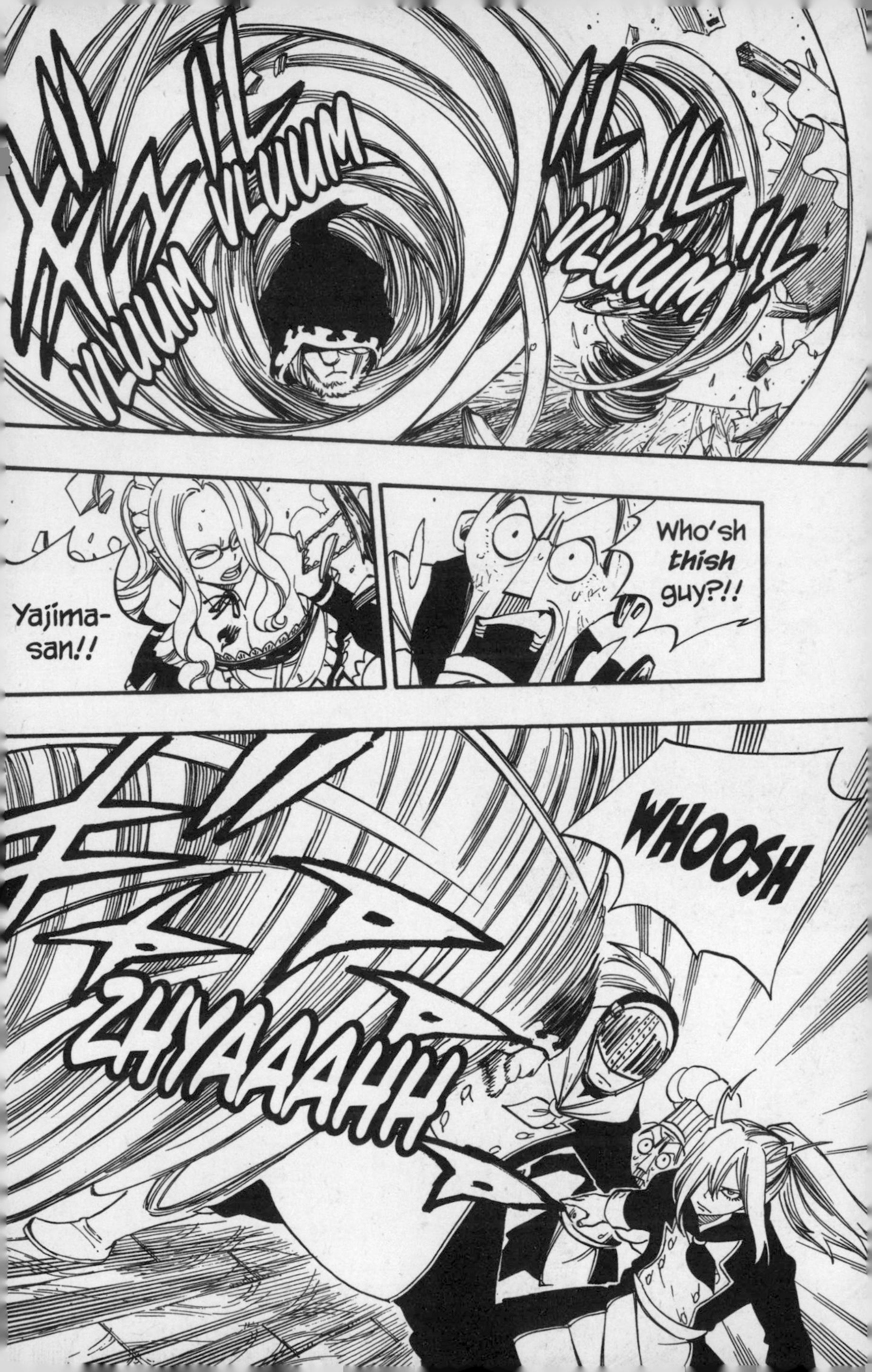
VLUUM
VLUUM
VLUUM
Who'sh thish guy?!!
Yajima-san!!
WHOOSH
ZHYAAAHH

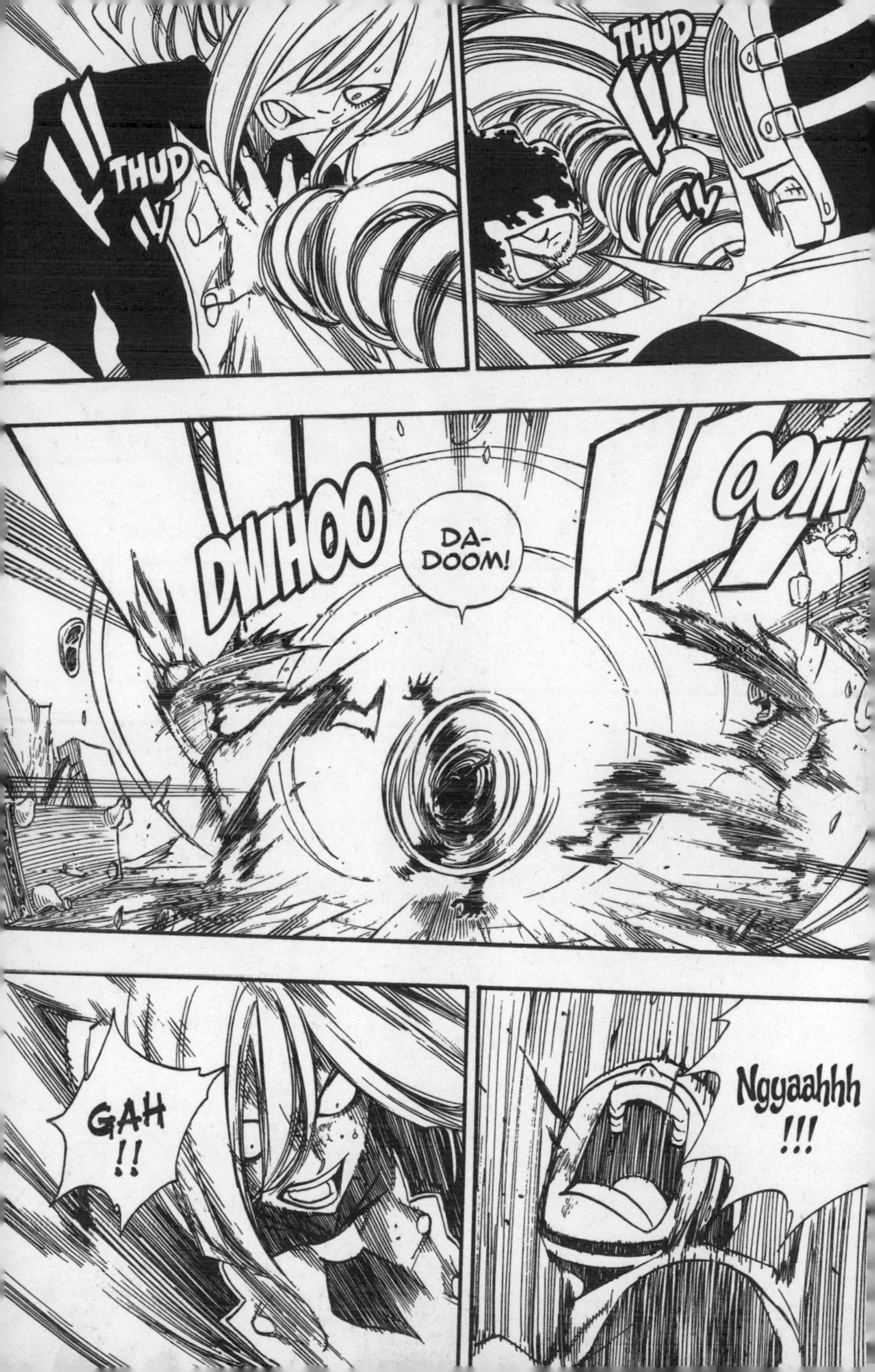
THUD
THUD
DWHOO
OOM
DA-DOOM!
Ngyaahhh!!!
GAH!!

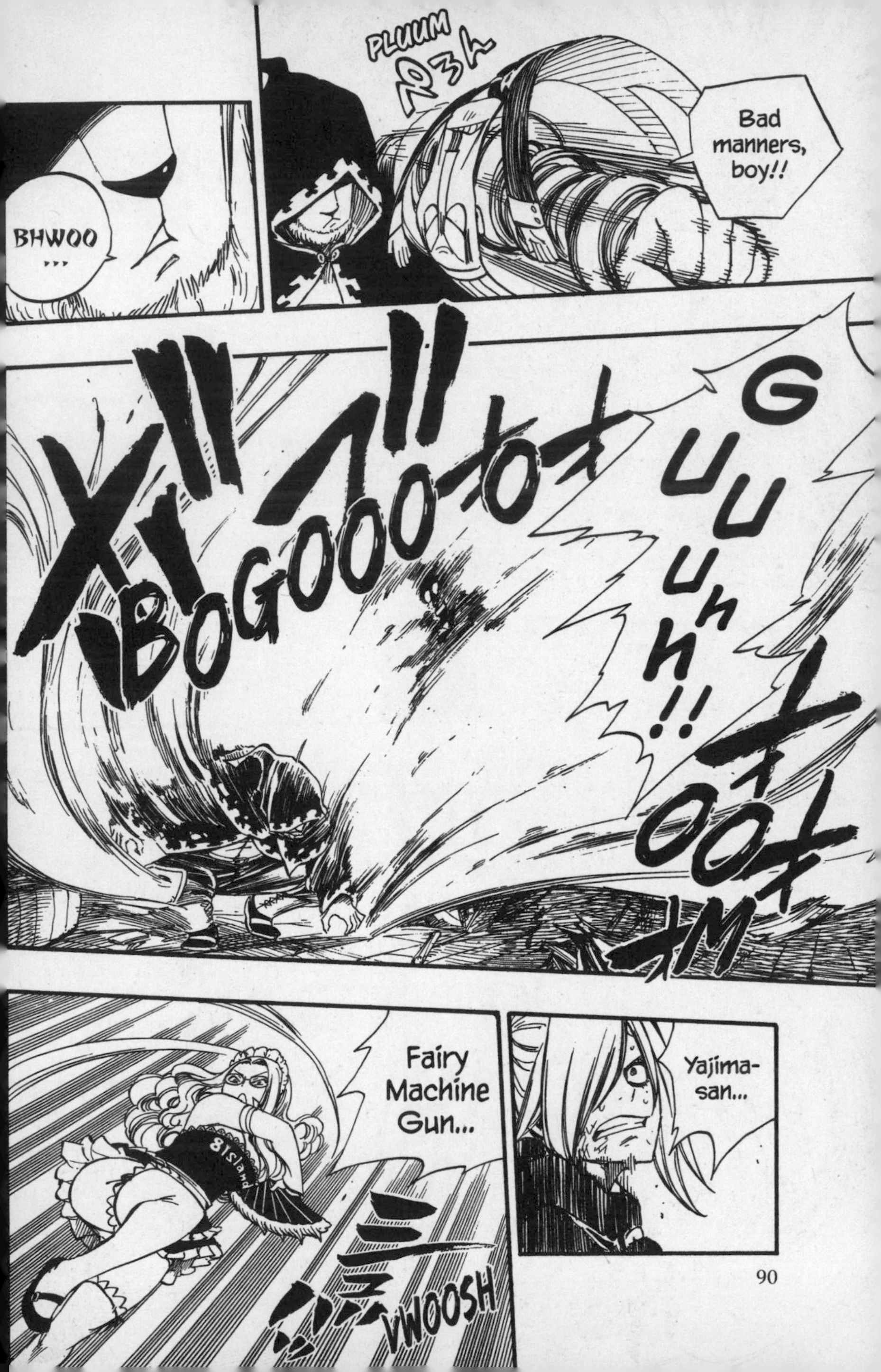
PLUUM
Bad manners, boy!!
BHWOO ...
GUUUunh!!
BOGOOO
OOM
Yajima-san...
Fairy Machine Gun...
8 Island
VWOOSH

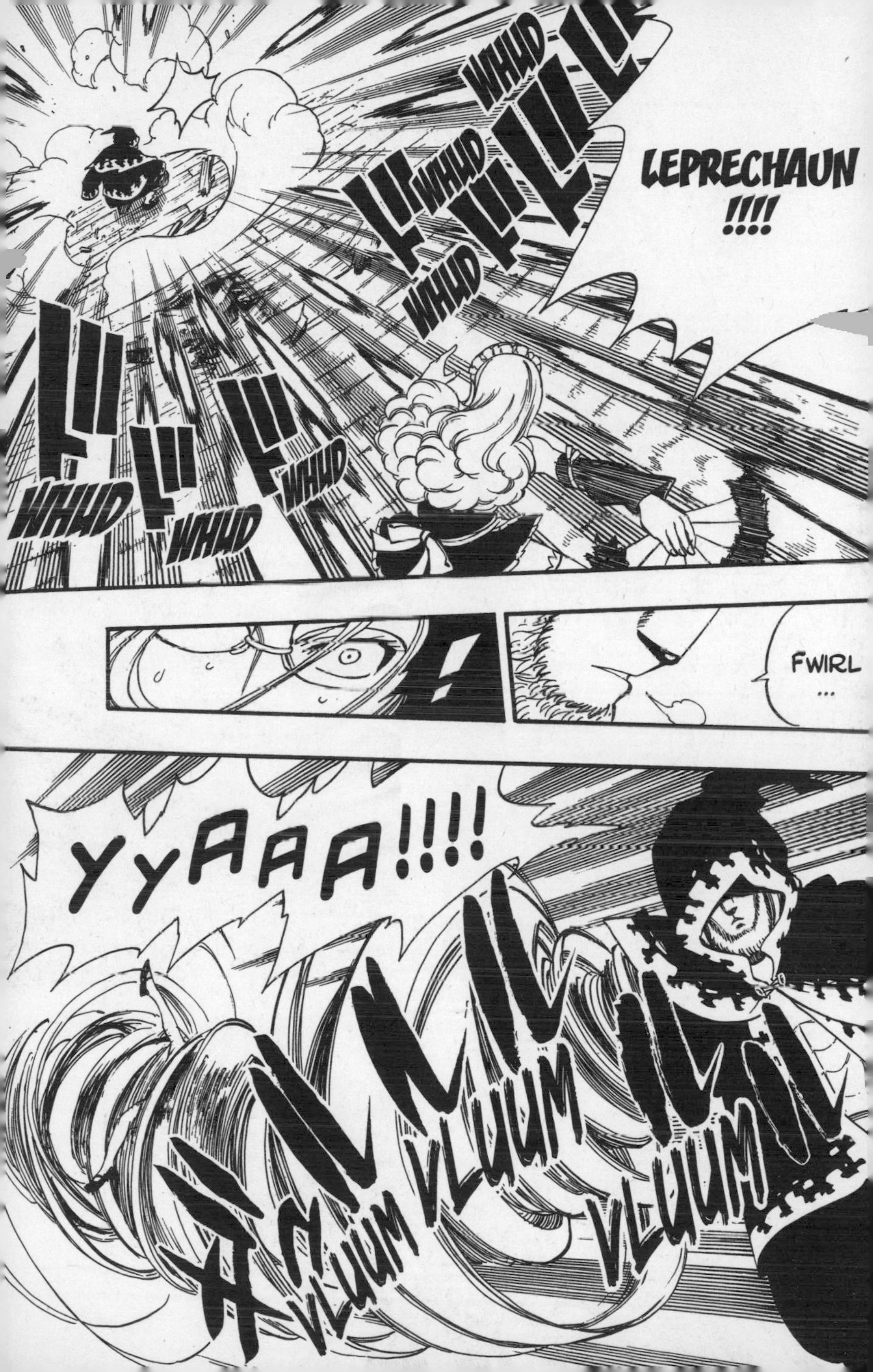
LEPRECHAUN !!!!
WHUD WHUD
WHUD WHUD
WHUD
WHUD
WHUD
FWIRL ...
!
YYAAAA!!!!
VLUUM VLUUM
VLUUM
VLUUM

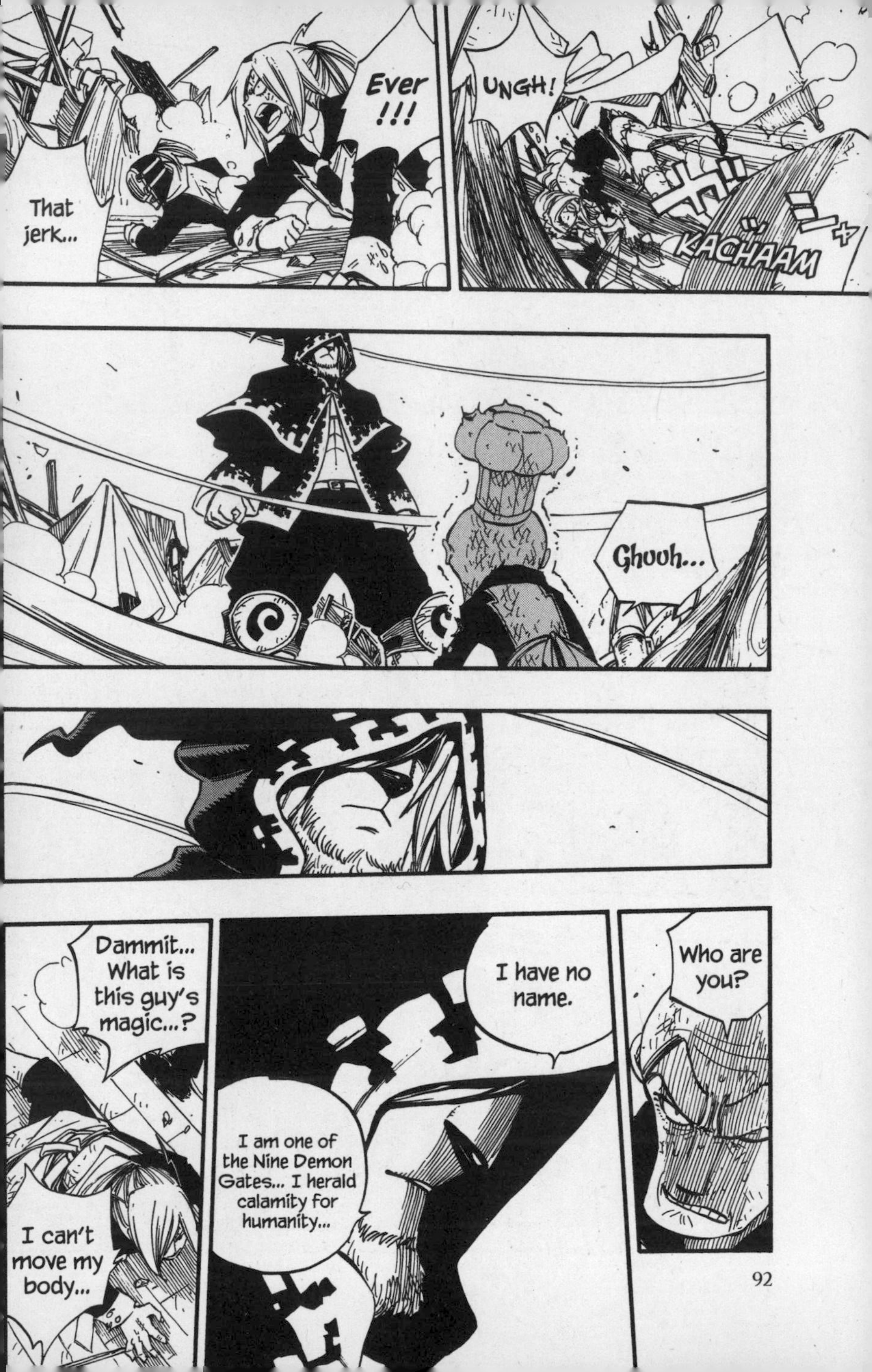
UNGH!
KACHAAM
Ever !!!
That jerk...
Ghuoh...
Who are you?
I have no name.
I am one of the Nine Demon Gates... I herald calamity for humanity...
Dammit... What is this guy's magic...?
I can't move my body...

The gate to the Underworld is open!

We are delivering mankind's rightful punishment!

Gugghh!

GRNN GRNN GRNN

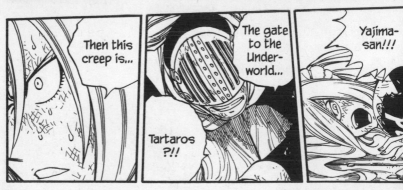

Then this creep is...

Tartaros?!!

The gate to the Under-world...

Yajima-san!!!

93

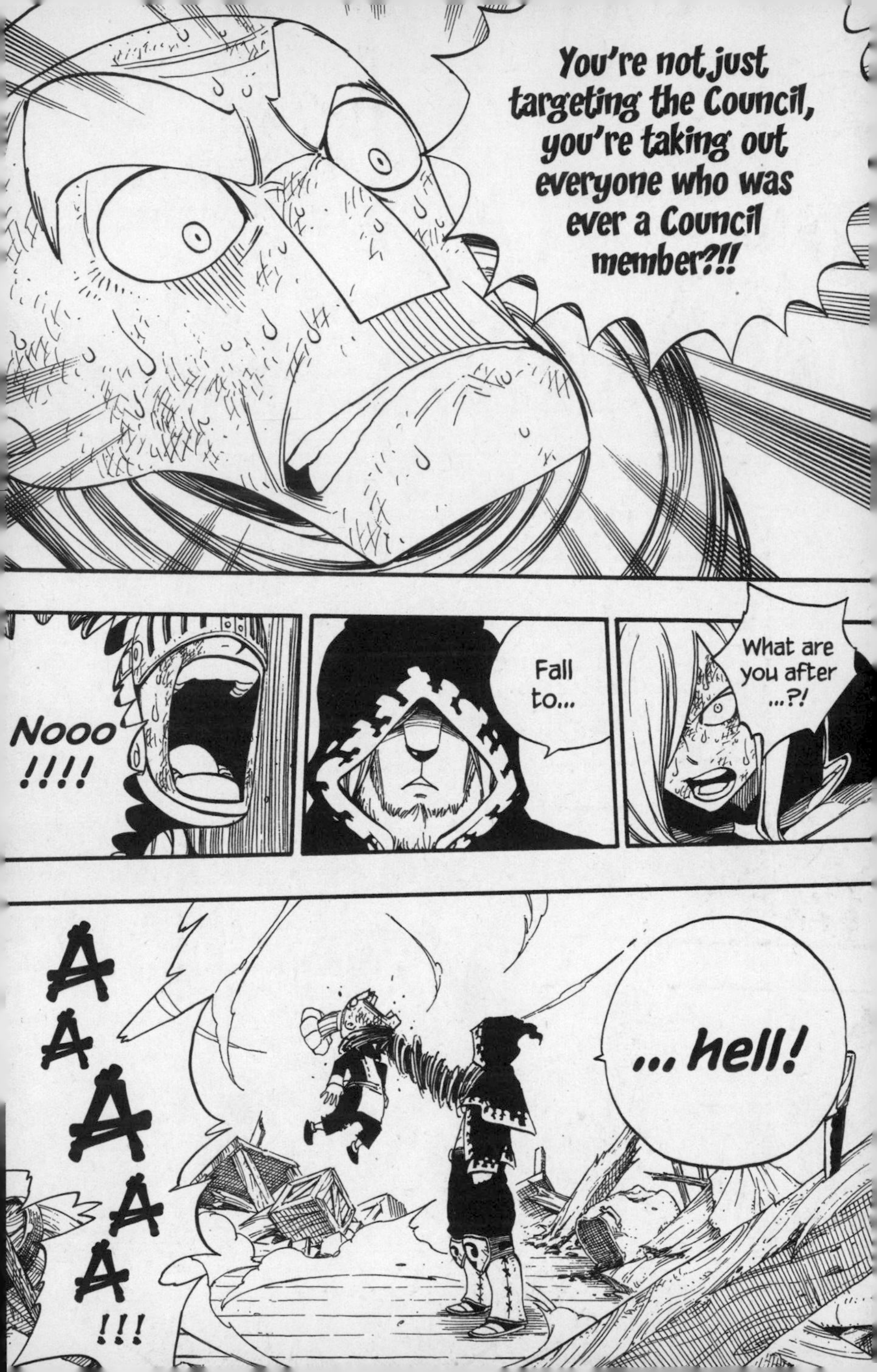
You're not just targeting the Council, you're taking out everyone who was ever a Council member?!!
What are you after ...?!
Fall to...
Nooo !!!!
...hell!
AAAAA !!!

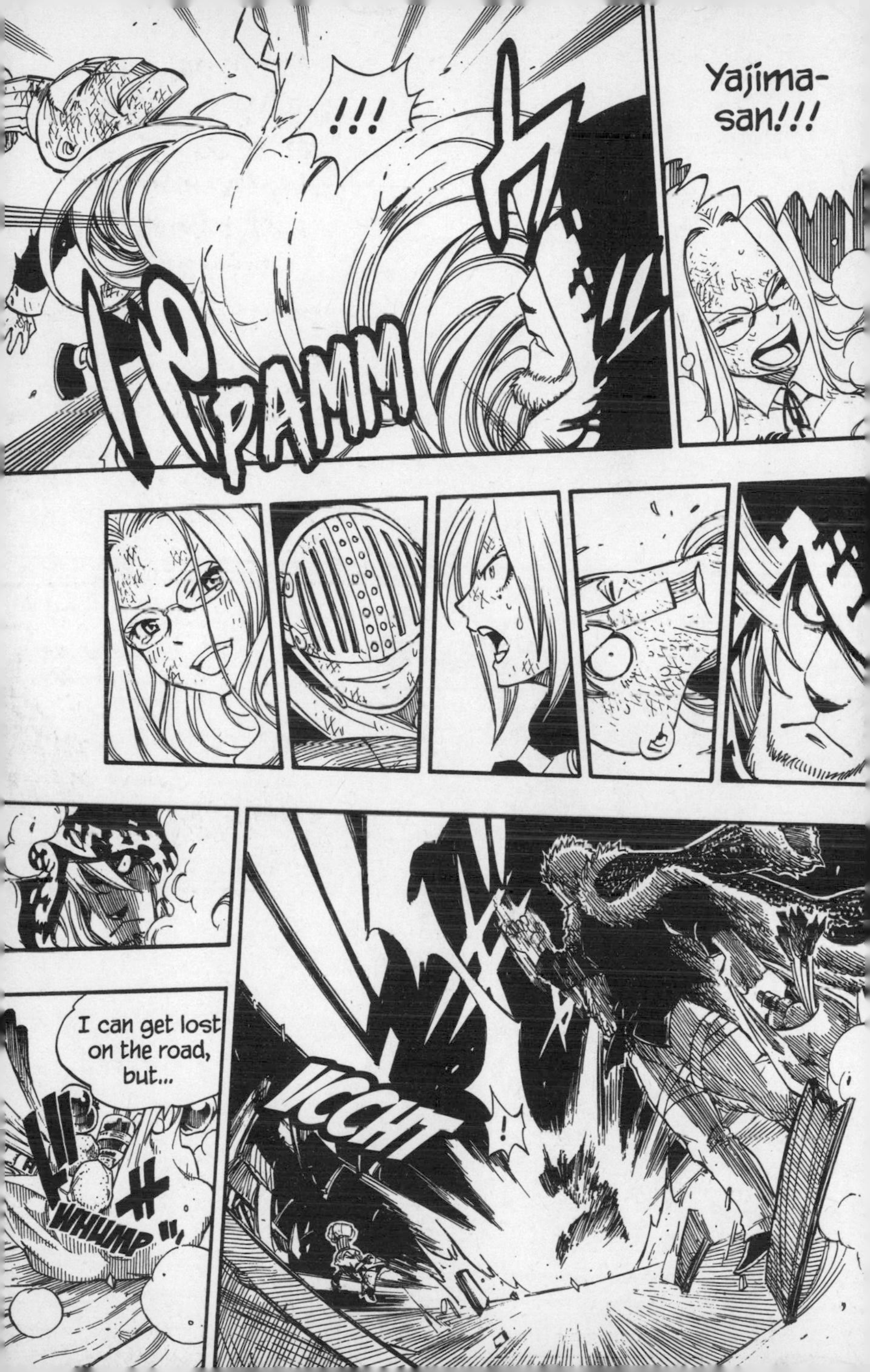
Yajima-
san!!!
!!!
PAMM
UCCHT
!
I can get lost
on the road,
but...
WHUMP

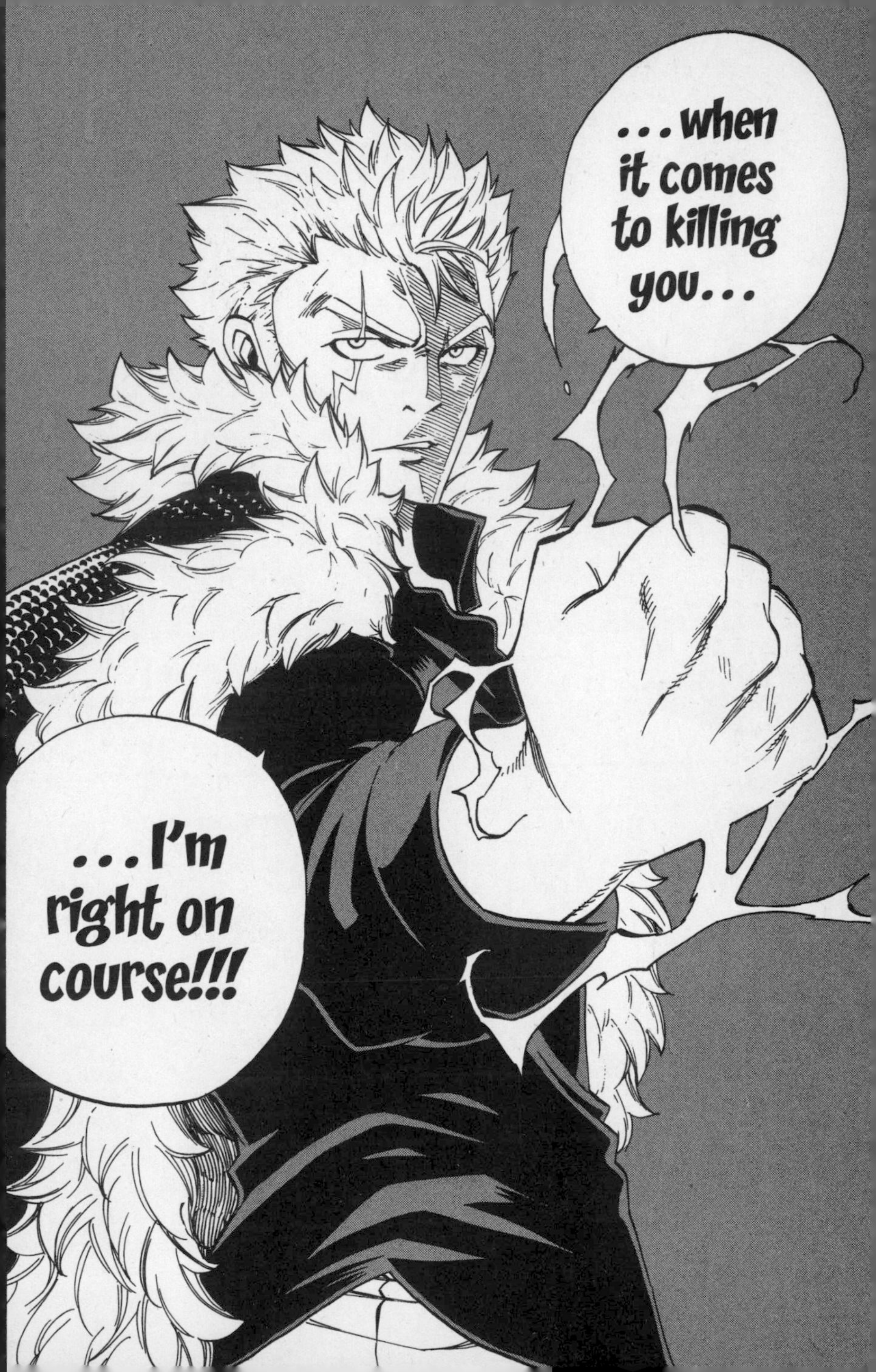
...when it comes to killing you...
...I'm right on course!!!

FAIRY TAIL

Chapter 358: The Devil Particles

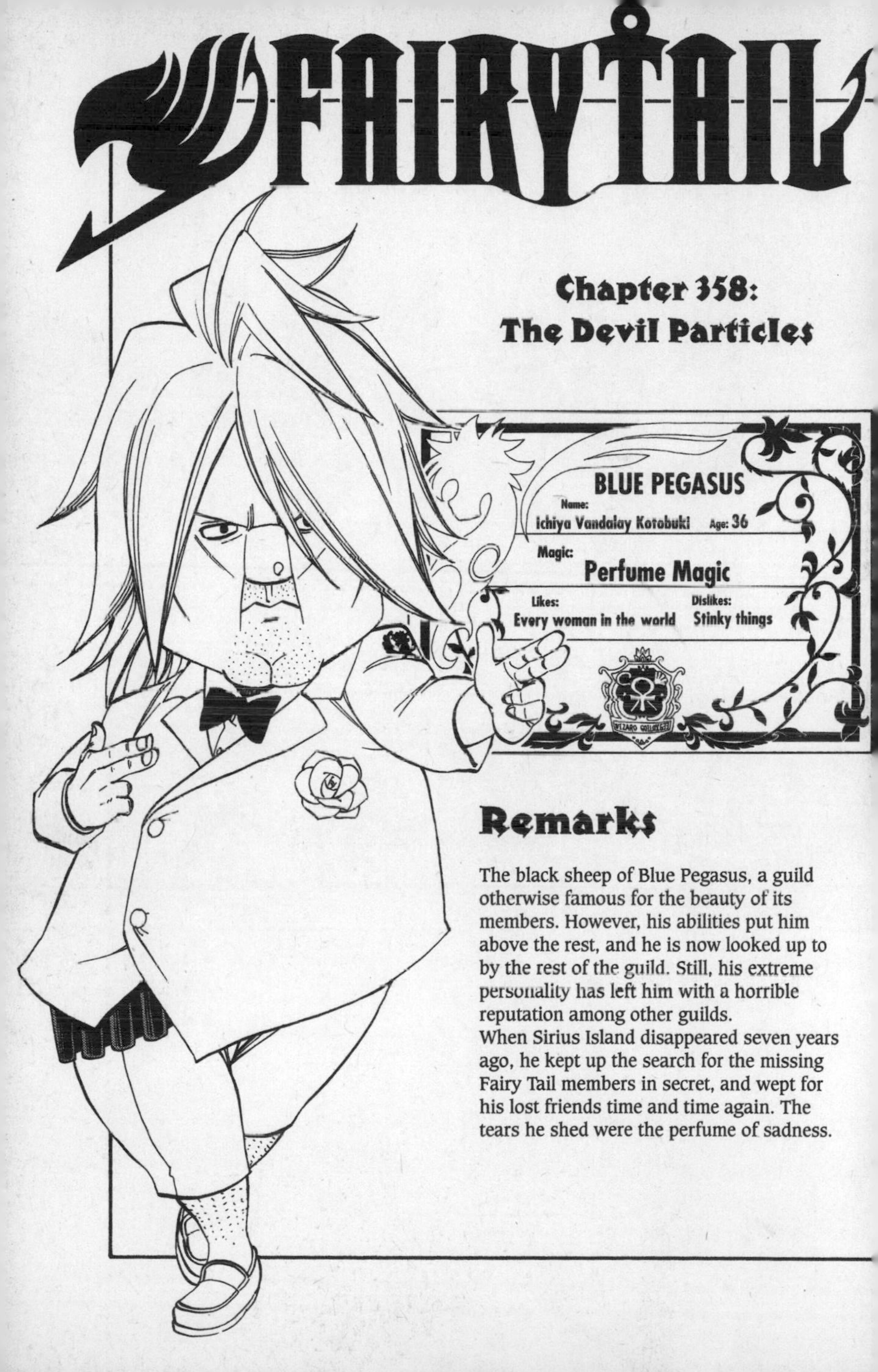

BLUE PEGASUS

Name: Ichiya Vandalay Kotobuki Age: 36

Magic: **Perfume Magic**

Likes: Every woman in the world

Dislikes: Stinky things

Remarks

The black sheep of Blue Pegasus, a guild otherwise famous for the beauty of its members. However, his abilities put him above the rest, and he is now looked up to by the rest of the guild. Still, his extreme personality has left him with a horrible reputation among other guilds.

When Sirius Island disappeared seven years ago, he kept up the search for the missing Fairy Tail members in secret, and wept for his lost friends time and time again. The tears he shed were the perfume of sadness.

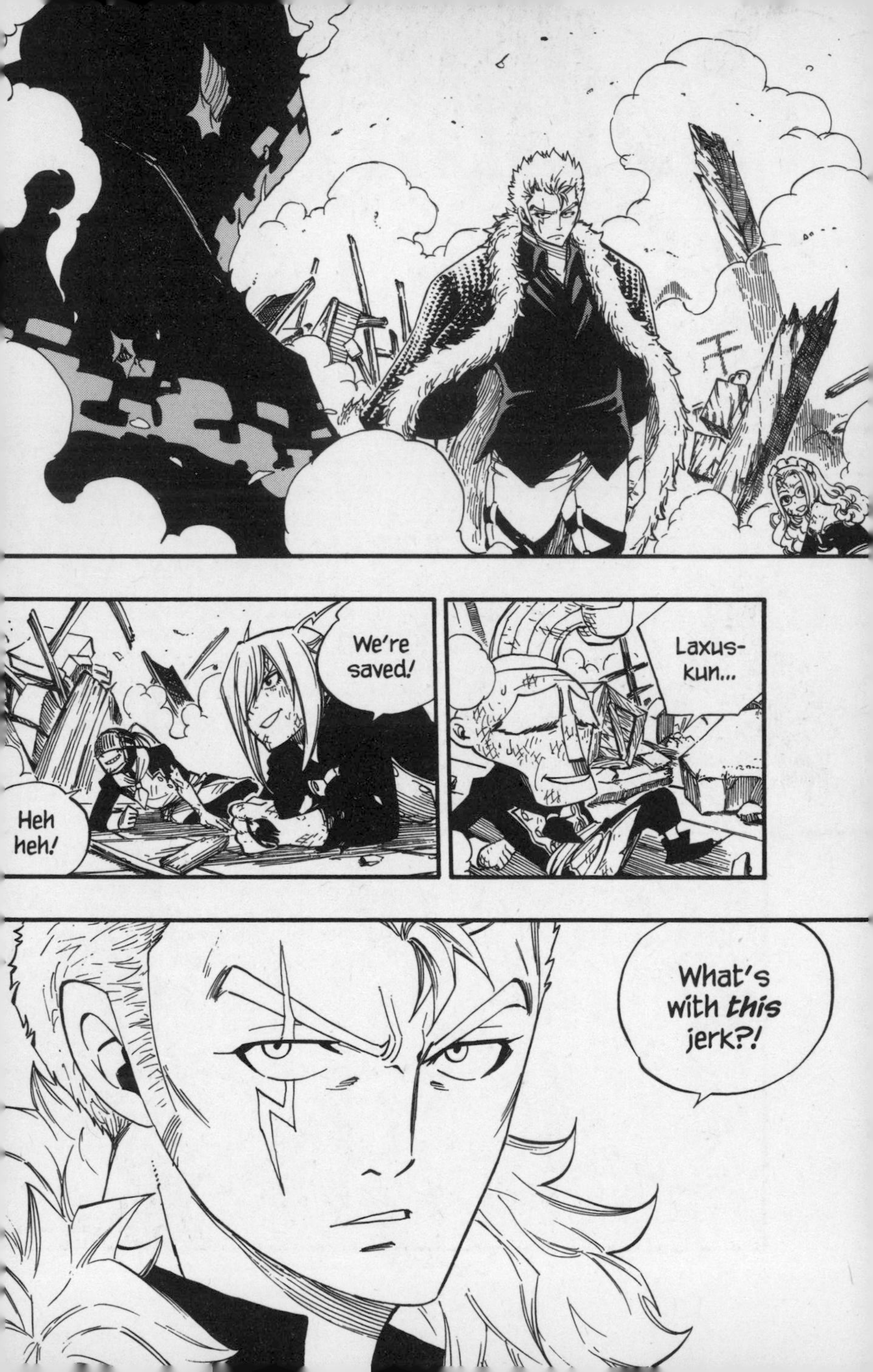
Laxus-kun...
We're saved!
Heh heh!
What's with *this* jerk?!

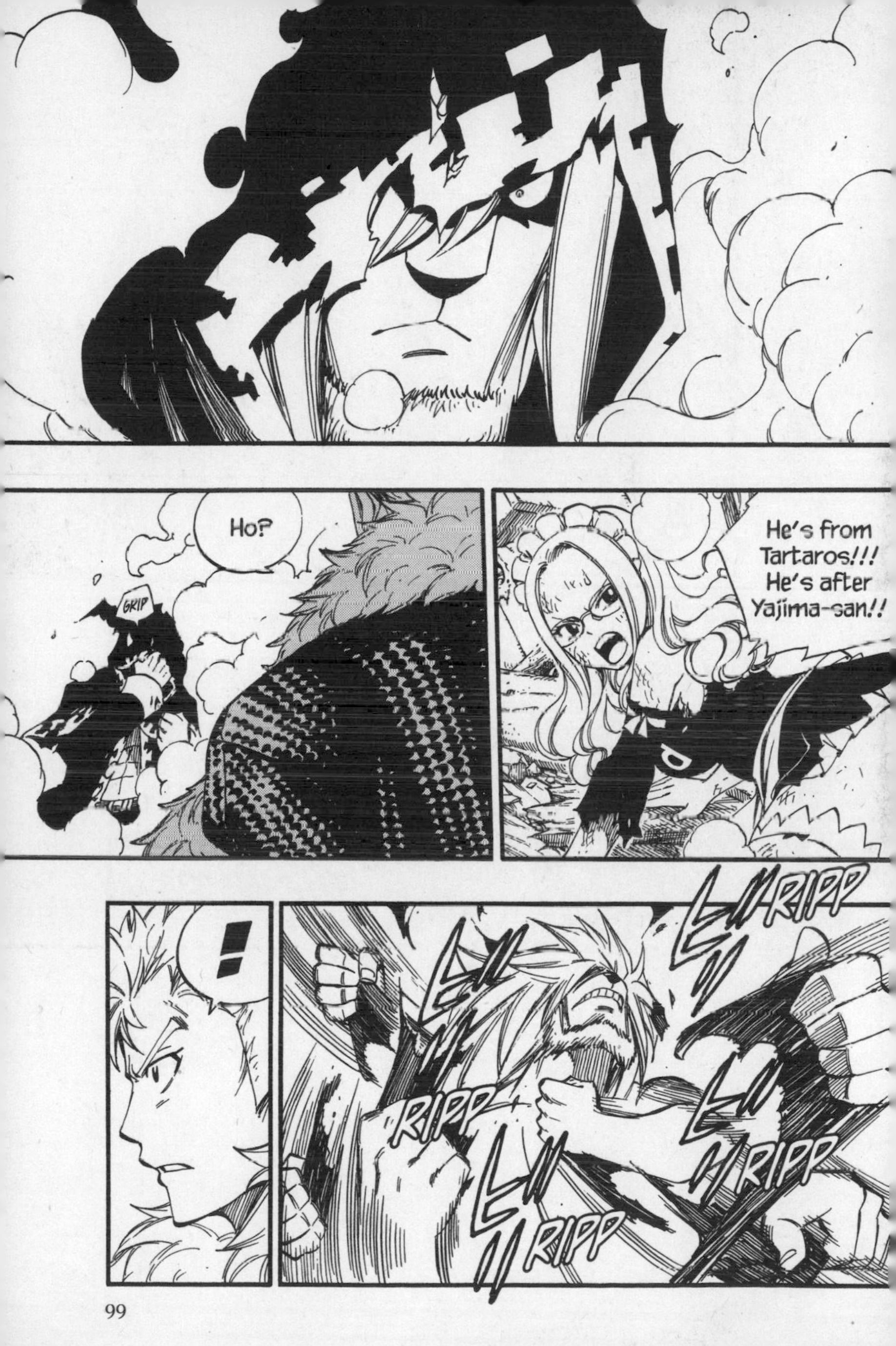
He's from Tartaros!!! He's after Yajima-san!!
Ho?
GRIP
RIPP
RIPP
RIPP
RIPP
!

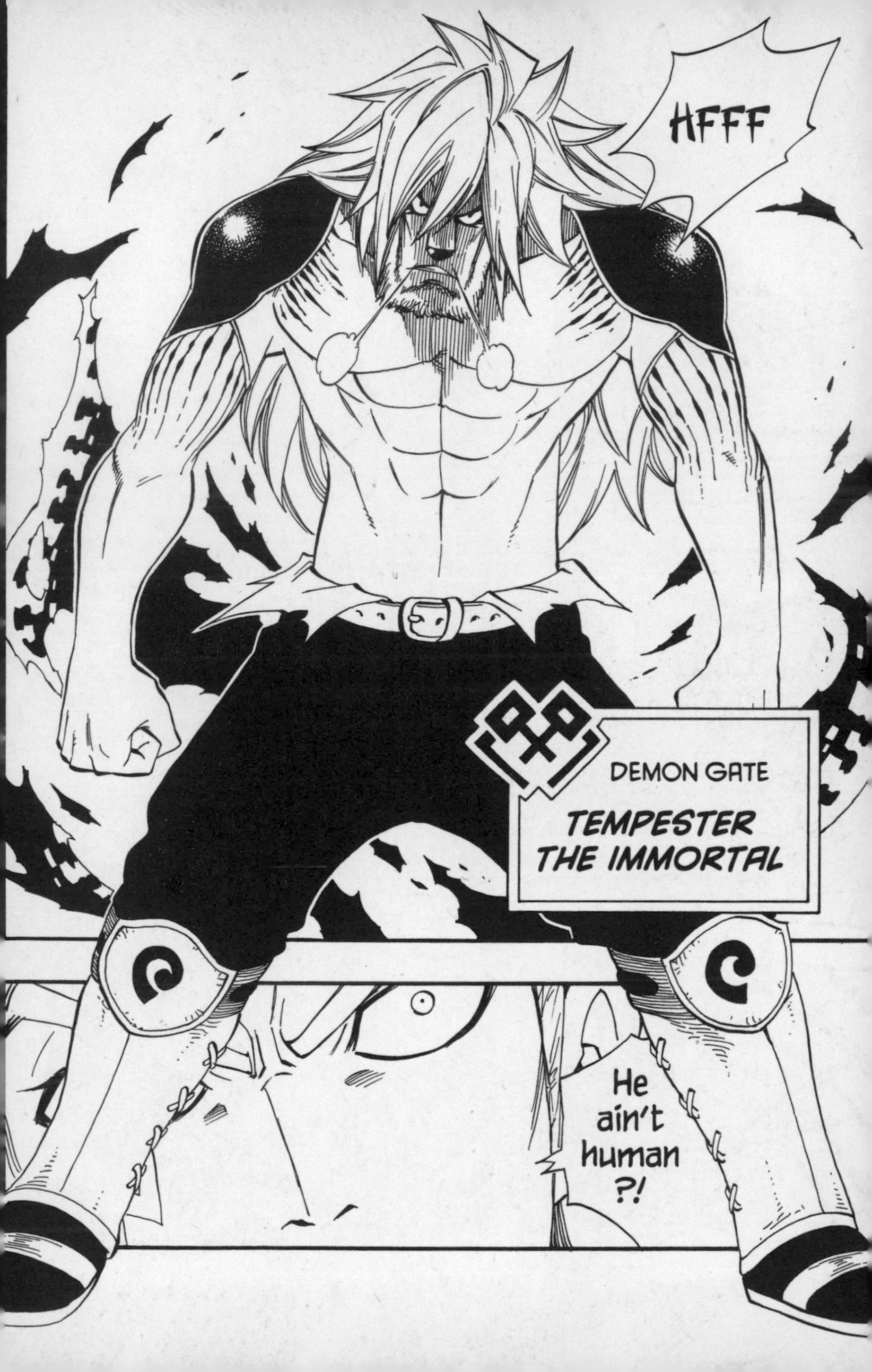
HFFF
DEMON GATE
TEMPESTER THE IMMORTAL
He ain't human ?!

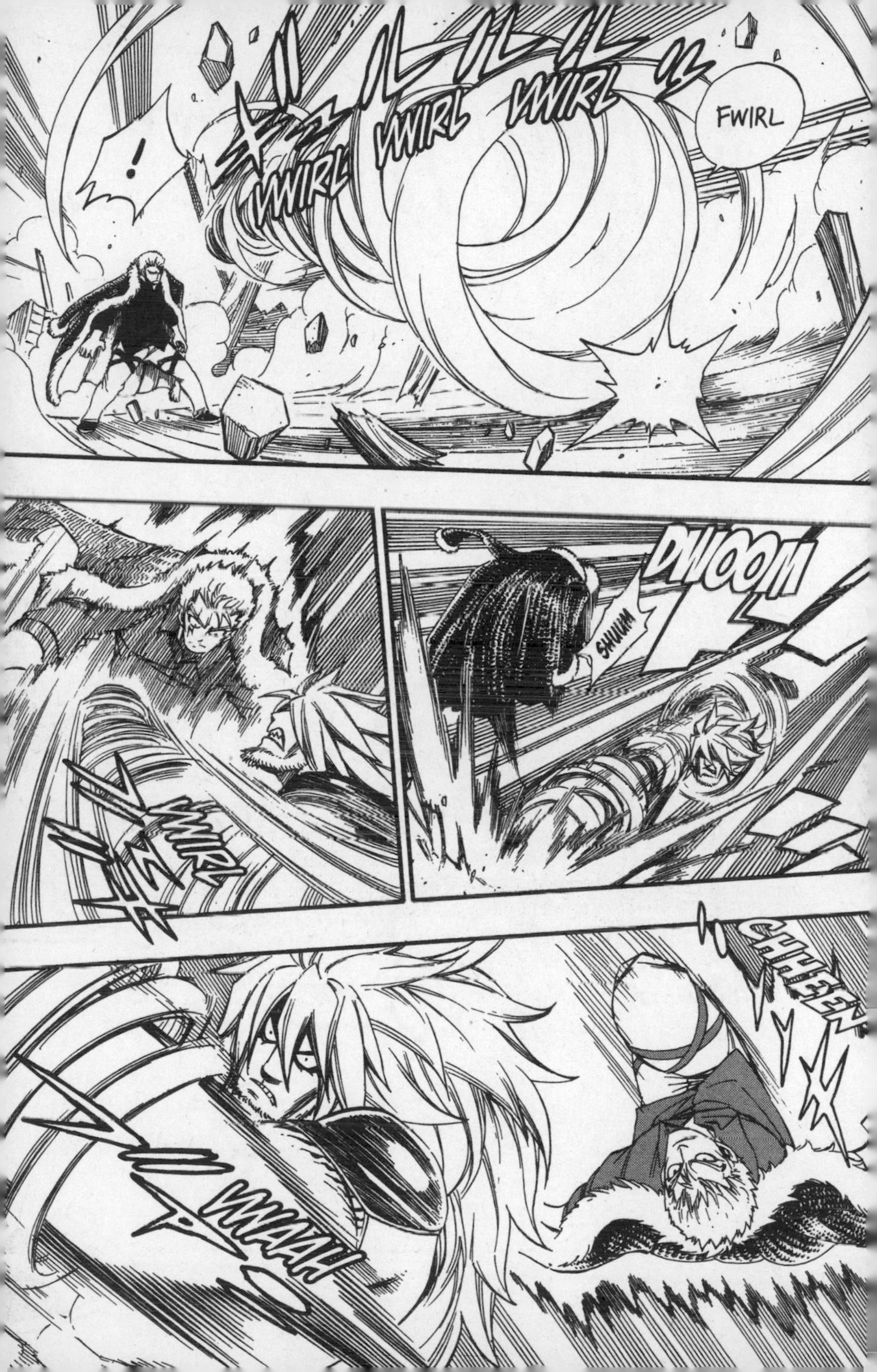
FWIRL
VWIRL VWIRL VWIRL
!
DWOOM
SHUUM
VWIRL
CHHEEN
VWAAH

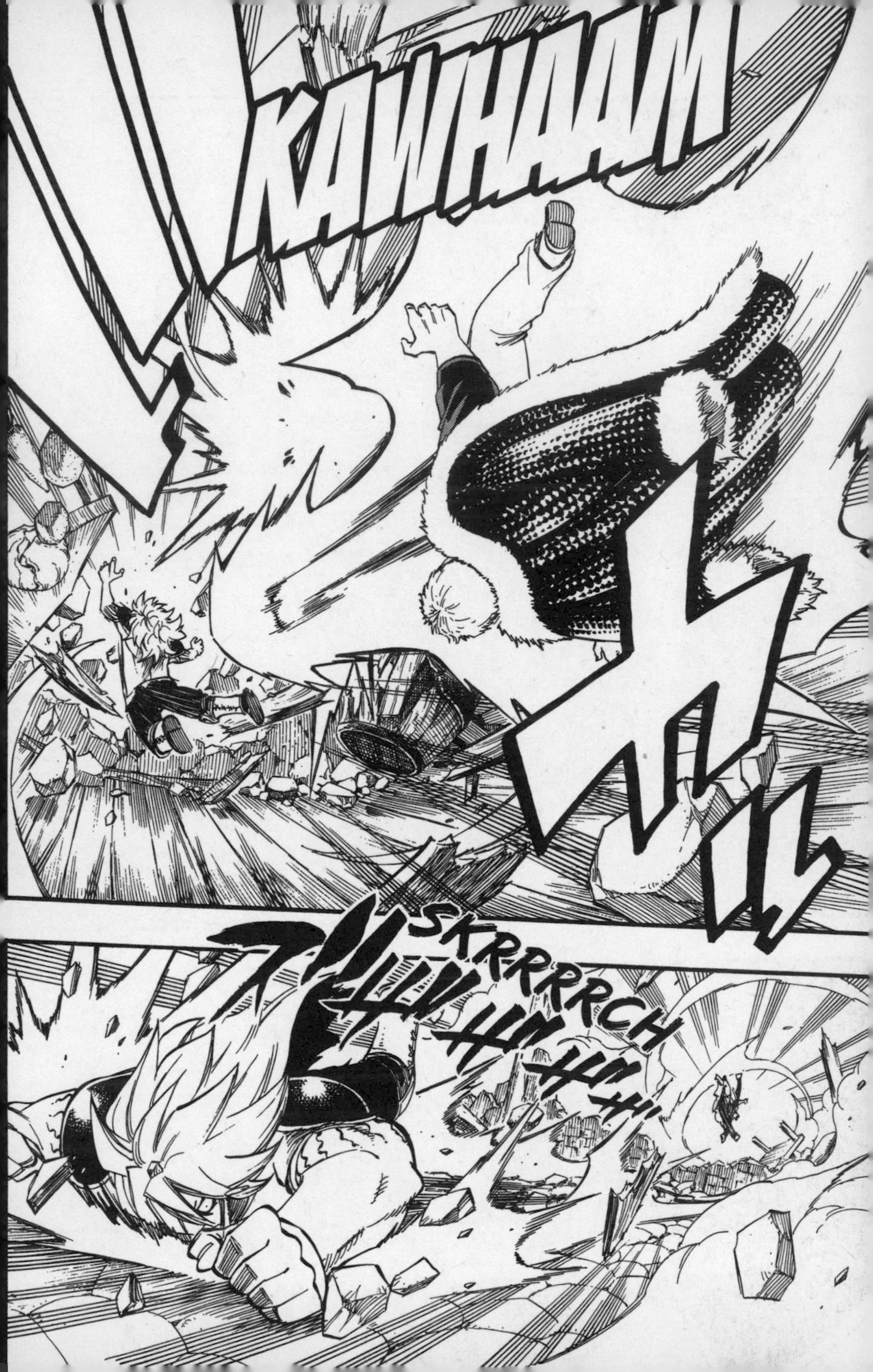
KAWHAAM
SKRRRRCH

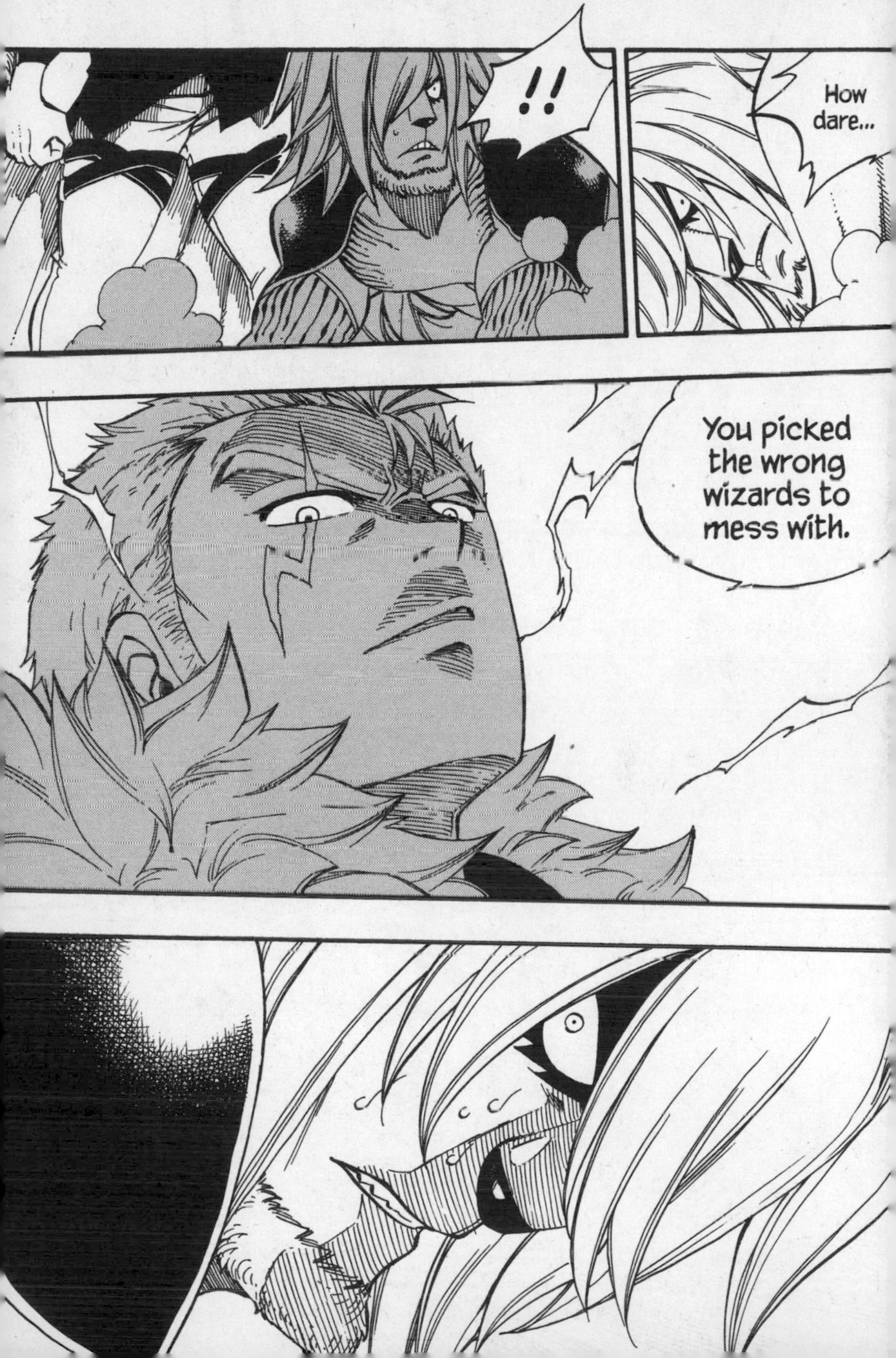
How dare...
!!
You picked the wrong wizards to mess with.

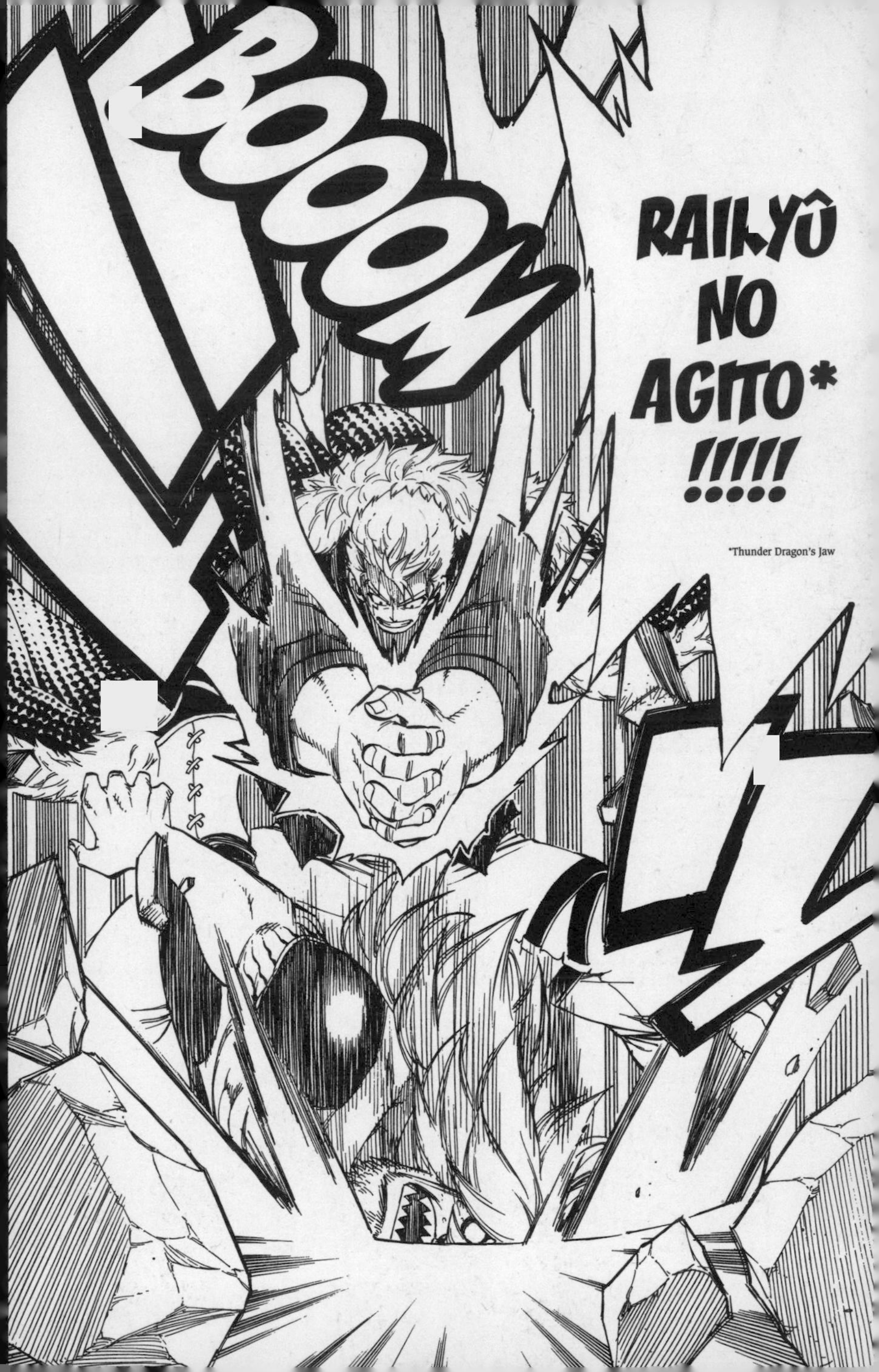
BOOOM
RAIKYÛ NO AGITO* !!!!!
*Thunder Dragon's Jaw

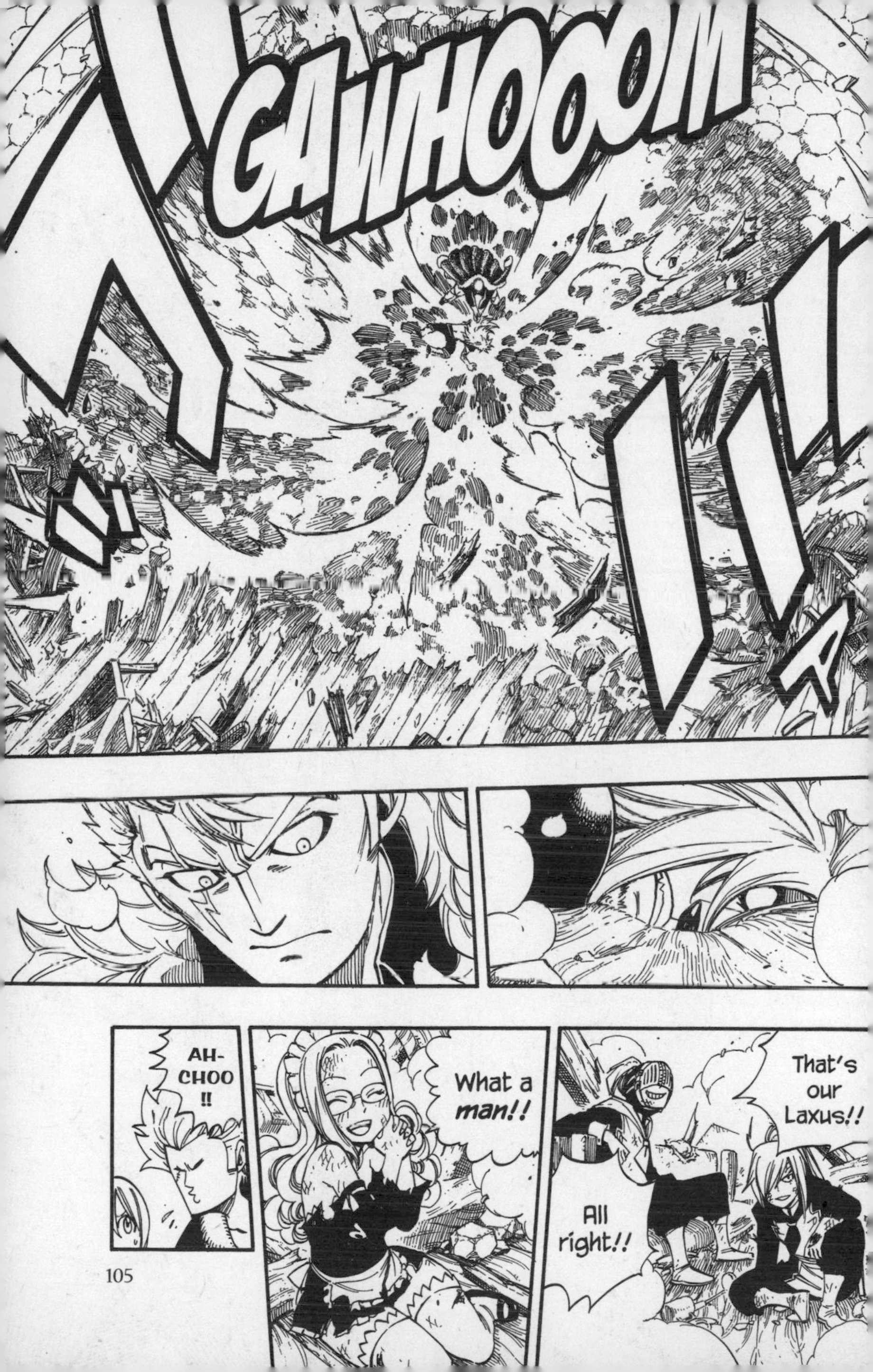
CAWHOOOM
That's our Laxus!!
All right!!
What a *man!!*
AH-CHOO !!

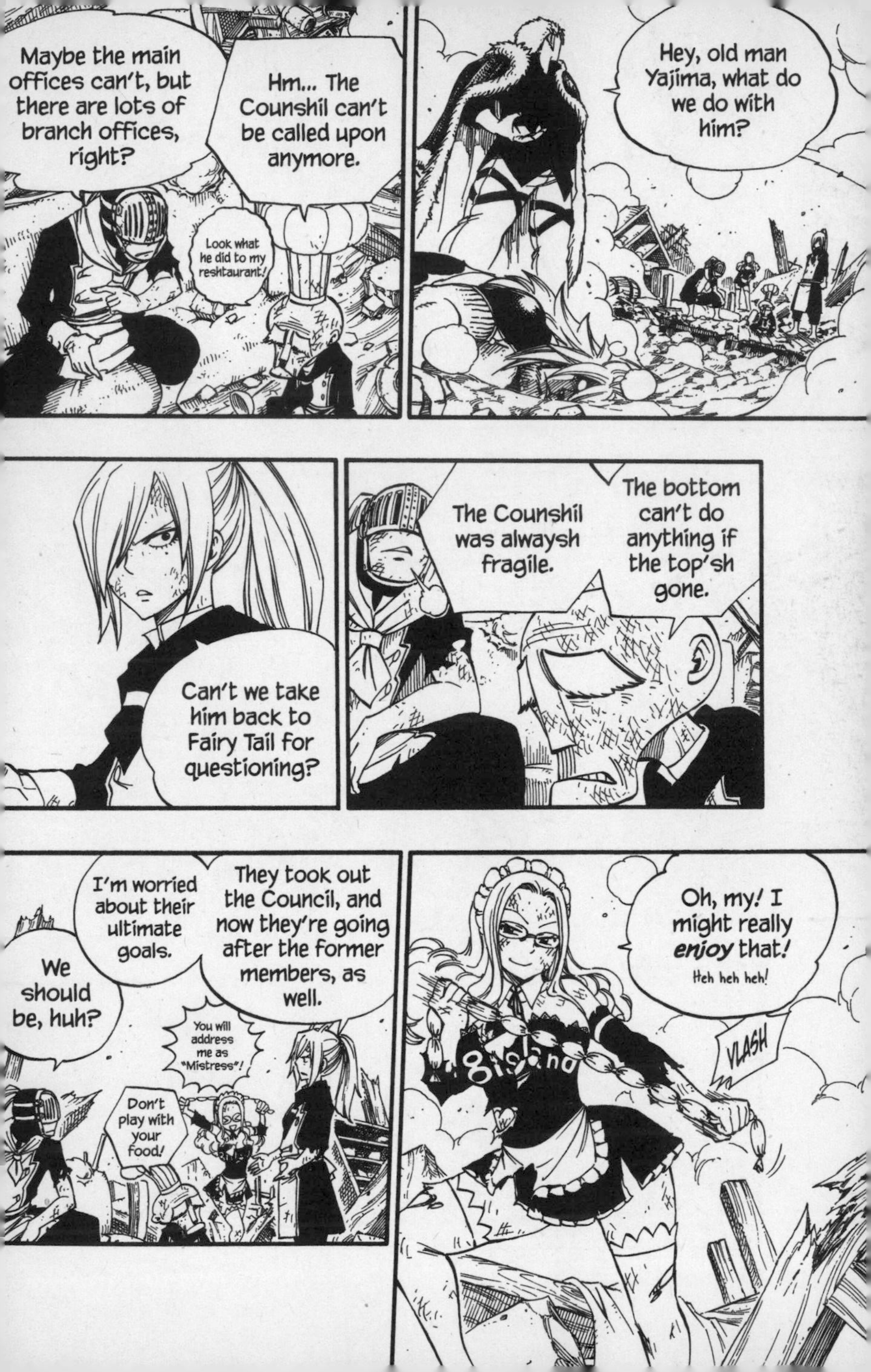
Hey, old man Yajima, what do we do with him?
Hm... The Counshil can't be called upon anymore.
Maybe the main offices can't, but there are lots of branch offices, right?
Look what he did to my reshtaurant!
The bottom can't do anything if the top'sh gone.
The Counshil was alwaysh fragile.
Can't we take him back to Fairy Tail for questioning?
Oh, my! I might really *enjoy* that!
Heh heh heh!
VLASH
They took out the Council, and now they're going after the former members, as well.
I'm worried about their ultimate goals.
We should be, huh?
You will address me as "Mistress"!
Don't play with your food!

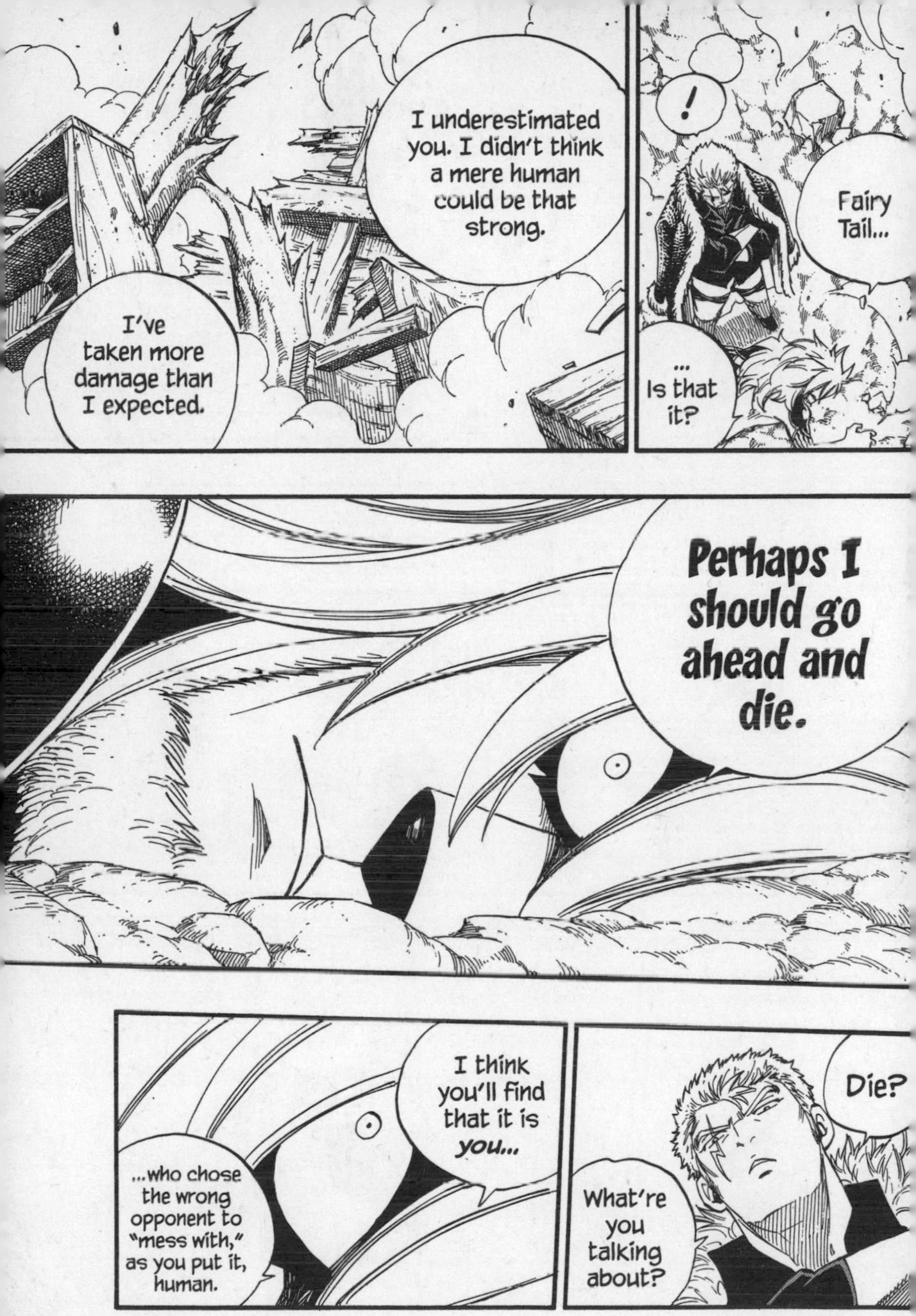
!
Fairy Tail...
... Is that it?
I underestimated you. I didn't think a mere human could be that strong.
I've taken more damage than I expected.
Perhaps I should go ahead and die.
Die?
What're you talking about?
I think you'll find that it is *you*...
...who chose the wrong opponent to "mess with," as you put it, human.

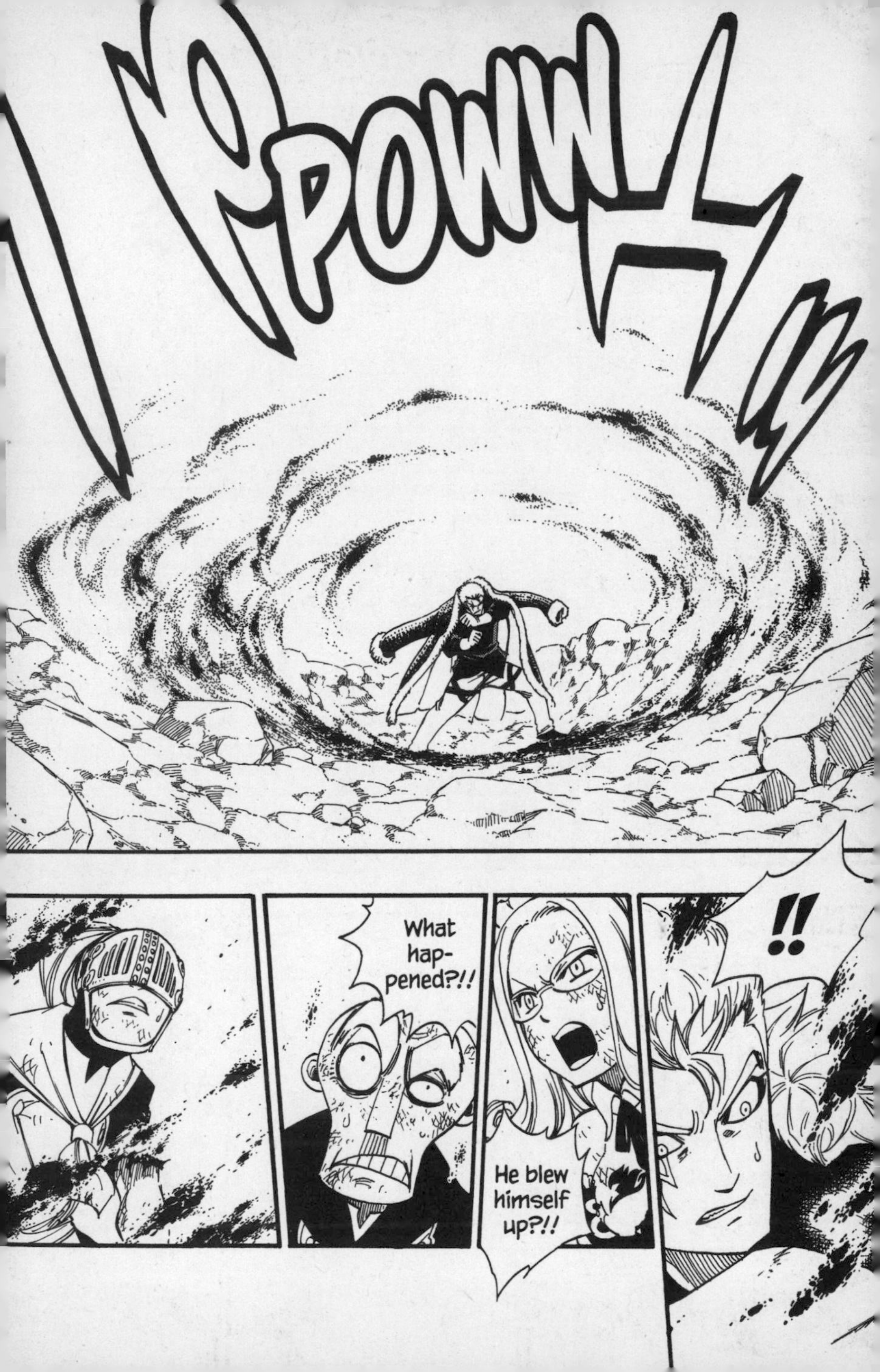
POWW
!!
He blew himself up?!!
What hap-pened?!!

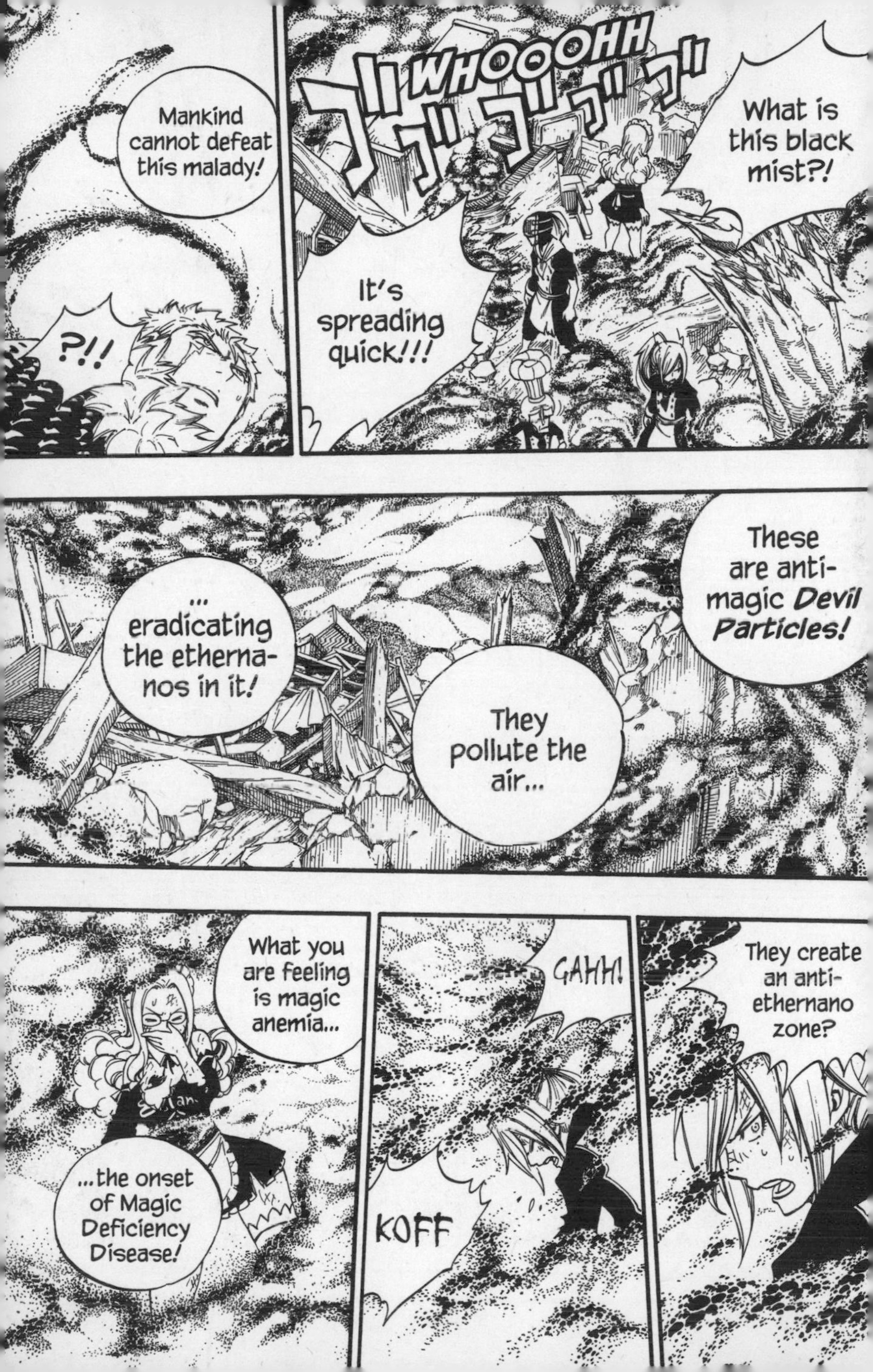
What is this black mist?!
WHOOOOHH
It's spreading quick!!!
Mankind cannot defeat this malady!
?!!
These are anti-magic *Devil Particles!*
They pollute the air...
... eradicating the etherna-nos in it!
They create an anti-ethernano zone?
GAHH!
KOFF
What you are feeling is magic anemia...
...the onset of Magic Deficiency Disease!

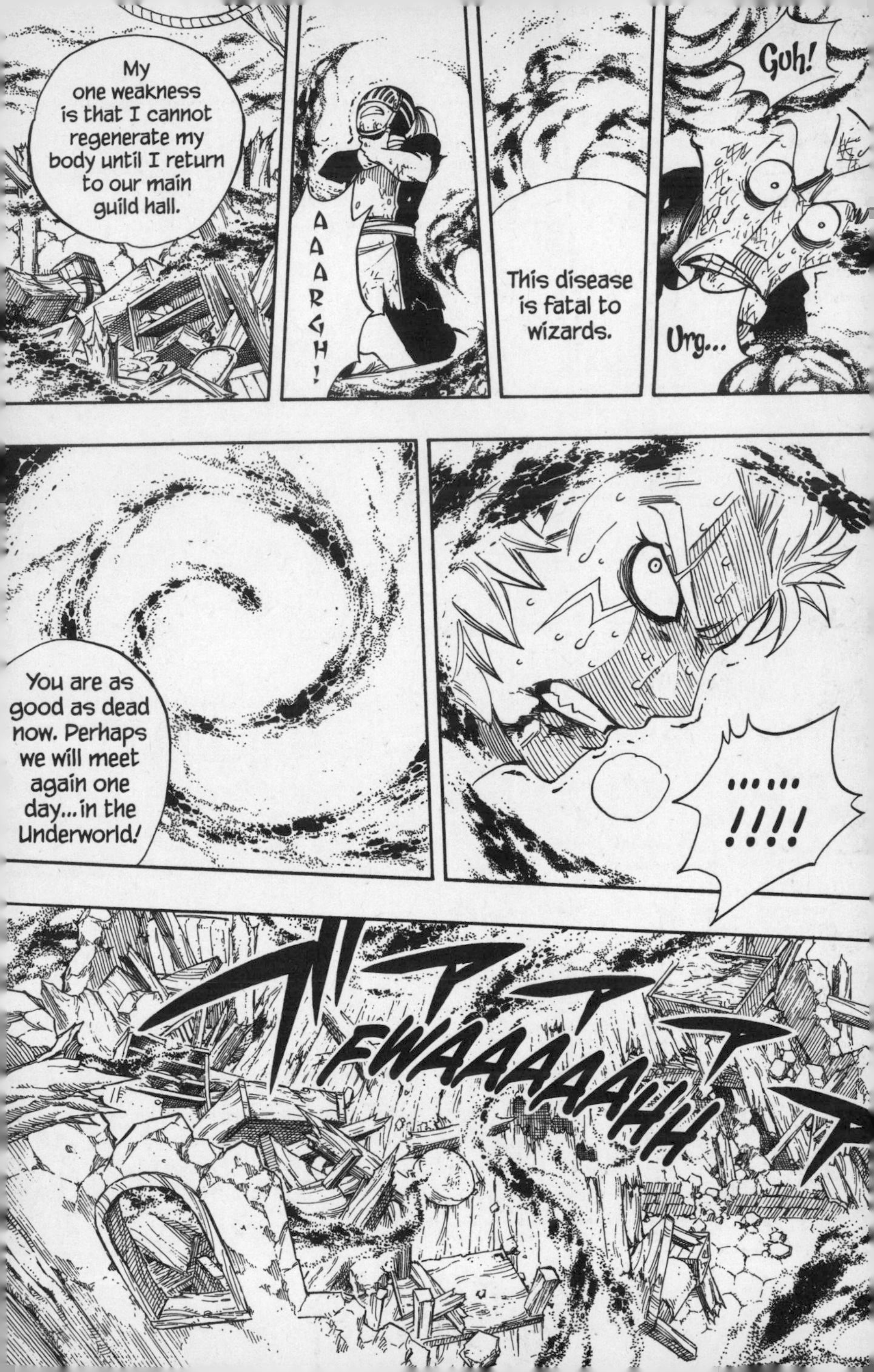
Guh!
Urg...
This disease is fatal to wizards.
AAAARGH!
My one weakness is that I cannot regenerate my body until I return to our main guild hall.
......
!!!!
You are as good as dead now. Perhaps we will meet again one day...in the Underworld!
FWAAAAAHH

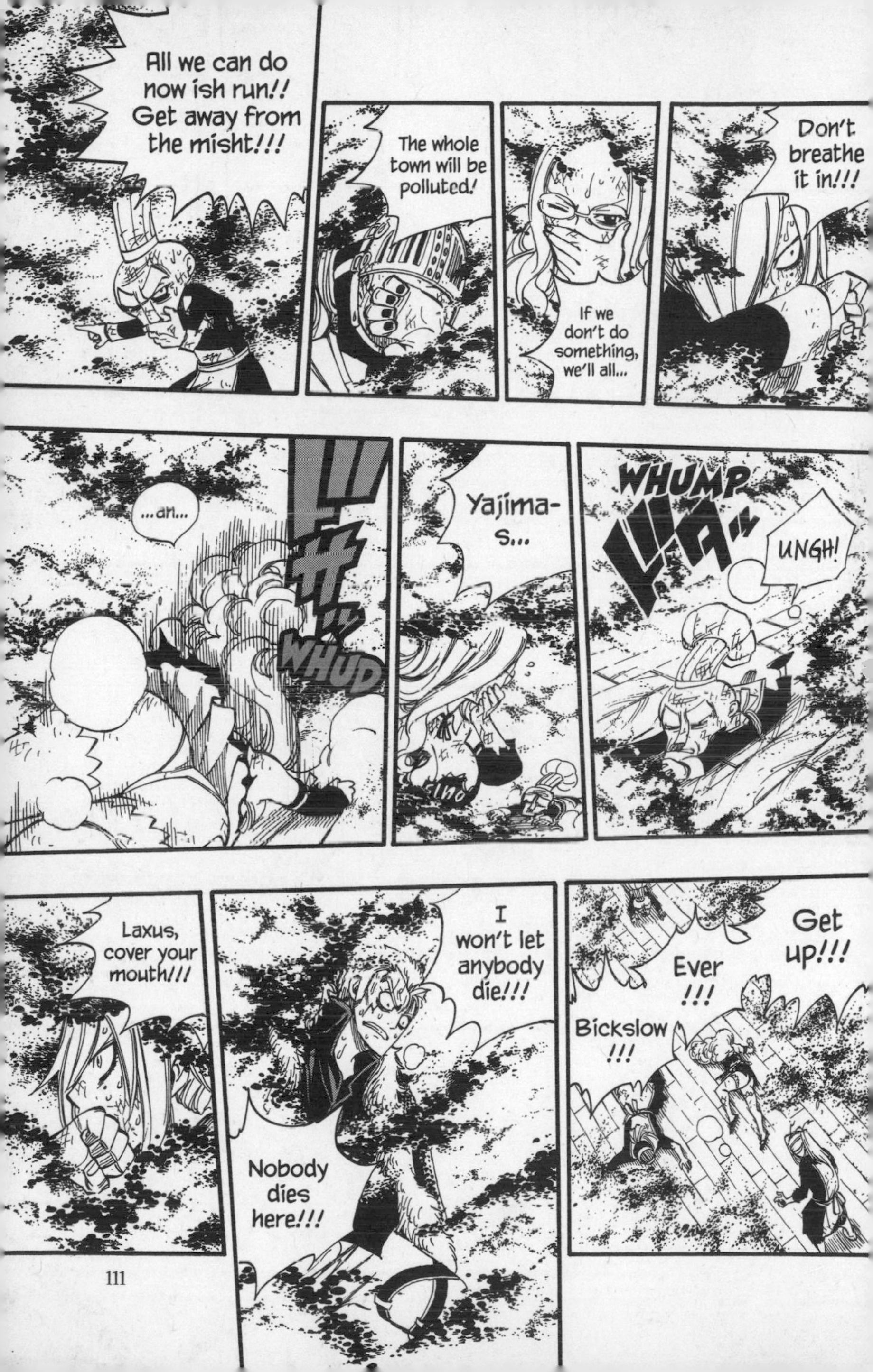
Don't breathe it in!!!
If we don't do something, we'll all...
The whole town will be polluted!
All we can do now ish run!! Get away from the misht!!!
WHUMP
UNGH!
Yajima-s...
WHUD
...an...
Get up!!!
Ever !!!
Bickslow !!!
I won't let anybody die!!!
Nobody dies here!!!
Laxus, cover your mouth!!!

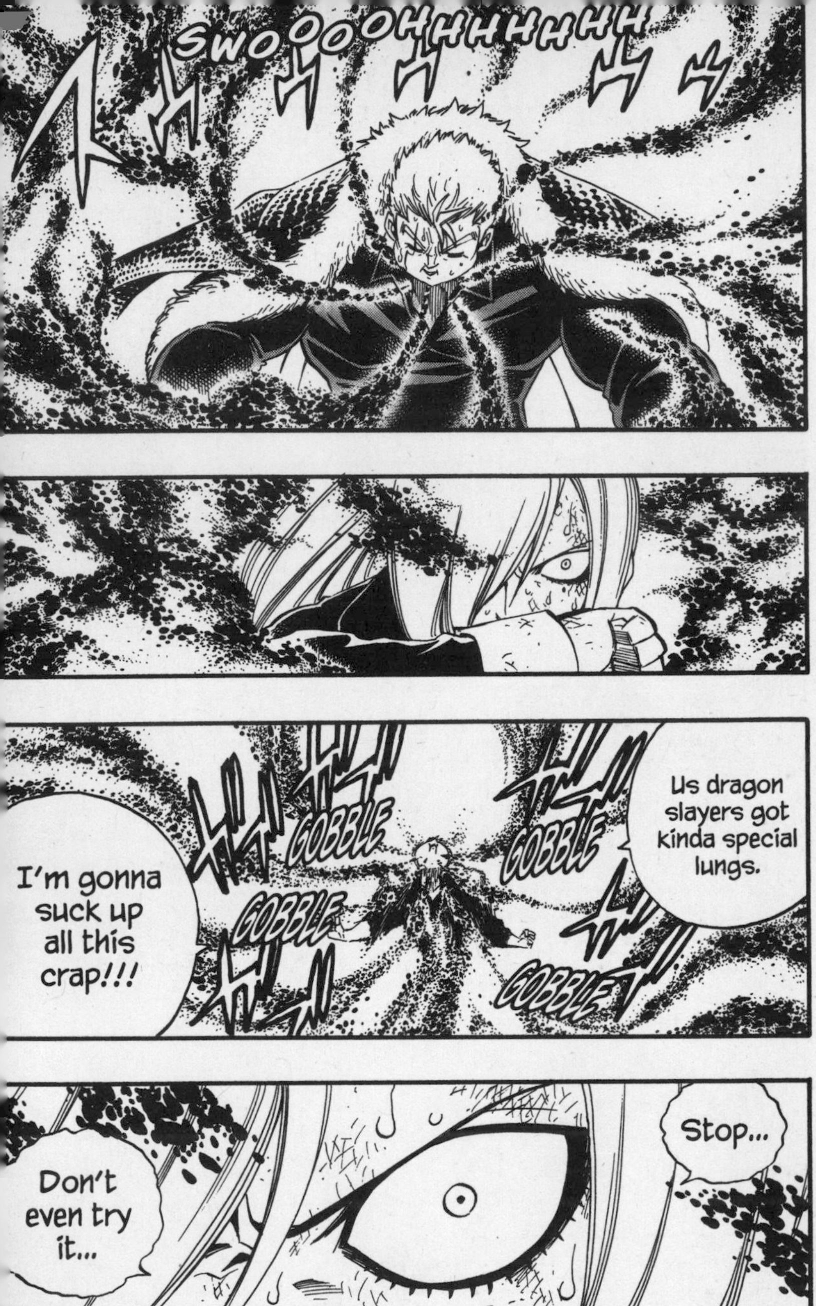
SWOOOOHHHHHHH
Us dragon slayers got kinda special lungs.
GOBBLE
GOBBLE
GOBBLE
GOBBLE
I'm gonna suck up all this crap!!!
Stop...
Don't even try it...

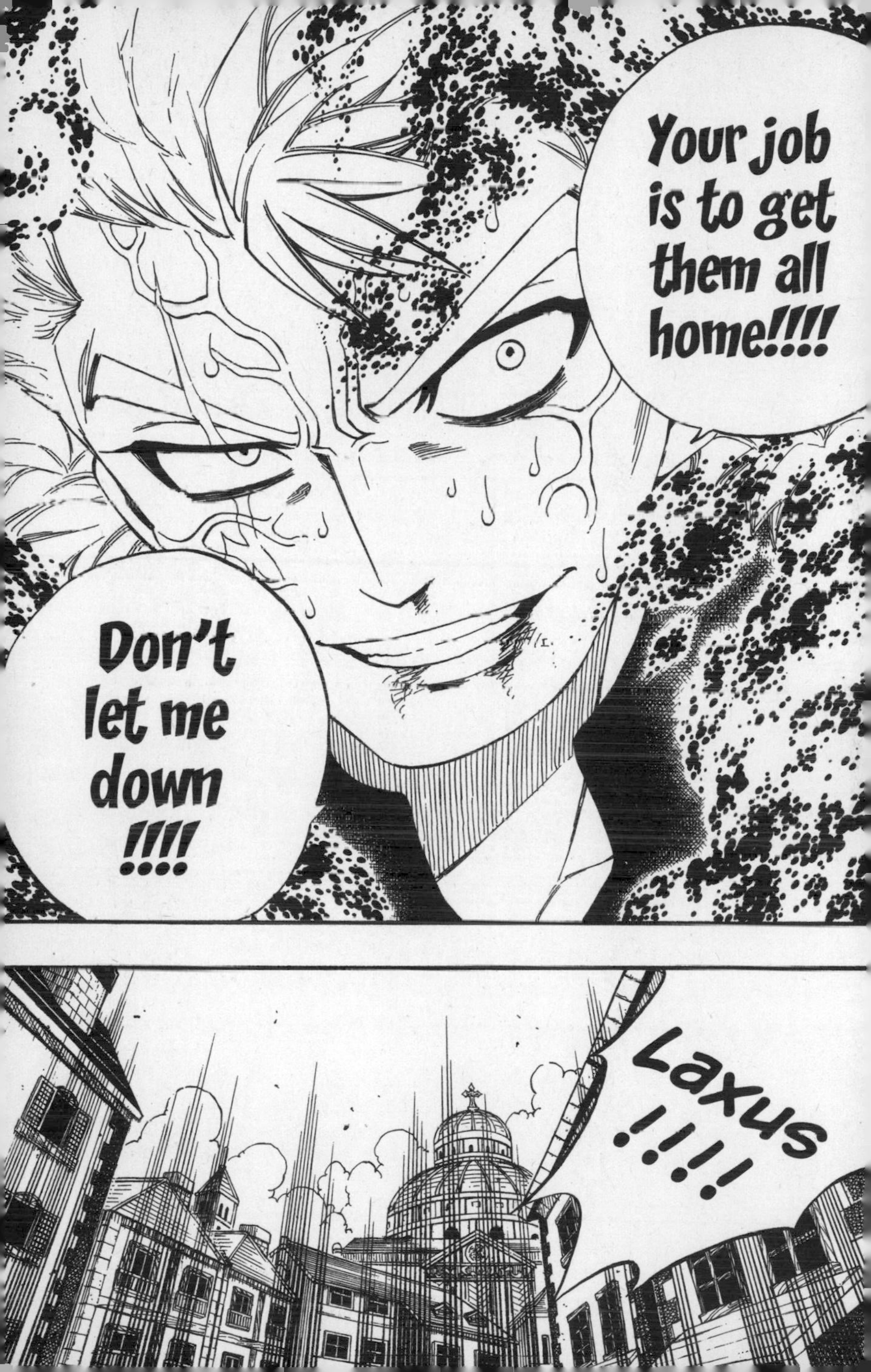
Your job is to get them all home!!!!
Don't let me down !!!!
Laxus !!!!

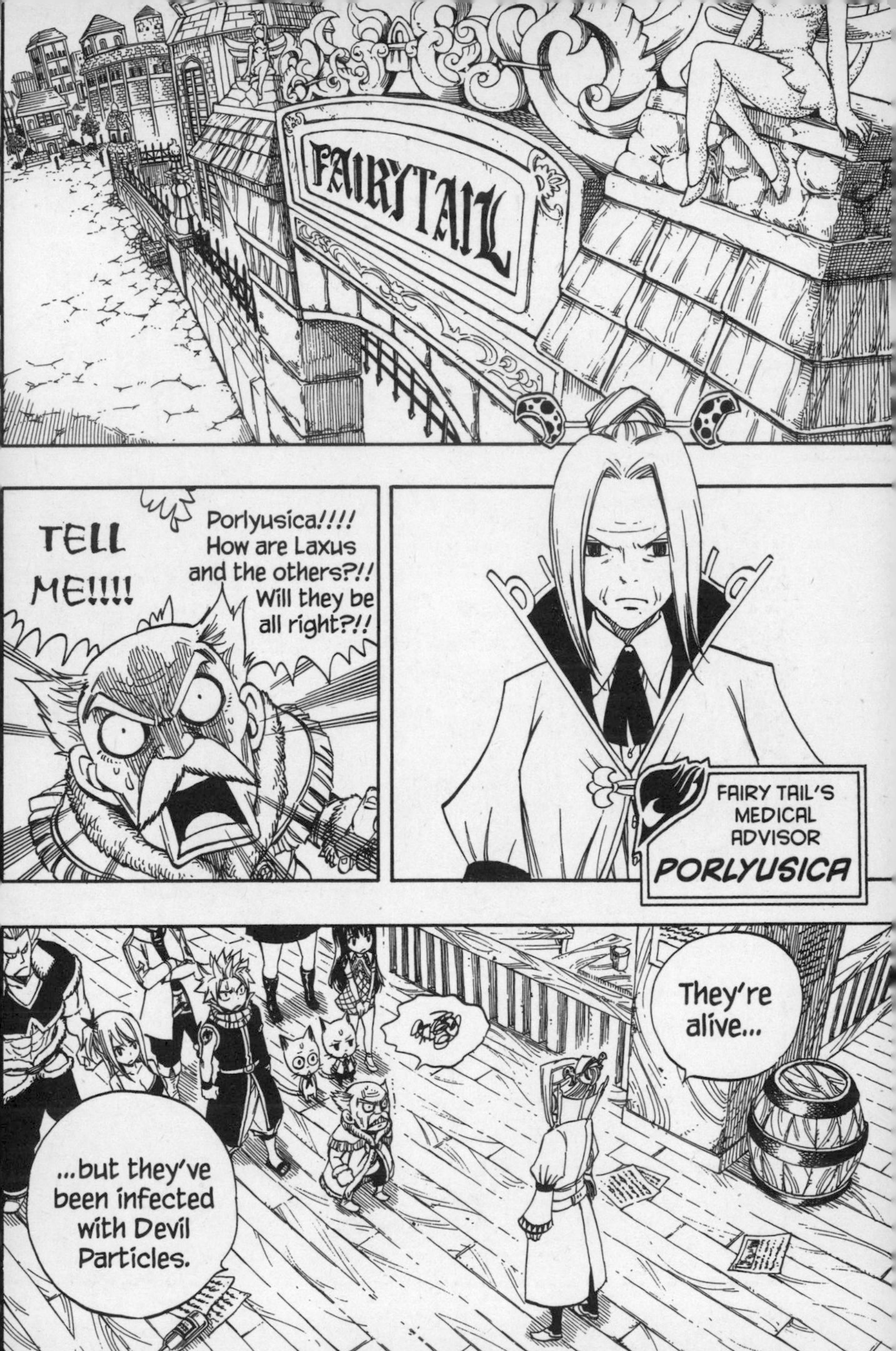
FAIRY TAIL
FAIRY TAIL'S MEDICAL ADVISOR PORLYUSICA
Porlyusica!!!! How are Laxus and the others?!! Will they be all right?!!
TELL ME!!!!
They're alive...
...but they've been infected with Devil Particles.

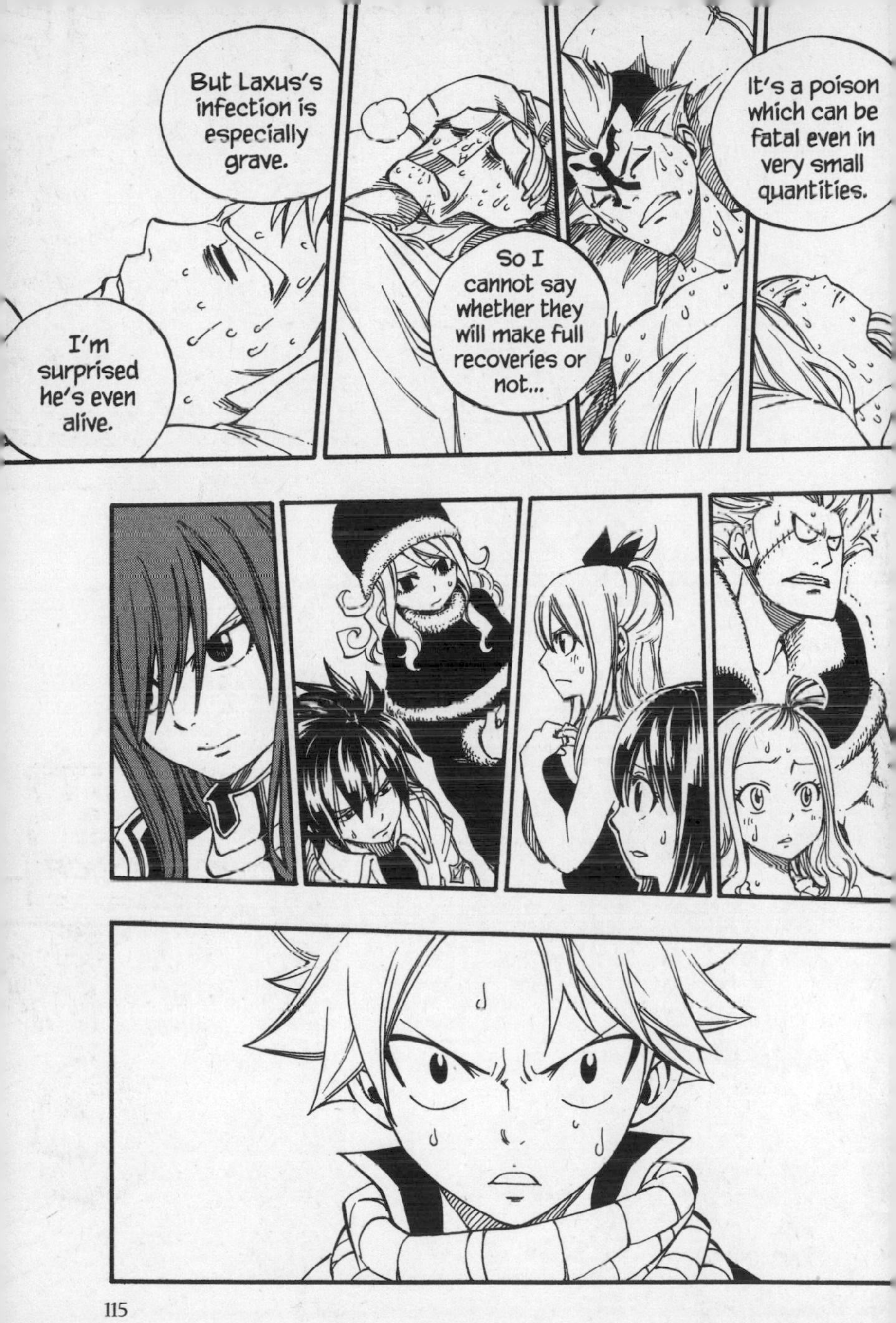
It's a poison which can be fatal even in very small quantities.
So I cannot say whether they will make full recoveries or not...
But Laxus's infection is especially grave.
I'm surprised he's even alive.

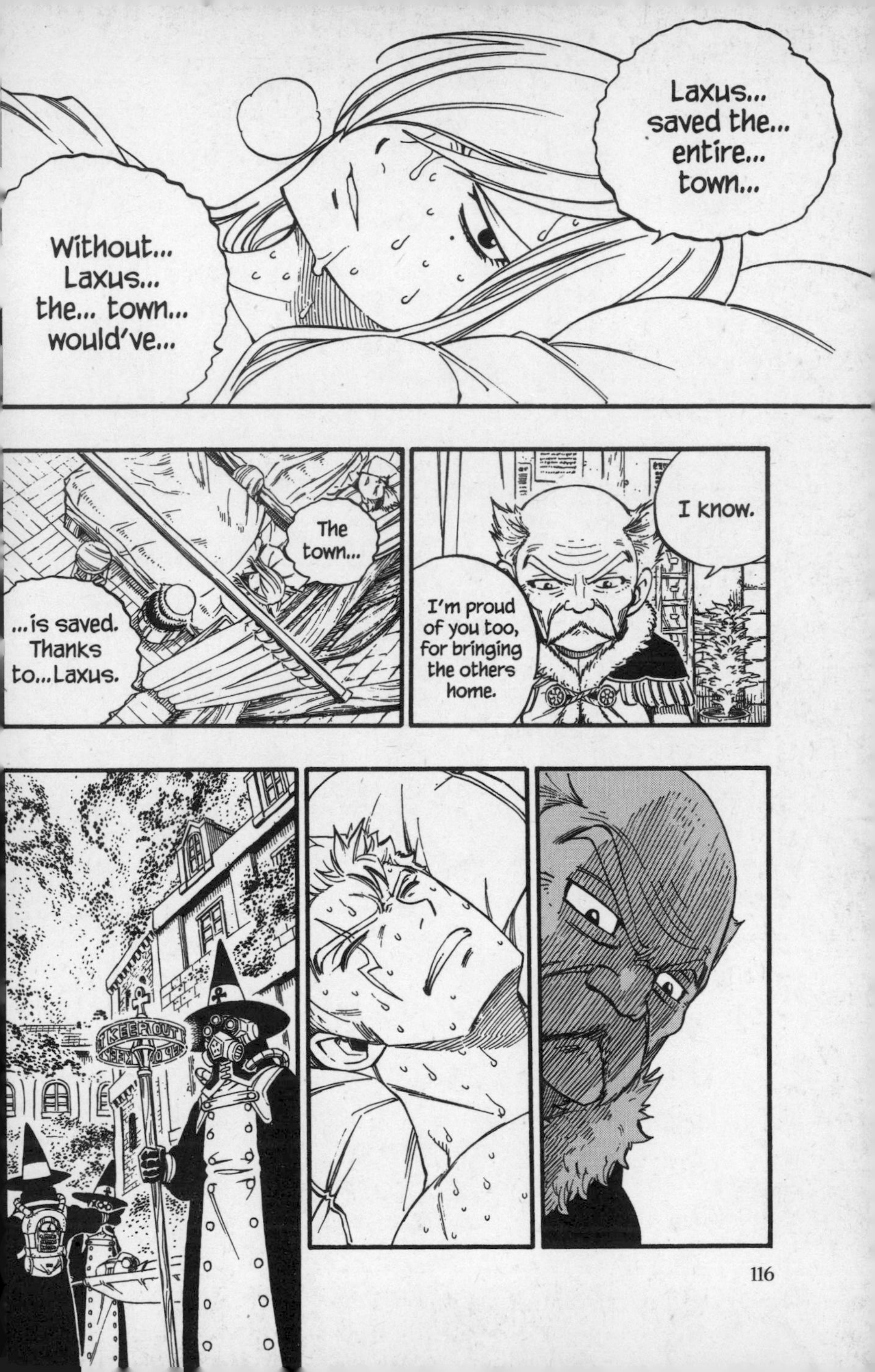
Laxus... saved the... entire... town...
Without... Laxus... the... town... would've...
I know.
I'm proud of you too, for bringing the others home.
The town...
...is saved. Thanks to...Laxus.
KEEP OUT

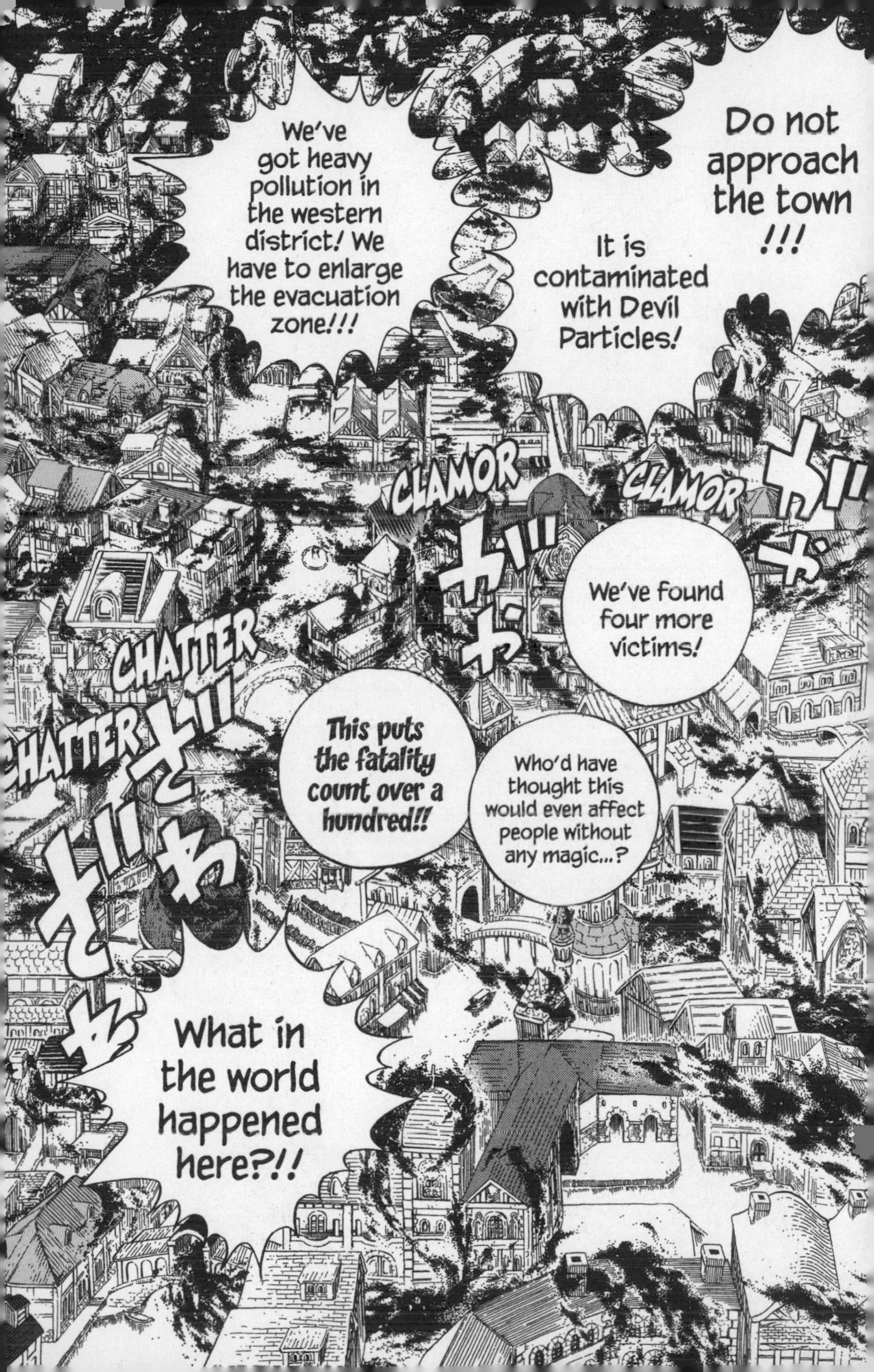
Do not approach the town!!!
It is contaminated with Devil Particles!
We've got heavy pollution in the western district! We have to enlarge the evacuation zone!!!
CLAMOR
CLAMOR
We've found four more victims!
Who'd have thought this would even affect people without any magic...?
This puts the fatality count over a hundred!!
CHATTER
CHATTER
What in the world happened here?!!

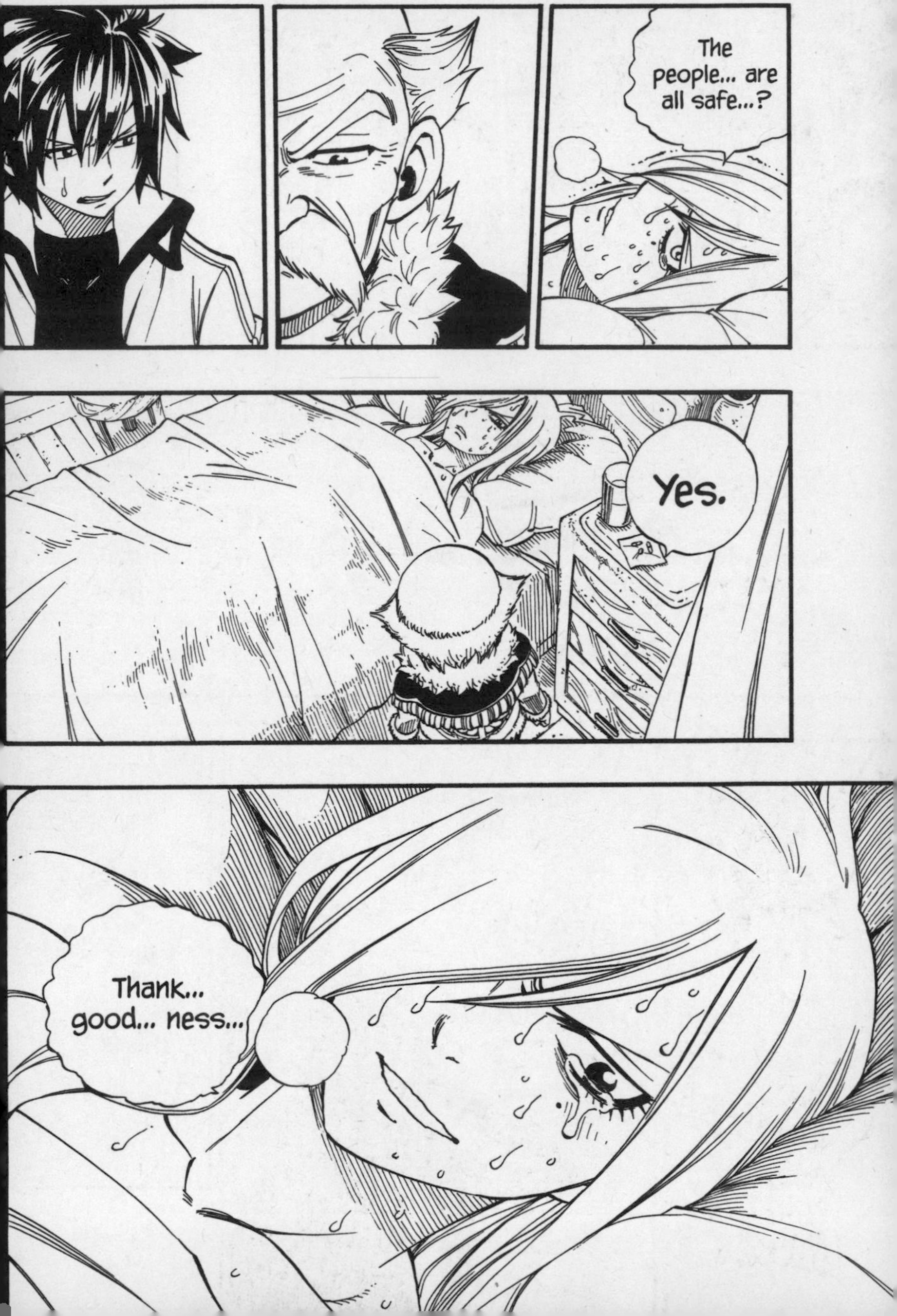
The people... are all safe...?
Yes.
Thank... good... ness...

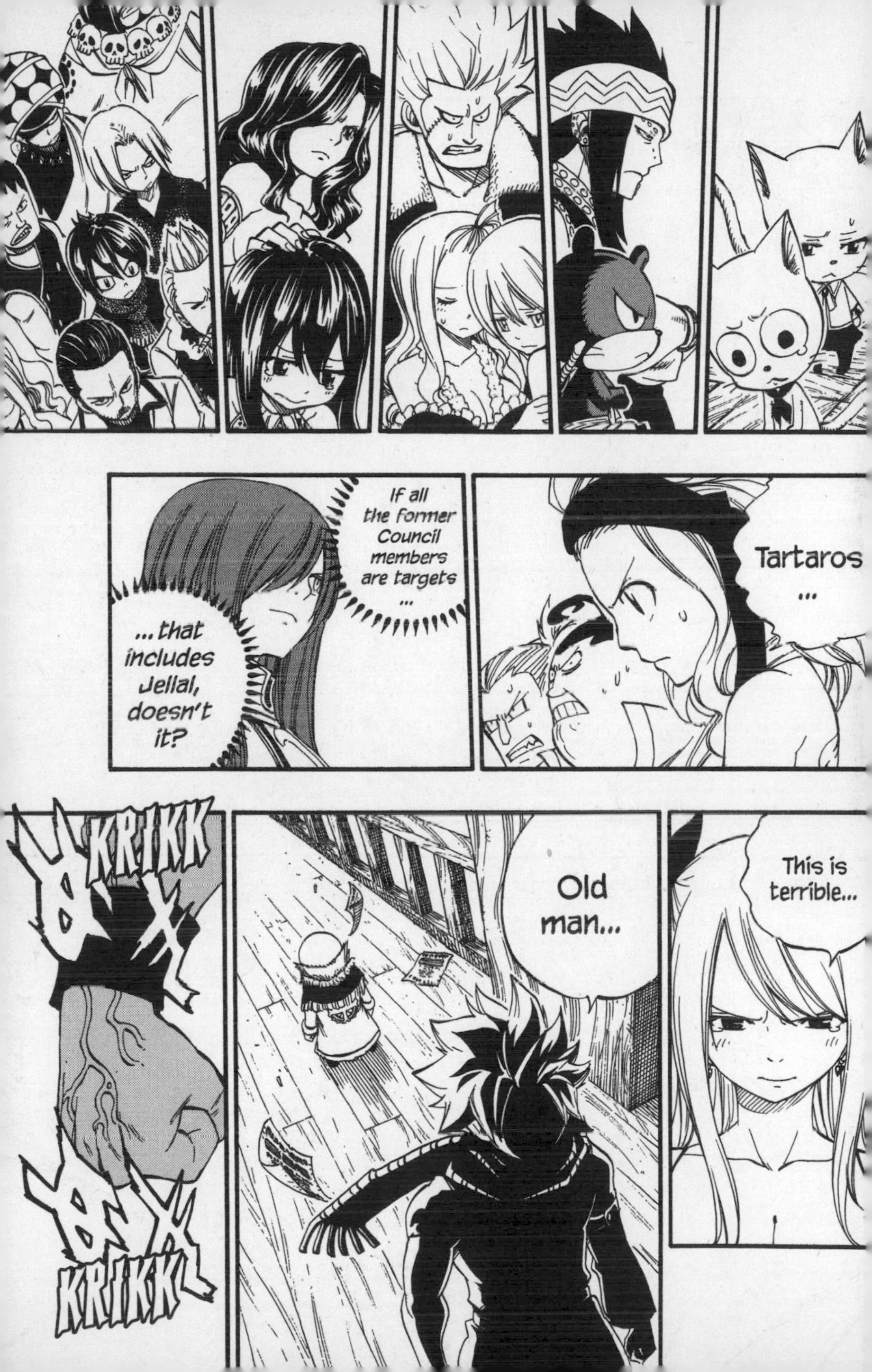
Tartaros ...
If all the former Council members are targets ...
...that includes Jellal, doesn't it?
This is terrible...
Old man...
KRIKK
KRIKK

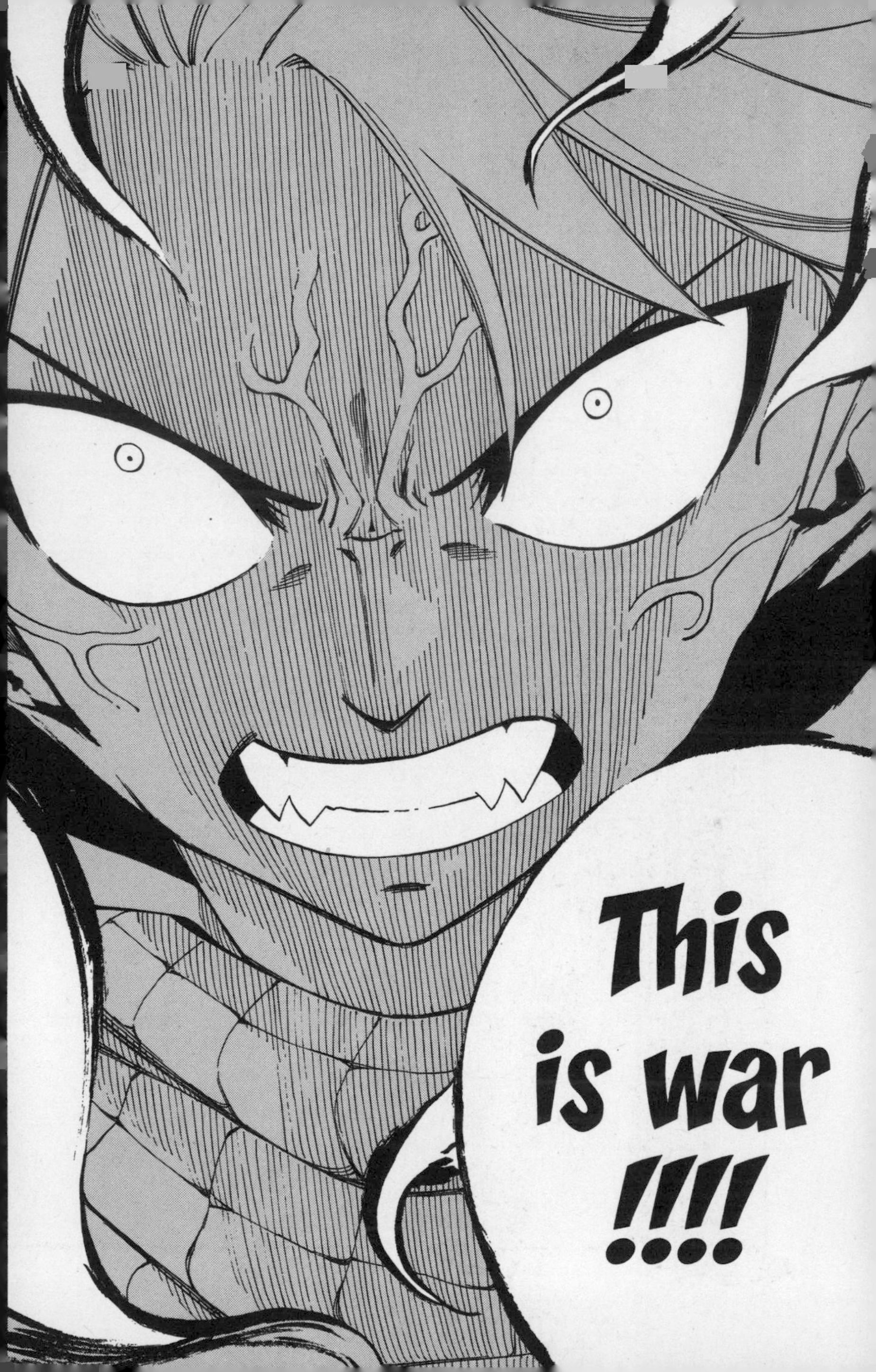
This is war !!!!

FAIRY TAIL

Chapter 359:
Fairies vs. the Underworld

BLUE PEGASUS

Name: Hibiki Letis   **Age:** 36

Magic:
Archive

Likes: **Dislikes:**

All women   **Bugs**

Remarks

He's held the top spot in the Weekly Sorcerer list of "Wizards I'd Like to Be My Boyfriend" for seven years running. He always has a number of girlfriends on hand, and none of them serious, but the editorial department of Weekly Sorcerer speculates that Jenny of Blue Pegasus is the one he truly loves. Over the past seven years, his speed with his Archive information retrieval has greatly increased. Recently, he's been working on miniaturizing his system.

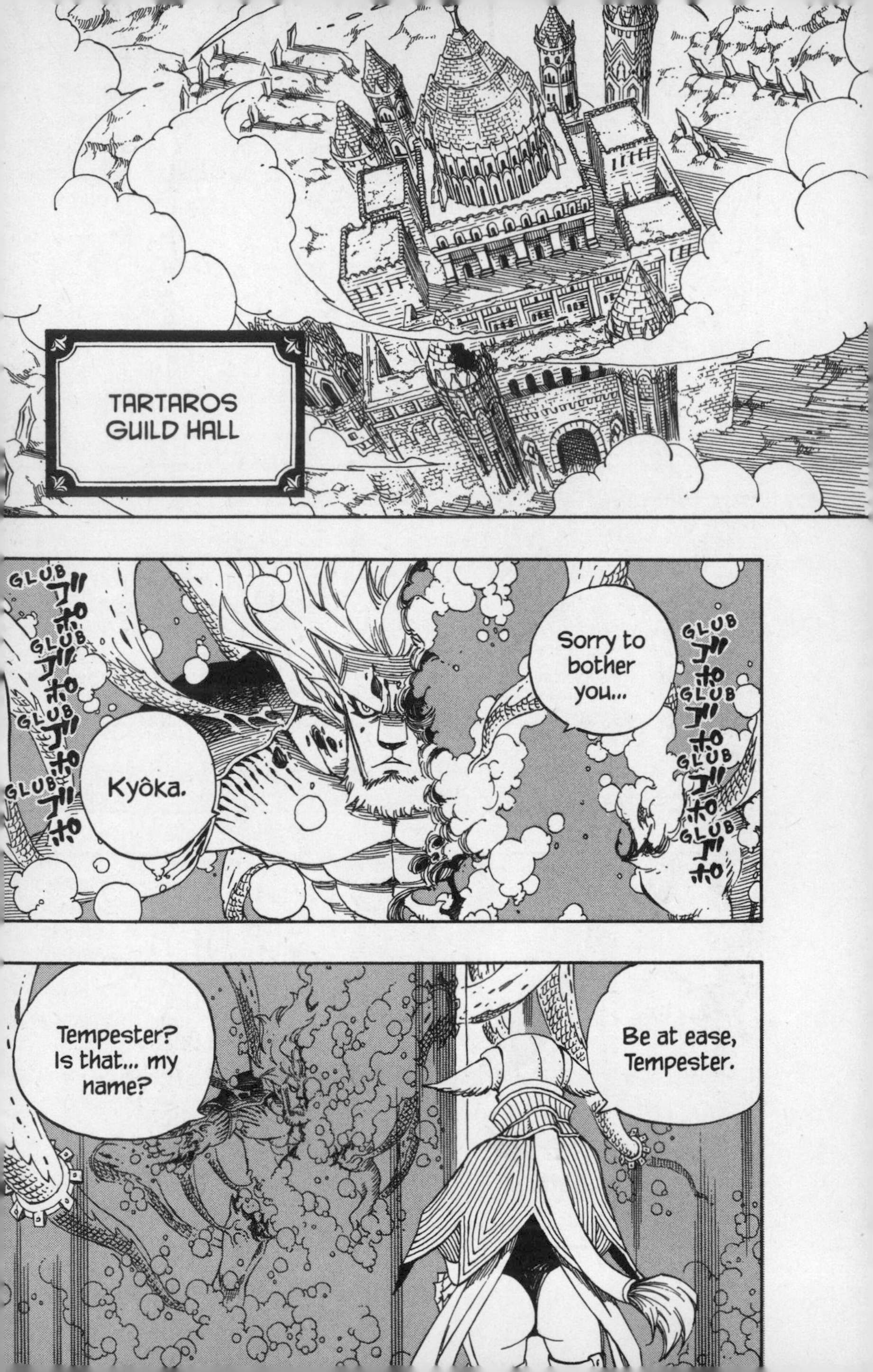
TARTAROS GUILD HALL
GLUB ゴボ GLUB ゴボ GLUB ゴボ GLUB ゴボ GLUB ゴボ
Sorry to bother you...
Kyôka.
GLUB ゴボ GLUB ゴボ GLUB ゴボ GLUB ゴボ
Be at ease, Tempester.
Tempester? Is that... my name?

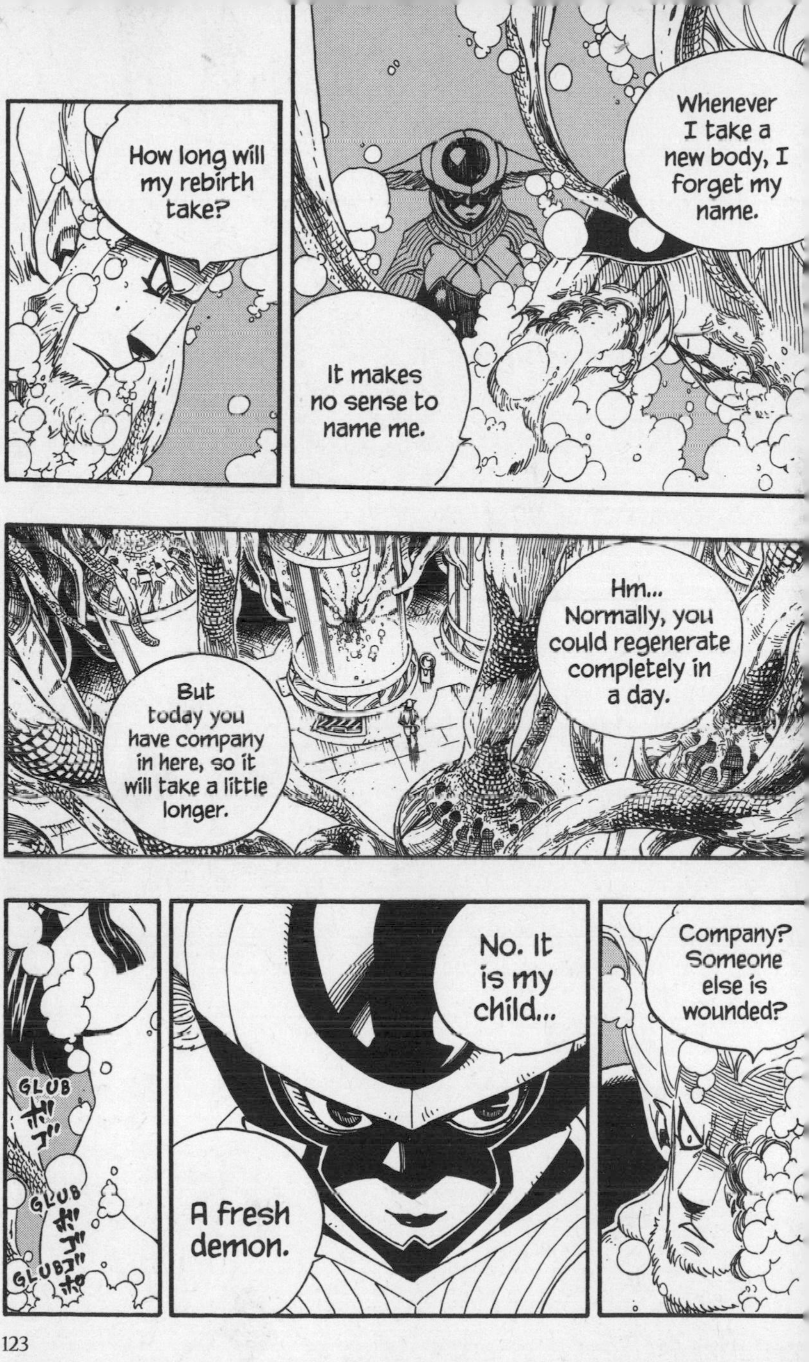
Whenever I take a new body, I forget my name.
It makes no sense to name me.
How long will my rebirth take?
Hm... Normally, you could regenerate completely in a day.
But today you have company in here, so it will take a little longer.
Company? Someone else is wounded?
No. It is my child...
A fresh demon.
GLUB
GLUB
GLUB

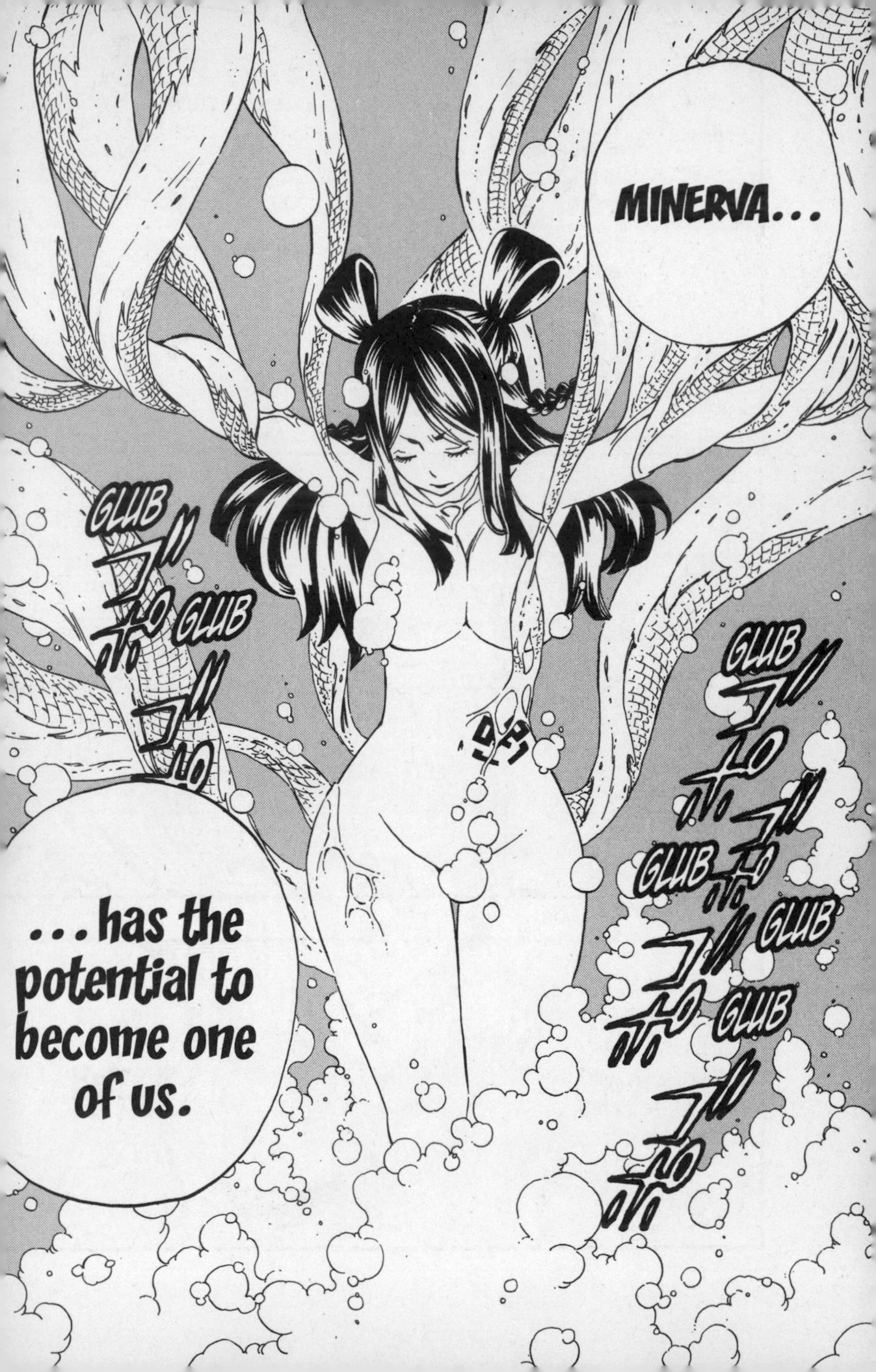
MINERVA...
GLUB
GLUB
GLUB
GLUB
GLUB
GLUB
...has the potential to become one of us.

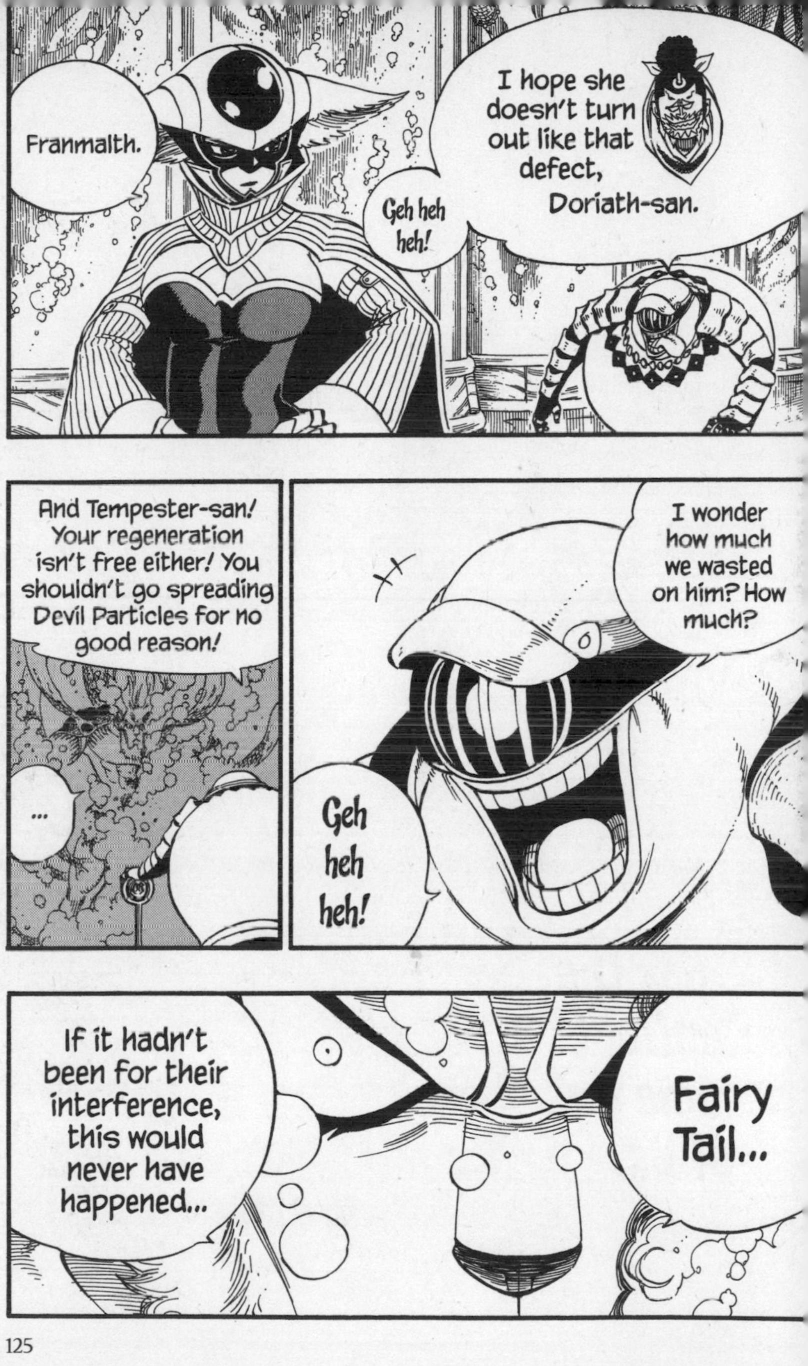
I hope she doesn't turn out like that defect, Doriath-san.
Geh heh heh!
Franmalth.
I wonder how much we wasted on him? How much?
Geh heh heh!
And Tempester-san! Your regeneration isn't free either! You shouldn't go spreading Devil Particles for no good reason!
...
Fairy Tail...
If it hadn't been for their interference, this would never have happened...

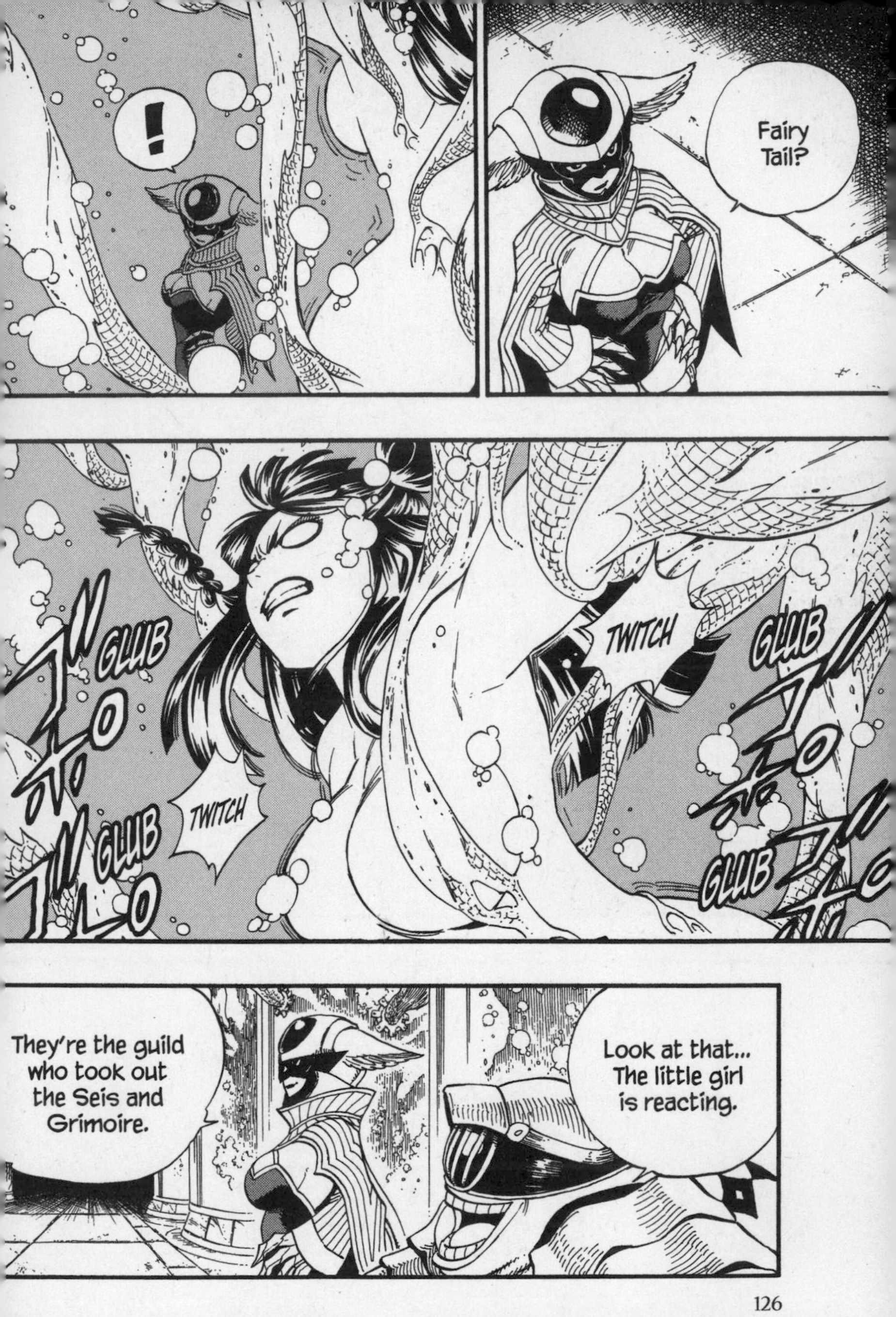

Fairy Tail?
!
GLUB
TWITCH
GLUB
GLUB
TWITCH
GLUB
Look at that... The little girl is reacting.
They're the guild who took out the Seis and Grimoire.

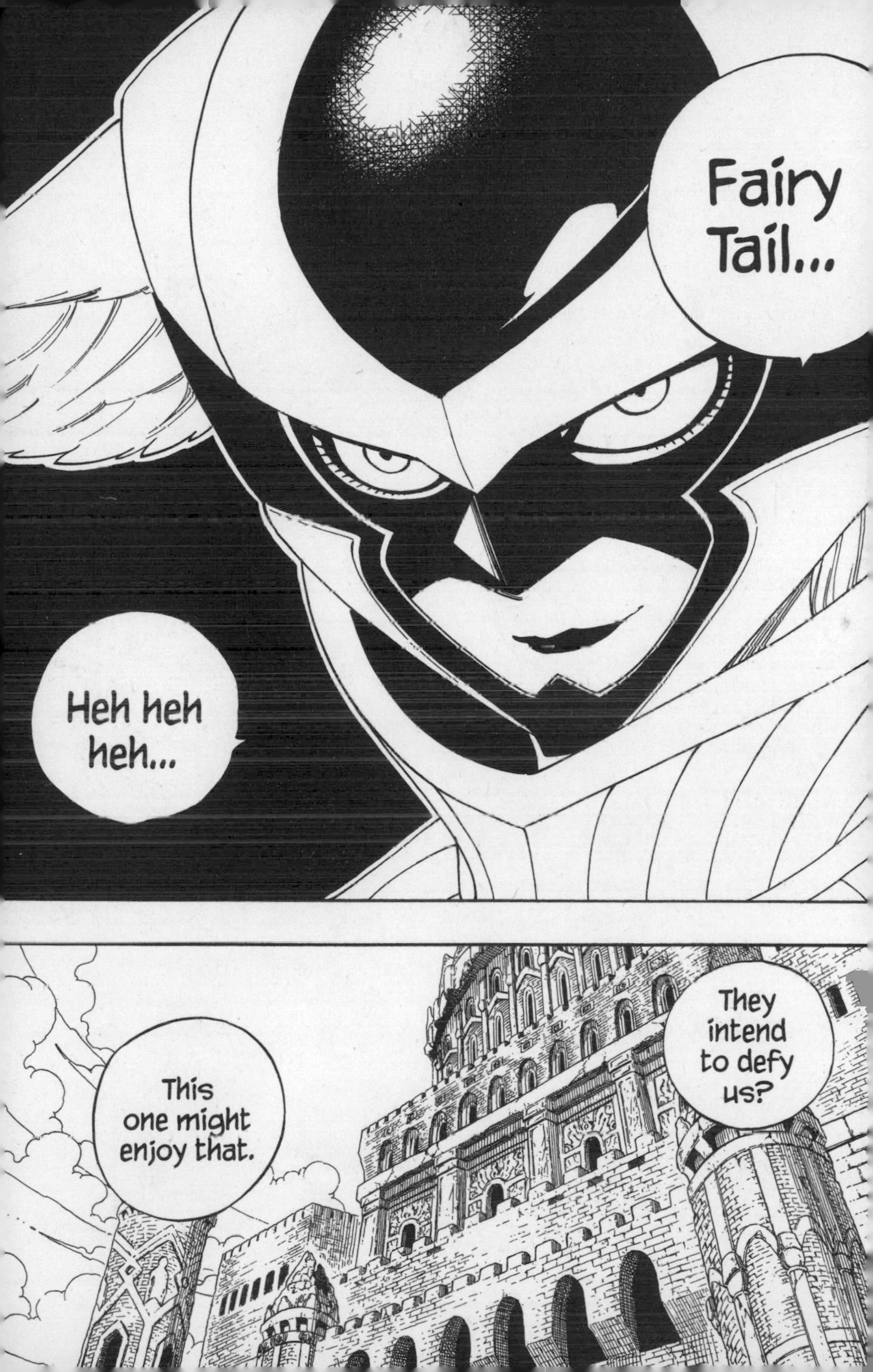
Fairy Tail...
Heh heh heh...
They intend to defy us?
This one might enjoy that.

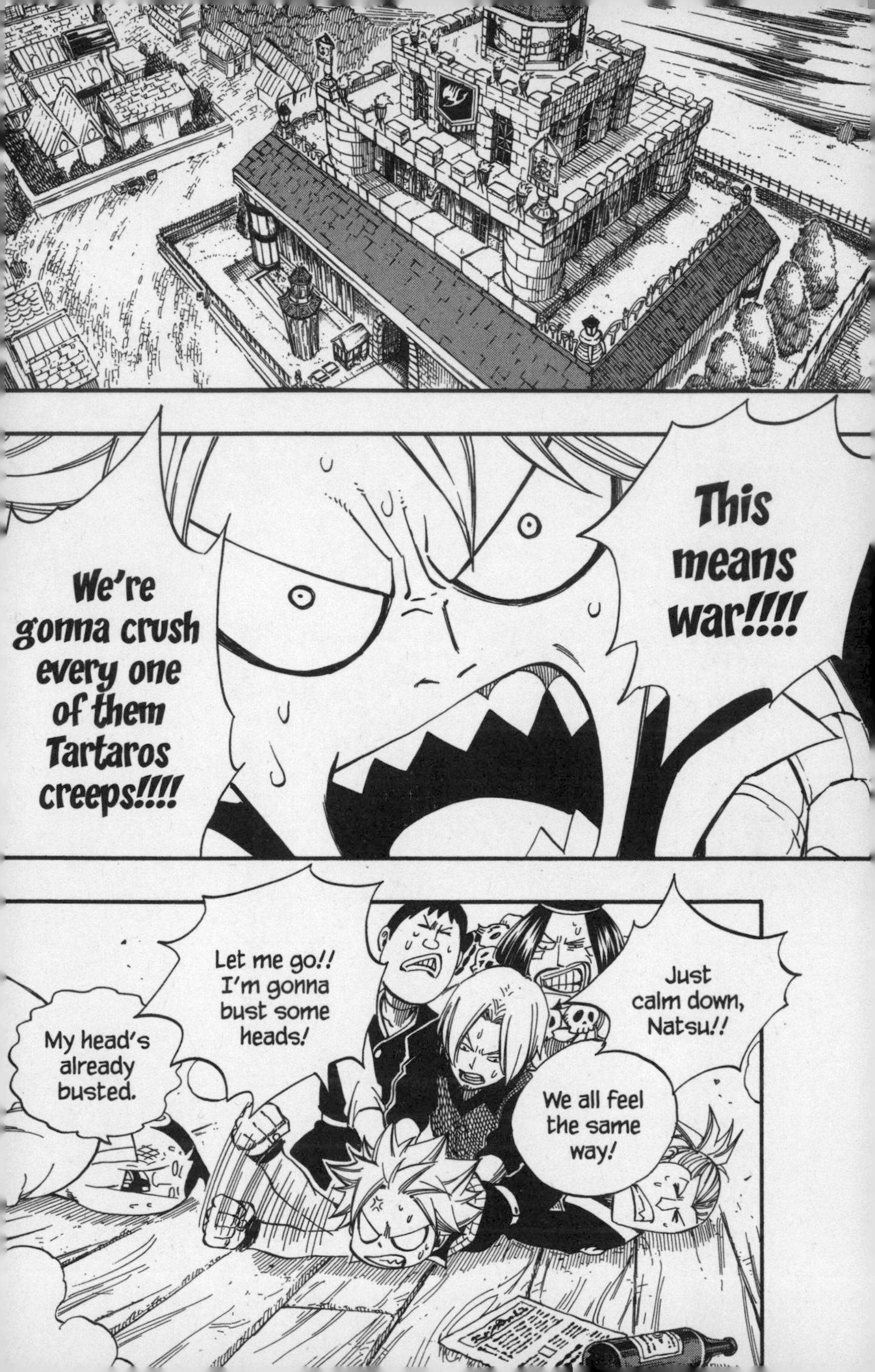
This means war!!!!
We're gonna crush every one of them Tartaros creeps!!!!
Just calm down, Natsu!!
Let me go!! I'm gonna bust some heads!
We all feel the same way!
My head's already busted.

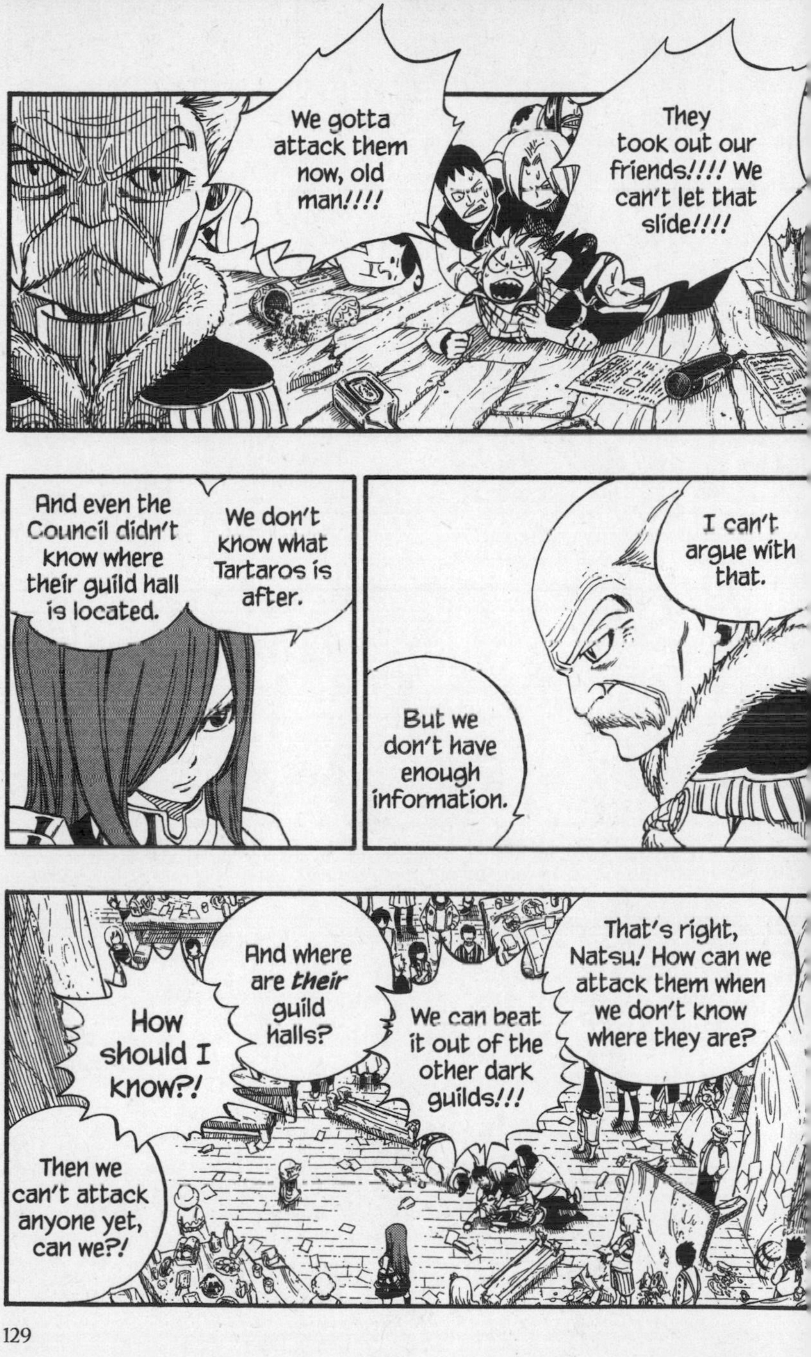

They took out our friends!!!! We can't let that slide!!!!
We gotta attack them now, old man!!!!
I can't argue with that.
But we don't have enough information.
We don't know what Tartaros is after.
And even the Council didn't know where their guild hall is located.
That's right, Natsu! How can we attack them when we don't know where they are?
We can beat it out of the other dark guilds!!!
And where are *their* guild halls?
How should I know?!
Then we can't attack anyone yet, can we?!

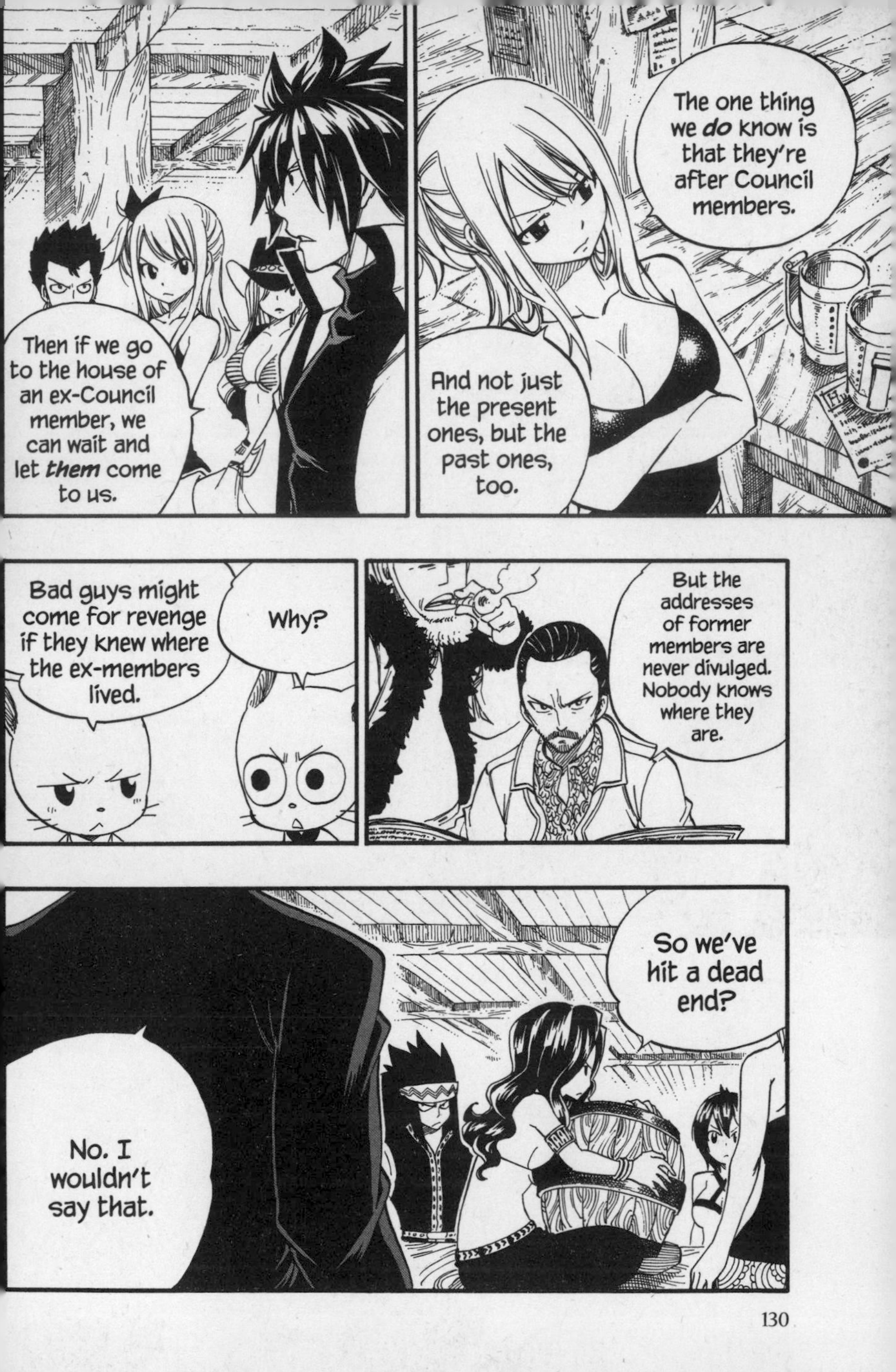
The one thing we *do* know is that they're after Council members.
And not just the present ones, but the past ones, too.
Then if we go to the house of an ex-Council member, we can wait and let *them* come to us.
But the addresses of former members are never divulged. Nobody knows where they are.
Why?
Bad guys might come for revenge if they knew where the ex-members lived.
So we've hit a dead end?
No. I wouldn't say that.

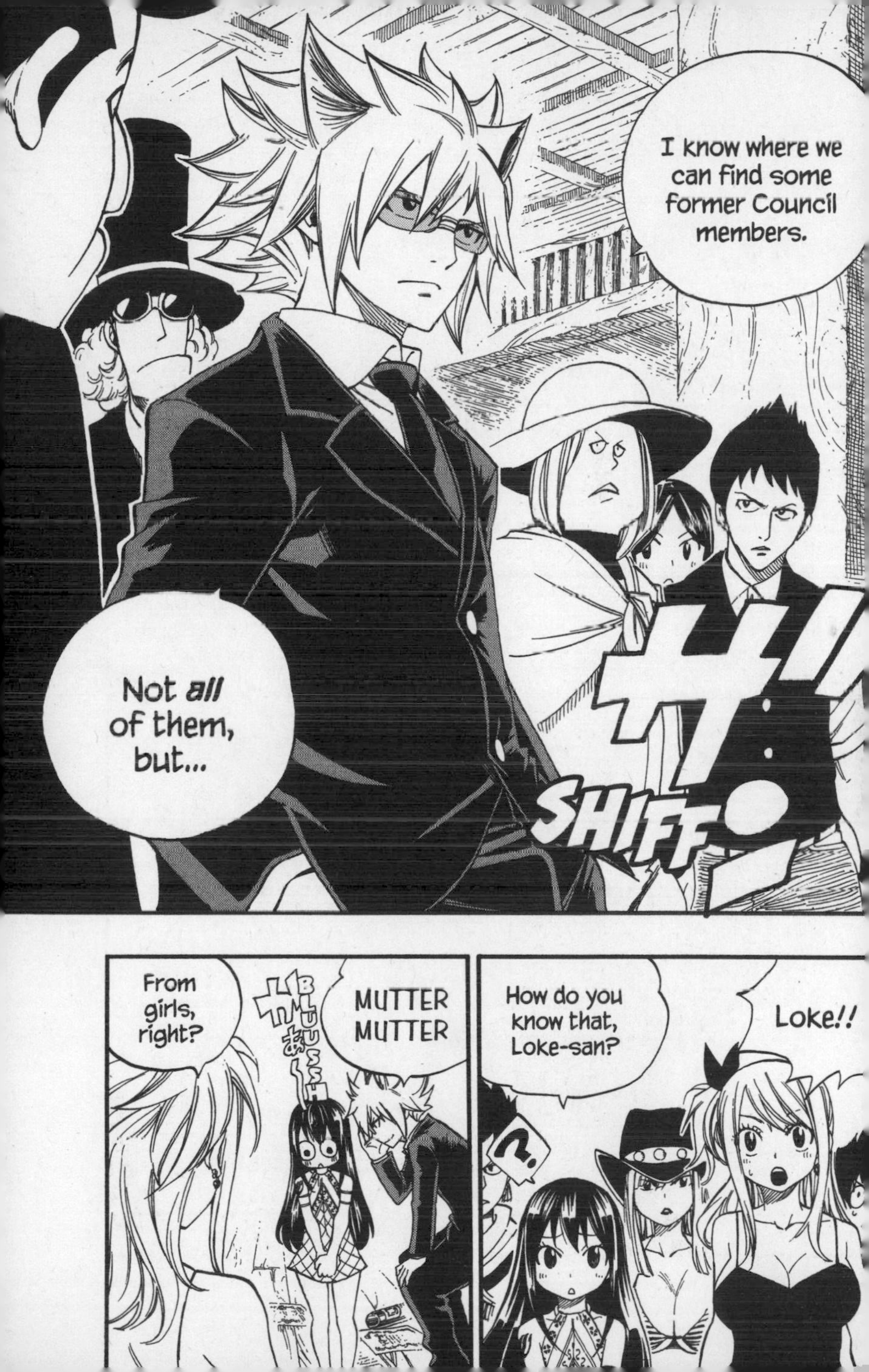
I know where we can find some former Council members.
Not *all* of them, but...
SHIFF
Loke!!
How do you know that, Loke-san?
MUTTER MUTTER
BLUUSH
From girls, right?

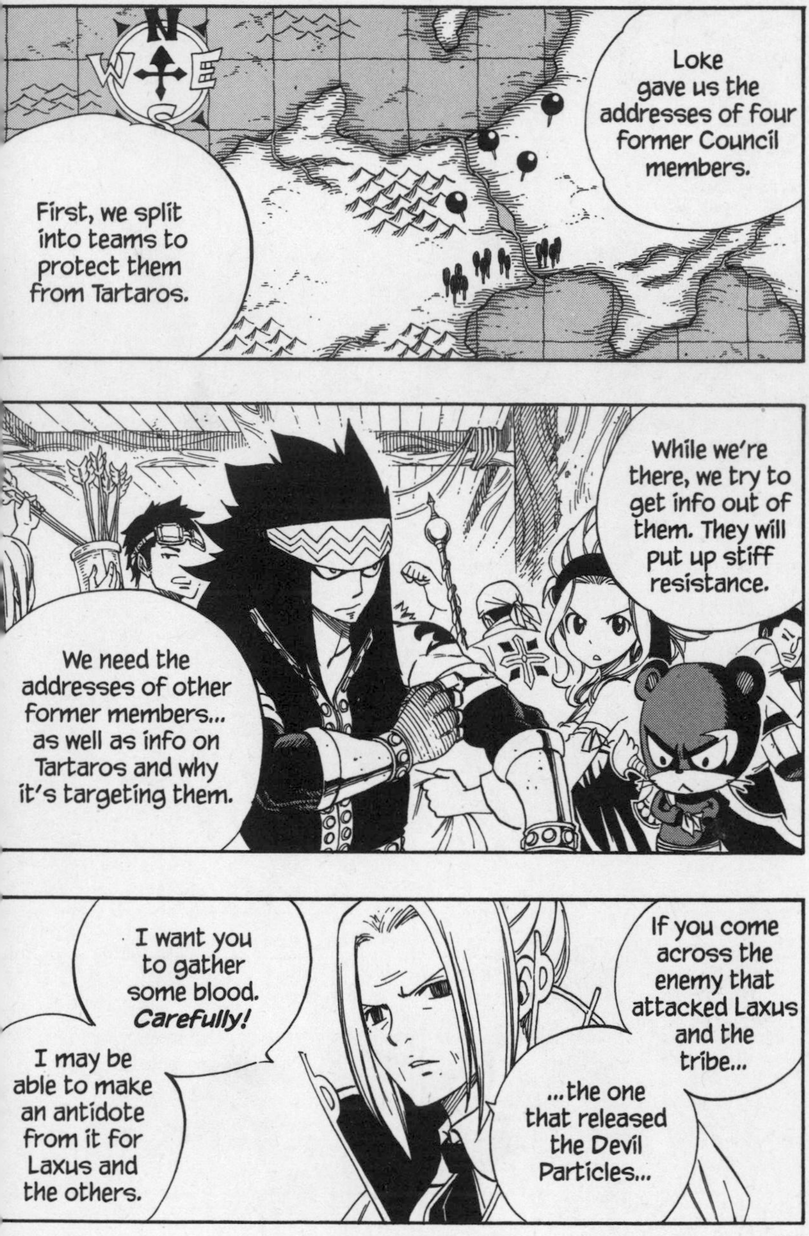
Loke gave us the addresses of four former Council members.
First, we split into teams to protect them from Tartaros.
While we're there, we try to get info out of them. They will put up stiff resistance.
We need the addresses of other former members... as well as info on Tartaros and why it's targeting them.
If you come across the enemy that attacked Laxus and the tribe...
...the one that released the Devil Particles...
I want you to gather some blood. *Carefully!*
I may be able to make an antidote from it for Laxus and the others.

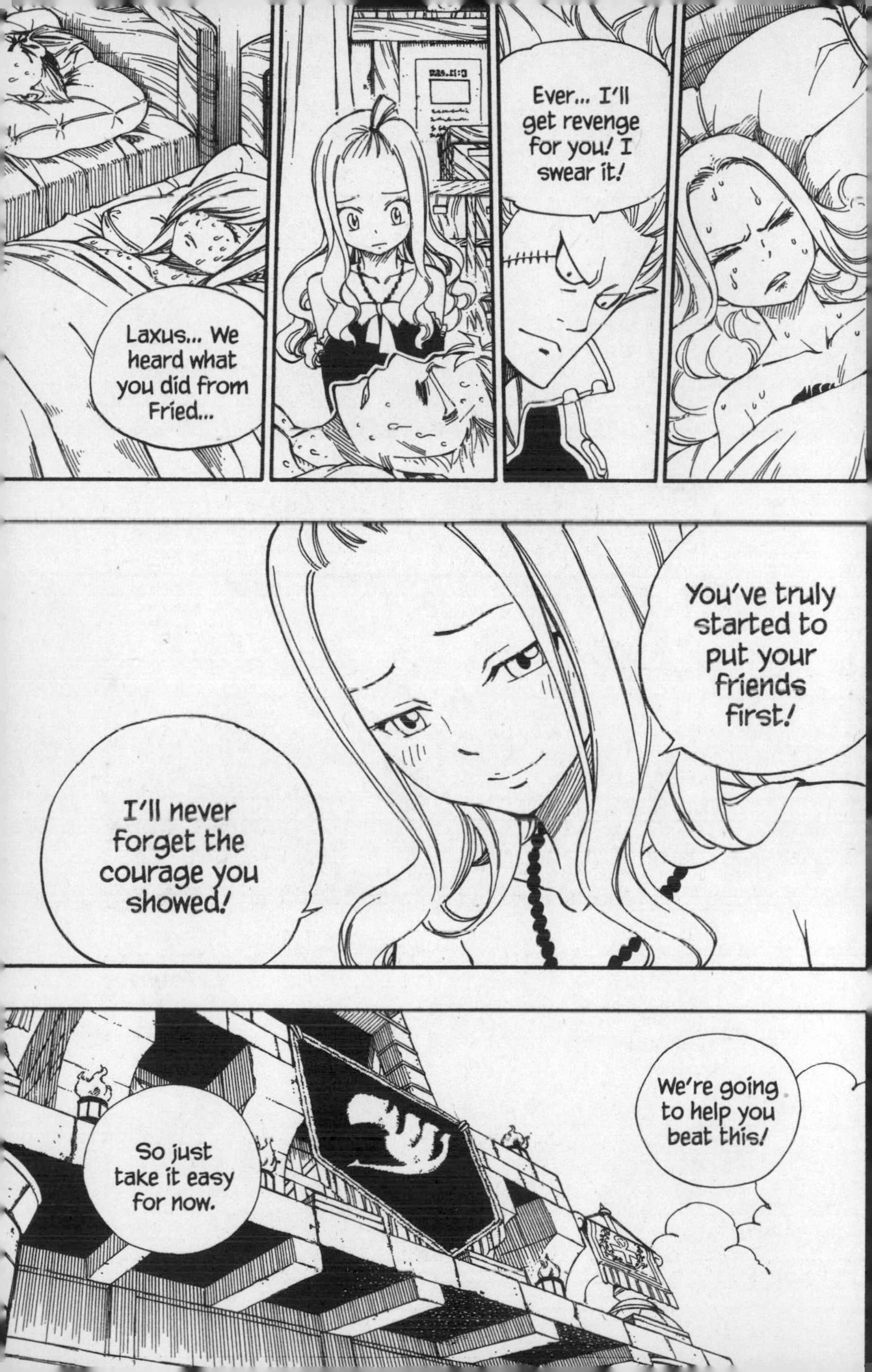
Ever... I'll get revenge for you! I swear it!
Laxus... We heard what you did from Fried...
You've truly started to put your friends first!
I'll never forget the courage you showed!
We're going to help you beat this!
So just take it easy for now.

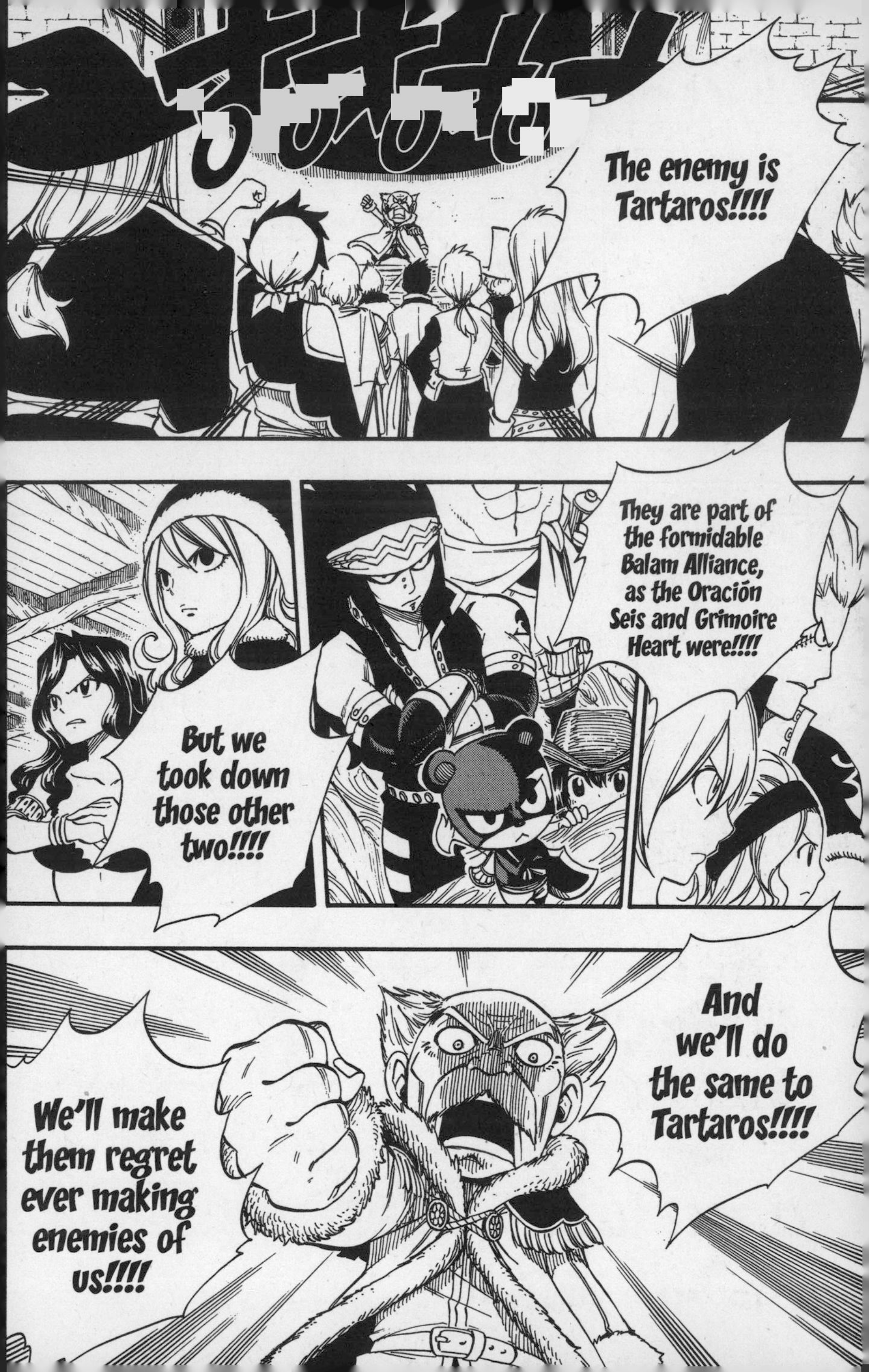
The enemy is Tartaros!!!!
They are part of the formidable Balam Alliance, as the Oración Seis and Grimoire Heart were!!!!
But we took down those other two!!!!
And we'll do the same to Tartaros!!!!
We'll make them regret ever making enemies of us!!!!

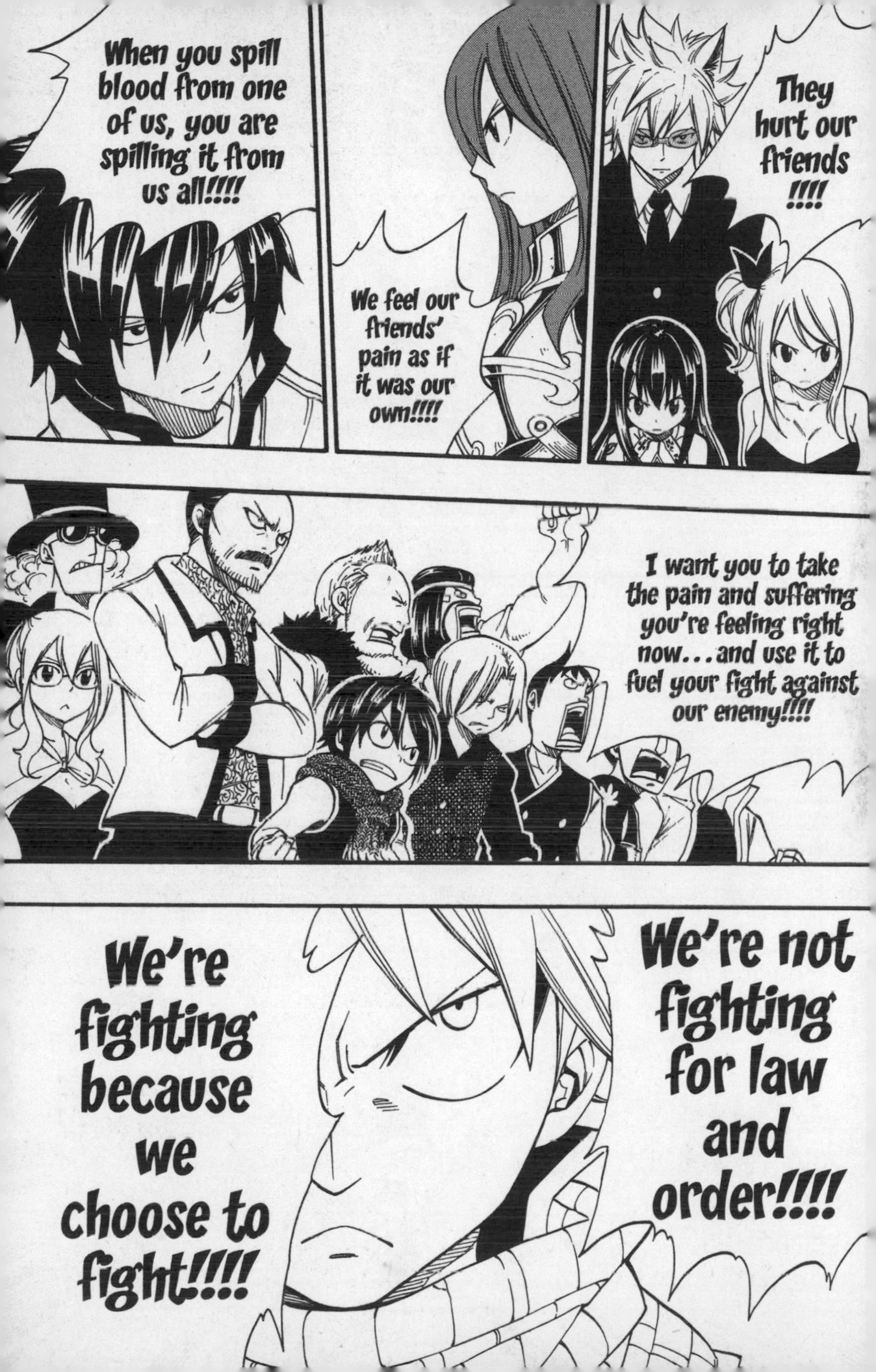
They hurt our friends!!!!
We feel our friends' pain as if it was our own!!!!
When you spill blood from one of us, you are spilling it from us all!!!!
I want you to take the pain and suffering you're feeling right now...and use it to fuel your fight against our enemy!!!!
We're not fighting for law and order!!!!
We're fighting because we choose to fight!!!!

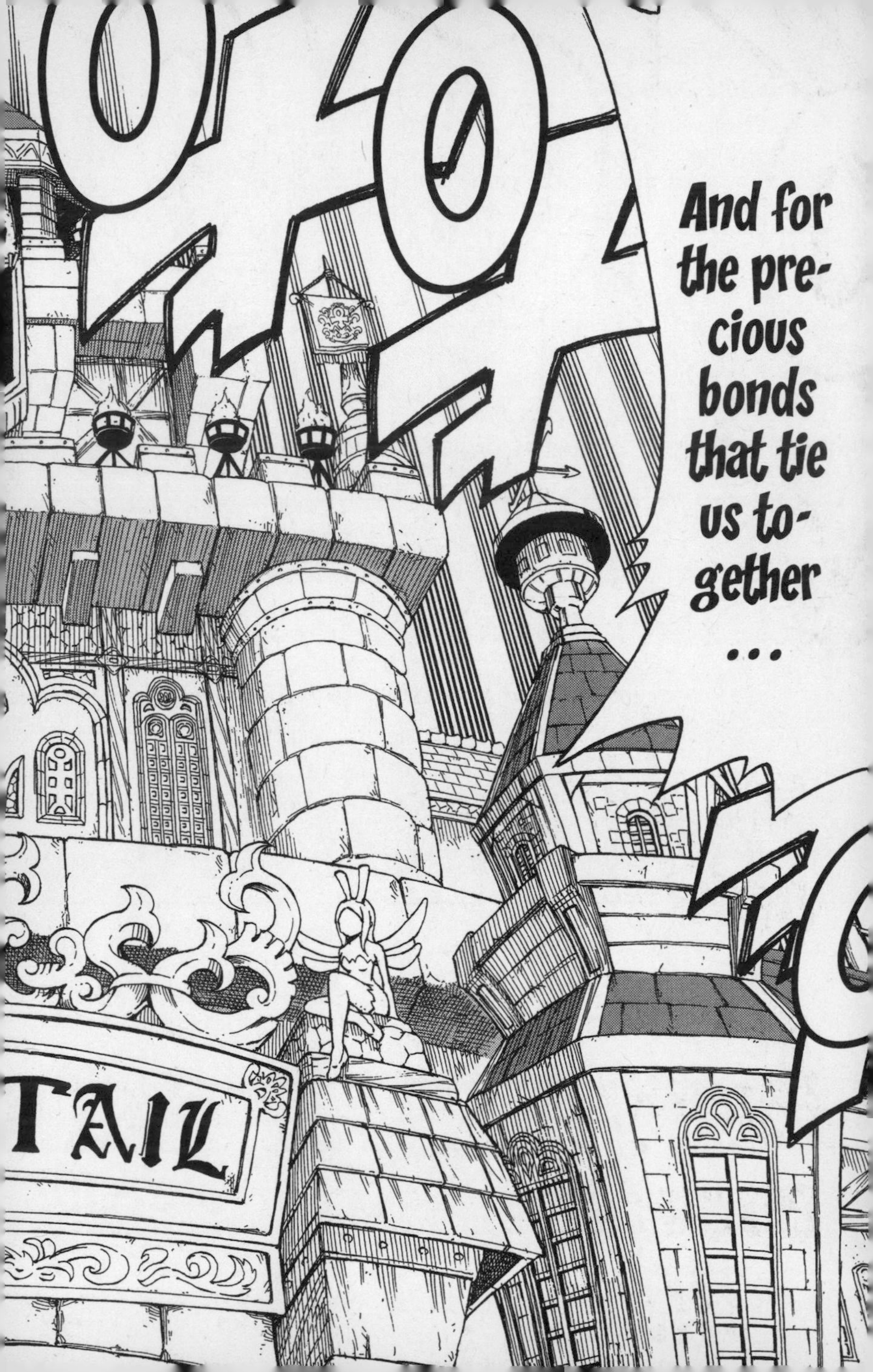
And for the pre-cious bonds that tie us to-gether ...
TAIL

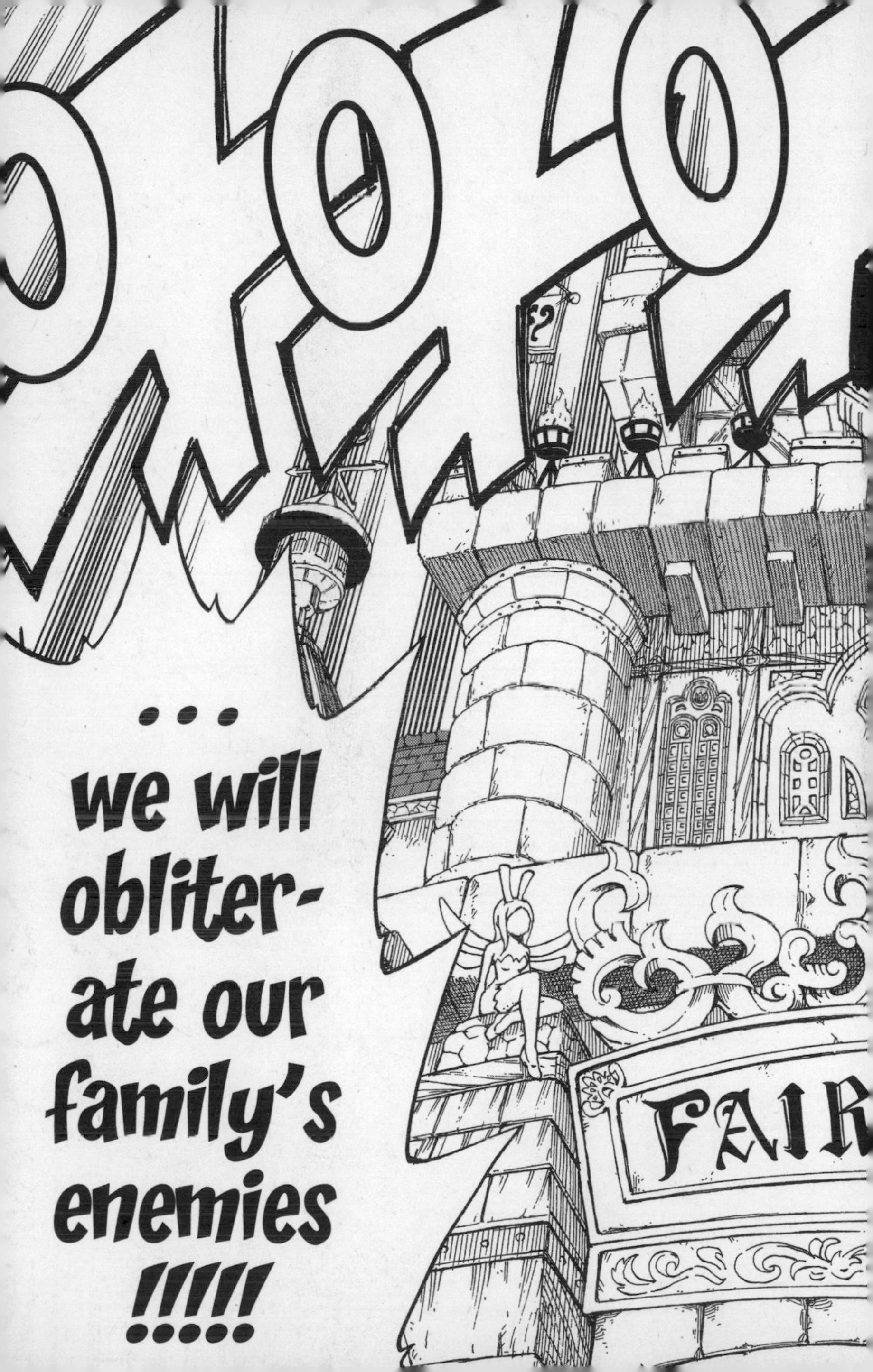
...
we will obliter-ate our family's enemies !!!!!
FAIR

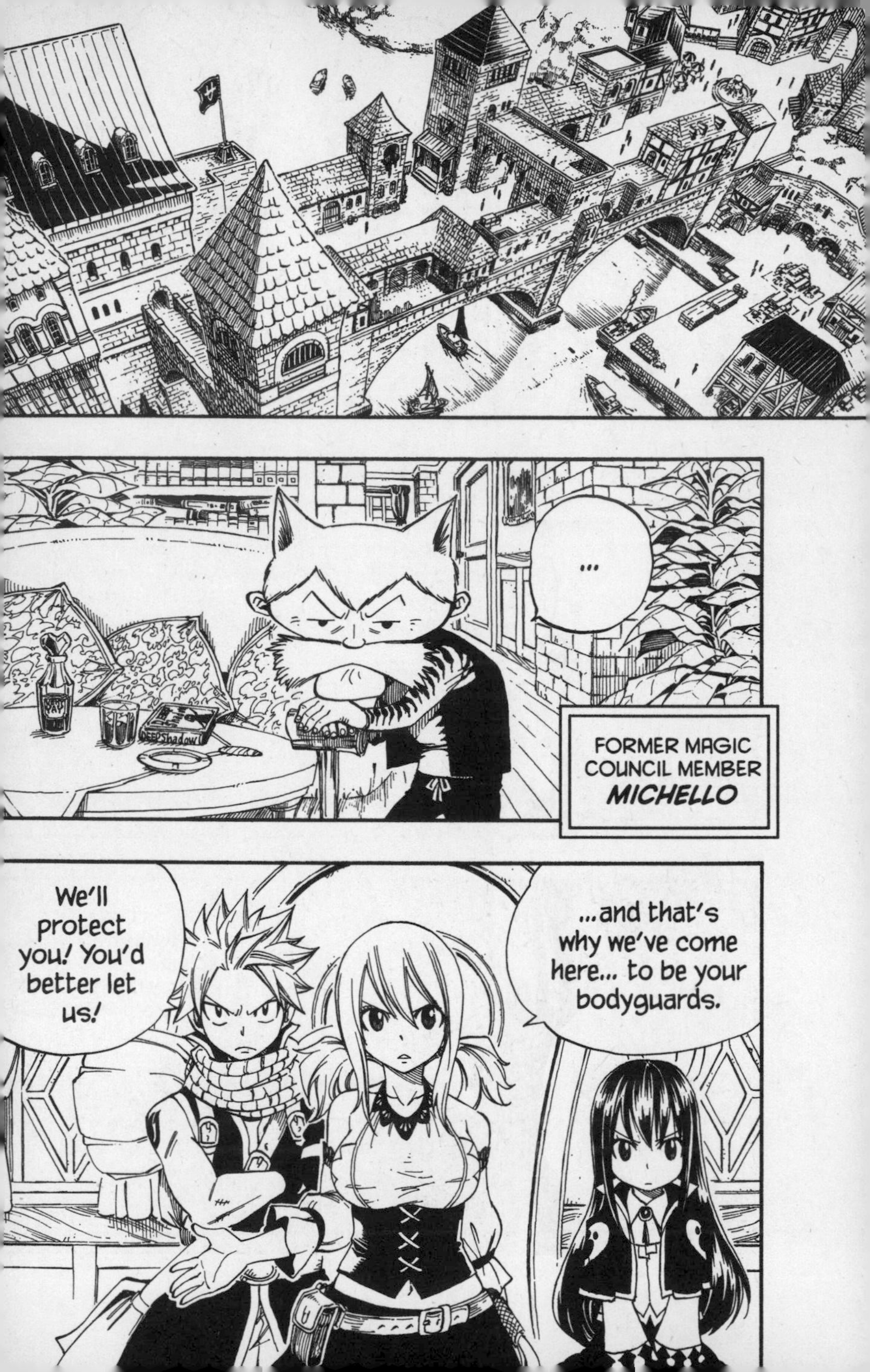
...
FORMER MAGIC COUNCIL MEMBER MICHELLO
...and that's why we've come here... to be your bodyguards.
We'll protect you! You'd better let us!

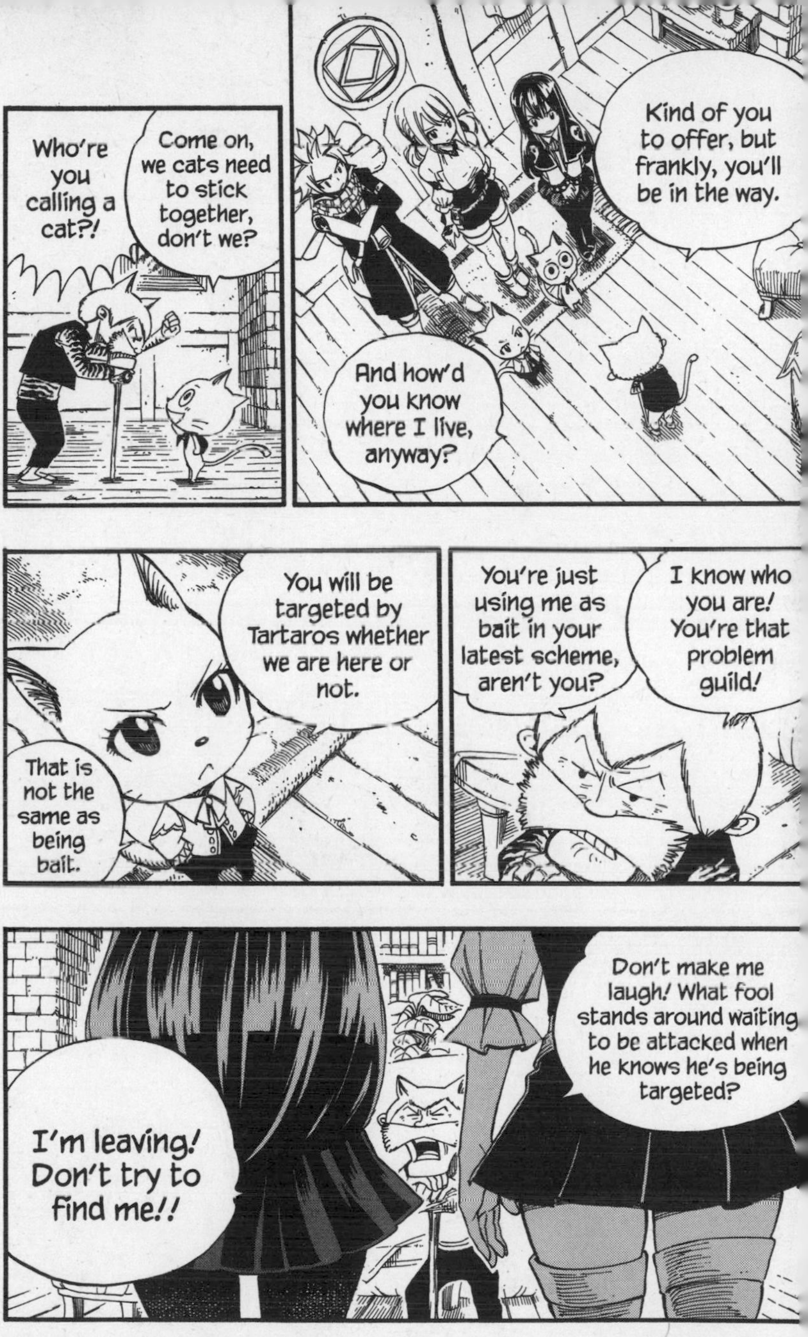
Kind of you to offer, but frankly, you'll be in the way.
And how'd you know where I live, anyway?
Come on, we cats need to stick together, don't we?
Who're you calling a cat?!
I know who you are! You're that problem guild!
You're just using me as bait in your latest scheme, aren't you?
You will be targeted by Tartaros whether we are here or not.
That is not the same as being bait.
Don't make me laugh! What fool stands around waiting to be attacked when he knows he's being targeted?
I'm leaving! Don't try to find me!!

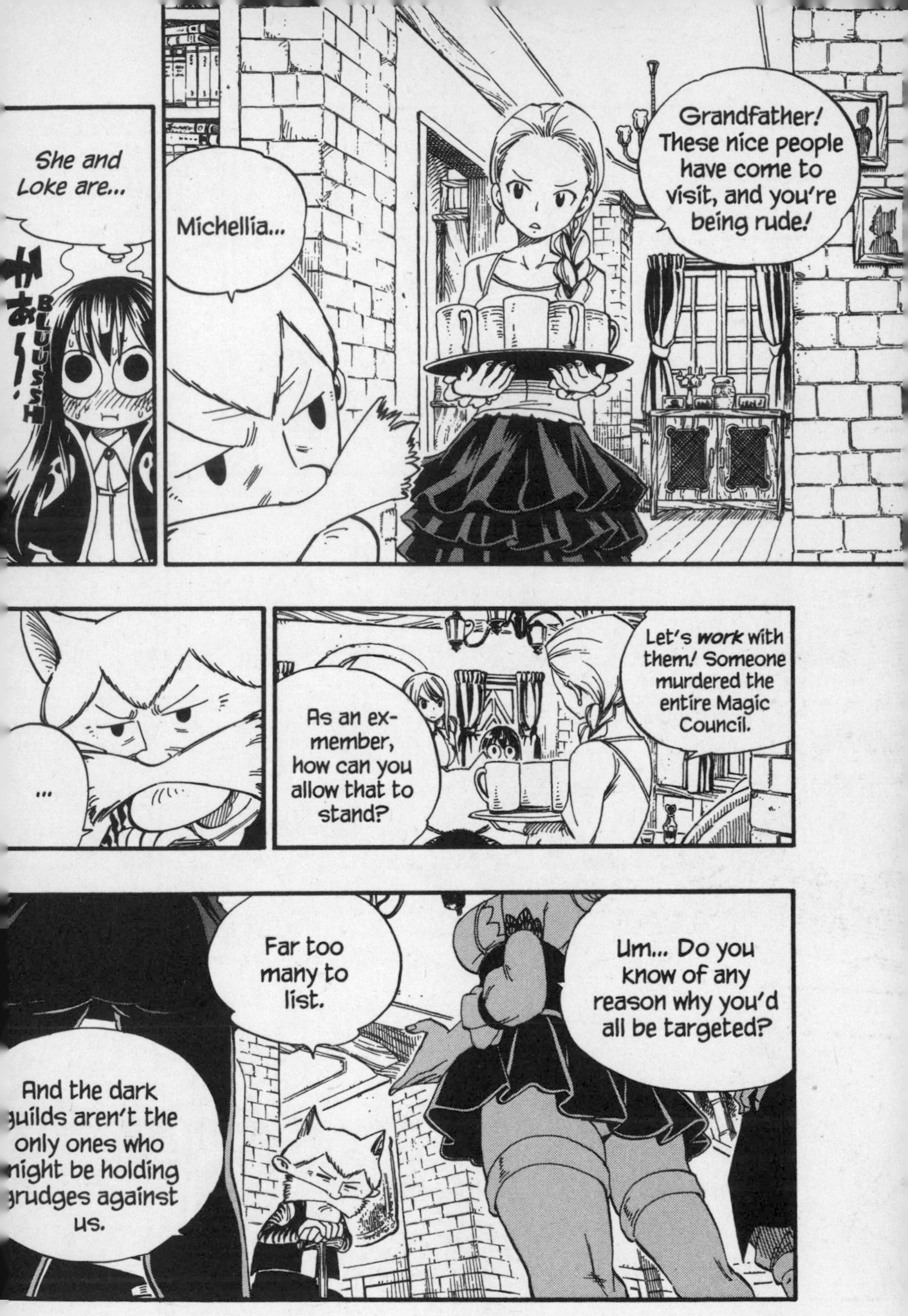
Grandfather! These nice people have come to visit, and you're being rude!
Michellia...
She and Loke are...
BLUUSSH
Let's *work* with them! Someone murdered the entire Magic Council.
As an ex-member, how can you allow that to stand?
...
Um... Do you know of any reason why you'd all be targeted?
Far too many to list.
And the dark guilds aren't the only ones who might be holding grudges against us.

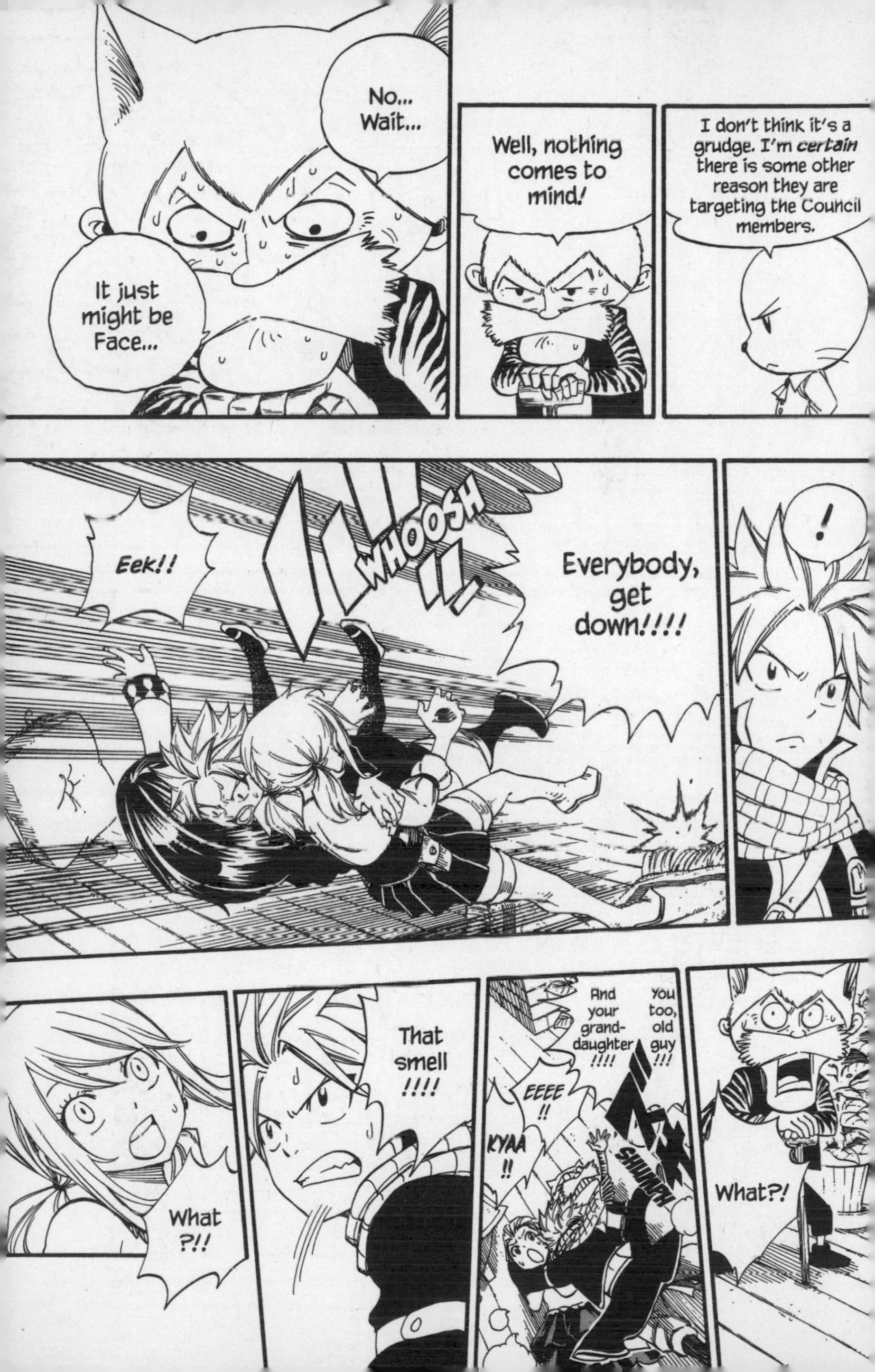
I don't think it's a grudge. I'm *certain* there is some other reason they are targeting the Council members.
Well, nothing comes to mind!
No... Wait...
It just might be Face...
!
Everybody, get down!!!!
WHOOSH
Eek!!
What?!
You too, old guy!!!
And your grand-daughter!!!!
EEEE!!
KYAA!!
That smell!!!!
What?!!

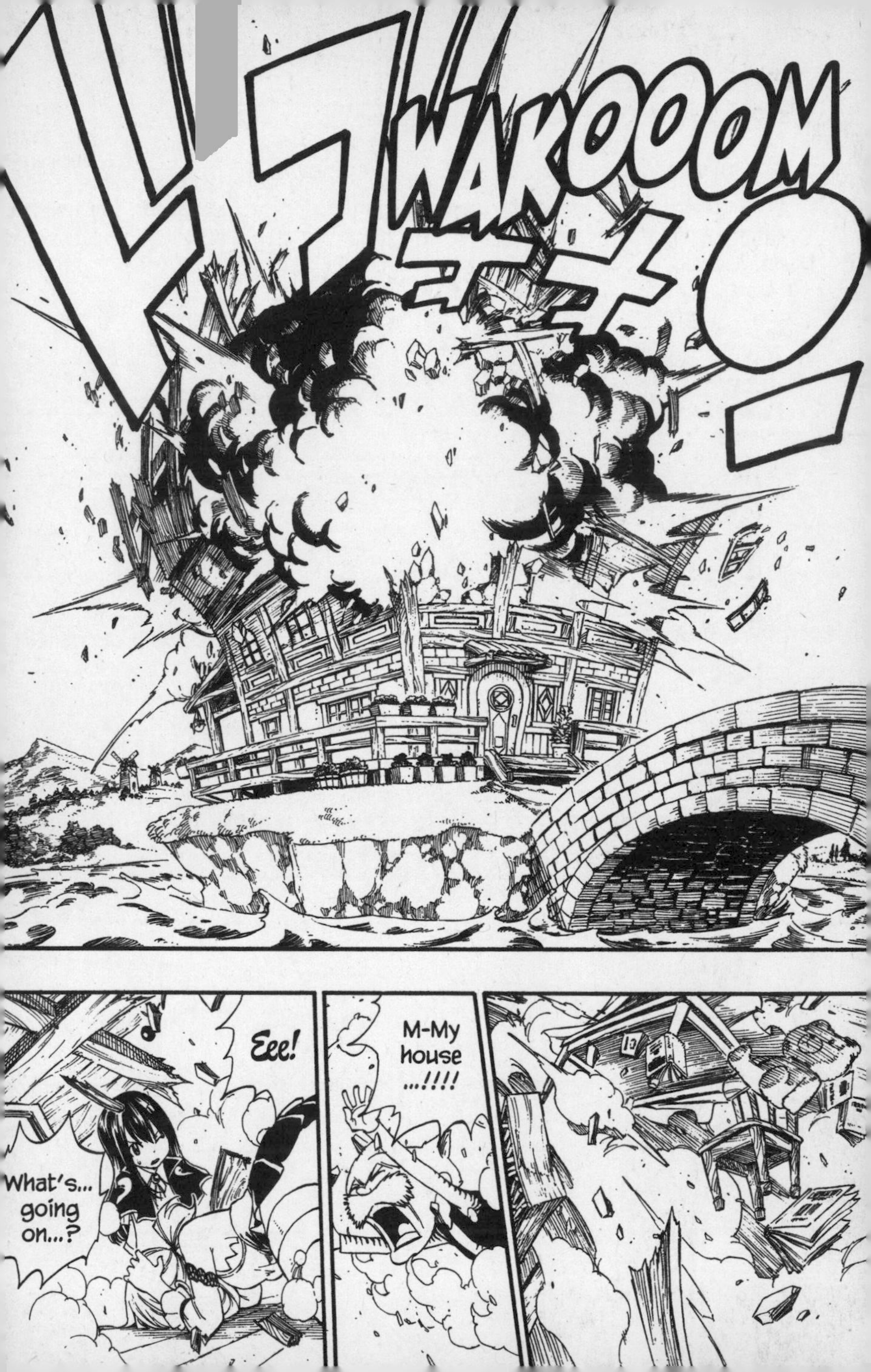
WAKOOOM
M-My house ...!!!!
Eee!
What's... going on...?

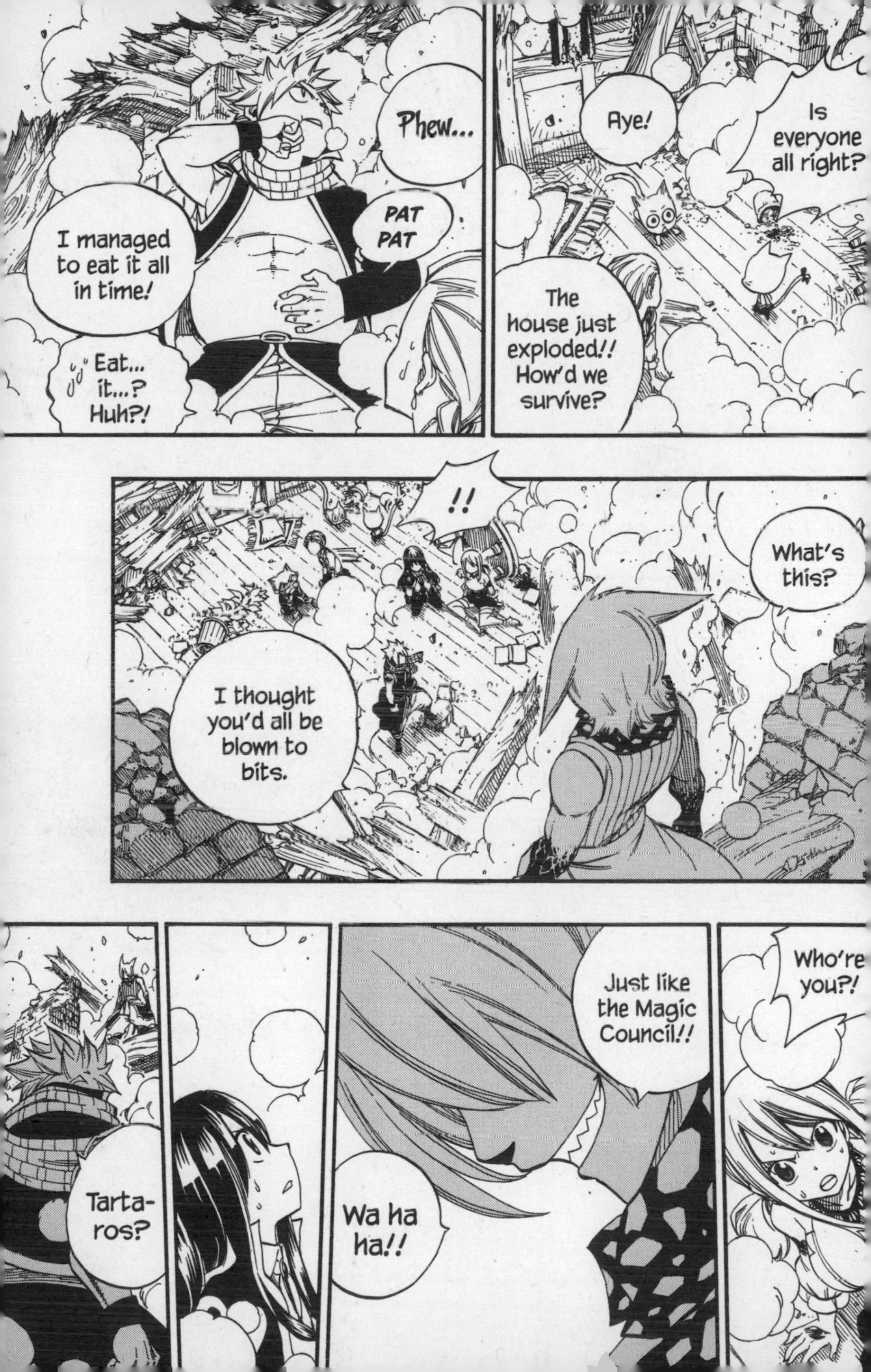
Is everyone all right?
Aye!
The house just exploded!! How'd we survive?
Phew...
PAT PAT
I managed to eat it all in time!
Eat... it...? Huh?!
!!
What's this?
I thought you'd all be blown to bits.
Who're you?!
Just like the Magic Council!!
Wa ha ha!!
Tarta-ros?

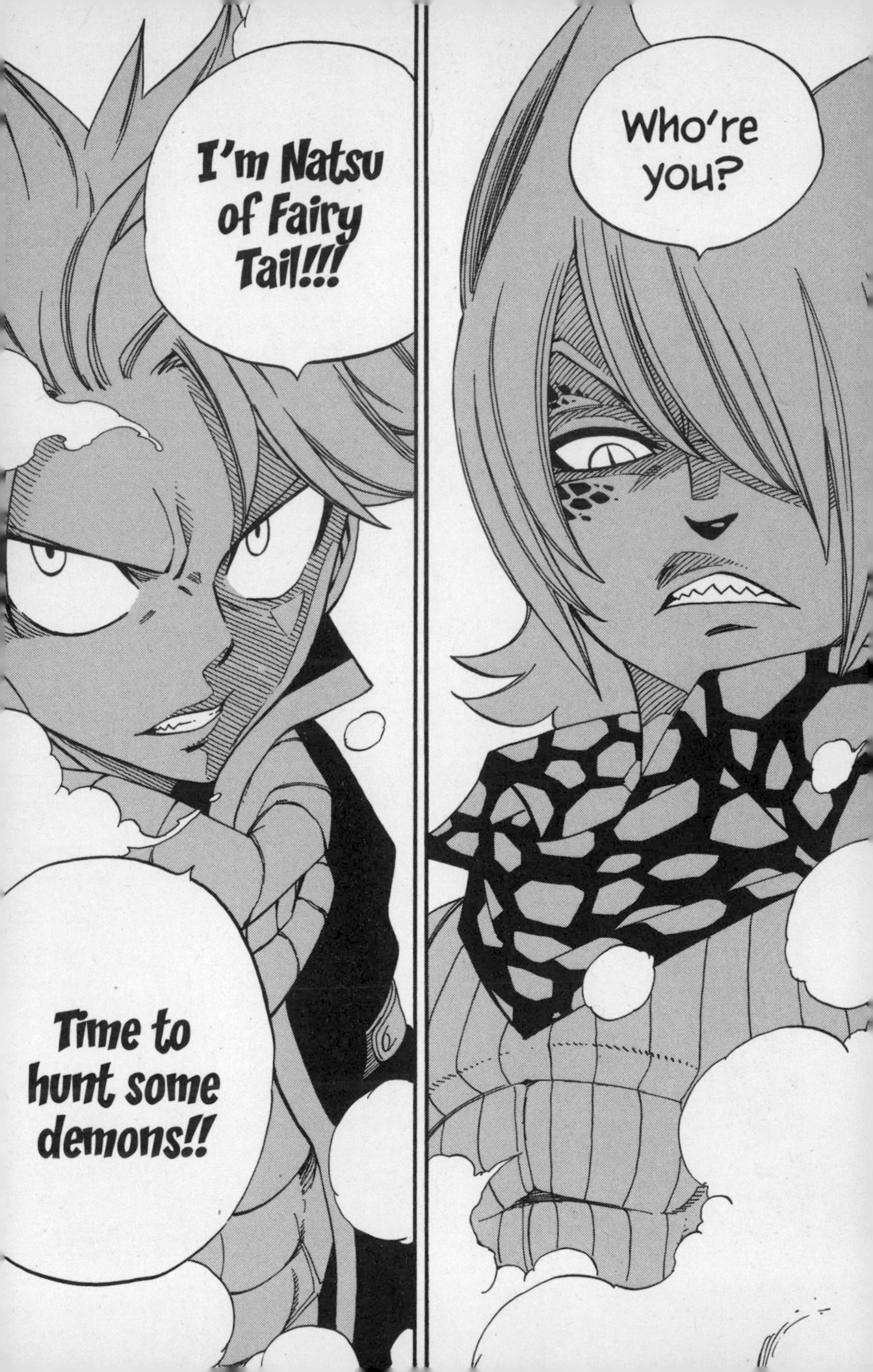
Who're you?
I'm Natsu of Fairy Tail!!!
Time to hunt some demons!!

FAIRY TAIL

Chapter 360:
The White Inheritance

BLUE PEGASUS

Name: Ren Akatsuki   Age: 27

Magic:
Air Magic

Likes: Dislikes:
Rabbits   **Pale skin**

Remarks

The *tsundere** of Blue Pegasus, he's very popular with the ladies. But seven years ago, he met Sherry of Lamia on a mission, and started dating her. Believe it or not, he's never dated another girl since. He's completely devoted to Sherry.
He was already "Big Brother Ren" to Sherria, and has a close relationship with her. The only person who opposes his relationship with Sherry is the master of Lamia, Ooba Babasaama. What will become of the star-crossed lovers separated by their guilds?!

*Tsundere means someone who is usually prickly but expresses affection during moments of weakness.

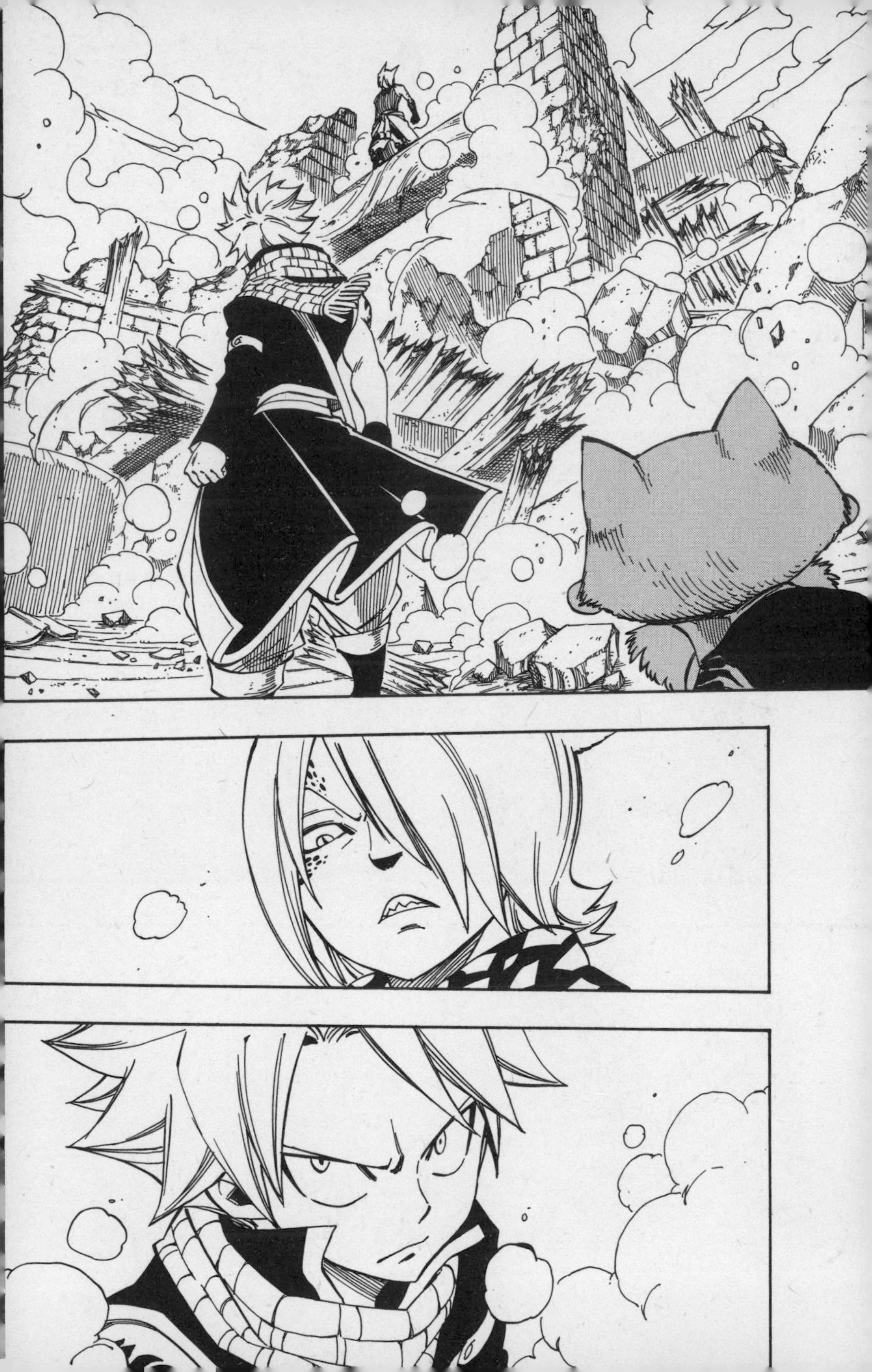

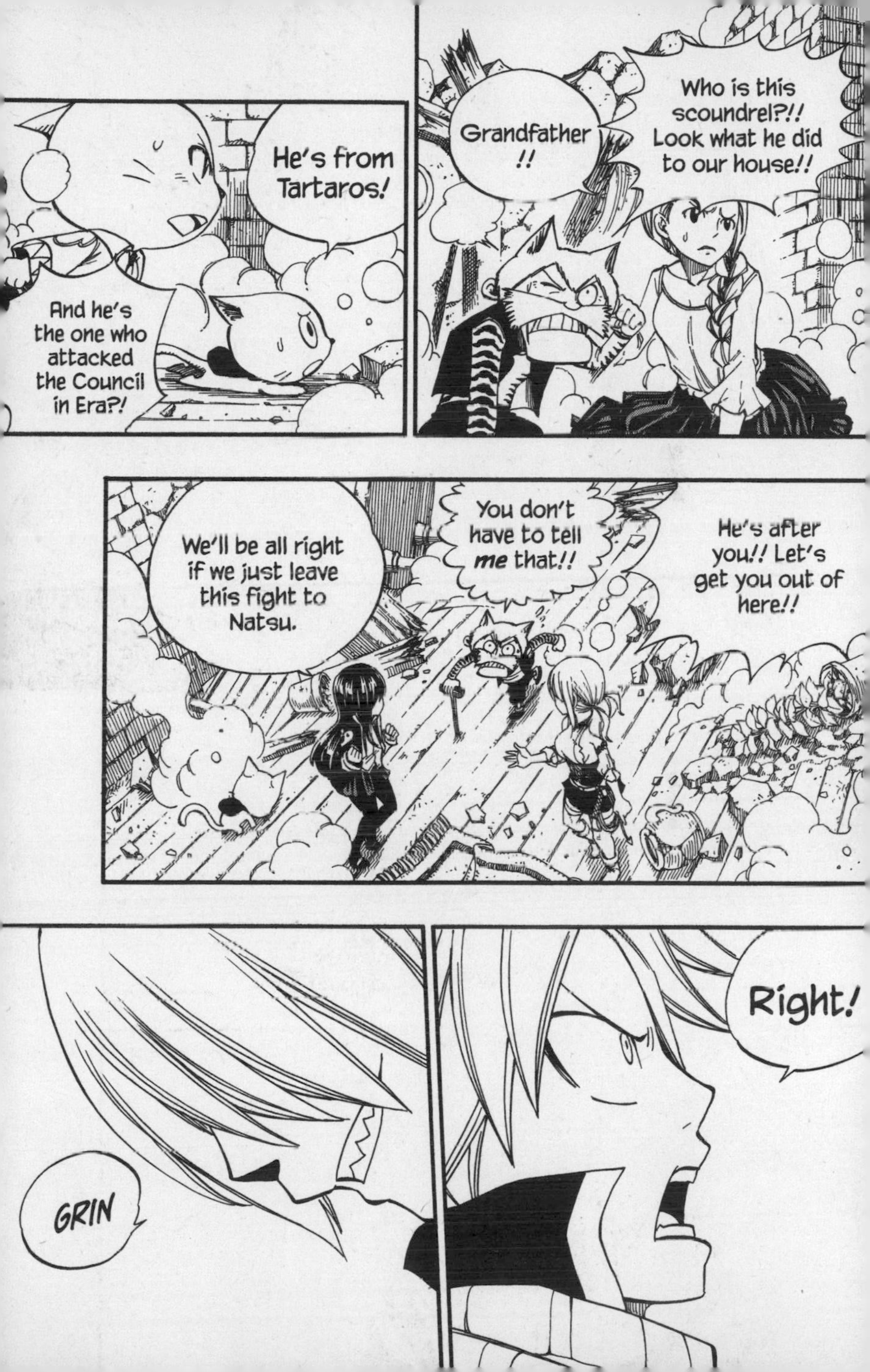
Who is this scoundrel?!! Look what he did to our house!!
Grandfather!!
He's from Tartaros!
And he's the one who attacked the Council in Era?!
He's after you!! Let's get you out of here!!
You don't have to tell *me* that!!
We'll be all right if we just leave this fight to Natsu.
Right!
GRIN

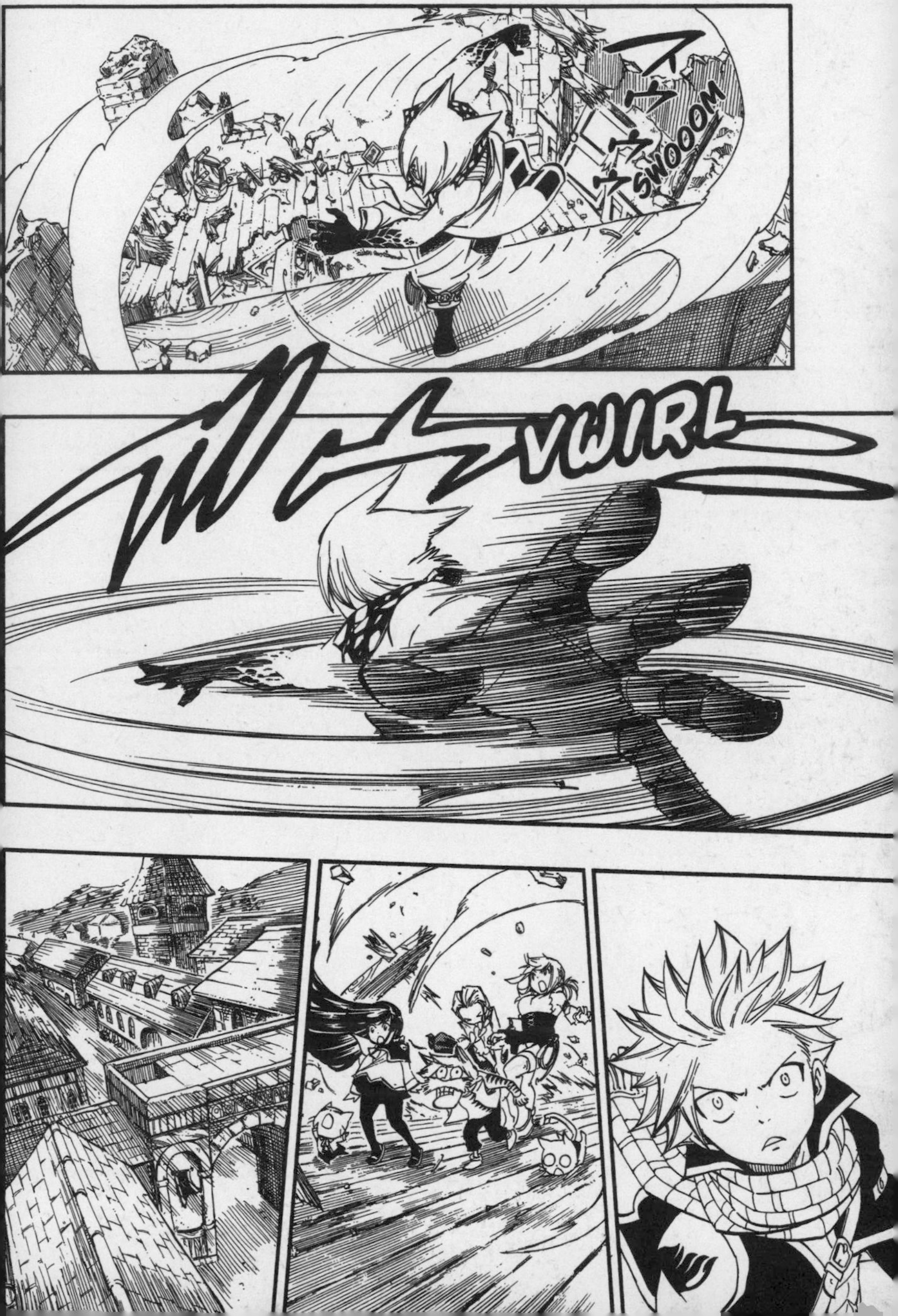
SWOOOM
VWIRL

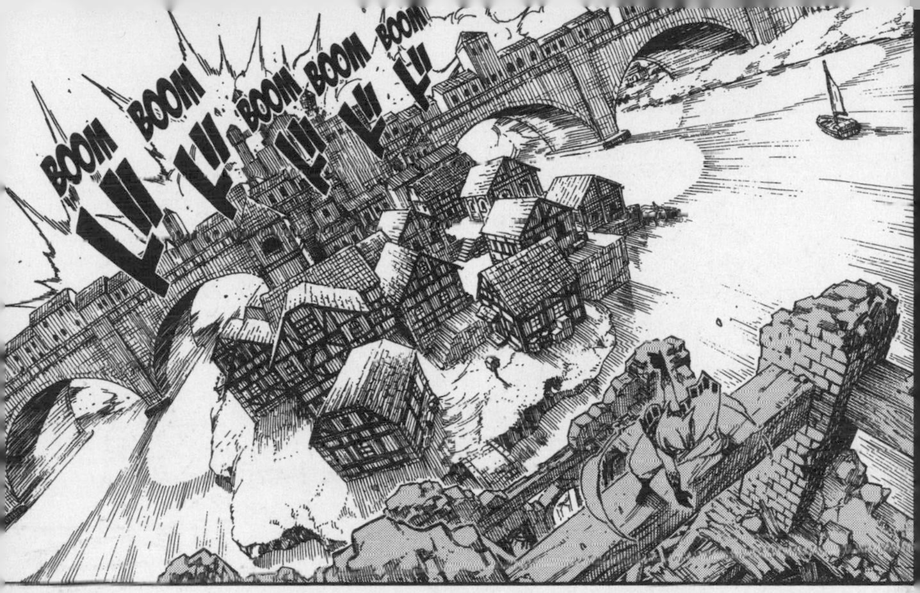
BOOM
BOOM
BOOM
BOOM
BOOM

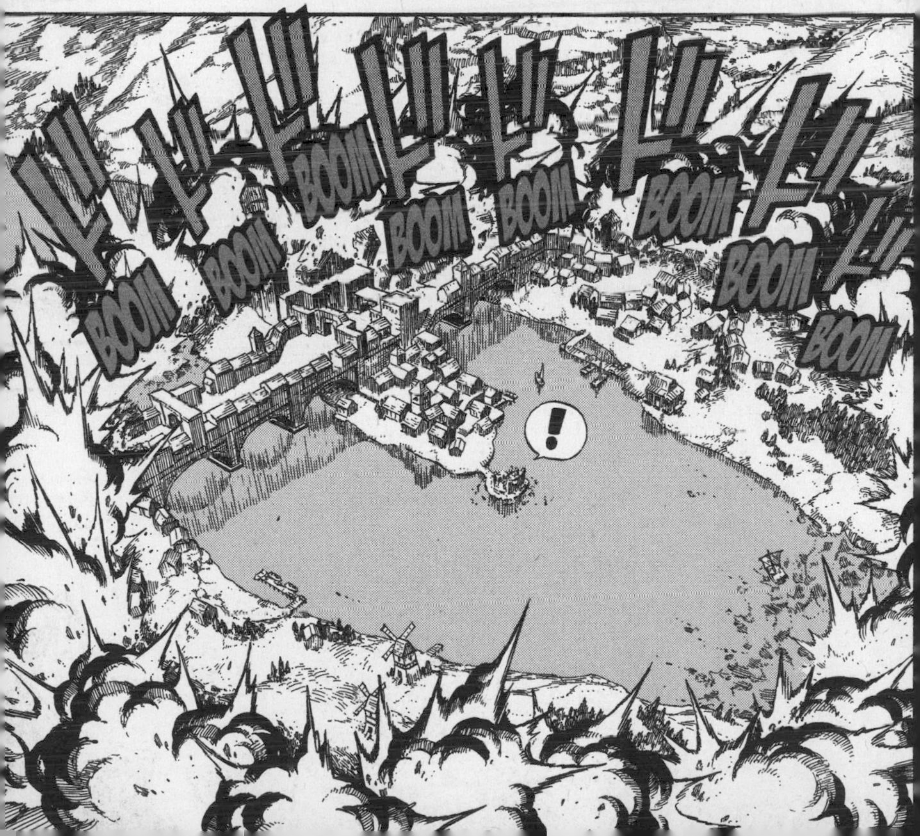
BOOM
BOOM
BOOM
BOOM
BOOM
BOOM
BOOM
BOOM
!

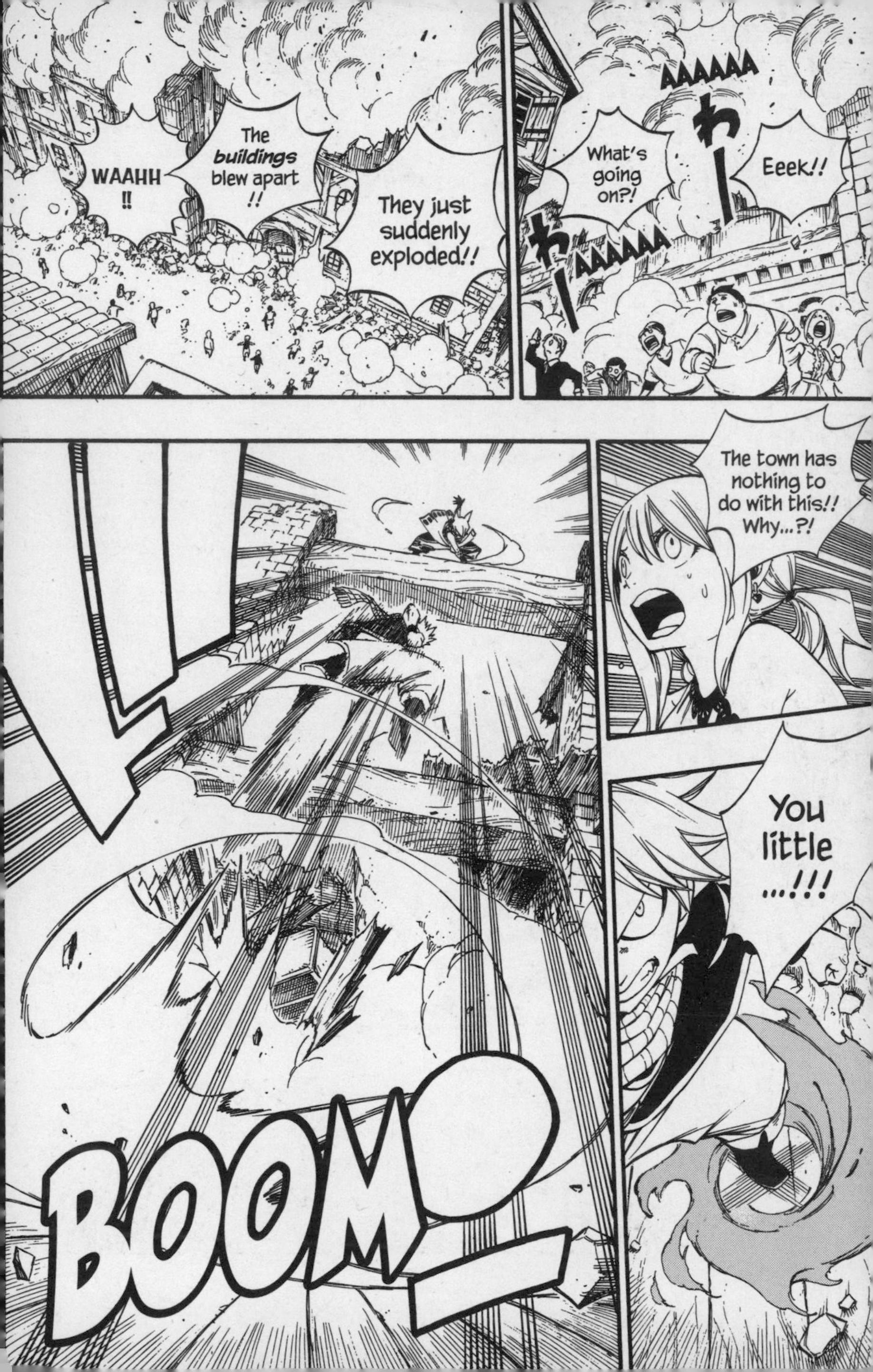
AAAAAA
わー
Eeek!!
What's going on?!
わー
AAAAAA
The *buildings* blew apart!!
They just suddenly exploded!!
WAAHH!!
The town has nothing to do with this!! Why...?!
You little ...!!!
BOOM

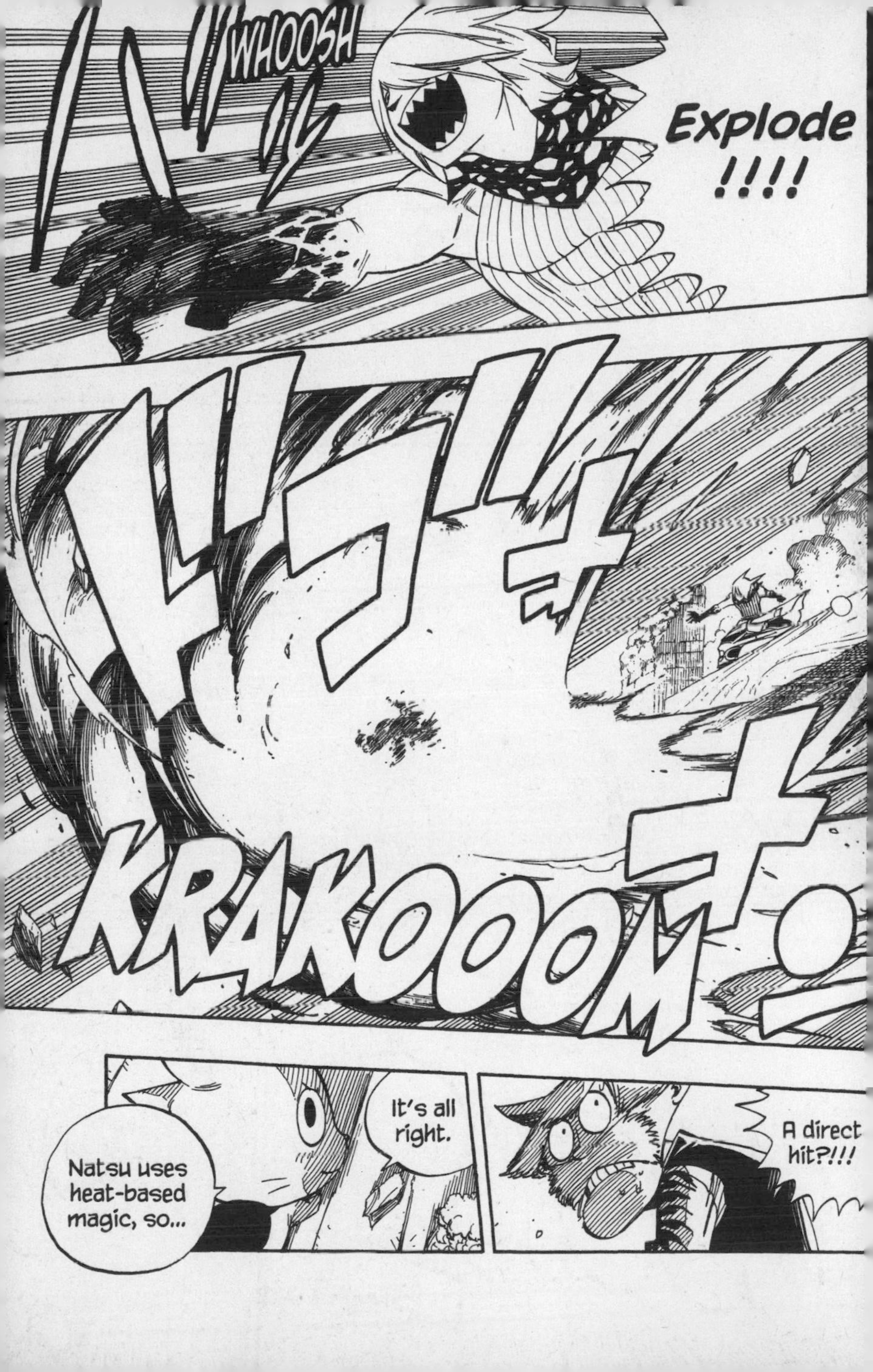
Explode !!!!
WHOOSH
KRAKOOOM!
A direct hit?!!!
It's all right.
Natsu uses heat-based magic, so...

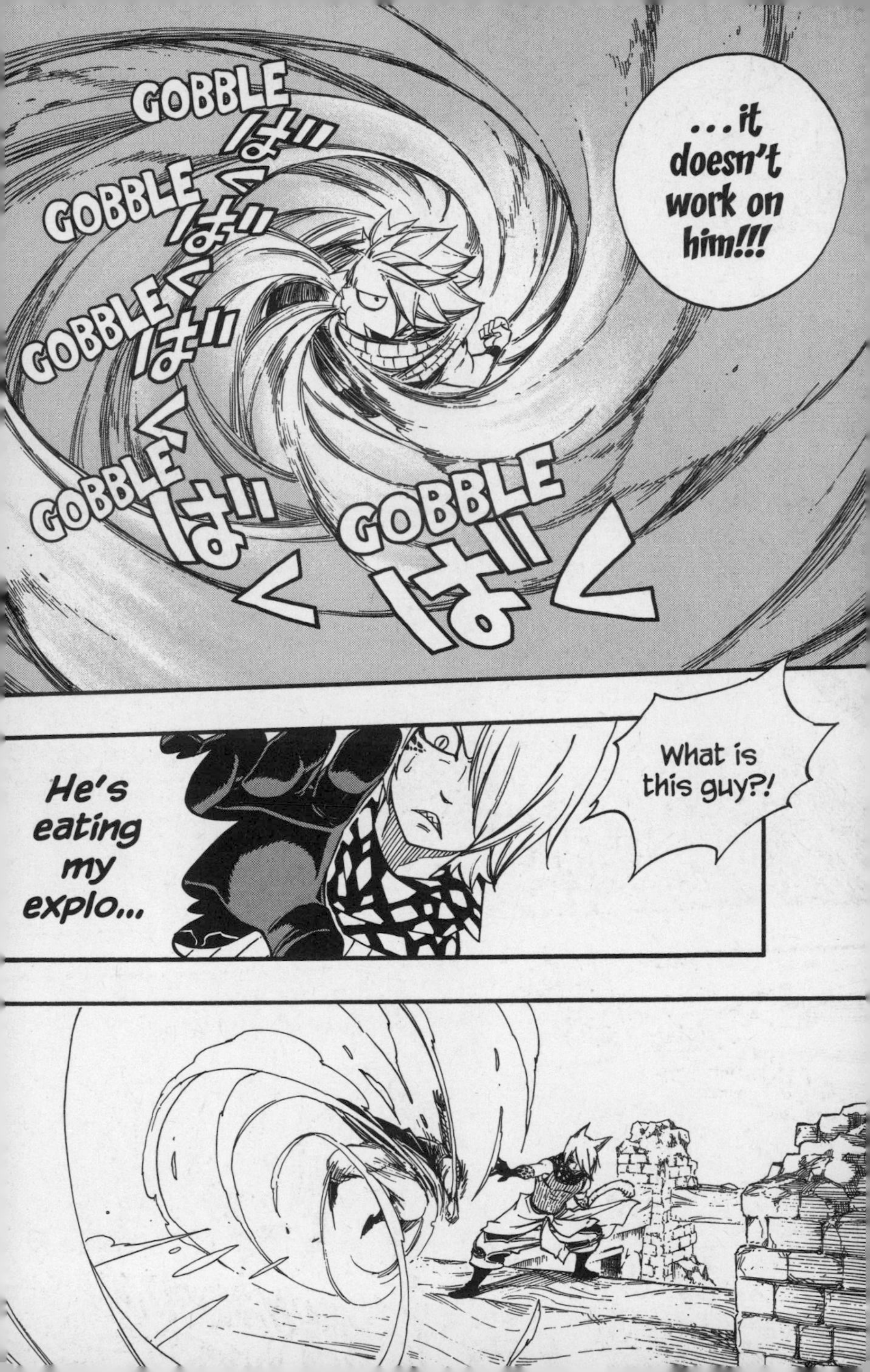
...it doesn't work on him!!!
GOBBLE ばく
GOBBLE ばく
GOBBLE ばく
GOBBLE ばく
GOBBLE ばく
What is this guy?!
He's eating my explo...

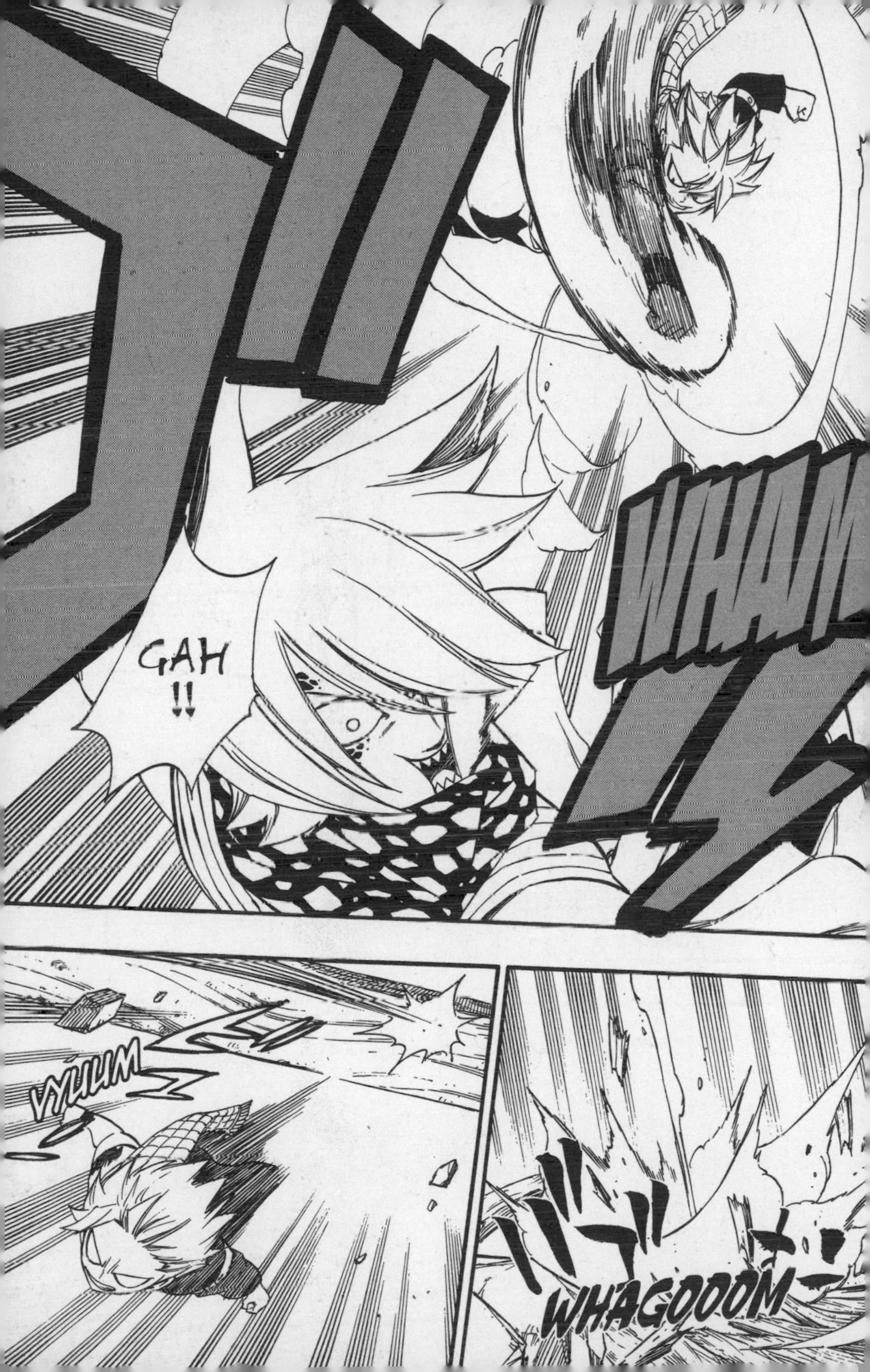
WHAM
GAH!!
WHAGOOOM
VYUUM

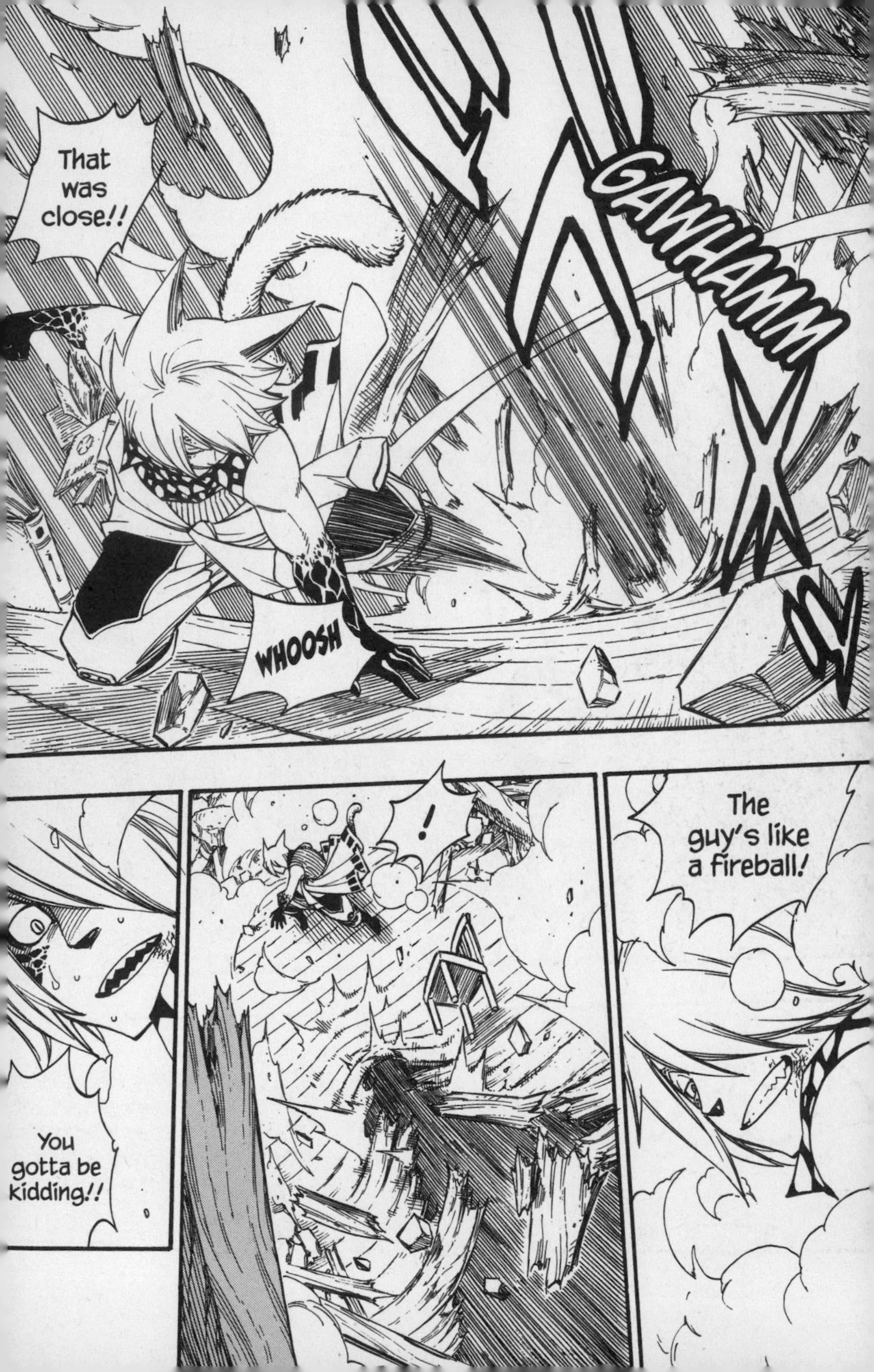
GAWHAMM
That was close!!
WHOOSH
The guy's like a fireball!
!
You gotta be kidding!!

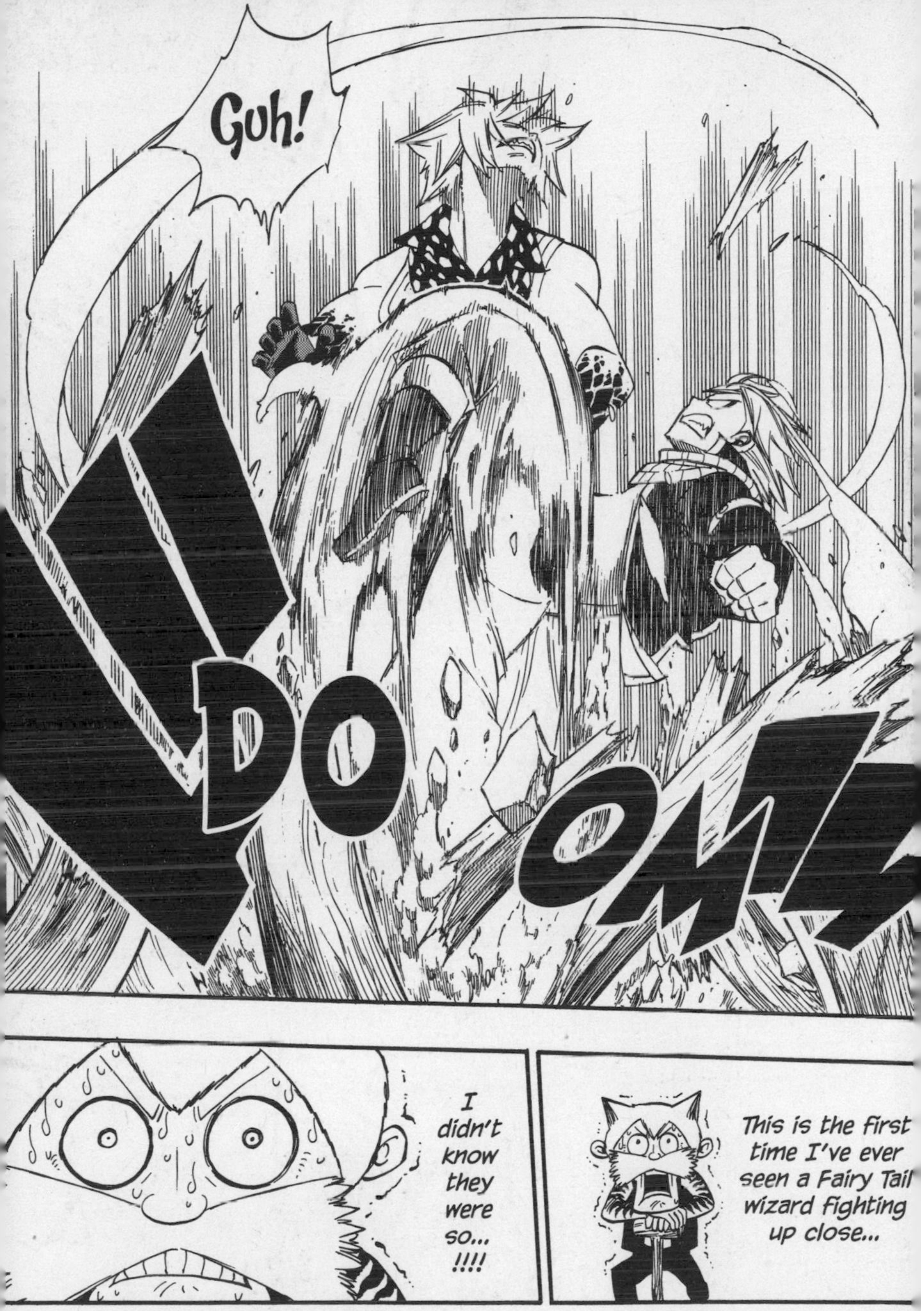
Guh!
DOOM
This is the first time I've ever seen a Fairy Tail wizard fighting up close...
I didn't know they were so... !!!!

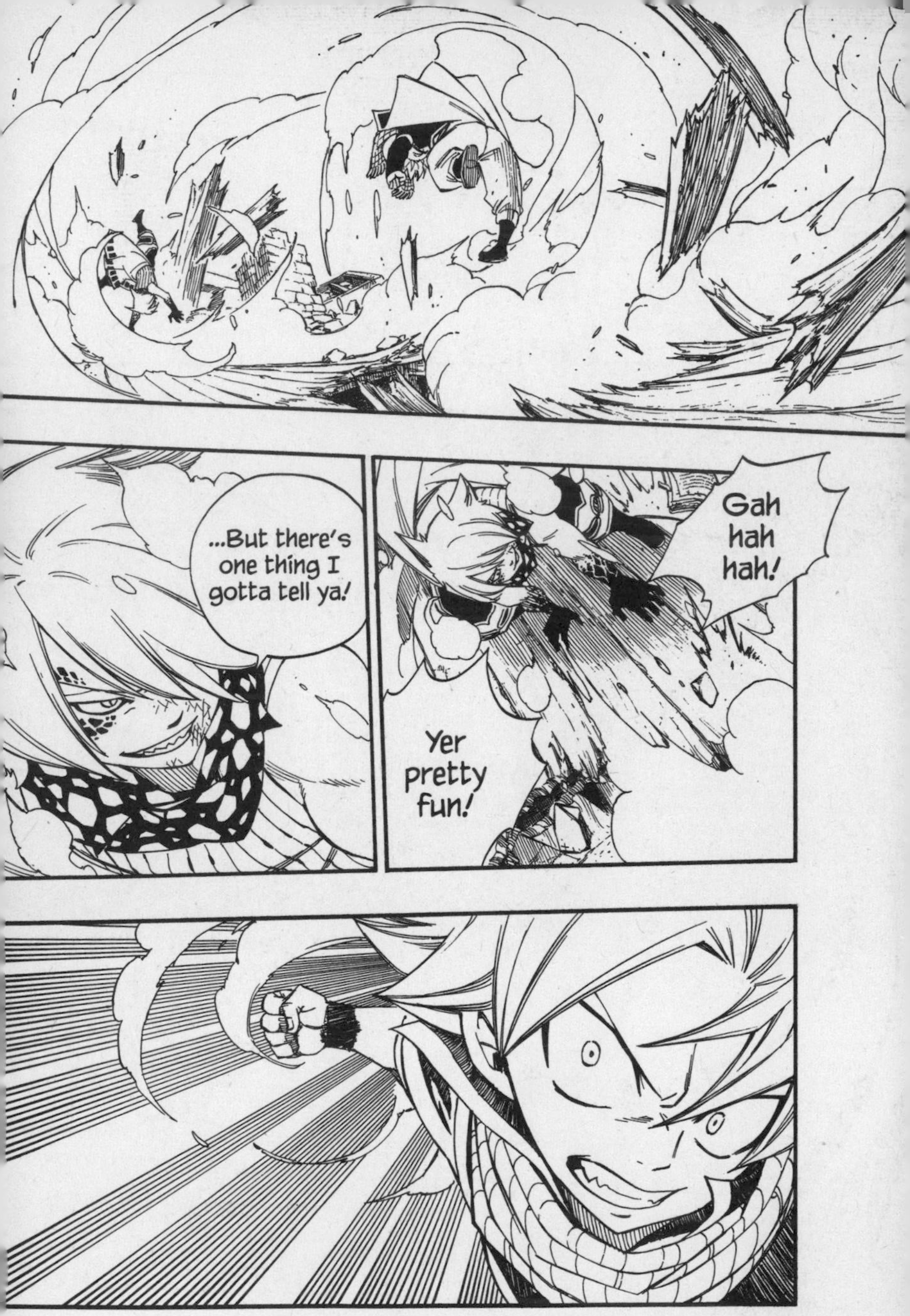
Gah hah hah!
Yer pretty fun!
...But there's one thing I gotta tell ya!

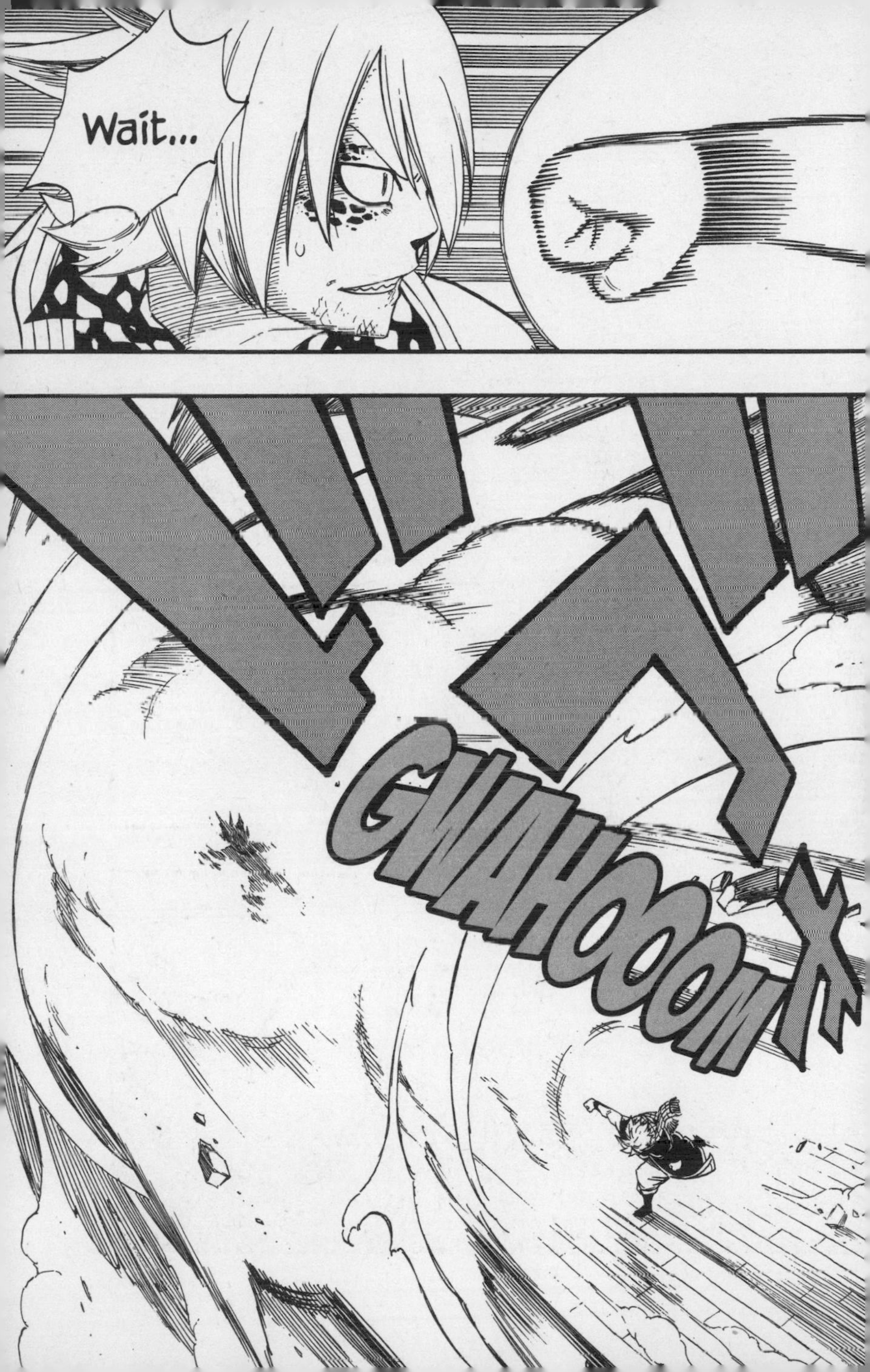
Wait...
GWAHOOOOM

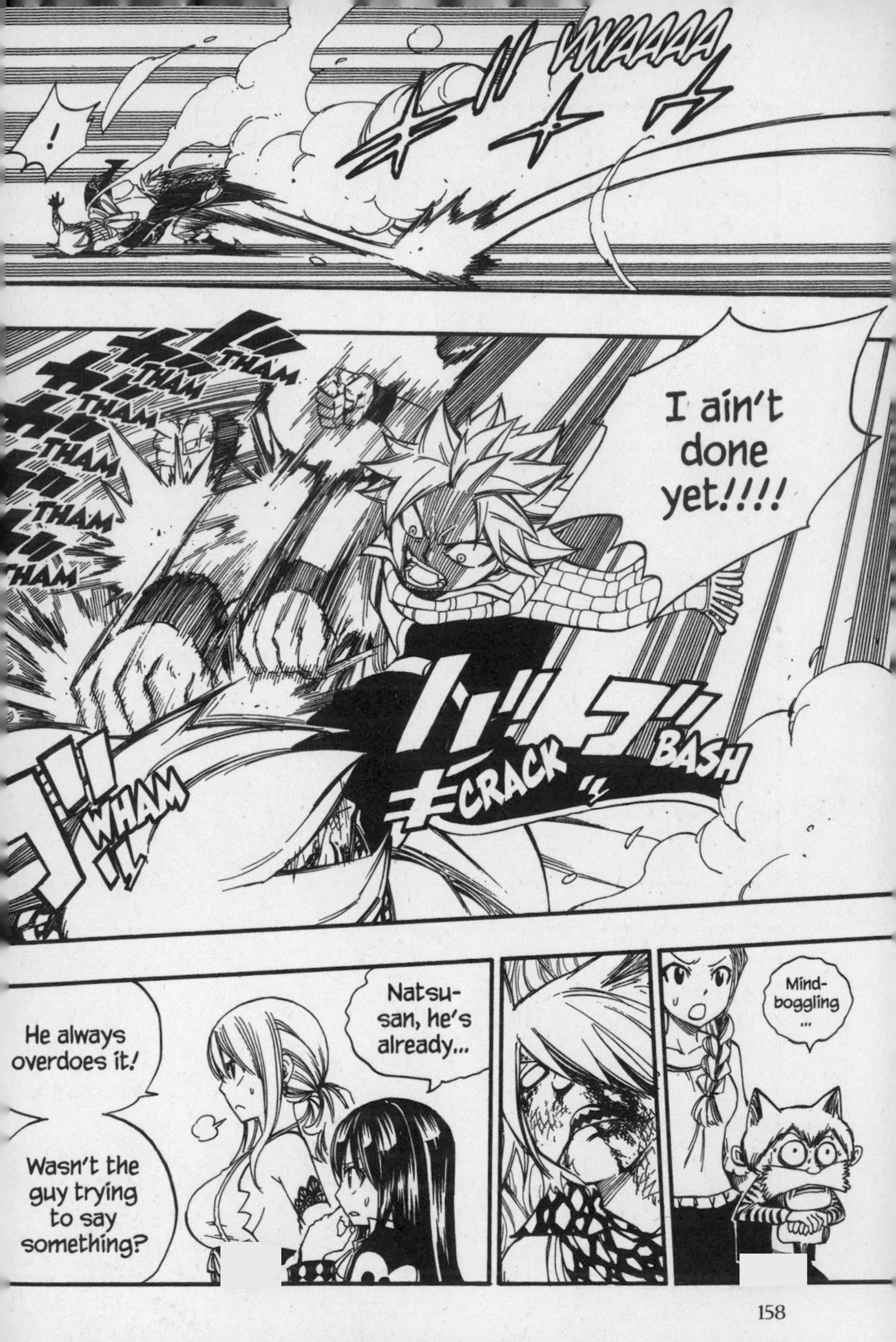
!
I ain't done yet!!!!
THAM
THAM
THAM
THAM
THAM
THAM
BASH
CRACK
WHAM
Mind-boggling ...
Natsu-san, he's already...
He always overdoes it!
Wasn't the guy trying to say something?

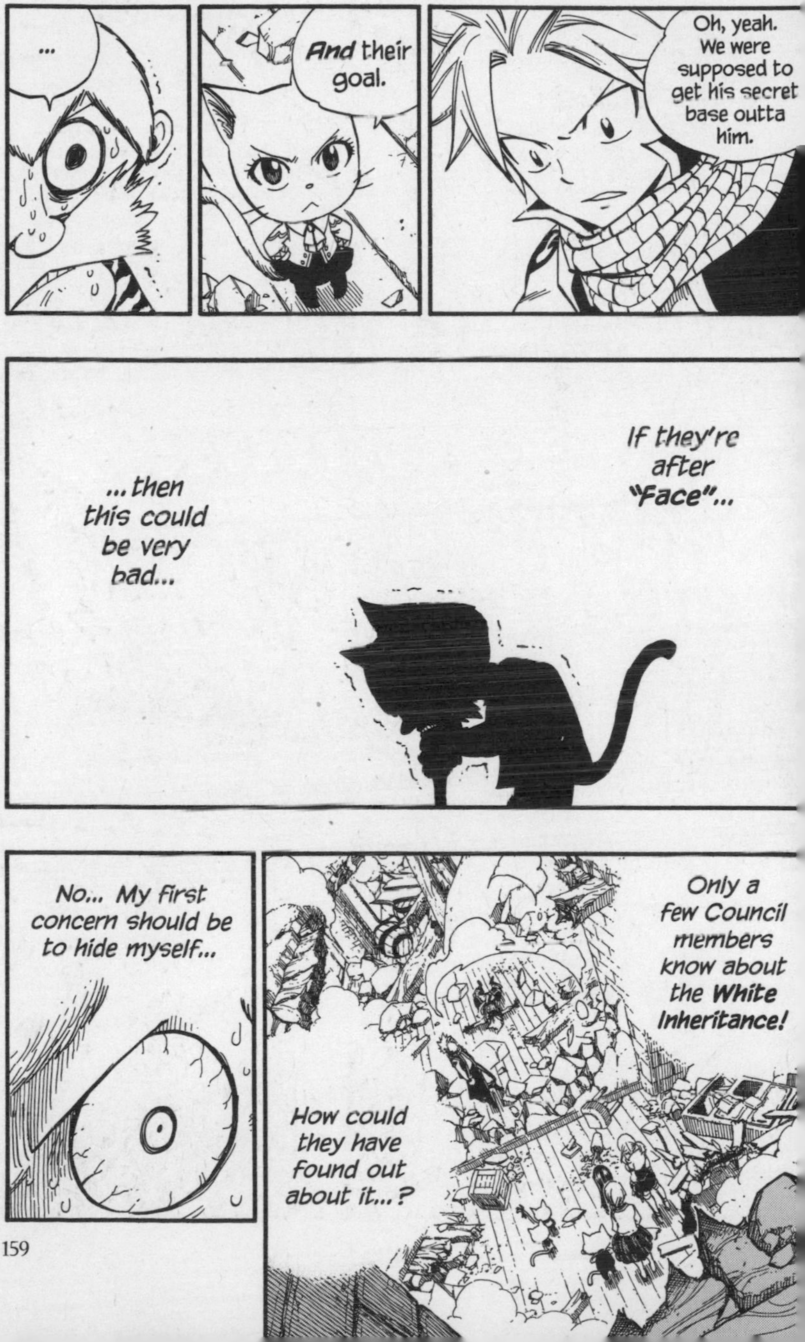

Oh, yeah. We were supposed to get his secret base outta him.
And their goal.
...
If they're after "Face"...
...then this could be very bad...
Only a few Council members know about the White Inheritance!
How could they have found out about it...?
No... My first concern should be to hide myself...

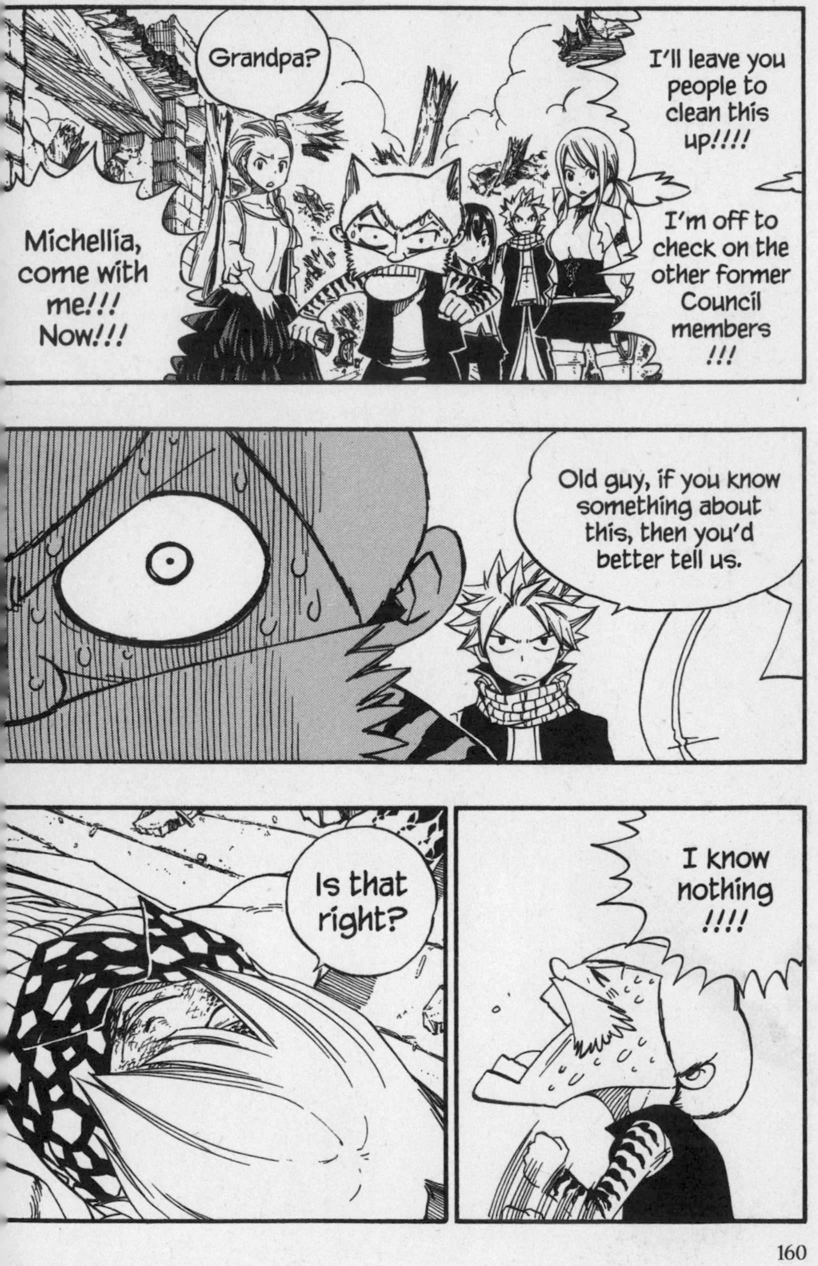
I'll leave you people to clean this up!!!!
Grandpa?
I'm off to check on the other former Council members!!!
Michellia, come with me!!! Now!!!
Old guy, if you know something about this, then you'd better tell us.
I know nothing!!!!
Is that right?

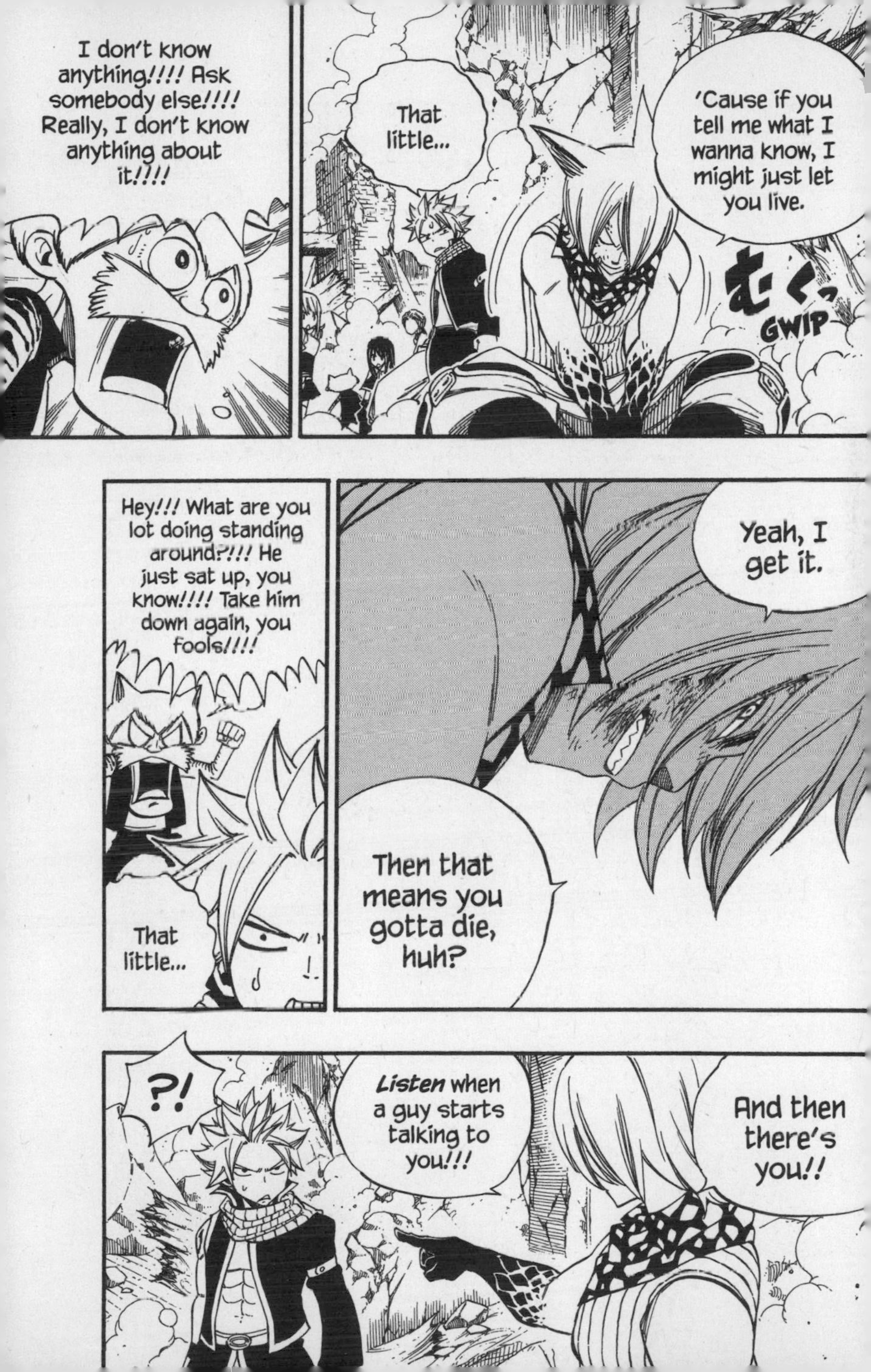
'Cause if you tell me what I wanna know, I might just let you live.
むくっ
GWIP
That little...
I don't know anything!!!! Ask somebody else!!!! Really, I don't know anything about it!!!!
Yeah, I get it.
Then that means you gotta die, huh?
Hey!!! What are you lot doing standing around?!!! He just sat up, you know!!!! Take him down again, you fools!!!!
That little...
And then there's you!!
Listen when a guy starts talking to you!!!
?!

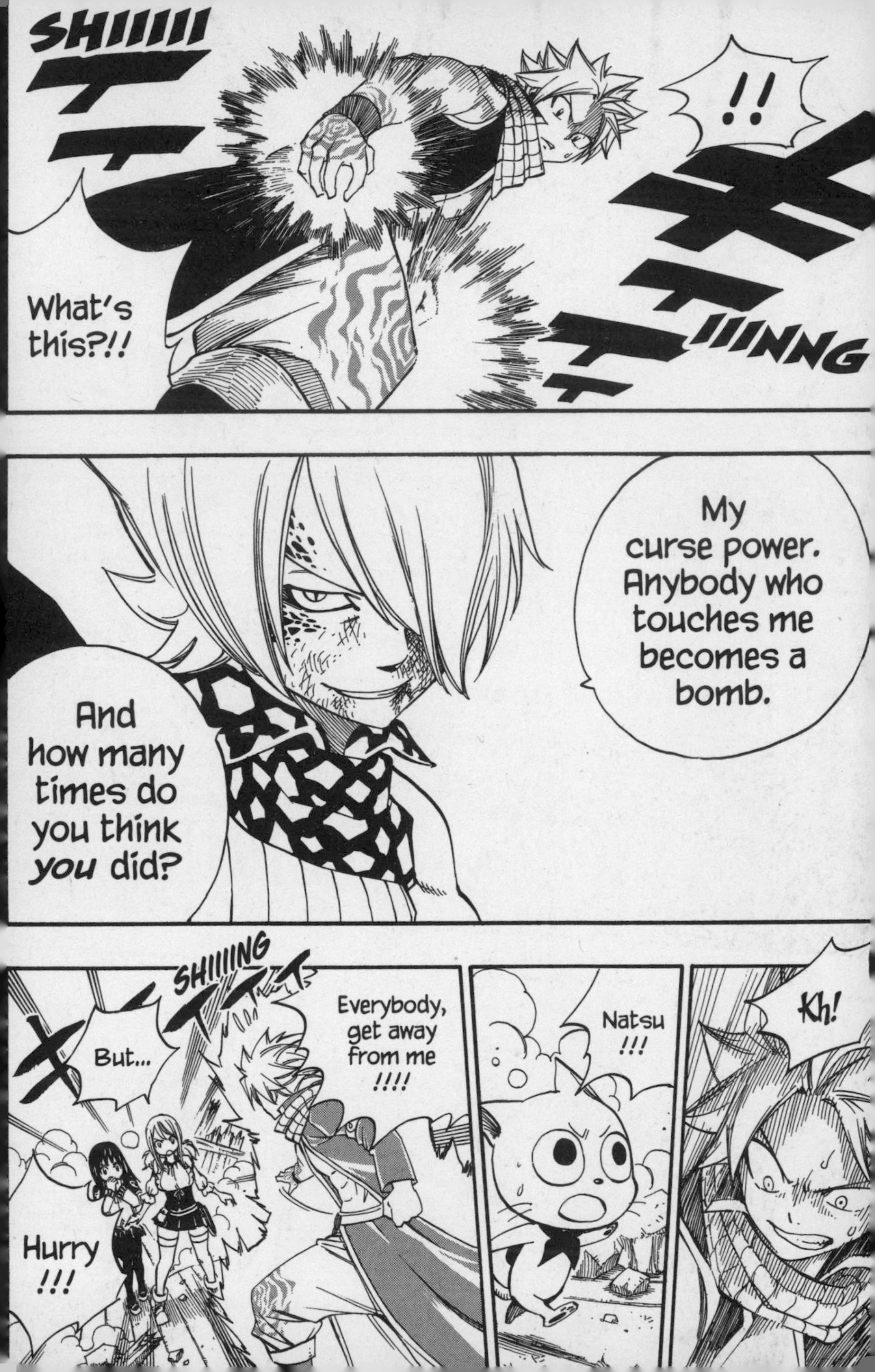
!!
SHIIIII
IIINNG
What's this?!!
My curse power. Anybody who touches me becomes a bomb.
And how many times do you think *you* did?
Kh!
Natsu !!!
Everybody, get away from me !!!!
SHIIIING
But...
Hurry !!!

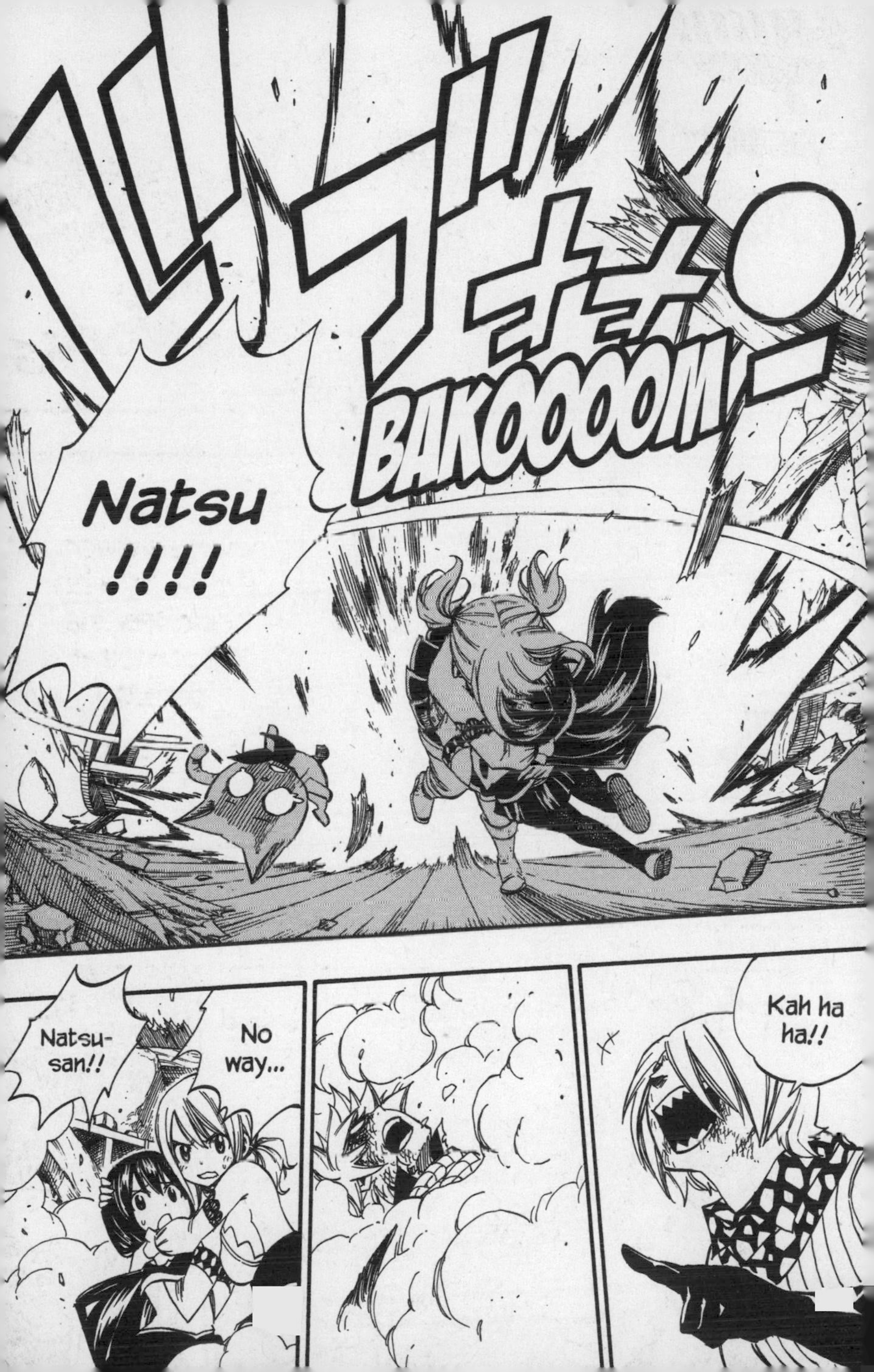
BAKOOOOM
Natsu!!!!
Kah ha ha!!
No way...
Natsu-san!!

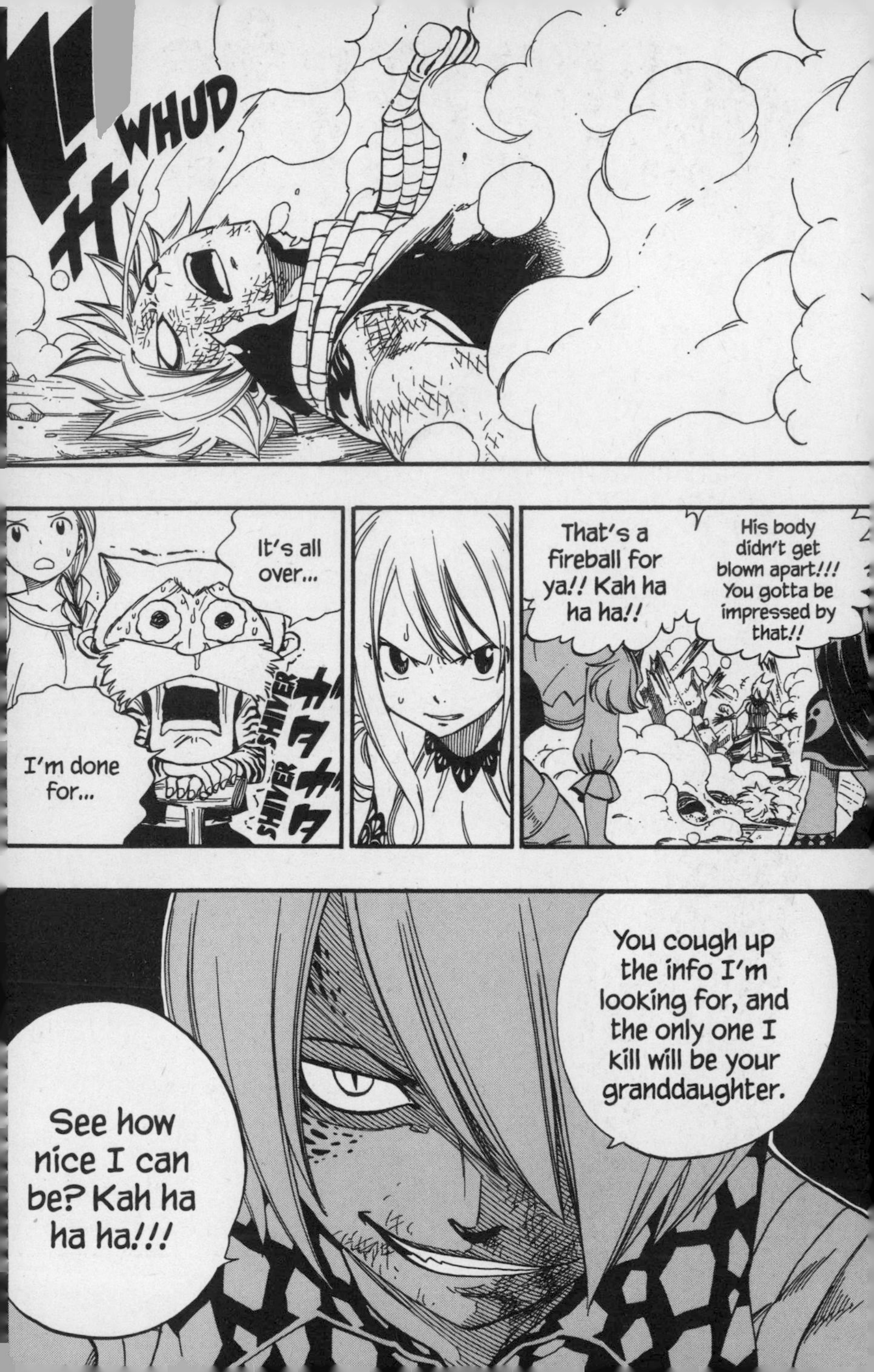
WHUD
His body didn't get blown apart!!! You gotta be impressed by that!!
That's a fireball for ya!! Kah ha ha ha!!
It's all over...
SHIVER SHIVER
I'm done for...
You cough up the info I'm looking for, and the only one I kill will be your granddaughter.
See how nice I can be? Kah ha ha ha!!!

FAIRY TAIL

Chapter 361: Two Bombs

BLUE PEGASUS

Name: Eve Tearm   Age: 23

Magic:
Snow Magic

Likes: Dislikes:
Big-sister-type girls   Bell peppers

Remarks

Before he joined Blue Pegasus, Eve was a member of the Magic Council's forces in the Arrest and Custody Division. At the time, he was considered a child prodigy, but for unknown reasons, he wound up in Blue Pegasus. One explanation attributes it to headhunting by Master Bob.

Once inside the guild, he played the part of everyone's little brother, but as he aged, he began to wonder how long he could keep that character going. Recently, he's been thinking of becoming a brainy type like Hibiki.

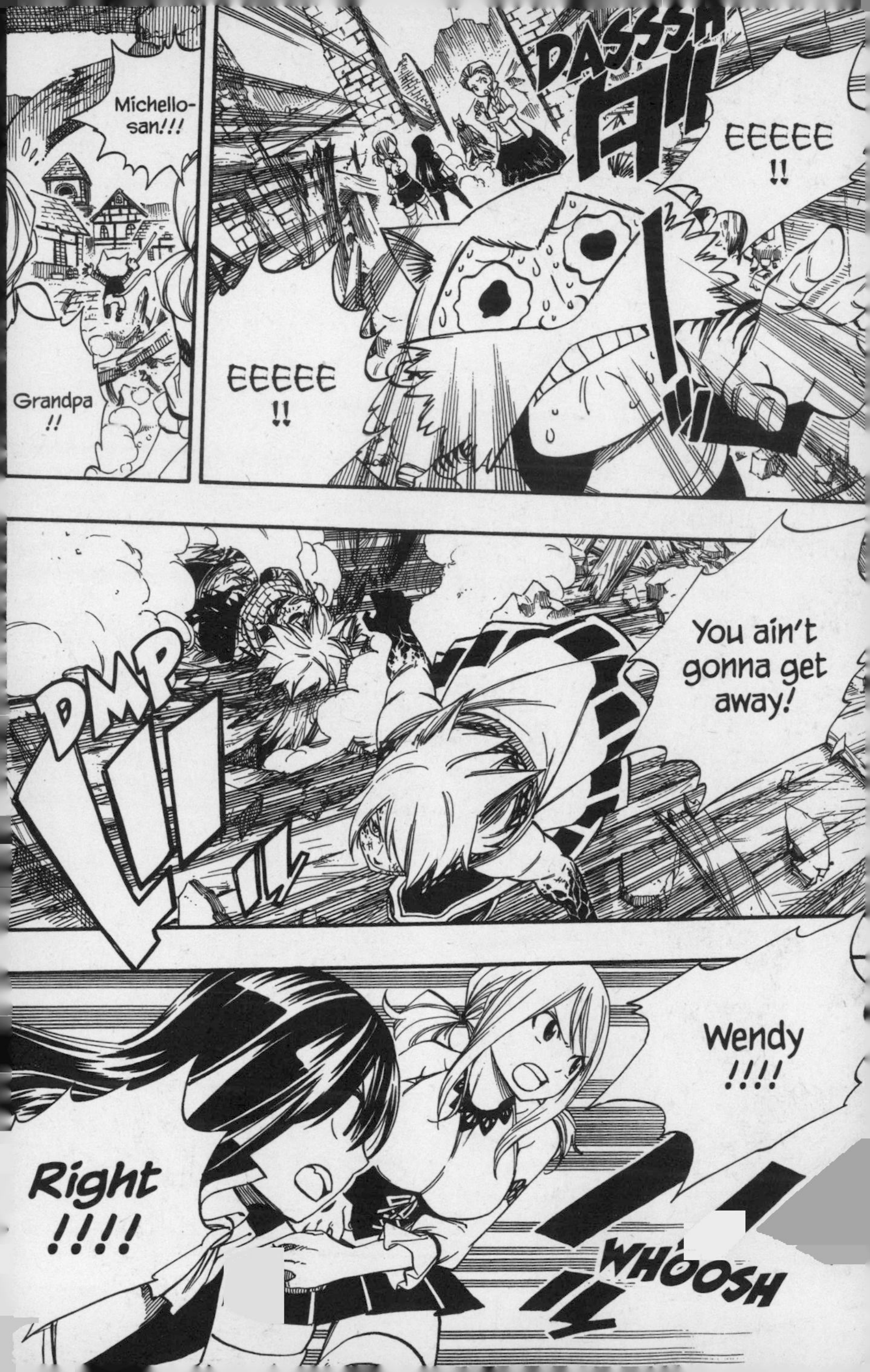
DASSSH
EEEEE !!
EEEEE !!
Michello-san!!!
Grandpa !!
You ain't gonna get away!
DMP
Wendy !!!!
Right !!!!
WHOOSH

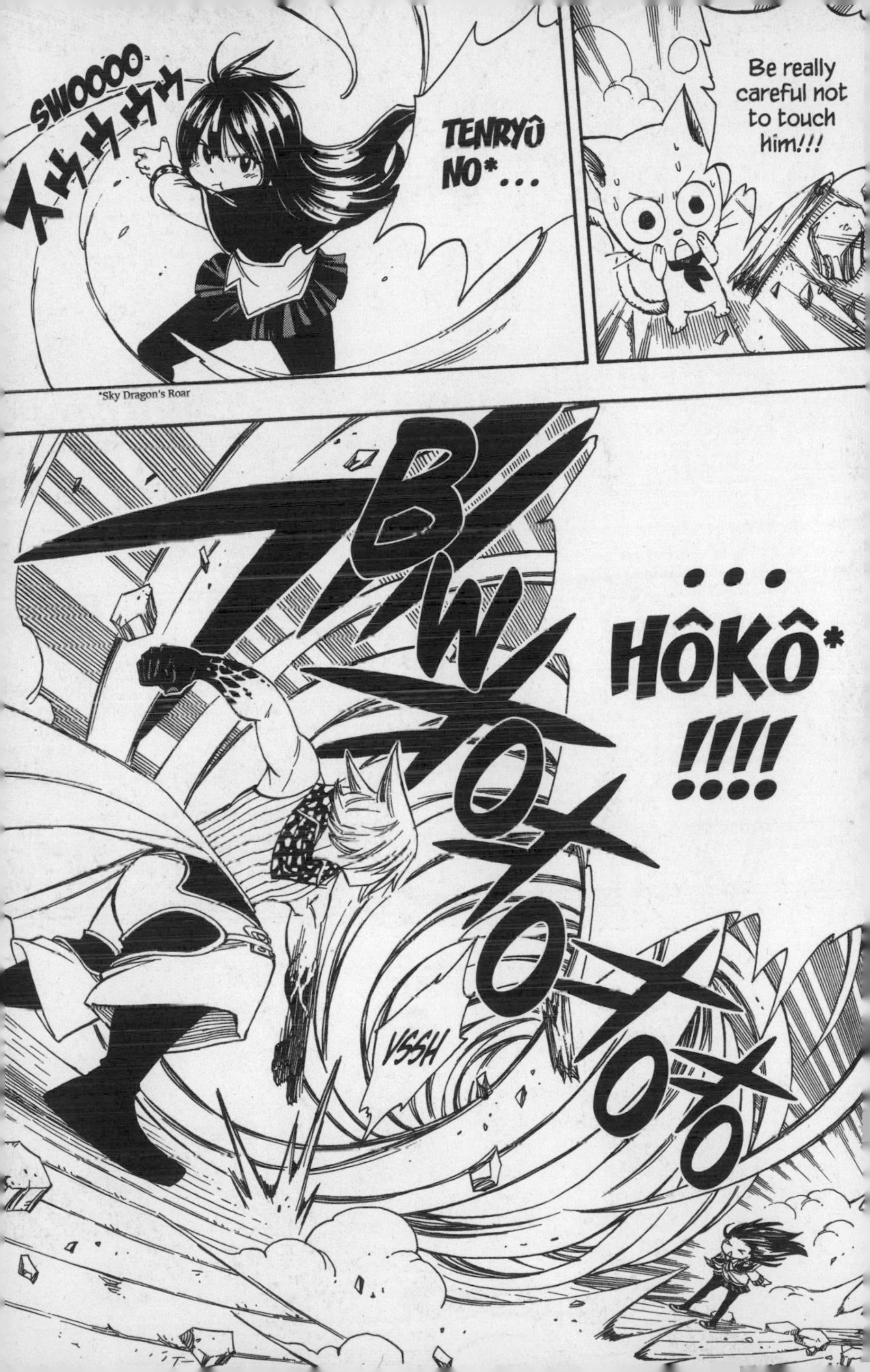
Be really careful not to touch him!!!
SWOOOO
TENRYÔ NO*...
*Sky Dragon's Roar
...HÔKÔ* !!!!
BWOOOOOO
VSSH

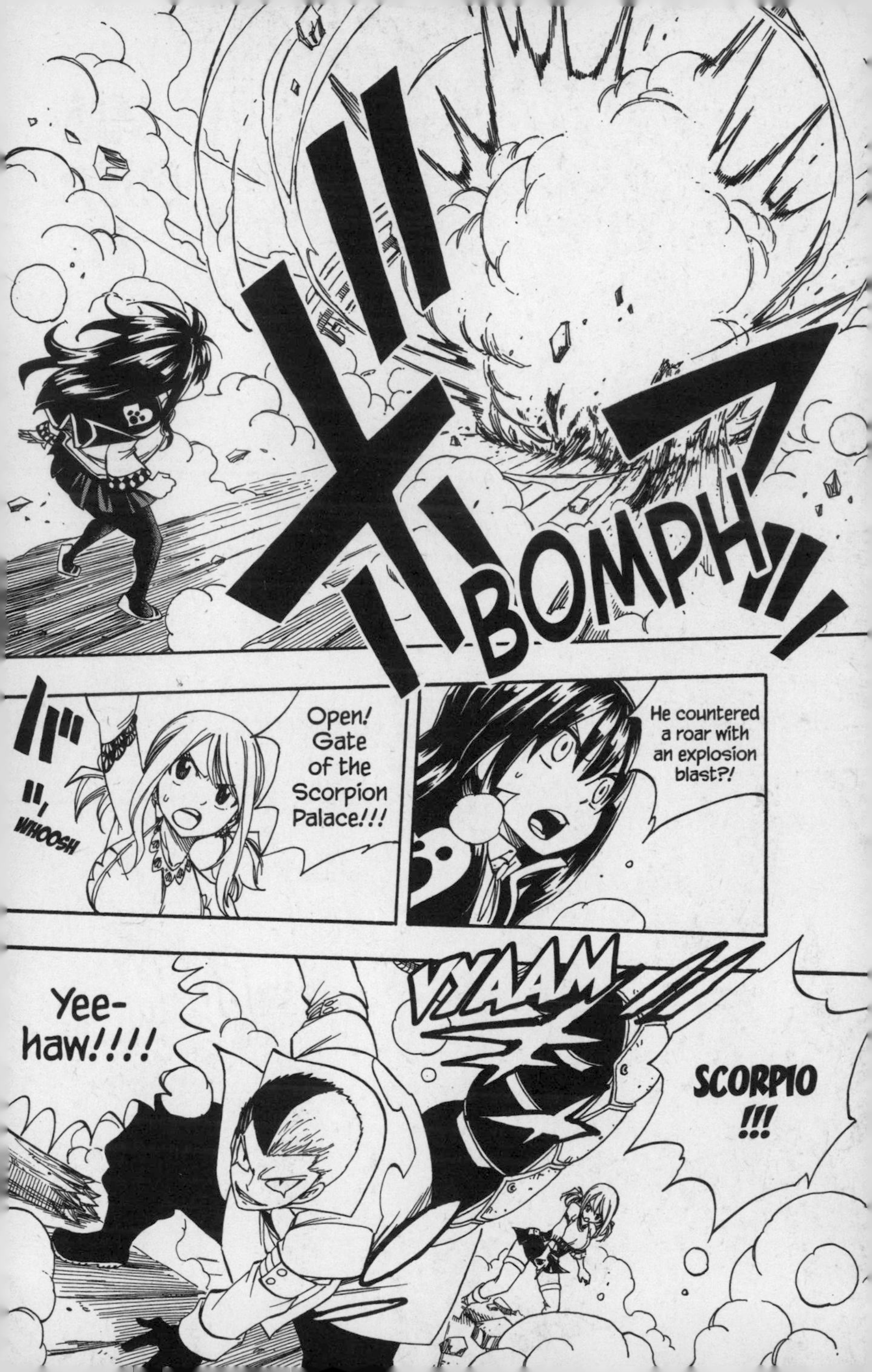
BOMPH
He countered a roar with an explosion blast?!
Open! Gate of the Scorpion Palace!!!
WHOOSH
VYAAM
SCORPIO!!!
Yee-haw!!!!

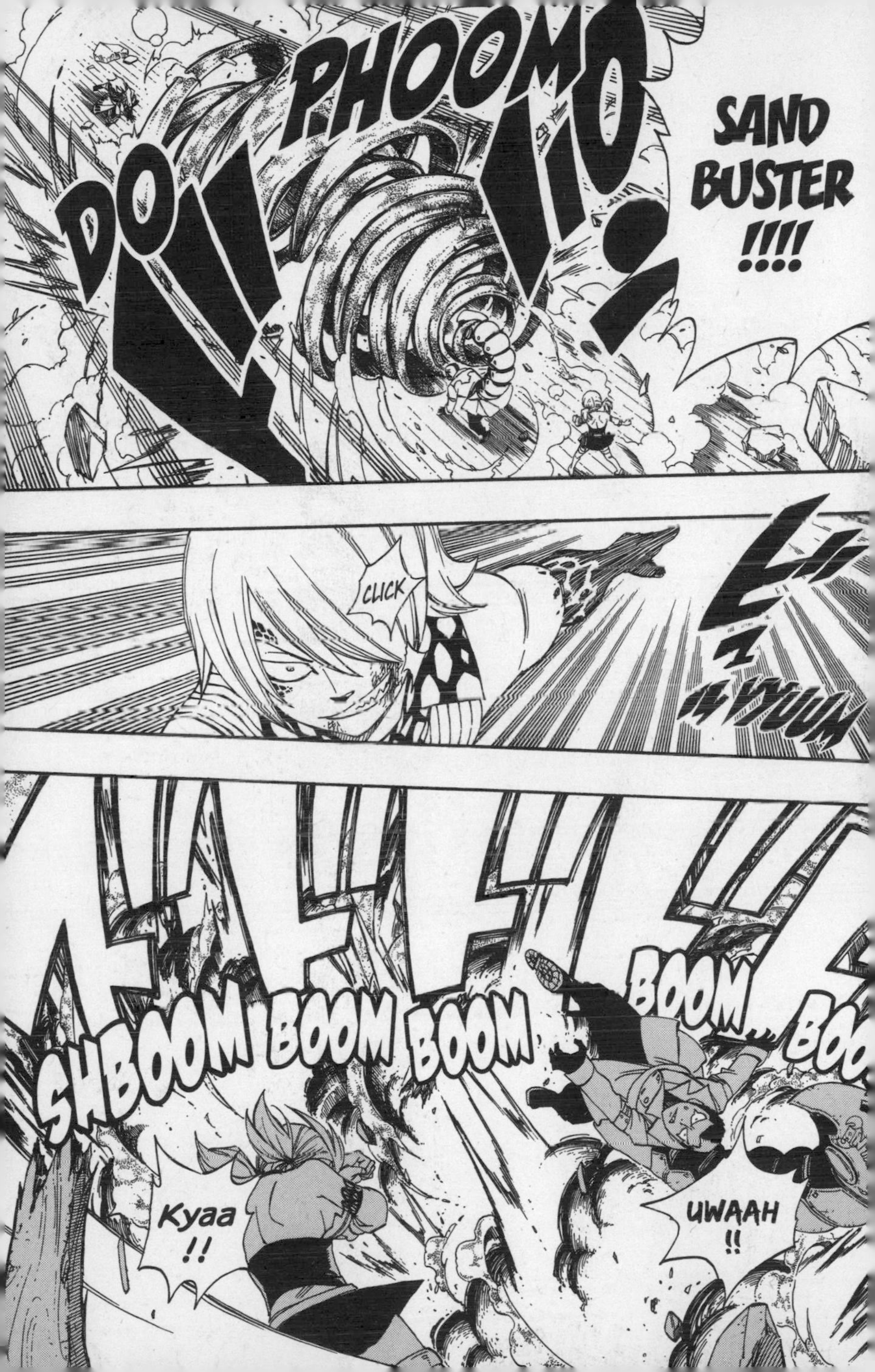
SAND BUSTER !!!!
CLICK
SHBOOM BOOM BOOM
BOOM... BOO
UWAAH !!
Kyaa !!

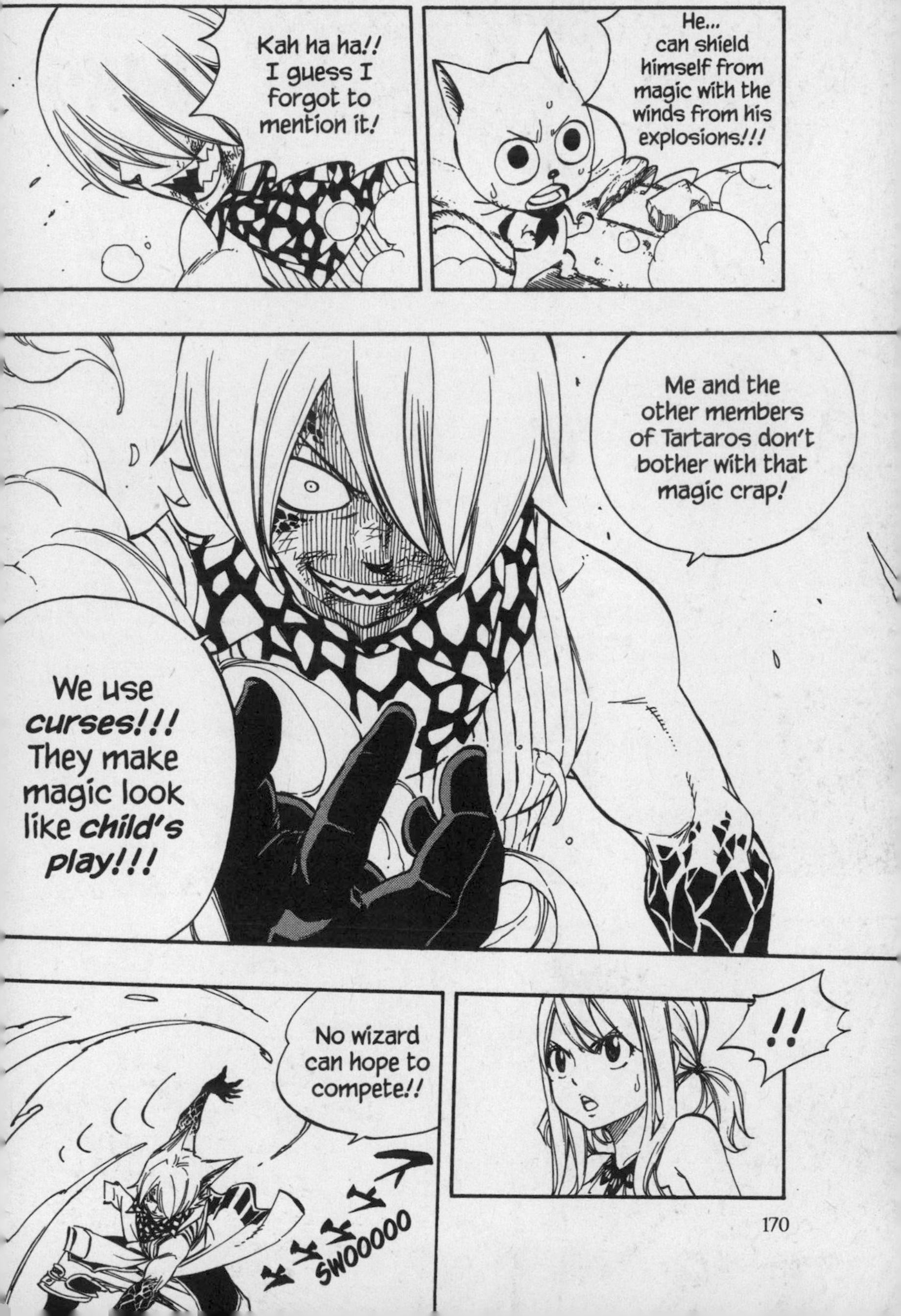
He... can shield himself from magic with the winds from his explosions!!!
Kah ha ha!! I guess I forgot to mention it!
Me and the other members of Tartaros don't bother with that magic crap!
We use *curses!!!* They make magic look like *child's play!!!*
!!
No wizard can hope to compete!!
SWOOOOO

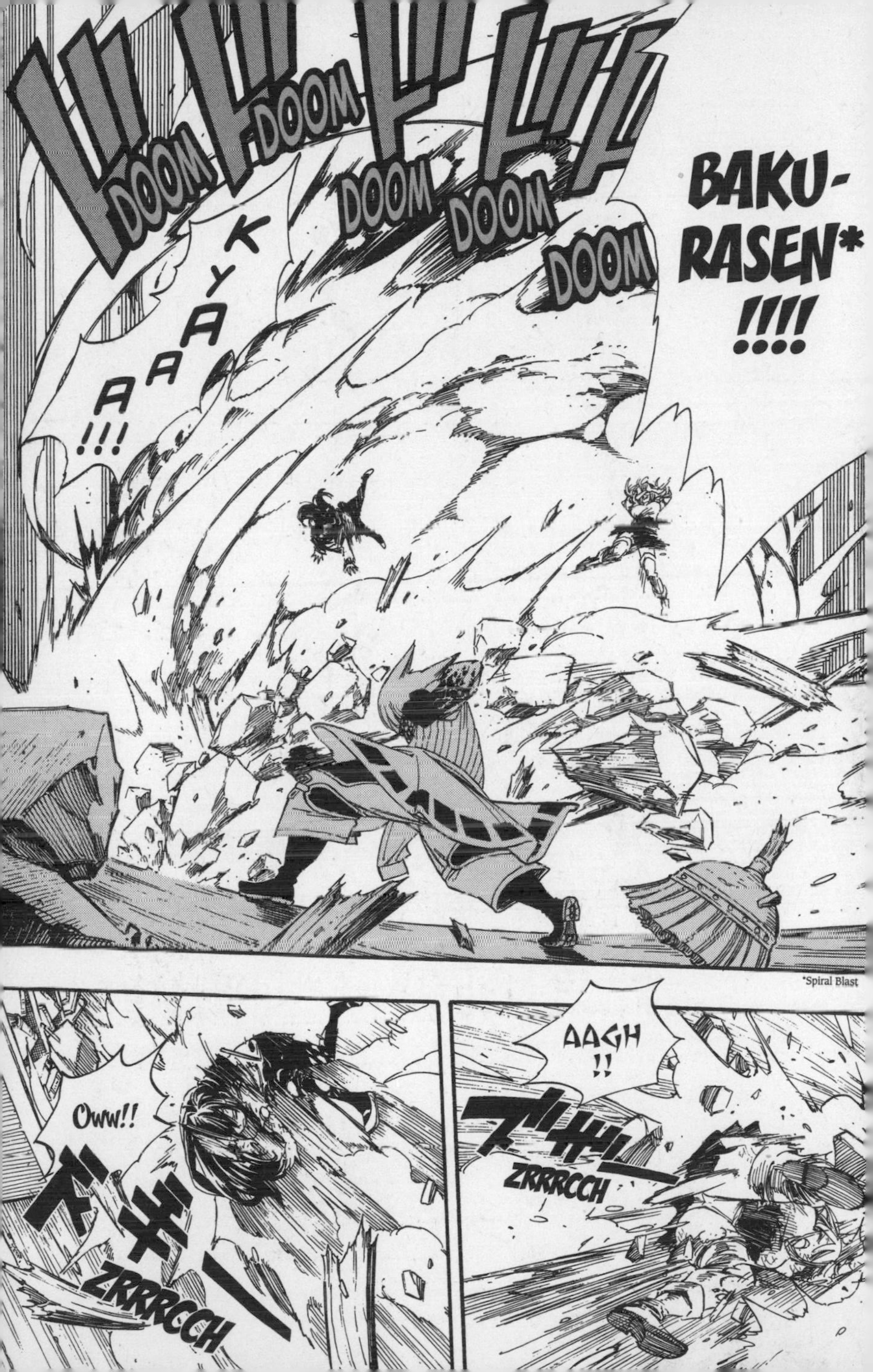
BAKU-RASEN*!!!!
DOOM DOOM DOOM DOOM DOOM
KYAAAA!!!
AAGH!!
ZRRRCCH
Oww!!
ZRRRCCH

*Spiral Blast

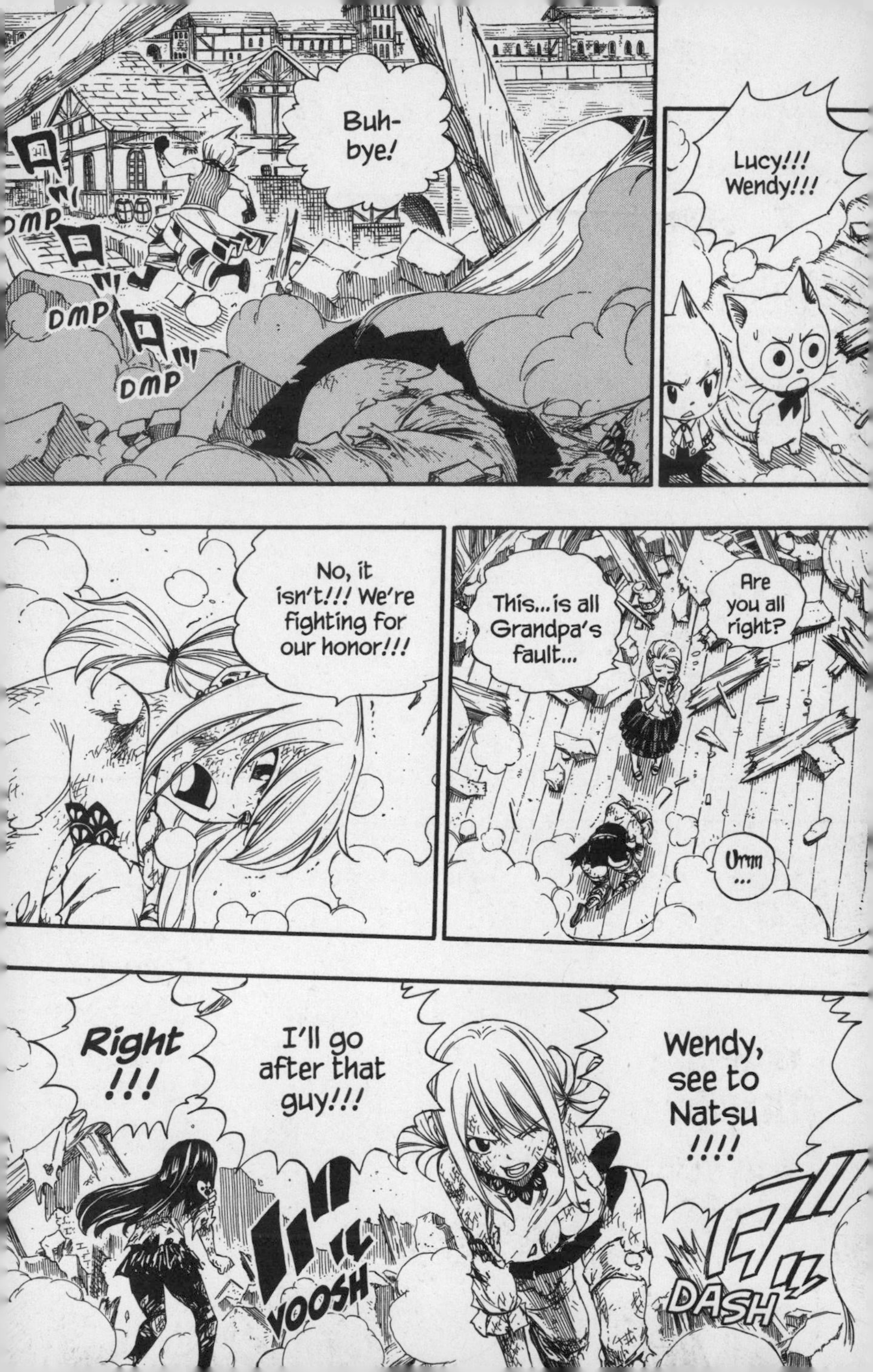
Lucy!!! Wendy!!!
Buh-bye!
DMP
DMP
DMP
Are you all right?
This...is all Grandpa's fault...
Urrn...
No, it isn't!!! We're fighting for our honor!!!
Wendy, see to Natsu!!!!
DASH
I'll go after that guy!!!
Right!!!
VOOSH

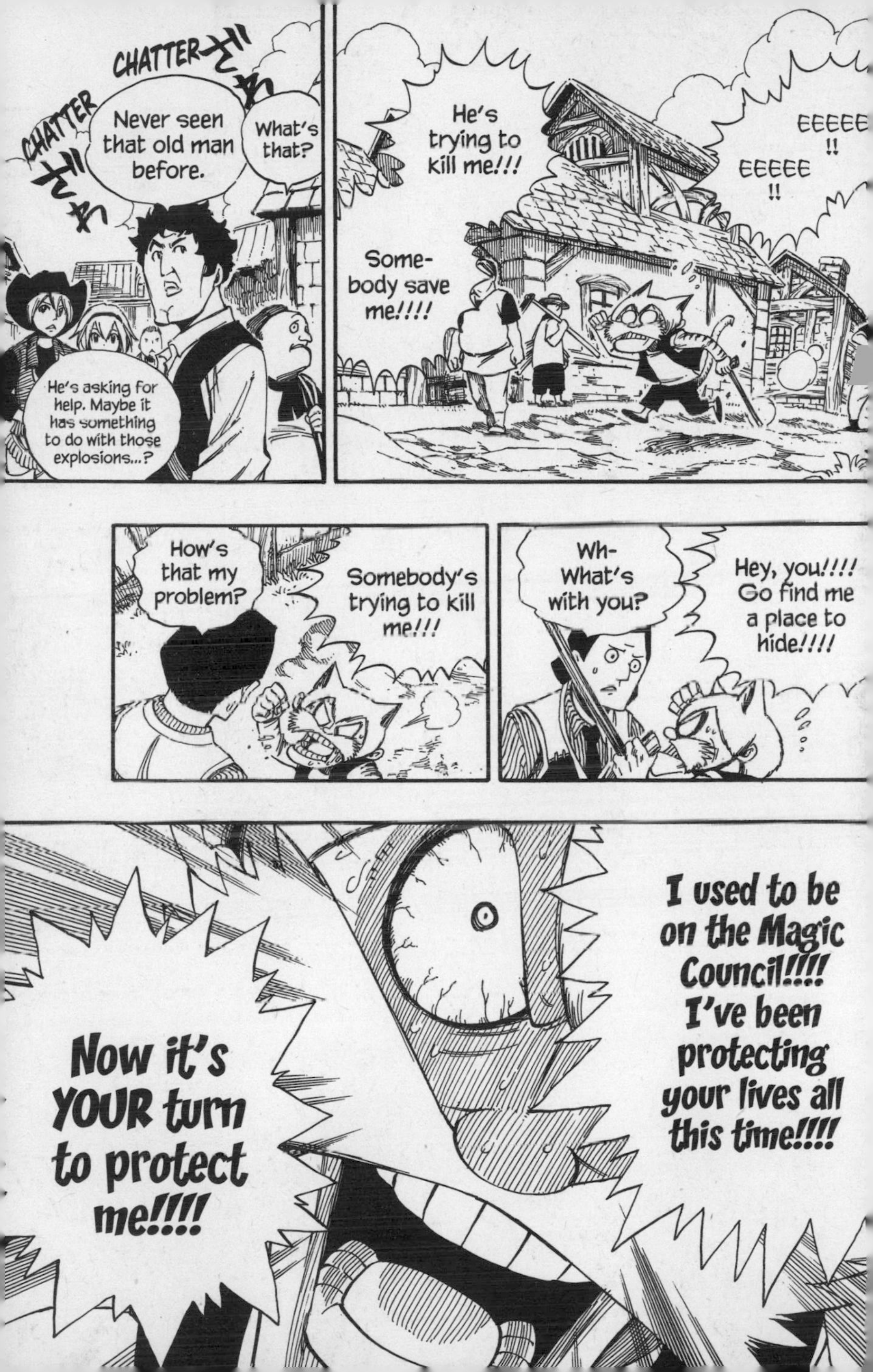
EEEEE!!
EEEEE!!
He's trying to kill me!!!
Some-body save me!!!!
What's that?
CHATTER
CHATTER
Never seen that old man before.
He's asking for help. Maybe it has something to do with those explosions...?
Hey, you!!!! Go find me a place to hide!!!!
Wh- What's with you?
Somebody's trying to kill me!!!
How's that my problem?
I used to be on the Magic Council!!!! I've been protecting your lives all this time!!!!
Now it's YOUR turn to protect me!!!!

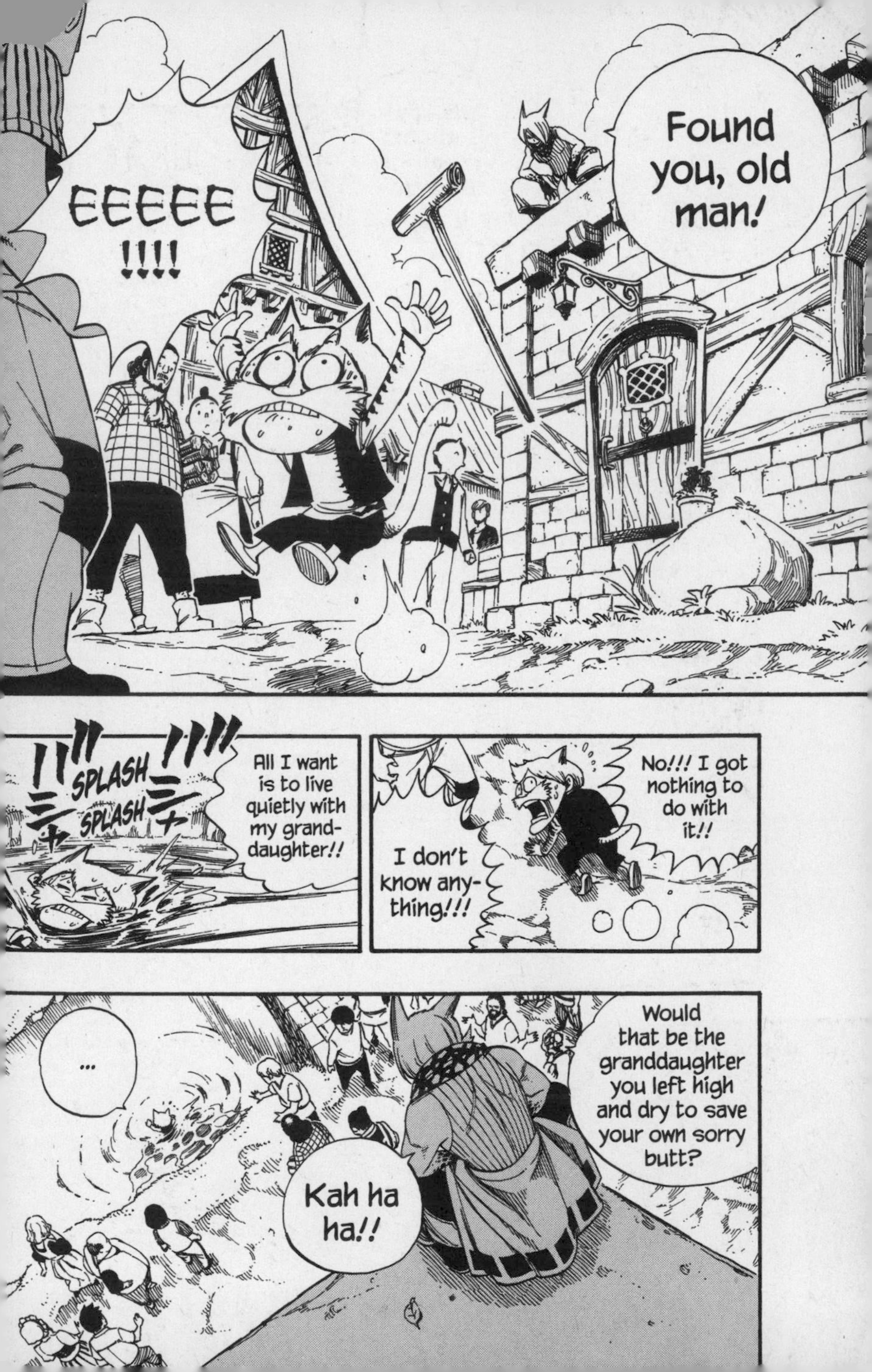

Found you, old man!
EEEEEE !!!!
No!!! I got nothing to do with it!!
I don't know any-thing!!!
All I want is to live quietly with my grand-daughter!!
SPLASH
SPLASH
Would that be the granddaughter you left high and dry to save your own sorry butt?
Kah ha ha!!
...

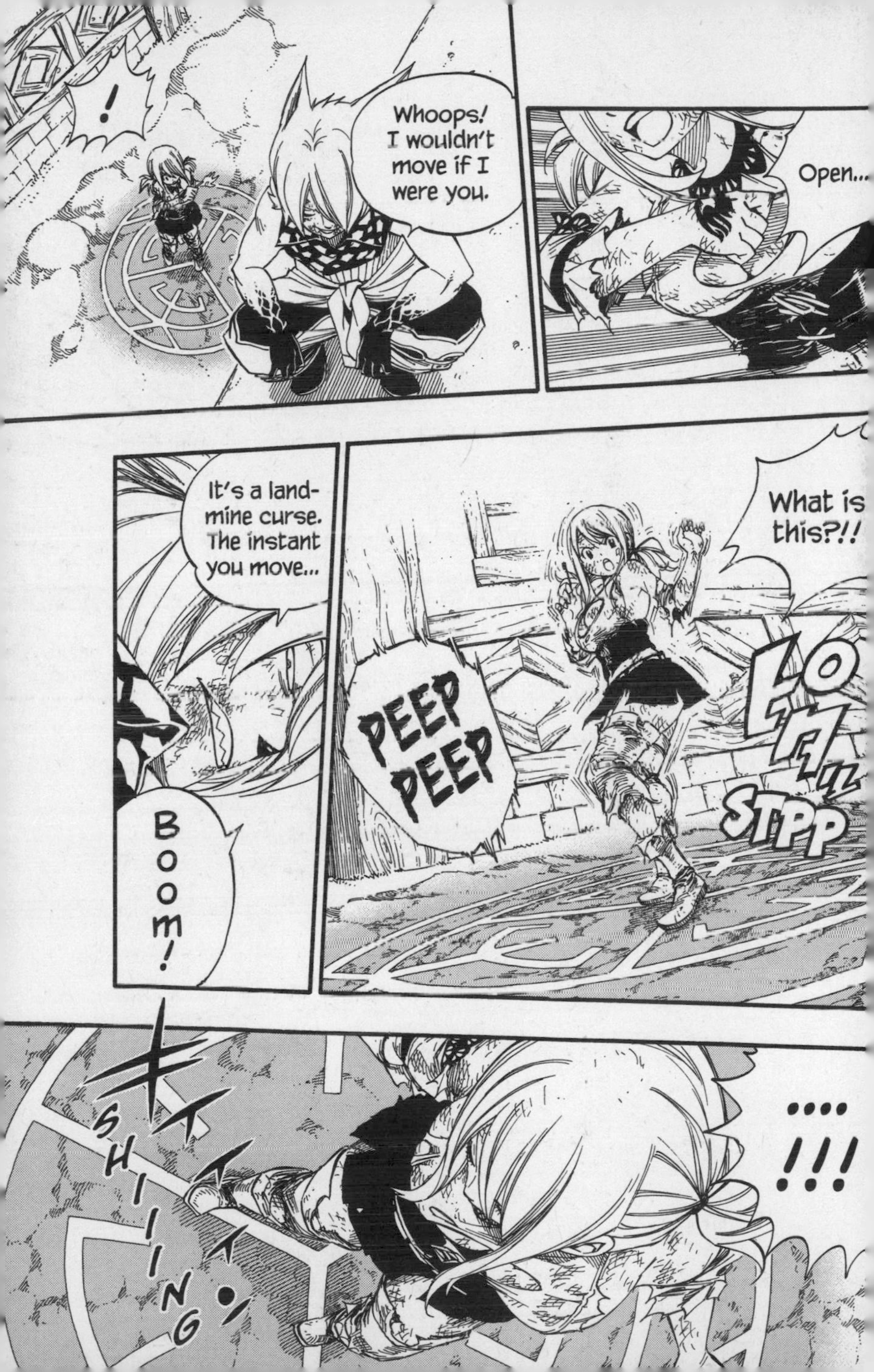
Open...
!
Whoops! I wouldn't move if I were you.
What is this?!!
STPP
PEEP PEEP
It's a land-mine curse. The instant you move...
Boom!
....
!!!
SHIIING

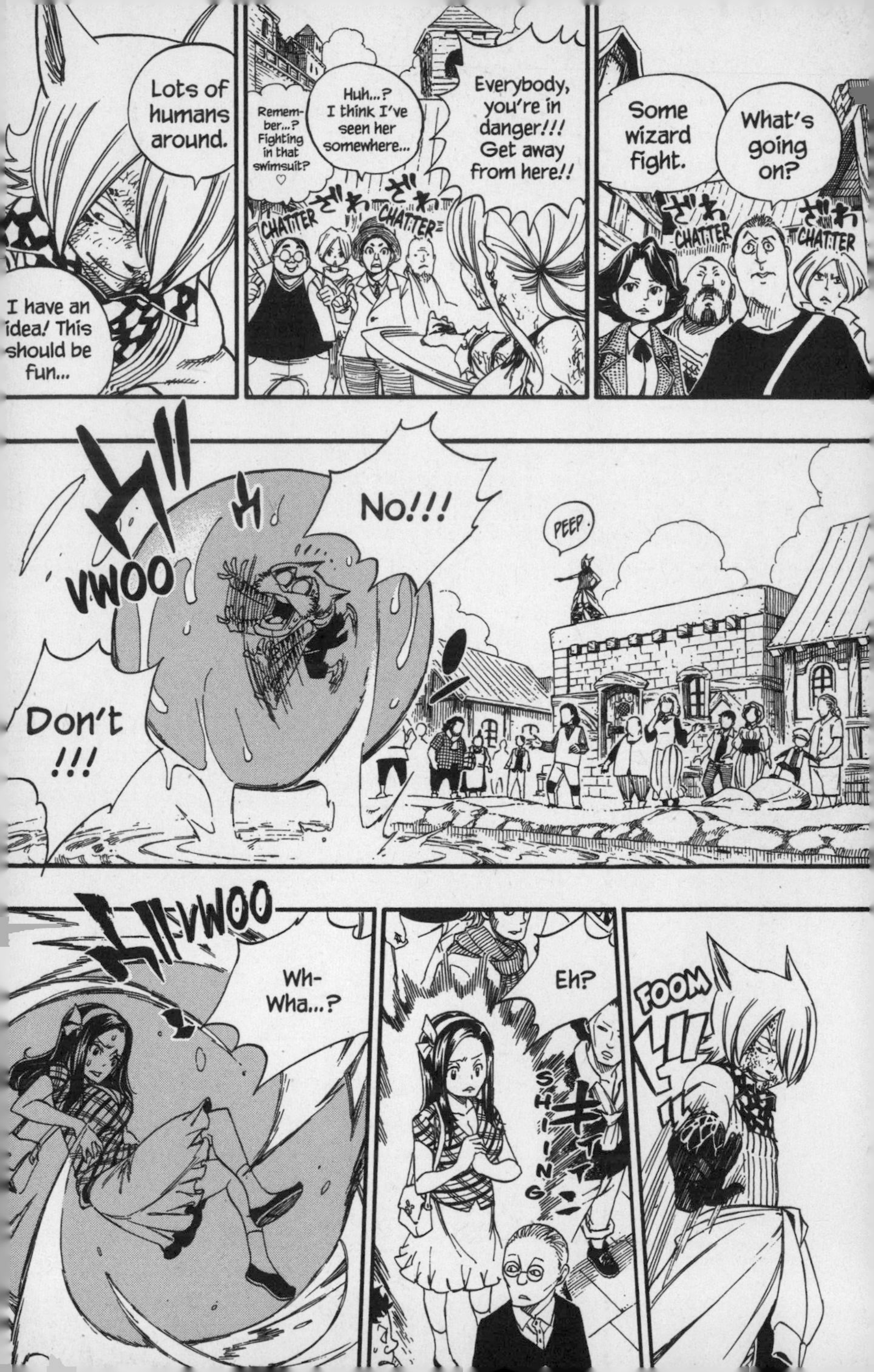
What's going on?
Some wizard fight.
ざわ CHATTER
ざわ CHATTER
Everybody, you're in danger!!! Get away from here!!
Huh...? I think I've seen her somewhere...
Remember...? Fighting in that swimsuit? ♡
ざわ CHATTER
ざわ CHATTER
Lots of humans around.
I have an idea! This should be fun...
PEEP.
No!!!
VWOO
Don't !!!
FOOM
Eh?
SHIIING
VWOO
Wh- Wha...?

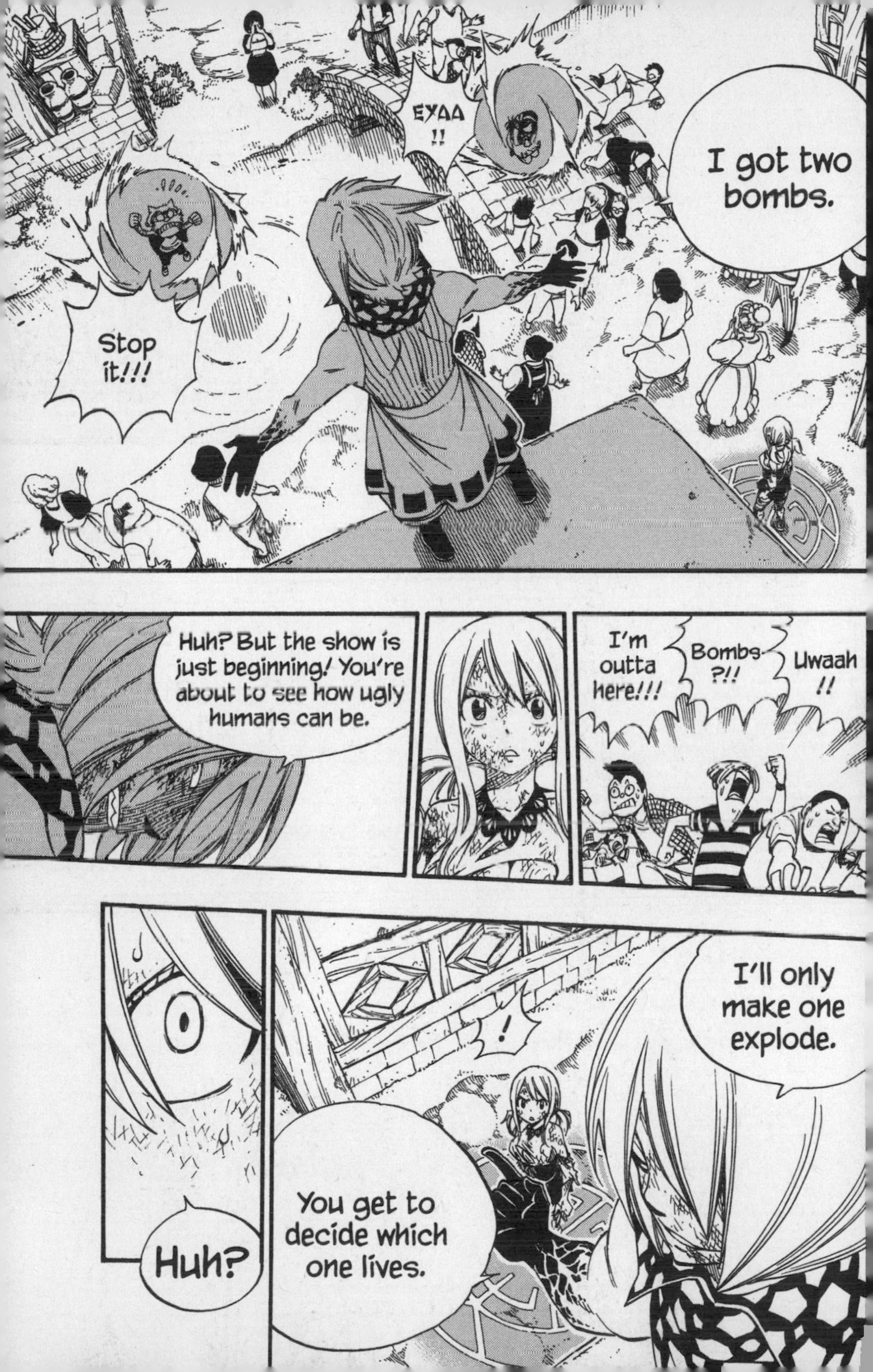

I got two bombs.
EYAA !!
Stop it!!!
Uwaah !!
Bombs ?!!
I'm outta here!!!
Huh? But the show is just beginning! You're about to see how ugly humans can be.
I'll only make one explode.
!
You get to decide which one lives.
Huh?

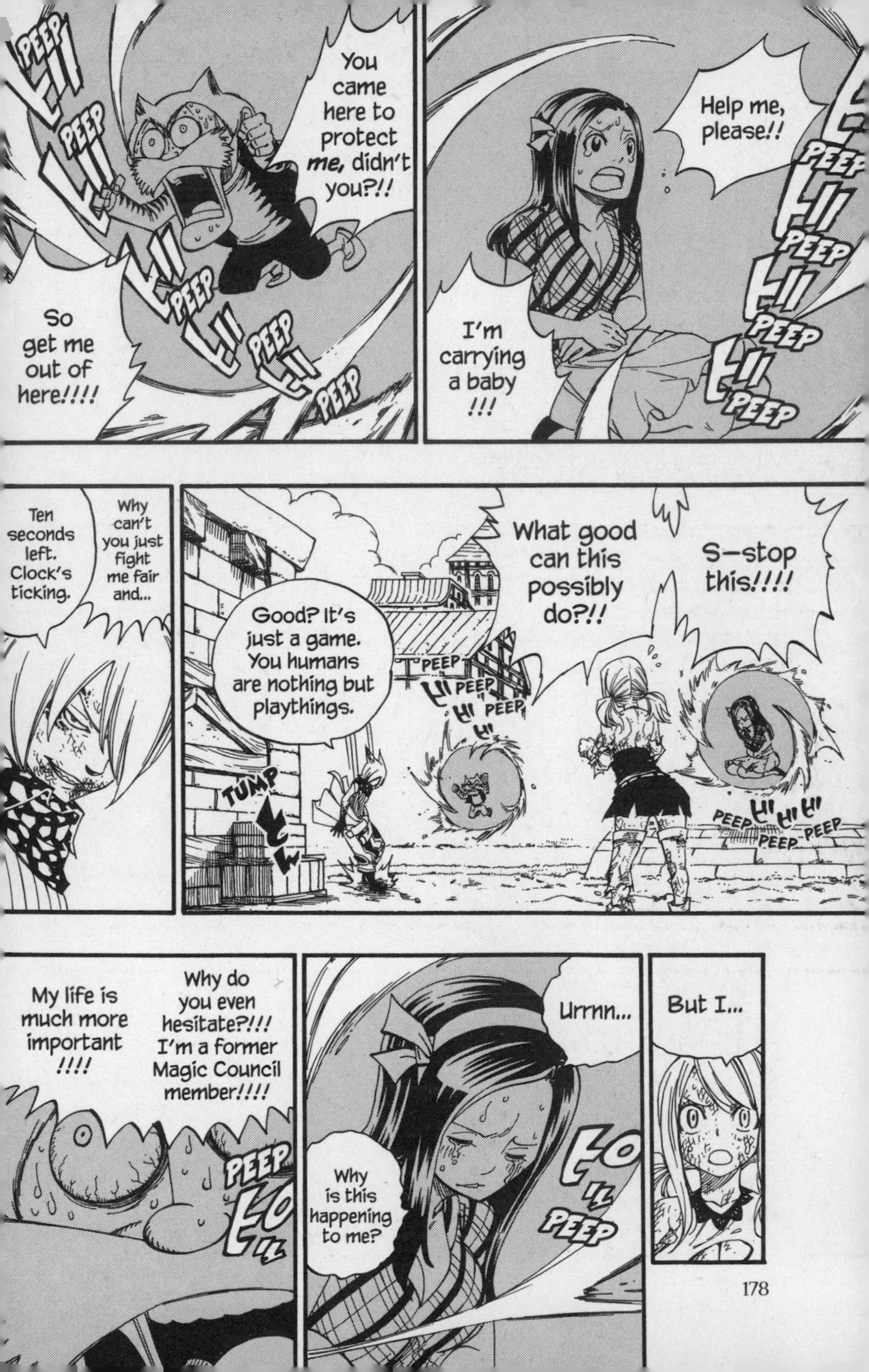
Help me, please!!
PEEP
PEEP
PEEP
PEEP
I'm carrying a baby!!!
You came here to protect *me,* didn't you?!!
PEEP
PEEP
PEEP
PEEP
PEEP
So get me out of here!!!!
S—stop this!!!!
What good can this possibly do?!!
Good? It's just a game. You humans are nothing but playthings.
PEEP
PEEP
PEEP
TUMP
PEEP
PEEP
PEEP
Why can't you just fight me fair and...
Ten seconds left. Clock's ticking.
But I...
Urrnn...
PEEP
Why is this happening to me?
Why do you even hesitate?!!! I'm a former Magic Council member!!!!
My life is much more important!!!!
PEEP

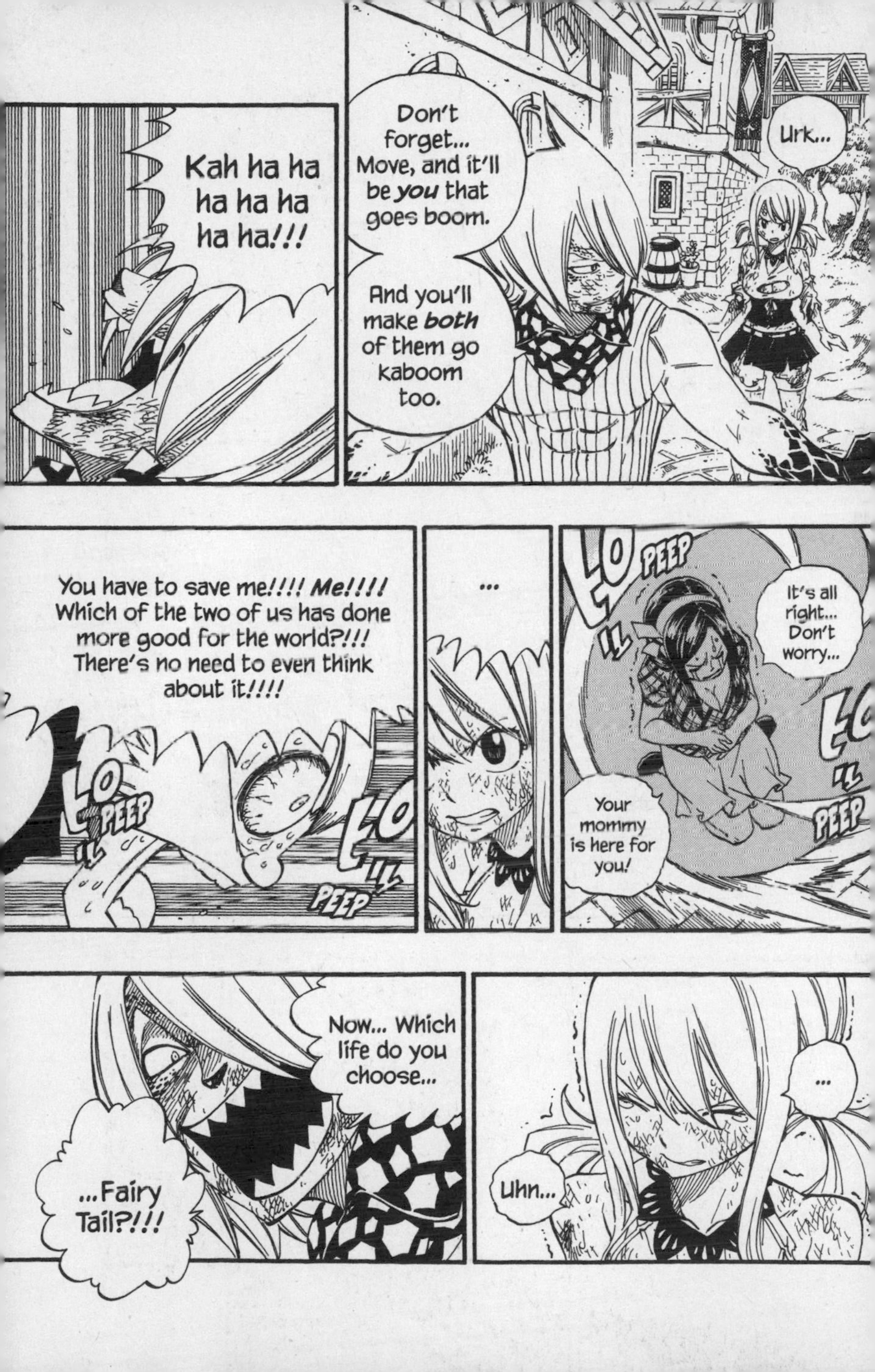
Urk...
Don't forget... Move, and it'll be *you* that goes boom.
And you'll make *both* of them go kaboom too.
Kah ha ha ha ha ha ha ha!!!
PEEP
It's all right... Don't worry...
PEEP
Your mommy is here for you!
...
You have to save me!!!! *Me!!!!* Which of the two of us has done more good for the world?!!! There's no need to even think about it!!!!
PEEP
PEEP
...
Uhn...
Now... Which life do you choose...
...Fairy Tail?!!!

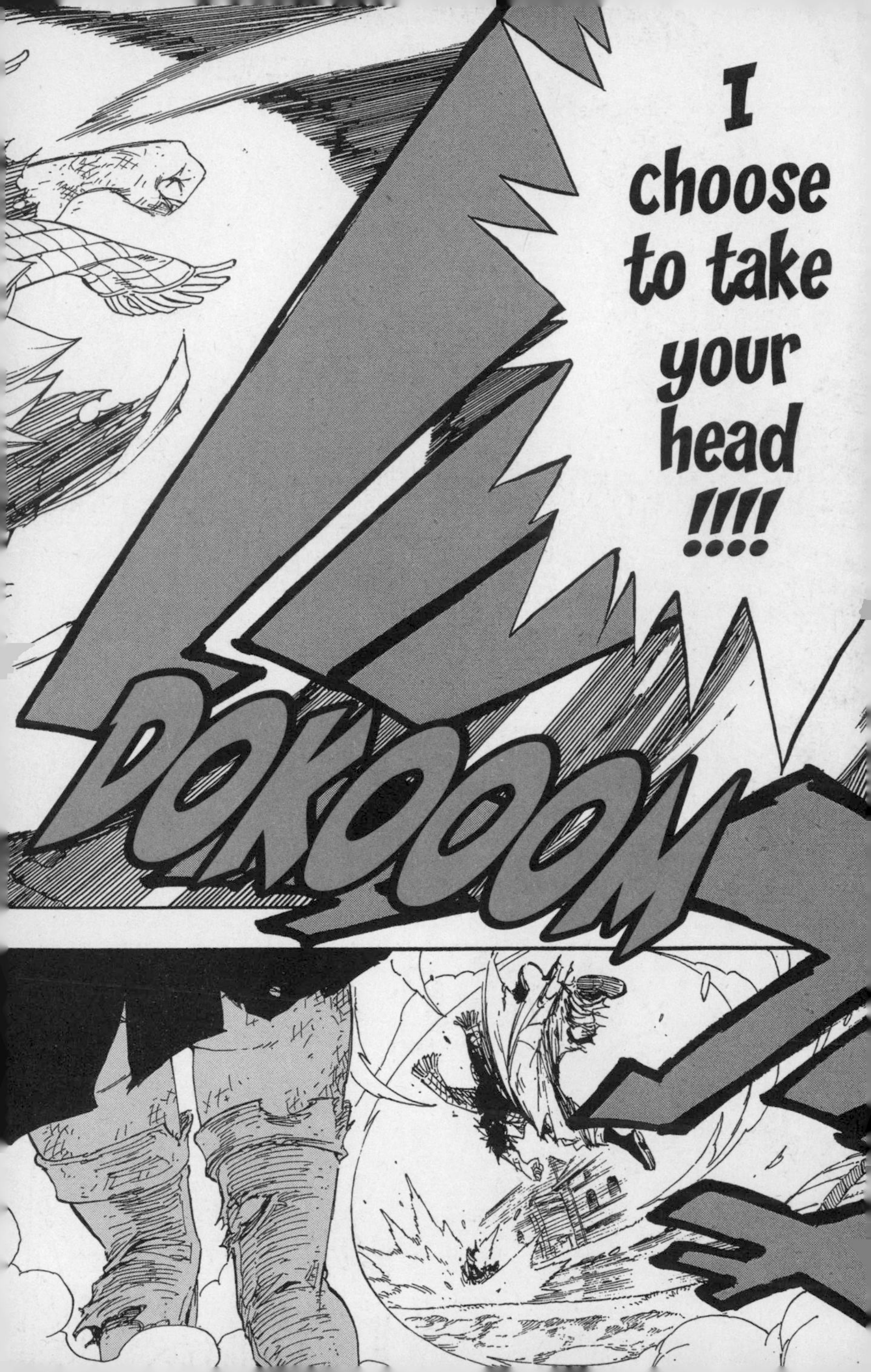
I choose to take your head!!!!
DOKOOOOM

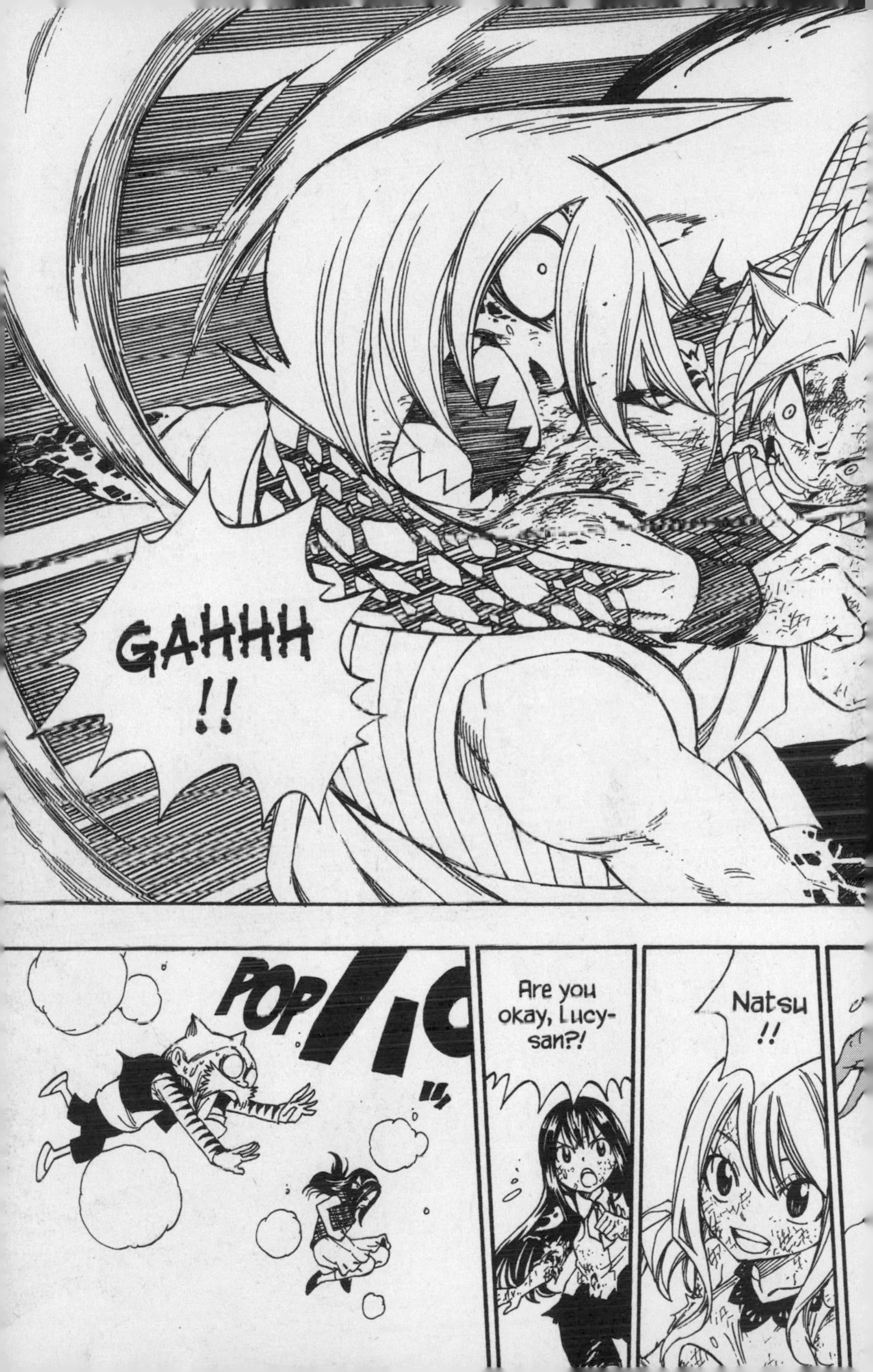
GAHHH !!
Natsu !!
Are you okay, Lucy-san?!
POP

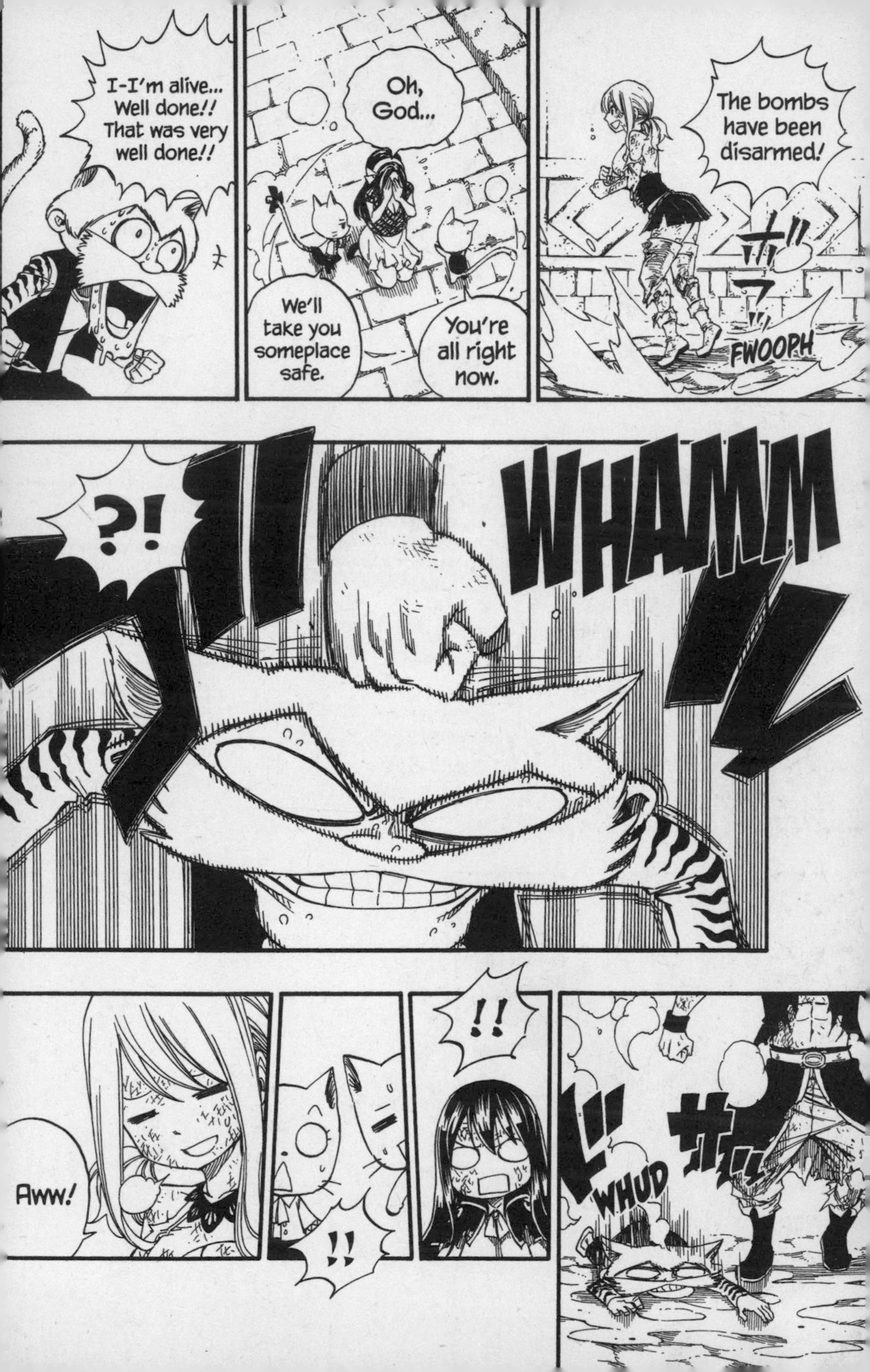
The bombs have been disarmed!
FWOOPH
Oh, God...
You're all right now.
We'll take you someplace safe.
I-I'm alive... Well done!! That was very well done!!
WHAMM
?!
WHUD
!!
!!
Aww!

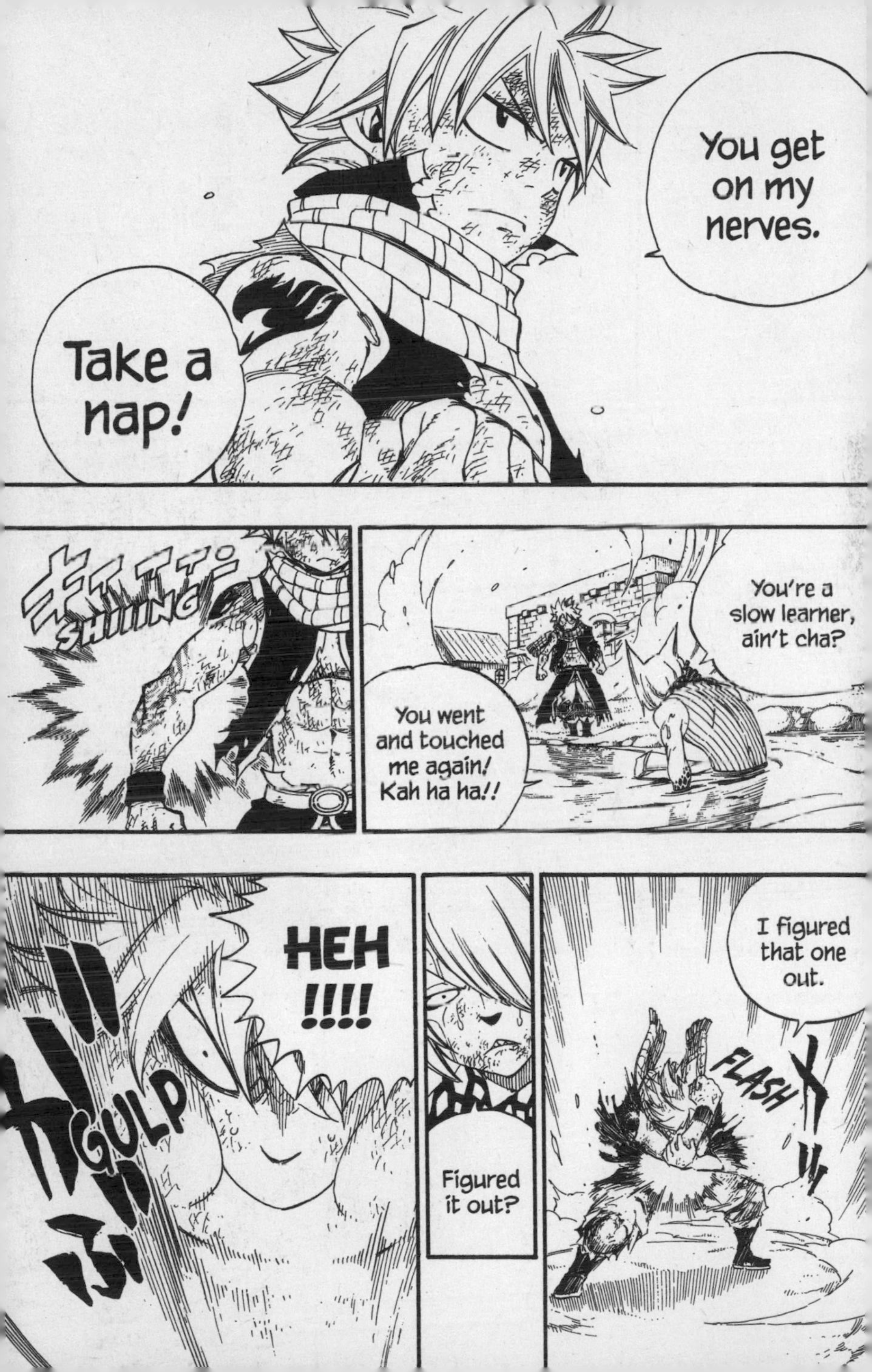
You get on my nerves.
Take a nap!
You're a slow learner, ain't cha?
You went and touched me again! Kah ha ha!!
SHIIING
I figured that one out.
FLASH
Figured it out?
HEH !!!!
GULP

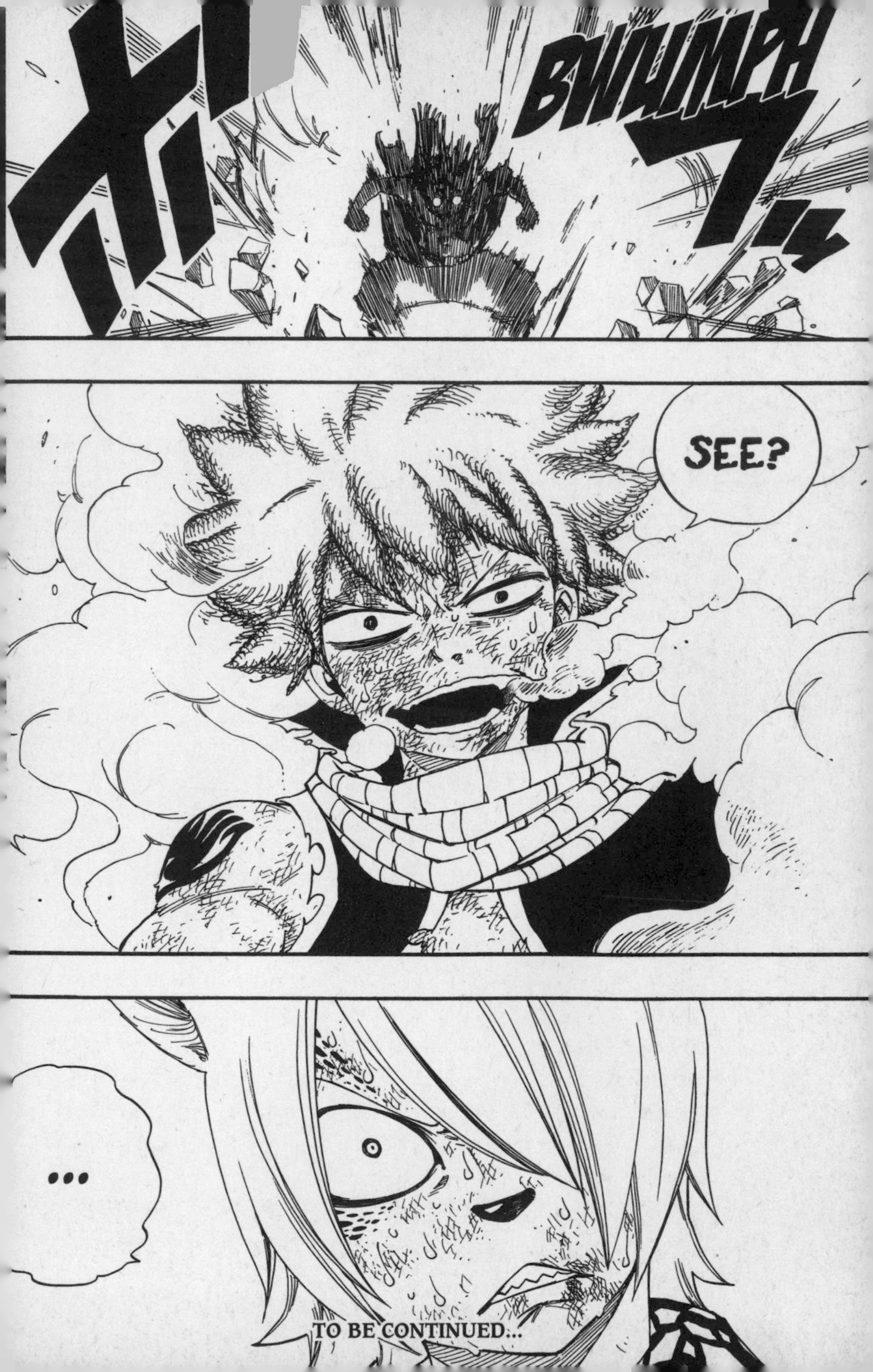
BWUMPH
SEE?
...
TO BE CONTINUED...

あとがき

Afterword

Now we've plunged into the Tartaros arc. For this, I changed up my methods a bit and am making a 6-7 chapter short arcs. And calling each of the small sections "prologue," "part 1," "part 2," and so on. That's how I'm thinking of going. And to tell the truth, I know how many parts this is supposed to run, but I'm going to keep it a secret because it'd be really embarrassing if the schedule got off-track. (Ha ha!)

On a different subject, there are going to be a lot of new characters appearing in this arc. I don't have much time, and some of them have complicated designs, but I have to say, I'm really enjoying the character of Kyôka. In the near future, she's going to be doing a bunch of cruel things.

One of the delights of a battle manga is imagining what would happen if this villain character faced off against that character from the hero's group. The same holds true for the author, since it's really cool setting up simulations in my mind when pitting one character against another to see if it's interesting. And then there are characters who are created especially to fight a battle against a specific character. In this case, that'd have to be Silver. When that person battles the person they're set up for, you can be sure there will be a few hot plot twists. This arc will clear up a large mystery that's been running through this entire series! It'd make me really happy if you'd read it all the way to its conclusion!

Continued from the left-hand page. ↓

Mira: I think the two of them have something within them that transcends words or existence.

Lucy: I see... In other words, they can sort of communicate from consciousness to consciousness?

Mira: Let us give it a try, huh?

 : Ow!

Mira: Lucy, I sense you're in pain.

 : That's because I just said, "Ow!"

Mira: Okay, next question.

> *Minerva wears striped panties, huh? That's cute.*

Wh...

When did that happen ?!!

Lucy: Hey, that isn't a question!!!

Mira: Mine are all lacey! ♥

 : You don't have to go announcing it!!!

 : And Lucy, you like to go au naturel under there, right?

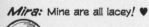 **:** I wear underwear!!!!

> *What is Duun?*

DUUN!

Lucy: How should I know?!!!

Mira: Hey, we have to answer this properly before the question corner is over!

Lucy: But there's no meaning to "Duun!" I mean, it's just, "Duun!"

Mira: Perhaps not. But even if, "Duun," has no meaning, "Superduun," has a meaning, right?

 : Huh?

 : Superduun is at least twice what Duun is.

Lucy: ...

Mira: It's a very super "duun."

Lucy: Um...

Mira: If I say it this way, it has a lot of meaning:

SUPERBEEN!

 : WHERE DID DUUN GO?!!!

Mira: I think that wraps things up with a duun!

Lucy: And in the end, *I'm* still the one complaining about what you say.

 : Yeah. What's that about?

Lucy: Okay... Now I'm exhausted...

EMERGENCY REQUEST! EXPLAIN THE MYSTERIES OF F.T.

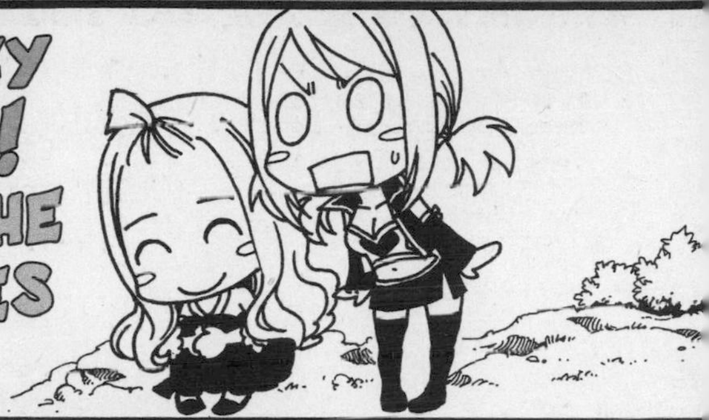

At the Fairy Tail counter...

Lucy: Hey, everybody!! Hi there!!

Mira: What's that about?!

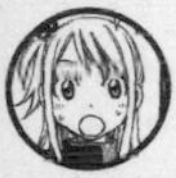: Huh?

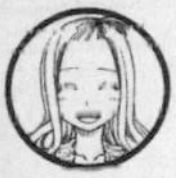: You know... You're always complaining about the first thing I say, so I thought it'd be cool to reverse that.♥

Lucy: But...I didn't say anything weird.

Mira: What's that about?!

Lucy: I get the feeling this time is going to wear me out.

Mira: First question.

If Zeref can't see or hear Mavis in Vol. 40, then how can they have a conversation?

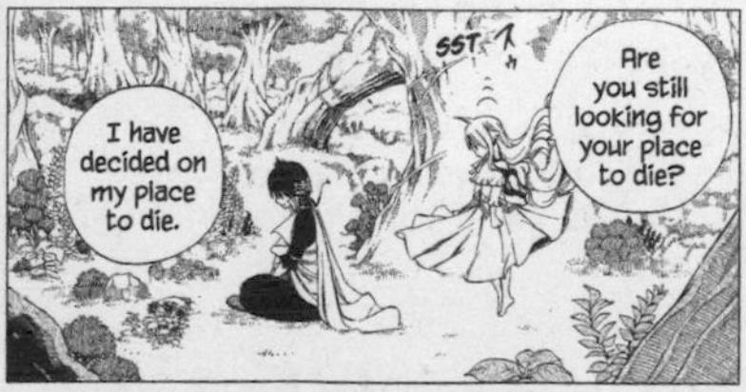
Are you still looking for your place to die?
SST
I have decided on my place to die.

Lucy: A lot of people wrote in wondering about that.

Mira: Who's "a lot" about?!

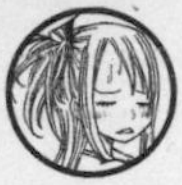: Sigh...

Mira: First, remember that the first master can hear Zeref's voice just fine.

Lucy: Now you're suddenly serious?!

Mira: So the problem is with Zeref, right? He isn't supposed to hear the first master's voice, but he can still carry on a conversation.

Lucy: So... telepathy or something?

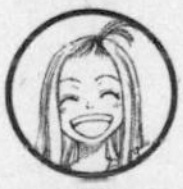: This isn't an ESP manga, dummy! (slap)

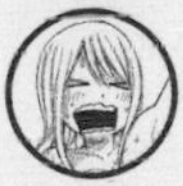: Ow! It's a magic manga.

Mira: So since it's magic, you think you can do anything you want, dummy? (Slap!)

Lucy: Ow!!

Mira: What's, "Ow!" about? (Slap!)

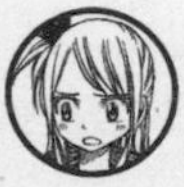: Come on, Mira-san! We aren't getting anywhere with this...

Mira: What's "Come on," about? (Slap slap!)

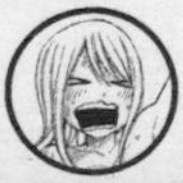: Ow, ow!!

Continued on the right-hand page.

TAIL

The Fairy Tail Guild is looking for illustrations! Please send in your art on a postcard or at postcard size, and do it in black pen, okay? Those chosen to be published will get a signed mini poster! ♪ Make sure you write your real name and address on the back of your illustration!

d'ART

Tokyo, Tomoka Sato

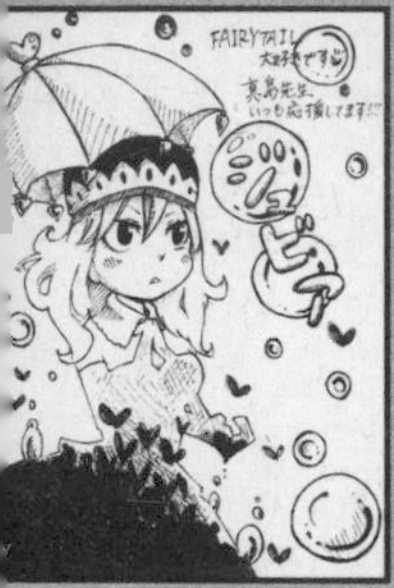
FAIRYTAIL

▲ Wow! You drew this really cute! Her outfit can only be found in a special version calendar making it a rare Juvia!

Chiba Prefecture, Okumura

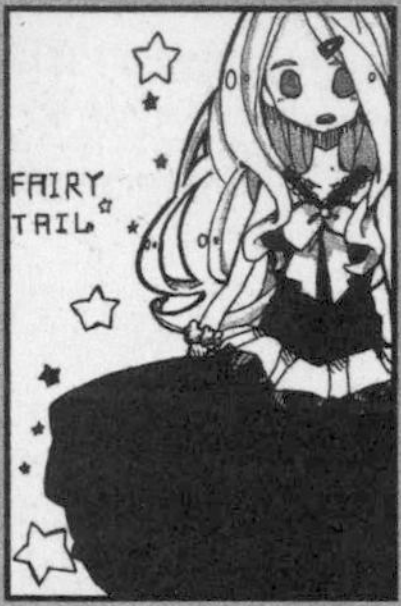
FAIRY TAIL

▲ What a great picture! It has this ethereal quality! Mira-chan is going to have a great part in this arc!

Kanagawa Prefecture, Kumi Ebizuka

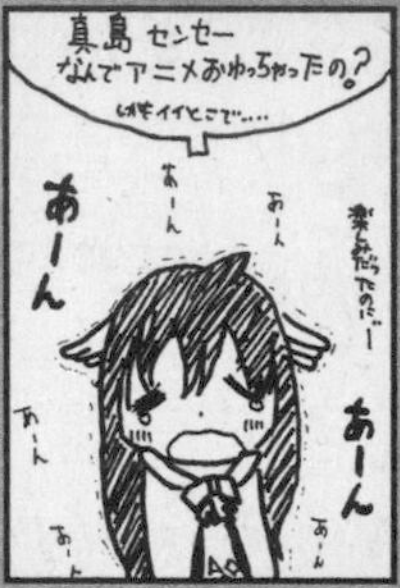

▲ The new series is about to start! Watch for it!!

Miyagi Prefecture, Seri

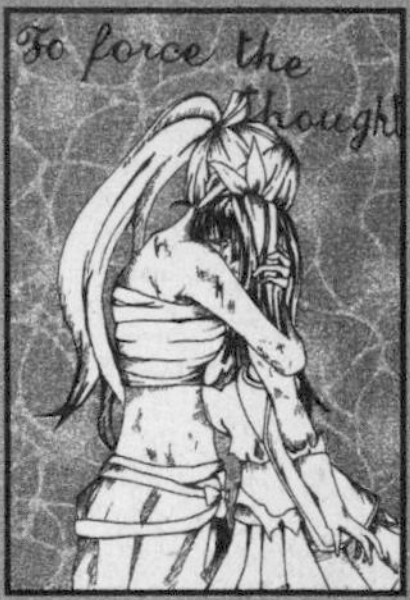

▲ I heard a lot of people say how much they love these two. Happiness binge!

Kagawa Prefecture, Sumiko

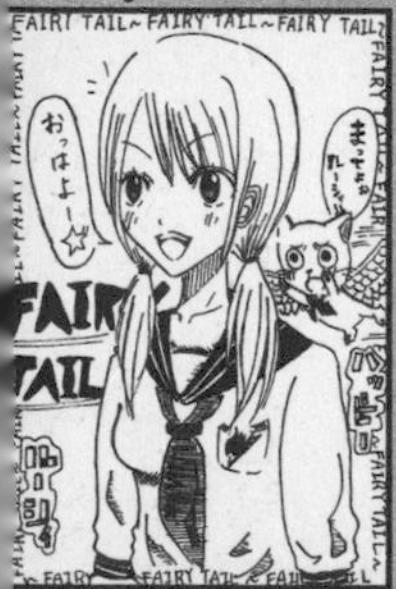
FAIRY TAIL

▲ Lucy in a sailor uniform! This is cute! Is she leaving Happy behind?

Tokyo, Yocchii

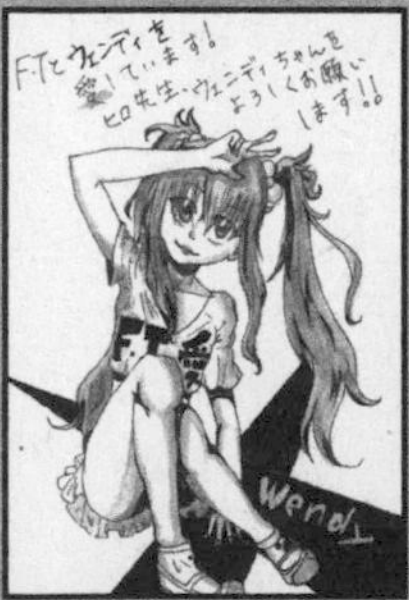
Wendy

▲ I'm sure Wendy will have a big part too! Be sure to watch for it, okay?

Aichi Prefecture, 3A Is the Best

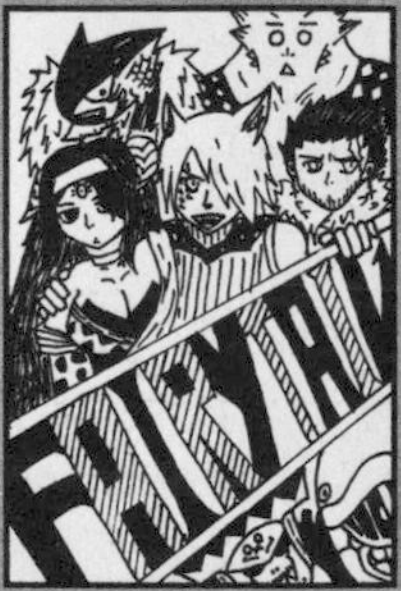

▲ The nine gates came really quickly! But we're missing two here...

Tokyo, Misa Matsuo

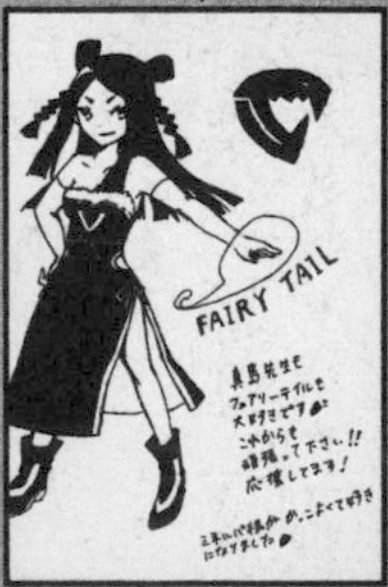
FAIRY TAIL

▲ Minerva has been rocketing up in popularity recently. I really like her too.

Send to Hiro Mashima, Kodansha Comics
451 Park Ave. South, 7th Floor New York, NY 10016

FAIRY GUILD

Hyogo Prefecture, Yui Kōsō

Who done it?!! I think the glancing Happy is really cute! ▶

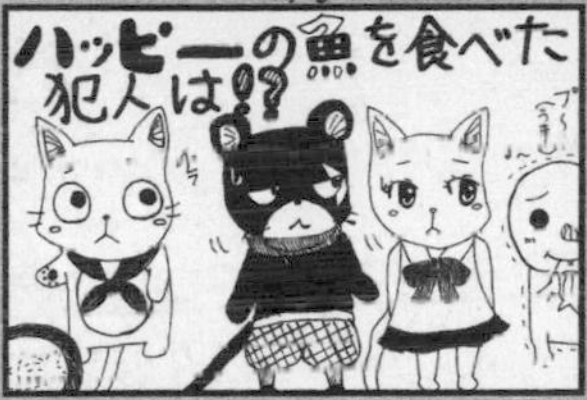
ハッピーの魚を食べた犯人は!?

Yamanashi Prefecture, Yuki

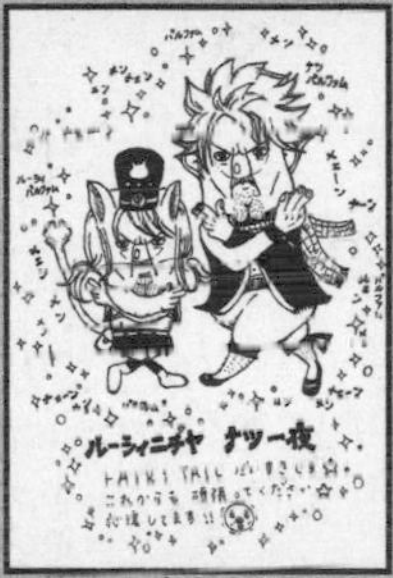

▲Ah ha ha! Why are they combined in this way?! It says Natsu Perfume...

Shizuoka Prefecture, Hyōsuke Ar

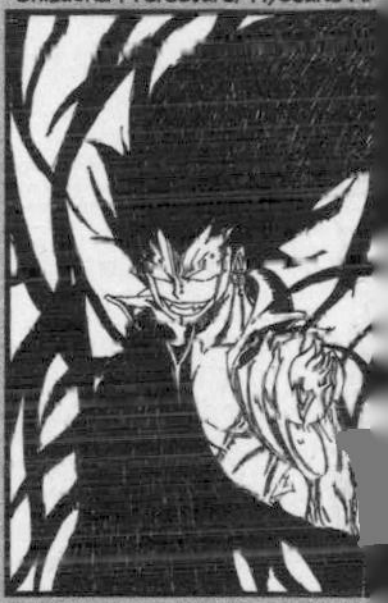

▲ Gajeel as the Iron-Shad Dragon version! He looks tough!

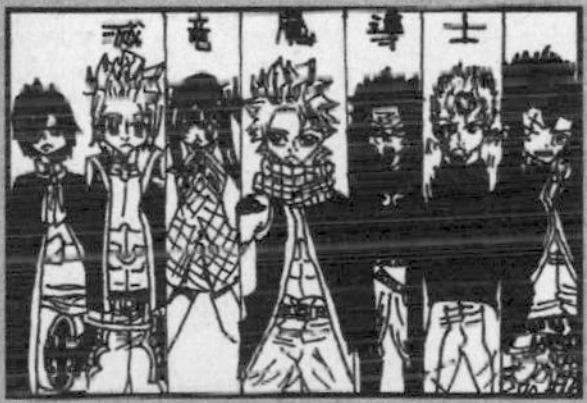
滅竜魔導士

Hyogo Prefecture, Kanon Yagi

◀All the dragon slayers unite!! I wonder if they're going to be able to fight dragons again?!

Shizuoka Prefecture, Chisato Shimoyama

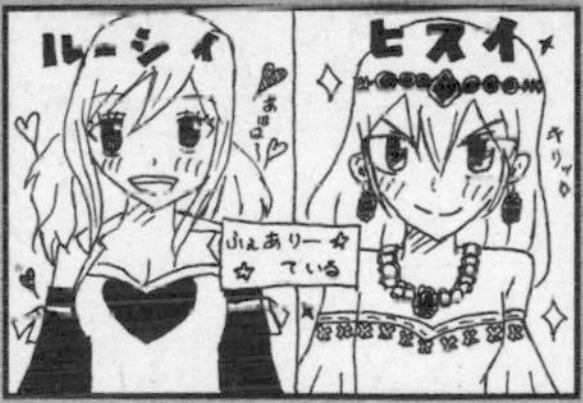
ルーシィ
ヒスイ
ふぇありー☆ている

▲ A combination of a former rich girl and a present princess. I wanted to draw more interaction between them.

Saitama Prefecture, Nanami Shima

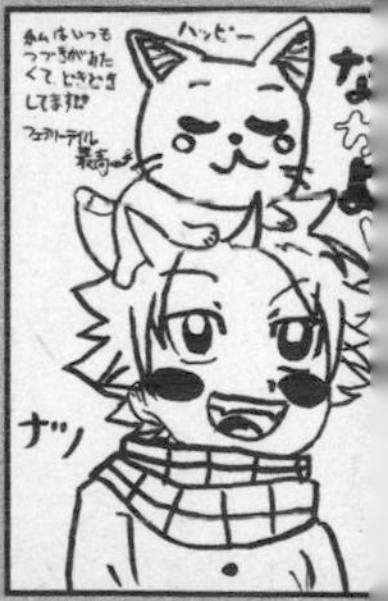
ハッピー
ナツ

▲Ohh! The two as kids! Now that's a cute image!

REJECTION CORNER

Wait... You're making a funny there, aren't you? Heh heh... ▶

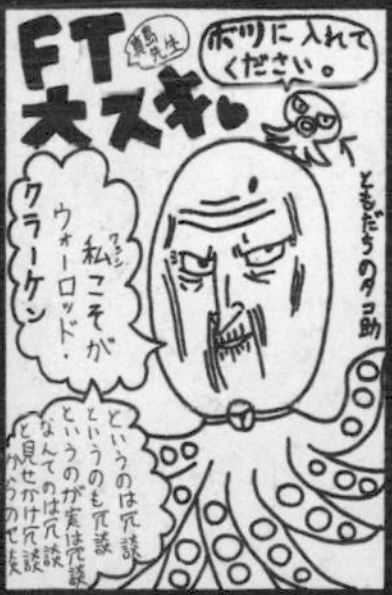
FT大スキ
ボツに入れてください。
私こそがウォーロッド・クラーケン

Fukuoka, Suzuna

By sending in letters or postcards, you give us permission to give your name, address, postal code, and any other information you include to the artist as-is. Please keep that in mind.

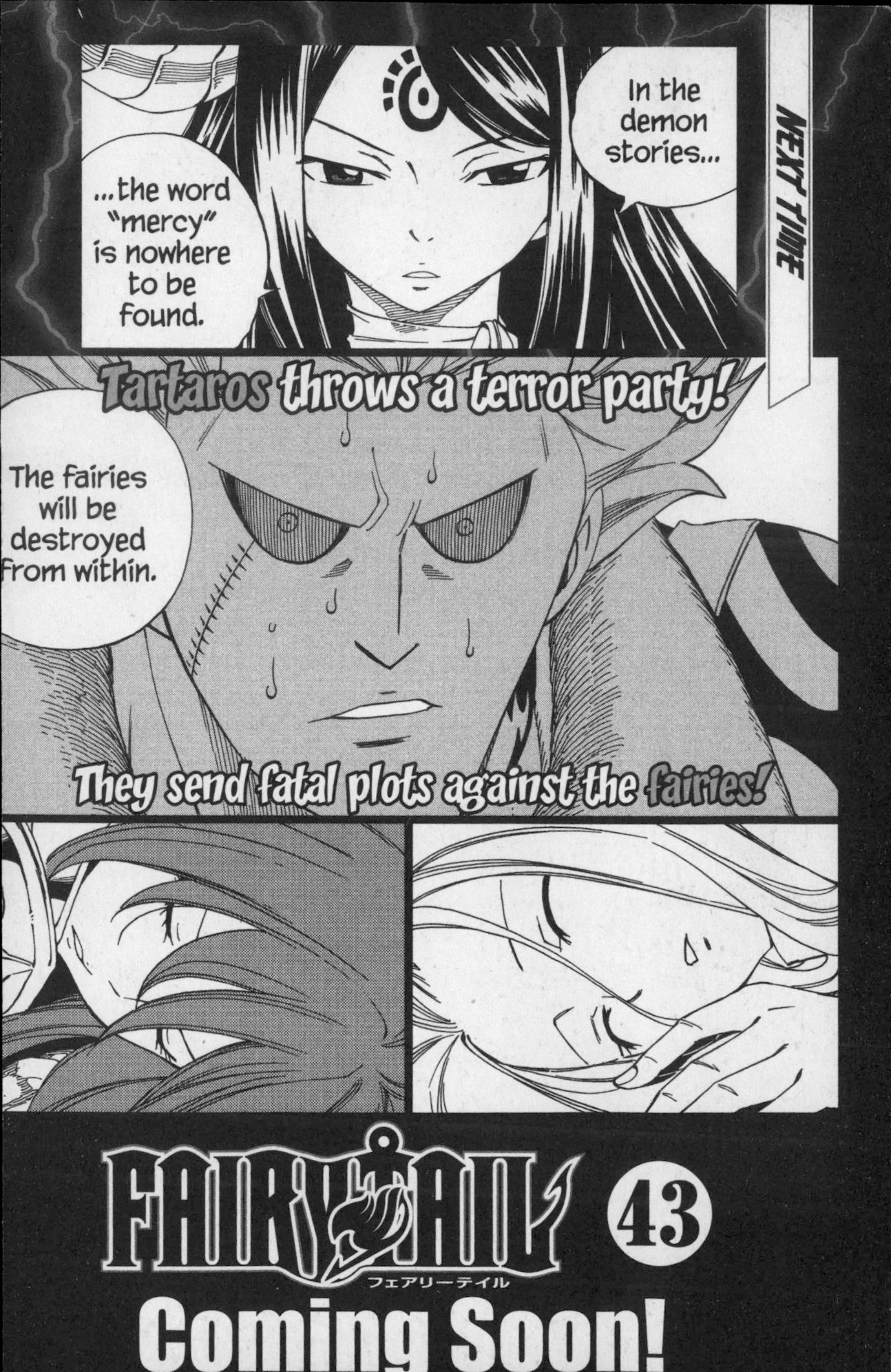
NEXT TIME
In the demon stories...
...the word "mercy" is nowhere to be found.
Tartaros throws a terror party!
The fairies will be destroyed from within.
They send fatal plots against the fairies!
FAIRY TAIL
43
フェアリーテイル
Coming Soon!

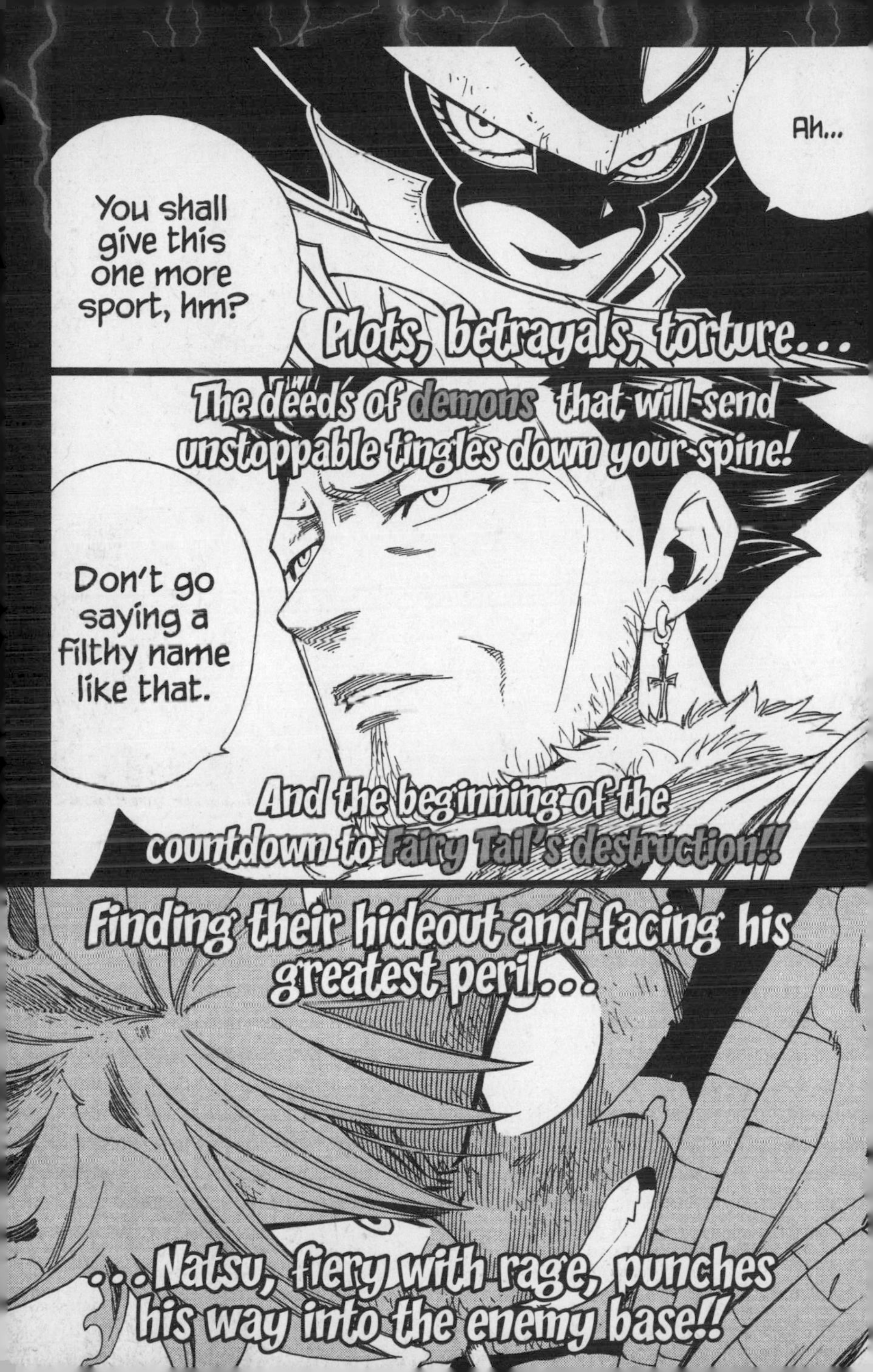
Ah...
You shall give this one more sport, hm?
Plots, betrayals, torture...
The deeds of demons that will send unstoppable tingles down your spine!
Don't go saying a filthy name like that.
And the beginning of the countdown to Fairy Tail's destruction!!
Finding their hideout and facing his greatest peril...
...Natsu, fiery with rage, punches his way into the enemy base!!

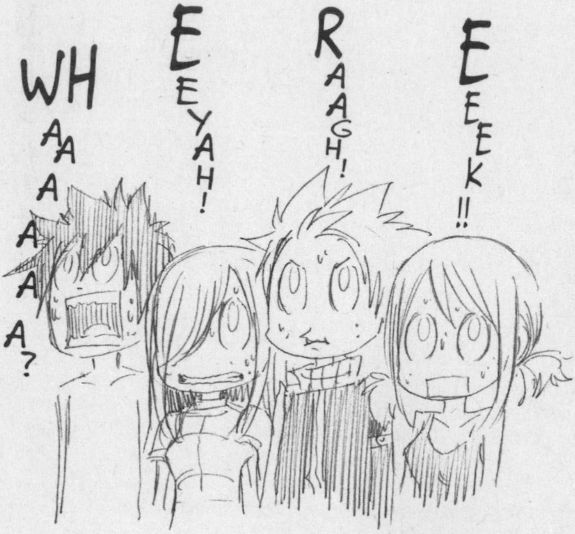
EEEEK!!
RAAAGH!
EEYAH!
WHAAAAAAA?

FAIRY TAIL 42

フェアリーテイル

FAIRY TAIL 42
WHERE'D THE COVER FOR THE GRAPHIC NOVEL GO...?

HIRO 真島ヒロ MASHIMA

FROM HIRO MASHIMA

The new TV anime series is just starting! It's been so long since I last saw everybody from the cast and staff, when I finally did see them, I was as happy as if I had just met up with everyone from my guild again! There will be little details where the new series will be a power-up of the old, so watch it! I'm sure you'll really enjoy it!

Original Jacket Design: Hisao Ogawa

Translation Notes:

Japanese is a tricky language for most Westerners, and translation is often more art than science. For your edification and reading pleasure, here are notes on some of the places where we could have gone in a different direction with our translation of the work, or where a Japanese cultural reference is used.

Page 20, Kyôka

Like Natsu (meaning "summer"), Kyôka is obviously a Japanese word, but unlike Natsu, Kyôka isn't one that is normally accepted as a Japanese name. So odds are her name is based on the meaning of a Japanese word pronounced *kyôka*. We can go over some of the words it probably isn't, like a bridge girder, a satirical poem or an offering of flowers, but one translation stands out as a probability. When she is first introduced, she describes her powers as making humans stronger, so we can assume the meaning of her name is the Japanese word *kyôka* which means to "enhance" or "strengthen." Another outside possibility is to "instruct" or "enlighten," but I would think "enhancing" is closer to her position (so far) in the story. Of course later events could prove me wrong.

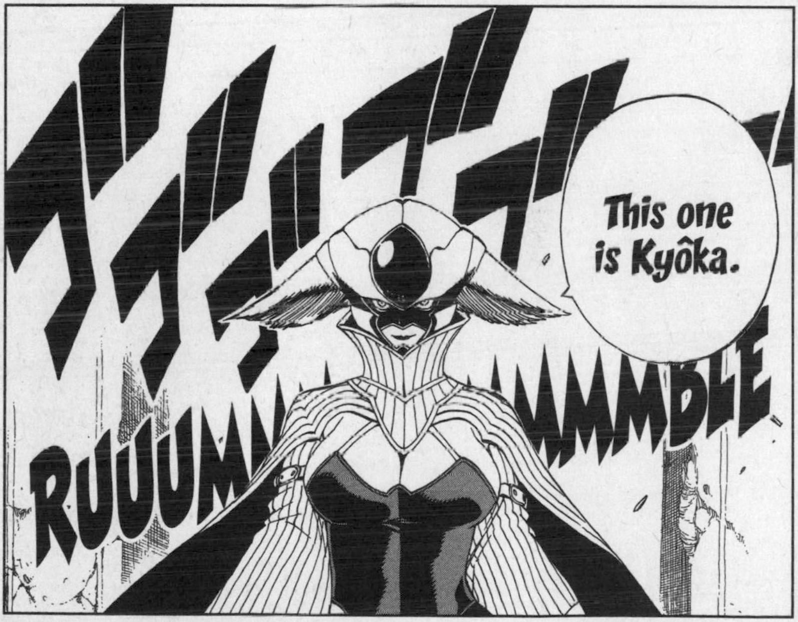
This one is Kyôka.
RUUUM
MMMBLE

Page 14, Women's bath

You may have heard that Japanese bathe in mixed company. It's true that there are mixed baths scattered here and there throughout the country, but they are rare. More common, even for small hot springs, is to section off women's baths from men's

Page 79, Dôjigiri

One of the most famous swords in Japan was said to have been made by the great sword maker Amakuni Yasutsuna in the Heian period (794-1185) of Japan's history. It got its name because of a legend where it was used to cut off the head of an *oni* (Japanese ogre) leader, Shuten Dôji, so its name translates to "Dôji cutter." The blade still exists and was displayed last year at the Tokyo National Museum. It is said that although it is more than 900 years old, the blade is as clear as the day it was made.

Page 104, *Agito*

Agito means "jaw," but it is considered a far cooler way of saying it than the more common word, *ago*. In fact, the word is consider cool enough to have a Kamen Rider series named after it in the early 2000s. Other anime and game characters have also been named Agito.

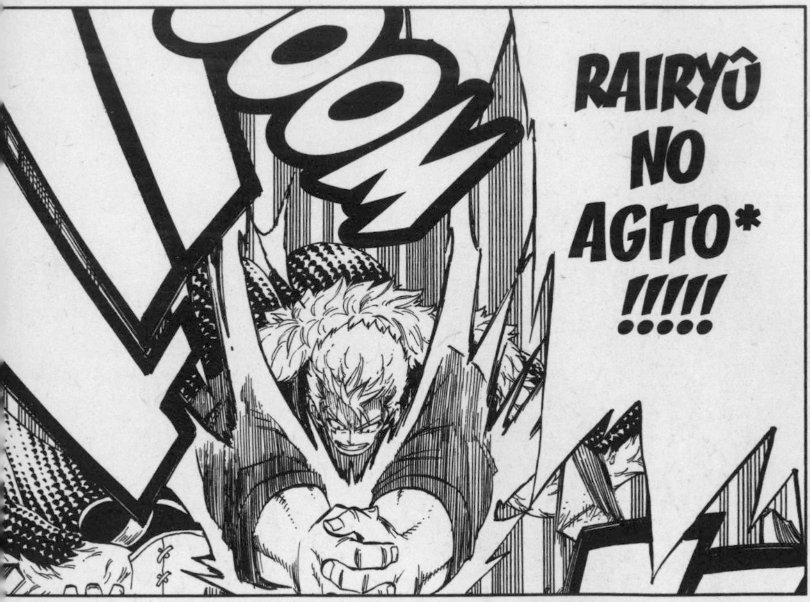
RAIRYÛ NO AGITO* !!!!!

Page 145, *Tsundere*

As mentioned in the notes for Volume 16, *tsundere* is a word for characters who pretend to be annoyed and unfeeling toward another character whereas they are actually madly in love. The word comes from two onomatopoetic words, *tsun tsun*, the sound of poking someone, and *dere dere*, the sound of cuddling. The two together refer to a type of personality that is angry and prickly at one moment, and loving the next. It's mostly used for female characters, although, as Ren demonstrates, there can be male *tsundere* characters, too.

SHERLOCK BONES

KC KODANSHA COMICS

DEDUCTIVE DOG DETECTIVE

When Takeru adopts a new pet, he's in for a surprise—the dog is none other than the reincarnation of Sherlock Holmes. With no one else able to communicate with Holmes, Takeru is roped into becoming Sherdog's assistant, John Watson. Using his sleuthing skills, Holmes uncovers clues to solve the trickiest crimes.

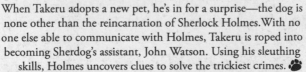

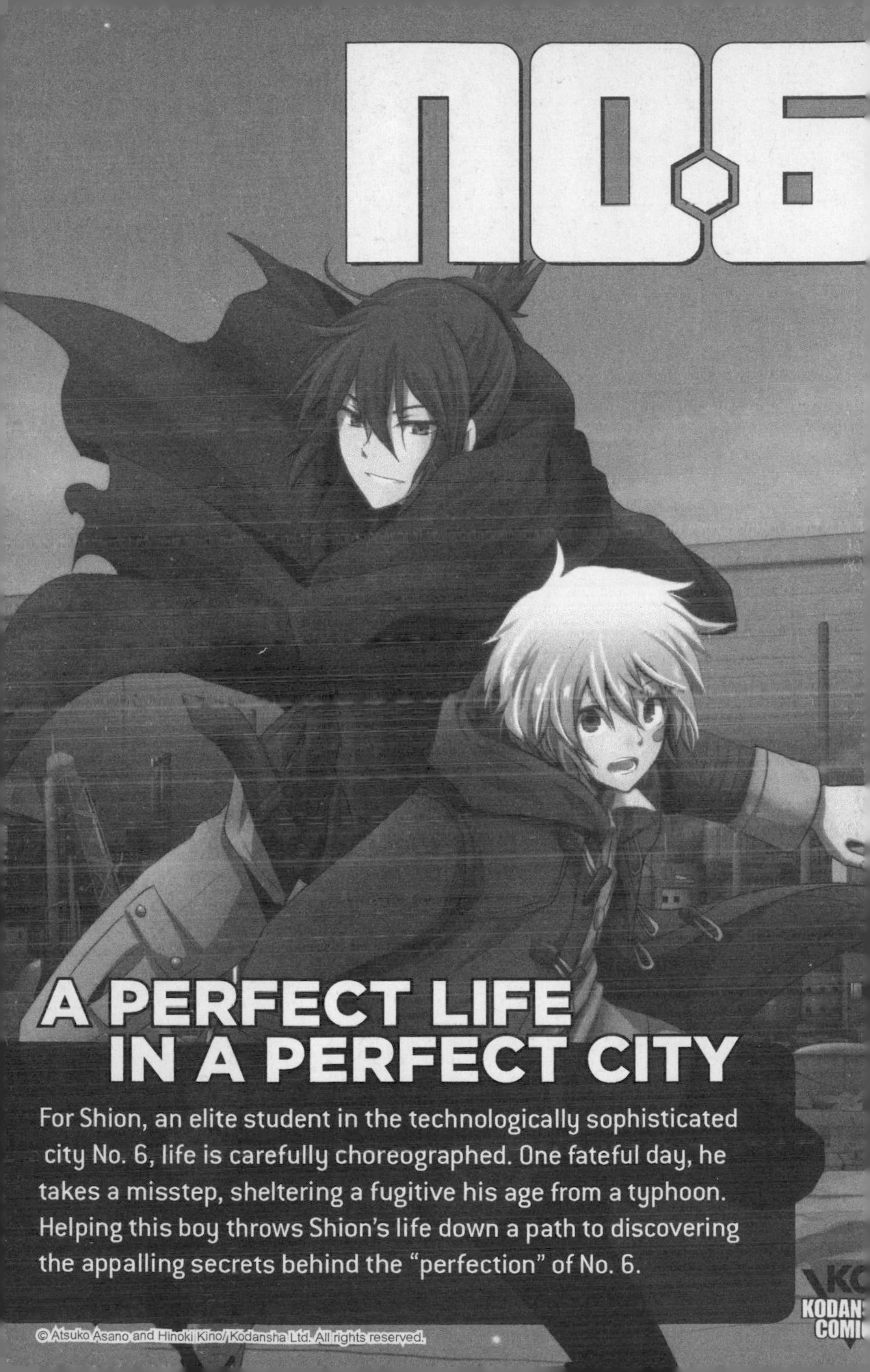
NO.6
A PERFECT LIFE
IN A PERFECT CITY
For Shion, an elite student in the technologically sophisticated city No. 6, life is carefully choreographed. One fateful day, he takes a misstep, sheltering a fugitive his age from a typhoon. Helping this boy throws Shion's life down a path to discovering the appalling secrets behind the "perfection" of No. 6.
© Atsuko Asano and Hinoki Kino/ Kodansha Ltd. All rights reserved.

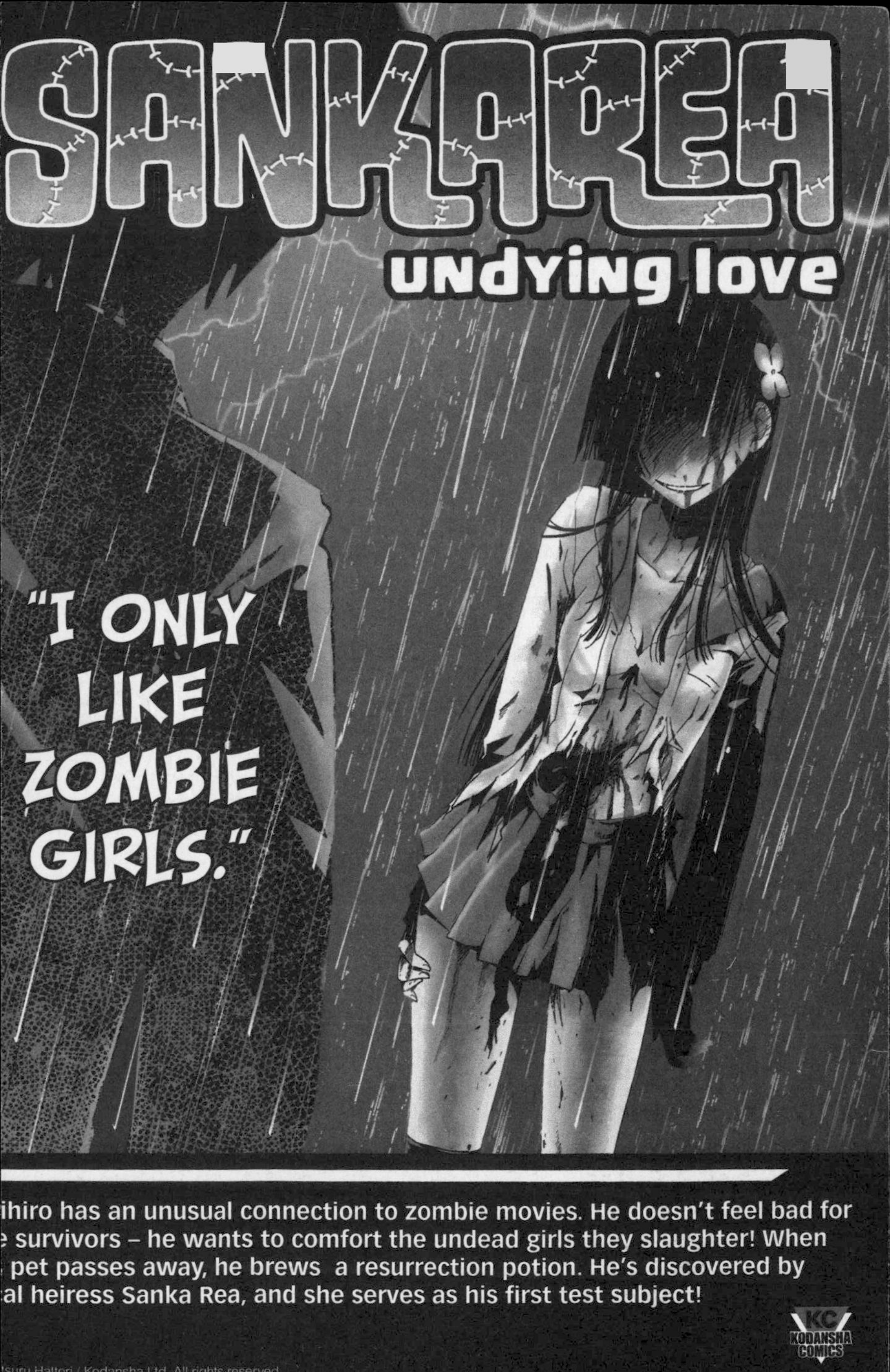
SANKAREA
undying love
"I ONLY LIKE ZOMBIE GIRLS."

ihiro has an unusual connection to zombie movies. He doesn't feel bad for e survivors – he wants to comfort the undead girls they slaughter! When pet passes away, he brews a resurrection potion. He's discovered by al heiress Sanka Rea, and she serves as his first test subject!

KC KODANSHA COMICS

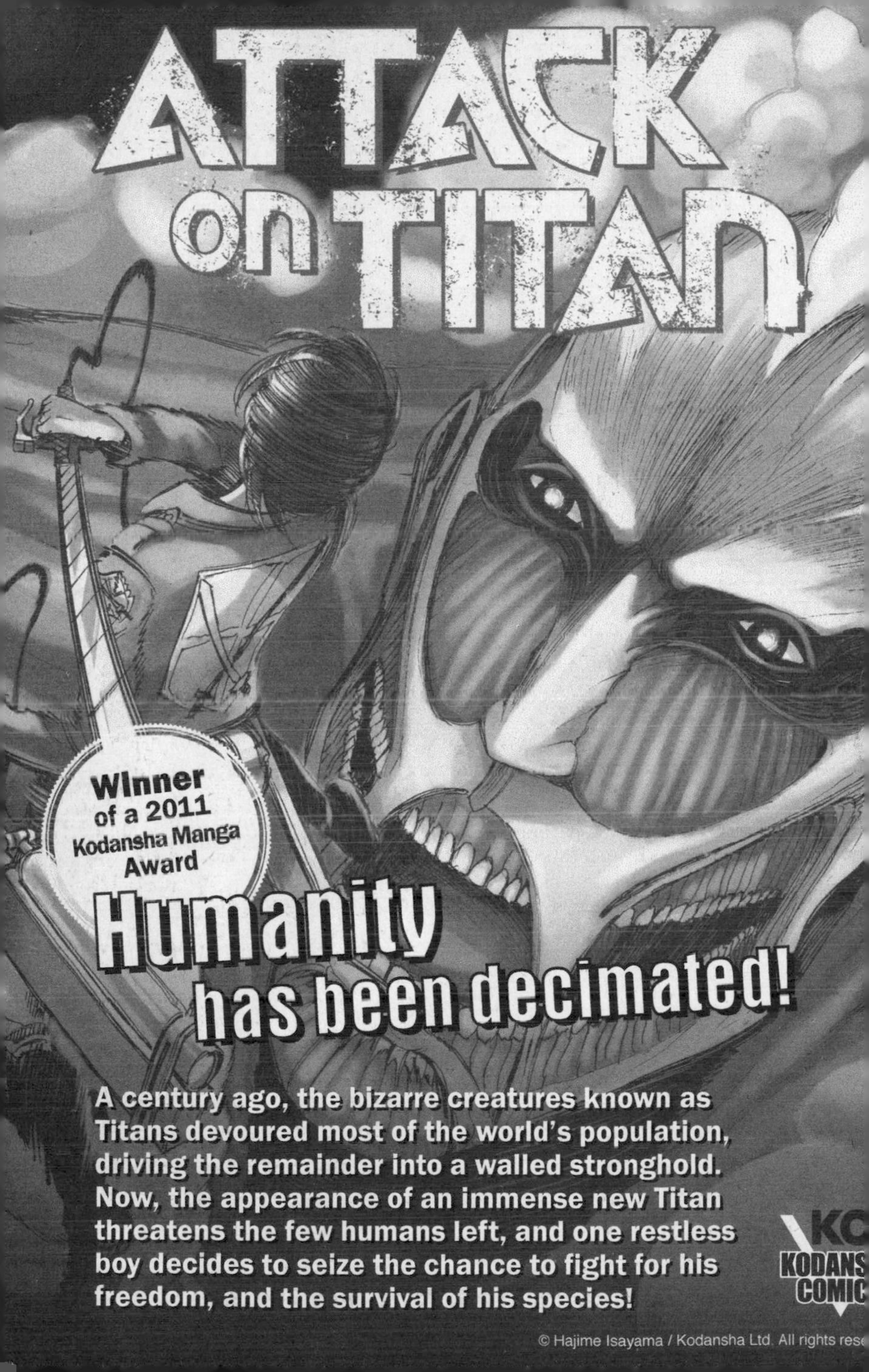
ATTACK on TITAN
Winner of a 2011 Kodansha Manga Award
Humanity has been decimated!
A century ago, the bizarre creatures known as Titans devoured most of the world's population, driving the remainder into a walled stronghold. Now, the appearance of an immense new Titan threatens the few humans left, and one restless boy decides to seize the chance to fight for his freedom, and the survival of his species!
KC
KODANS
COMIC
© Hajime Isayama / Kodansha Ltd. All rights rese

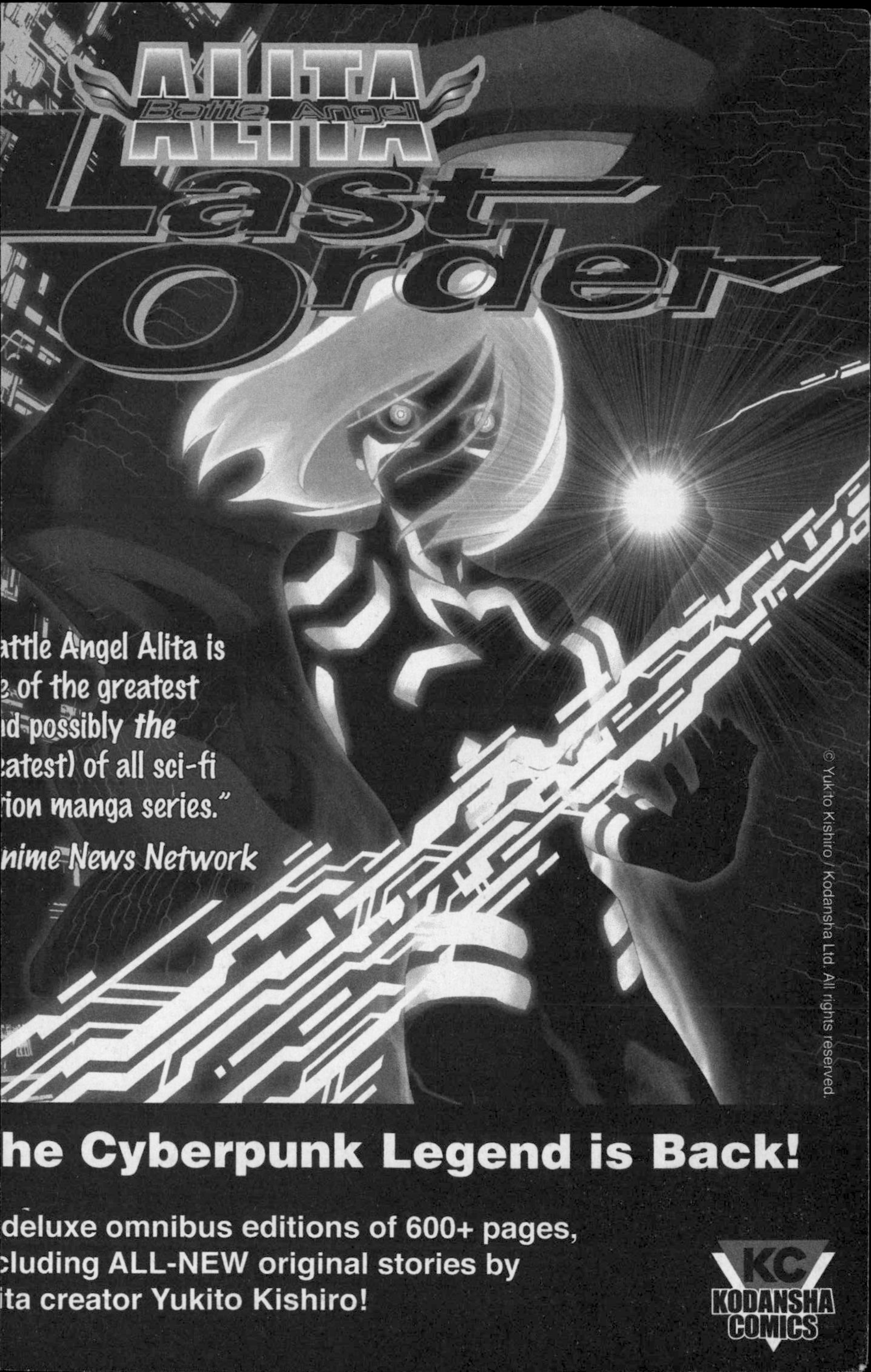
ALITA
Battle Angel
ALITA
Last Order
attle Angel Alita is
e of the greatest
nd possibly *the*
eatest) of all sci-fi
tion manga series."
nime News Network
© Yukito Kishiro / Kodansha Ltd. All rights reserved.

My Little Monster

OPPOSITES ATTRACT...MAYBE?

Haru Yoshida is feared as an unstable and violent "monster." Mizutani Shizuku is a grade-obsessed student with no friends. Fate brings these two together to form the most unlikely pair. Haru firmly believes he's in love with Mizutani and she firmly believes he's insane.

KC
KODANSHA COMICS

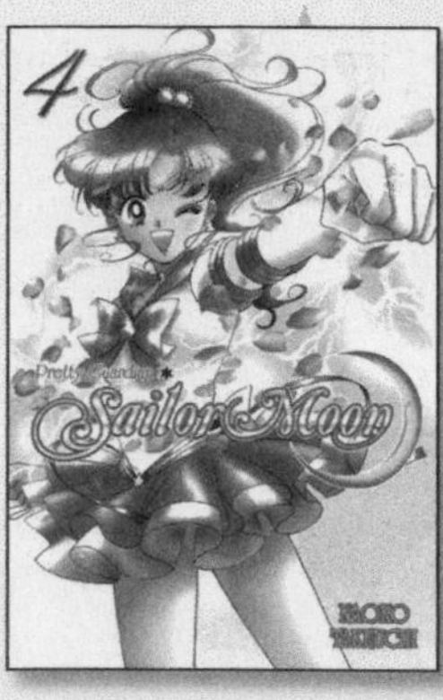
4
Pretty Guardian
Sailor Moon
NAOKO TAKEUCHI

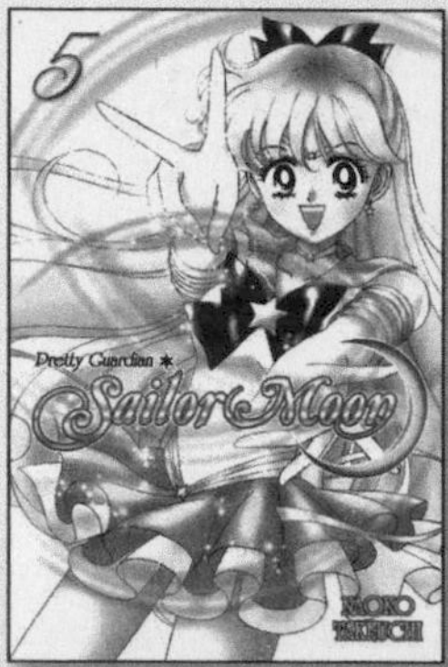
5
Pretty Guardian
Sailor Moon
NAOKO TAKEUCHI

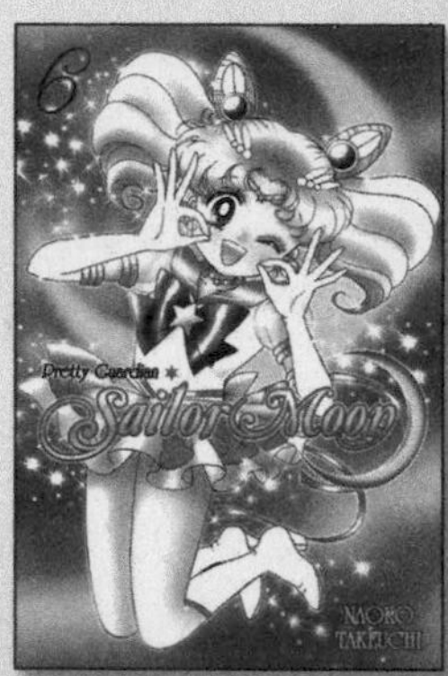
6
Pretty Guardian
Sailor Moon
NAOKO TAKEUCHI

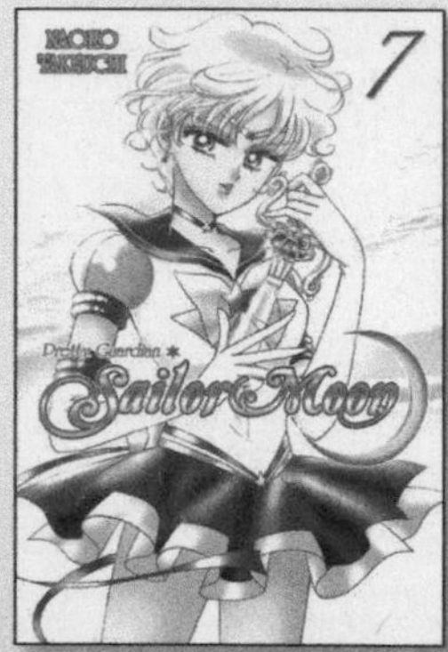
NAOKO TAKEUCHI
7
Pretty Guardian
Sailor Moon

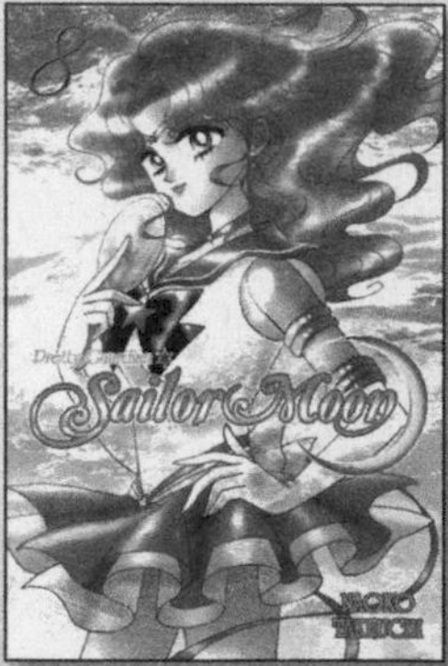
8
Sailor Moon
NAOKO TAKEUCHI

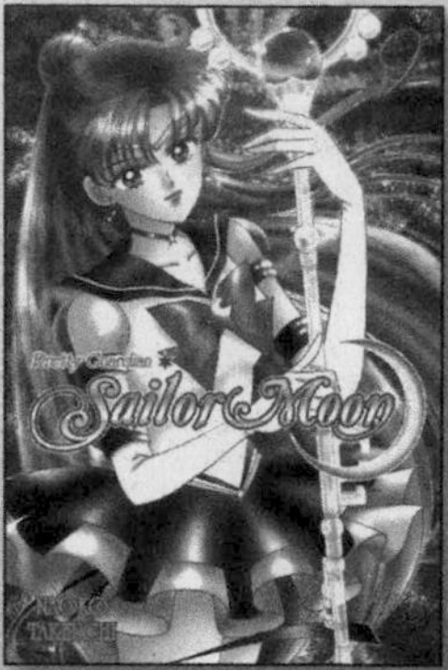
Pretty Guardian
Sailor Moon

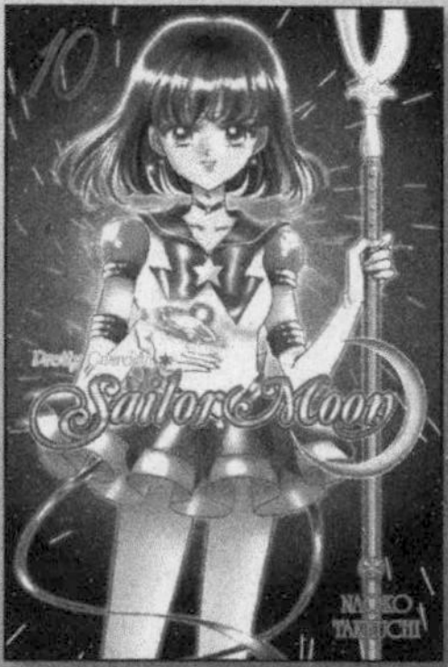
10
Sailor Moon
NAOKO TAKEUCHI

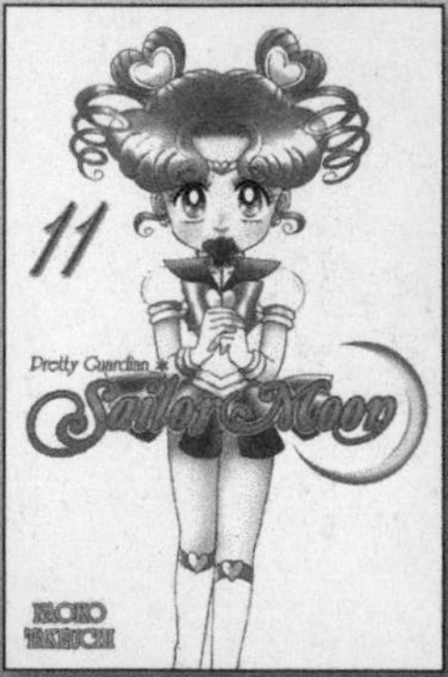
11
Pretty Guardian
Sailor Moon
NAOKO TAKEUCHI

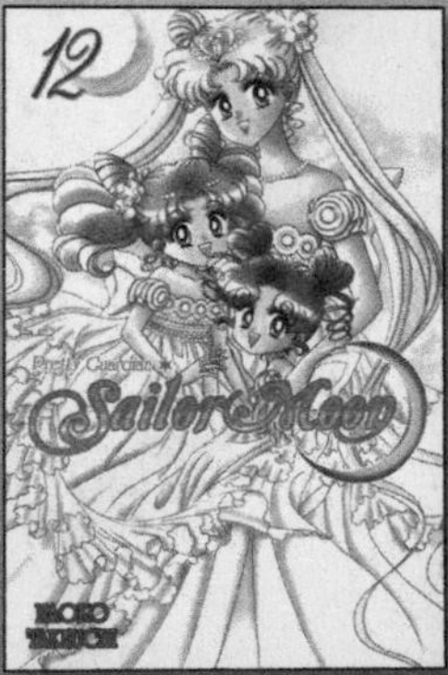
12
Pretty Guardian
Sailor Moon
NAOKO TAKEUCHI

The Pretty Guardians are back!

★

Kodansha Comics is proud to present *Sailor Moon* with all new translations.

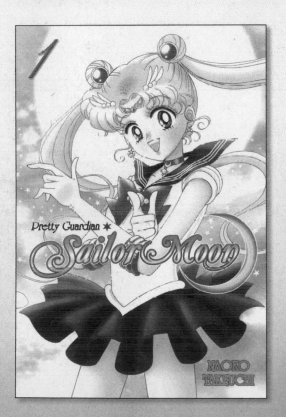

For more information, go to **www.kodanshacomics.com**

Praise for the anime:

"The show provides a pleasant window on the highs and lows of young love with two young people who are first timers at the real thing."

-The Fandom Post

"Always it is smarter, more poetic, more touching, just plain better than you think it is going to be."

-Anime News Network

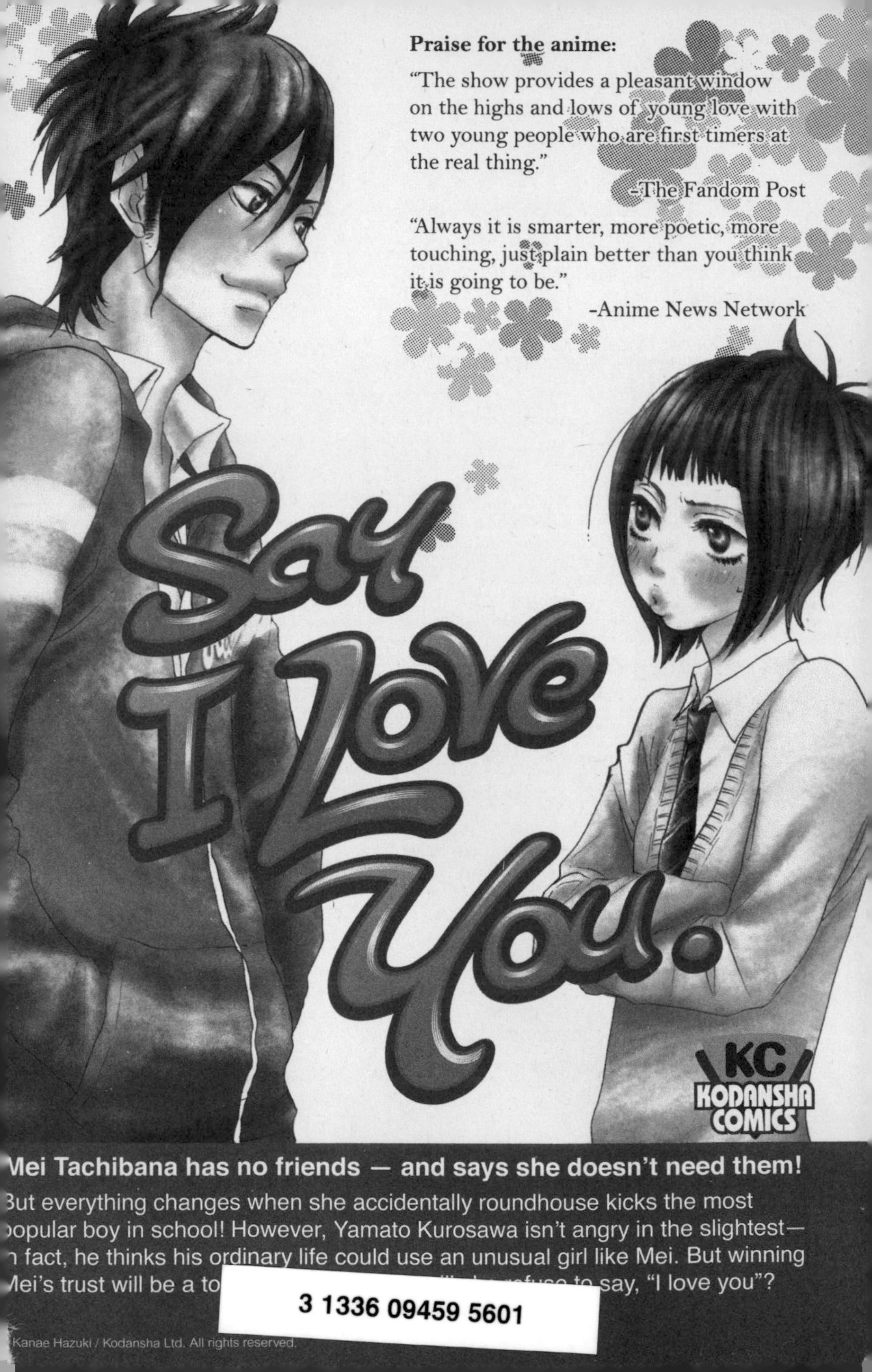
Say I Love You.
KC
KODANSHA COMICS

Mei Tachibana has no friends — and says she doesn't need them!

But everything changes when she accidentally roundhouse kicks the most popular boy in school! However, Yamato Kurosawa isn't angry in the slightest—in fact, he thinks his ordinary life could use an unusual girl like Mei. But winning Mei's trust will be a to [illegible] refuse to say, "I love you"?

A Kodansha Comics Trade Paperback Original.

Published in the United States by Kodansha Comics, an imprint of Kodansha USA Publishing, LLC, New York.

Publication rights for this English edition arranged through Kodansha Ltd., Tokyo.

First published in Japan in 2014 by Kodansha Ltd., Tokyo
ISBN 978-1-61262-561-4

Printed in the United States of America.

www.kodanshacomics.com

9 8 7 6 5 4 3 2 1

Translation: William Flanagan
Lettering: AndWorld Design
Editing: Ben Applegate

TOMARE!

止まれ

[STOP!]

You're going the wrong way!

Manga is a completely different
type of reading experience.

To start at the *beginning,*
go to the *end!*

hat's right! Authentic manga is read the traditional Japanese way—
om right to left, exactly the *opposite* of how American books are
ead. It's easy to follow: Just go to the other end of the book and read
ach page—and each panel—from right side to left side, starting at
e top right. Now you're experiencing manga as it was meant to be!